D1807466

OXFORD CLASSICAL & PHILOSOPHICAL
MONOGRAPHS

Editorial Committee
J. L. ACKRILL   W. G. G. FORREST
J. BOARDMAN   P. H. J. LLOYD-JONES
K. J. DOVER   R. G. M. NISBET

HIERONYMUS OF CARDIA

Jane Hornblower

OXFORD UNIVERSITY PRESS
1981

Oxford University Press, Walton Street, Oxford OX2 6DP
London Glasgow New York Toronto
Delhi Bombay Calcutta Madras Karachi
Kuala Lumpur Singapore Hong Kong Tokyo
Nairobi Dar es Salaam Cape Town
Melbourne Auckland
and associate companies in
Beirut Berlin Ibadan Mexico City

Published in the United States by
Oxford University Press, New York

© Jane Hornblower 1981

All rights reserved. No part of this publication may be reproduced,
stored in a retrieval system, or transmitted, in any form or by any means,
electronic, mechanical, photocopying, recording, or otherwise, without
the prior permission of Oxford University Press

British Library Cataloguing in Publication Data

Hornblower, Jane
Hieronymus of Cardia. – (Oxford classical
and philosophical monographs)
I. Title
930'.07'202   D56.52.H6/
ISBN 0-19-814717-1

Set by Western Printing Services Ltd
and Printed in Great Britain
at the University Press, Oxford
by Eric Buckley
Printer to the University

to
SIMON

Preface and Acknowledgements

I wish especially to thank the following for their help, academic or moral, during the writing of this book: Dr O. Murray and Professor A. Andrewes for casting a critical eye on the work in its early stages; St. Anne's College, Oxford, for a Junior Research Fellowship; the Fondation Hardt at Geneva for its hospitality during 1975, and the Craven Committee of Oxford University for a grant which enabled me to study there; the British School of Archaeology in Athens for hospitality in 1981 during the last stages of preparation for publication; E. J. Brill of Leiden, and the Akademie der Wissenschaften der D.D.R. for their permission to reproduce material printed in the appendices. Professors F. W. Walbank and J. K. Davies made valuable comments on an earlier version. Professors N. G. L. Hammond and C. M. Robertson have helped me by correspondence on specific points. To Professor P. A. Brunt I am grateful for his honest criticism and for many helpful suggestions, also for letting me see the typescript of his edition of Arrian and of other material in advance of publication. I am especially indebted to Mr P. M. Fraser for saving me from errors and for sharing some of his wisdom on the Hellenistic world: the faults that remain are my own. I thank my mother for educating me well, and my father for firing an interest in the exotic past. Miss Rosemary Morris was a loyal friend and an example during the vicissitudes of research. My husband Simon has made it possible to keep 'Hieronymus' up to date at a time when I could not often visit libraries, and has fostered the book during periods of neglect by its author: to his wide bibliographic knowledge, his surefootedness on all the paths of Greek history, and his unfailing encouragement, I owe more than can easily be expressed.

JANE HORNBLOWER

22nd May 1981

Contents

List of Short Abbreviations

AC   *Acta Classica*

ACl.   *Antiquité classique*

Am. Hist. Rev.   *American Historical Review*

AJA   *American Journal of Archaeology*

AJP   *American Journal of Philology*

Aymard, *Études*   A. Aymard, *Études d'histoire ancienne*, Paris, 1967

Badian, *Studies*   E. Badian, *Studies in Greek and Roman History*, Oxford, 1964

BCH   *Bulletin de correspondance hellénique*

BMC   *Catalogue of Greek Coins in the British Museum*, London, 1873–1927

BSA   *Papers of the British School at Athens*

CAH   *Cambridge Ancient History*

Class. et Med.   *Classica et Mediaevalia*

CP   *Classical Philology*

CR   *Classical Review*

CRAI   *Comptes rendus de l'academie des inscriptions et belles lettres*

CQ   *Classical Quarterly*

CW   *Classical Weekly*

F. Gr. Hist.   F. Jacoby, *Die Fragmente der griechischen Historiker*, 14 vols., Berlin–Leiden, 1923–58

FHG   C. Müller, *Fragmenta Historicorum Graecorum*, Paris, 1841–70

GRBS   *Greek, Roman and Byzantine Studies*

Head, *HN*²   B. V. Head, *Historia Numorum*. second edition, Oxford, 1911

Holleaux, *Études*   M. Holleaux, *Études d'epigraphie et d'histoire grecques*, edited L. Robert, 6 vols., Paris, 1938–68

HSCP   *Harvard Studies in Classical Philology*

IG   *Inscriptiones Graecae*

JEA   *Journal of Egyptian Archaeology*

JHS   *Journal of Hellenic Studies*

JOAI   *Jahreshefte des Österreichisches Archaeologisches Instituts in Wien*

Journ. Hist. Ideas   *Journal of the History of Ideas*

JRS   *Journal of Roman Studies*

J. Th. St.   *Journal of Theological Studies*

Mus. Helv.   *Museum Helveticum*

Num. Chron.   *Numismatic Chronicle*

OCD²   *Oxford Classical Dictionary*, second edition, Oxford, 1970

OGIS   *Orientis Graeci Inscriptiones Selectae*

PACA   *Proceedings of the African Classical Society*

Par. d. Pass. *Parola del Passato*
PBSR *Papers of the British School at Rome*
PCPS *Proceedings of the Cambridge Philological Society*
Proc. Brit. Acad. *Proceedings of the British Academy*
PSI *Papiri della Societa Italiana*
RE Pauly–Wissowa–Kroll, *Real Encyclopaedie*
REA *Revue des études anciennes*
REG *Revue des études grecques*
Rév. de Phil. *Revue de philologie*
Rh. Mus. *Rheinisches Museum*
Riv. Fil. *Rivista di Filologia*
Robert, *Hellenica* *Recueil d'epigraphie, de numismatique et d'antiquités grecques*, publié par Louis Robert, 13 vols., Limoges–Paris, 1940–65
Rostovtzeff, *SEHHW* M. Rostovtzeff, *Social and Economic History of the Hellenistic World*, 3 vols., Oxford, 1941
SEG *Supplementum Epigraphicum Graecum*
SNG von Aulock H. S. von Aulock, *Sylloge Nummorum Graecorum*, Berlin, 1957–68
Syll.[3] W. Dittenberger, *Sylloge Inscriptionum Graecarum*, third edition, Leipzig, 1915–24
TAPS *Transactions of the American Philosophical Society*, Philadelphia
Walbank, *HCP* F. W. Walbank, *A Historical Commentary on Polybius*, 3 vols., Oxford, 1957–79
Welles, *RC* C. B. Welles, *Royal Correspondence in the Hellenistic Period*, New Haven, 1934
YCS *Yale Classical Studies*
ZPE *Zeitschrift für Papyrologie und Epigraphik*

Introduction

'No one can bear to read Hieronymus through to the end,' said the literary critic Dionysius of Halicarnassus.[1] This was the epitaph which the ancient world accorded to Hieronymus of Cardia, the contemporary eye-witness historian of Alexander's Successors. His work in its original form is, apart from a few citations, entirely lost; but in modern times it has been ranked alongside the histories of Thucydides and Polybius[2]—an opinion founded chiefly on the epitome, in three extant books, made by the Augustan writer Diodorus of Sicily.

The peculiar interest of this writer is the position he occupied in the history of his times. He was the friend and companion in turn of Eumenes the Cardian, Antigonus Monophthalmus, Demetrius, and Antigonus Gonatas; possibly he had also accompanied Alexander's expedition; and he held important administrative and diplomatic posts under his various masters. The great range of his experience and his close relationship to many of the leading figures of the age made Hieronymus uniquely qualified to record one of the most dramatic evolutions of Greek history: the passing of the classical world, into which he had been born, and the creation of the Hellenistic kingdoms. Such was the authority of his work that even a detractor like Dionysius sometimes felt obliged to consult it on points of fact;[3] and it was used by epitomizers and biographers of the Roman period as the standard history of the Diadochi. The literary critics, however, deplored the style in which it was written—in the same passage of Dionysius the author voices his objections to nearly the whole of Greek historiography in the Hellenistic period—and we must blame the taste of Dionysius' generation for the loss of Hieronymus' history in the original, along with so many other casualties of Hellenistic literature.

Not only was Hieronymus' style unfashionable in the Augustan era: specialized works on the Macedonian period had only a limited appeal to Romans. Dionysius found Hieronymus useful where, in recounting Pyrrhus' Italian expedition, he had touched on the history of Rome; but in general few were concerned to preserve histories of long dead

---

[1] Dion. Hal. *De Comp. Verb.* iv.30 = *F. Gr. Hist.* 154 T12.
[2] Cf. E. A. Barber, *CAH* vii, p. 259; J. B. Bury, *The Ancient Greek Historians*, p. 177; W. W. Tarn, *Antigonos Gonatas* (Oxford, 1913), p. 247; C. Wachsmuth, *Einleitung in das Studium der alten Geschichte* (Leipzig, 1895), pp. 580 f.
[3] Dion. Hal. *Ant. Rom.* i.5.4 = *F. Gr. Hist.* 154 F13. For Dionysius' use of Hieronymus in his narrative of Pyrrhus' wars see P. Lévêque, *Pyrrhos* (Paris, 1957), p. 56 n. 10.

kings and cities in eclipse, whose affairs would be of marginal interest to the educated reading public.[4] It is only by chance that we still have so much of Polybius.[5] The first century BC saw a great development in encyclopaedic writing, and the general trend was towards abbreviation. 'Universal' historians like Diodorus, Trogus, and Nicolaus reduced the histories of their predecessors to readable synopses, or absorbed them into their own works without acknowledgement; the biographers plundered them for accounts of interesting individuals, and the strategical writers for specimens of military expertise. Later Justin, compiling what was, in effect, the epitome of an epitome, described himself without shame as an anthologist: 'veluti florum corpusculum feci.'

A spirit of antiquarianism in the imperial period nevertheless helped to preserve knowledge of a few Hellenistic works. Thus Zosimus showed an interest in Polybius which his contemporaries must have regarded as eccentric;[6] and Arrian, imbued with the nostalgia of the Second Sophistic, sought out copies of Ptolemy and Aristobulus for his history of Alexander, and apparently drew on Hieronymus for his τὰ μετὰ Ἀλέξανδρον, which is partially preserved in the Photian epitome and on a Vatican codex;[7] Plutarch, too, may have had access to Hieronymus. Two papyrus fragments of the second century AD have been found this century which come from histories of the Diadochi: one seems to be a fragment of Arrian's work, the other part of the exercise of a private student who had set himself to abridge a Rhodian historian drawing on Hieronymus.[8] No true fragment of Hieronymus has yet appeared on papyrus, but if a manuscript was still available in the second century—presumably in Athens—for Plutarch and Arrian to read, hope is not lost that a copy may yet emerge from the sands of Egypt. There is rather greater probability, perhaps, that more of Arrian's *Successors* may be recovered. Arrian seems to have intended to replace earlier accounts of Macedonian history by his own more fashionable versions, and his writings did survive into the Byzantine

[4] Cf. Paus. i.6.1 on the loss of Hellenistic histories; C. Préaux, *Le Monde hellénistique* Paris (1979), i, p. 28.
[5] Cf. A. Momigliano, *Entretiens Fondation Hardt* xx (1973), pp. 374 ff.; 'Polybius between the English and the Turks', Seventh J. L. Myres Memorial Lecture, Oxford, 1974, *passim*.
[6] Zosimus *Hist. Nov.* i.1.1. Cf. Momigliano, opp. citt.
[7] Arrian, *F. Gr. Hist.* 156 (henceforth cited as Arr. *Succ.*) F1–11. On Plutarch and Hieronymus cf. ch. 2, pp. 67 ff. For the antiquarianism of the Trajanic and Hadrianic period see E. L. Bowie, 'The Greeks and their Past in the Second Sophistic', *Studies in Ancient Society*, London, 1974, pp. 166 ff: esp. pp. 191–5 (on Arrian).
[8] V. Bartoletti, *PSI* xii. 2 (1951), pp. 158 ff. no. 1284; P. Berl. 11632 = *F. Gr. Hist.* 533, Anhang. See below, ch. 2, pp. 30 ff.

period. Himself really only another epitomator, he was exceptional, at least, in his choice of sources, and the recovery of his work on the Diadochi would be of inestimable value to our knowledge of Hieronymus.[9]

In the present state of our knowledge, a handful of citations of Hieronymus—twelve testimonia and eighteen fragments—are preserved; and these provide valuable information about the historian's life.[10] Paradoxically, however, most of what we know about his work comes not from the named fragments, but from derivative accounts in which Hieronymus is not acknowledged, or only acknowledged for particular details. Accordingly, a separate commentary on the fragments is appended to the present study, and an appreciation of Hieronymus' writing has to be based on that section of Diodorus Siculus' world history—Books xviii–xx—which recounts the history of the Diadochi. In this, the most extended literary treatment of the period which survives from antiquity, there is evidence not only that Hieronymus was Diodorus' main source, but that for long sections Diodorus merely paraphrased or extracted, without addition or interpretation except of the simplest kind. It will be evident that the exact nature of this derivation is the central issue in a discussion of Hieronymus. The present work is largely a study in method, which aims to throw light on two Hellenistic historians: Hieronymus himself, and incidentally on Hieronymus' medium, Diodorus, a naïve but puzzling writer, whose method is of general interest to the study of Greek and Roman Republican history.

The intention, however, is not merely to reaffirm or modify the conclusions long since reached in a general way by the traditional methods of source criticism. The loss of most Hellenistic historiography makes the century before Polybius begins a twilight zone, in which we have only glimpses of the contemporary account of Hieronymus—a guide, as Tarn said, to be more than thankful for:[11] but the fact that one historian appears to have dominated the tradition in a poorly documented period suggests the need for especial caution, and the limits of Hieronymus' celebrated trustworthiness need to be defined. An attempt will also be made to estimate his outlook and characterize his writing as a product of its time, since the unique relationship between Diodorus and his sources, which has become increasingly

[9] On Arrian's lack of originality as a historian (against the exalted estimate of E. Schwartz *et al.*) see P. A. Brunt, Loeb edition of Arrian, vol. ii (forthcoming), App. xxviii. I am grateful to Professor Brunt for allowing me to see the typescript of this volume in advance of publication.

[10] F. Jacoby, *F. Gr. Hist.* IIB 154 (henceforth cited as Hier. T and F).

[11] Tarn, *Antigonos Gonatas*, App. i, p. 411.

apparent during the last century, allows us to perceive something of both the substance and the tone of the authors he used.

Hieronymus has attracted the attention of commentators sporadically since the beginnings of modern scholarship. G. J. Voss included a short essay on Hieronymus in his pioneer work on the Greek historians in the early seventeenth century, in which he discussed the most important evidence for his life and tried to distinguish him from his namesakes Hieronymus of Egypt and Hieronymus of Rhodes.[12] In the first part of the eighteenth century the abbé Sévin contributed a discussion of Hieronymus to the *Mémoires de l'académie des inscriptions et belles lettres* of 1737 (a volume which also included essays on Philistus and Timagenes), and in this he attempted to relate the historian to his historical background, but made a number of mistakes in identification. These errors were corrected and serious analysis begun by the German scholar Brückner in his dissertation *De Vita et Scriptis Hieronymi Cardiani* of 1842, which is the foundation of later commentaries.[13] Fr. Reuss's monograph of 1876 was the first extended treatment of Hieronymus, amplifying all Brückner's points and adding an analysis of authors apparently drawing on Hieronymus.[14] Numerous analyses of the sources for the Diadochi followed;[15] but few have considered in a comprehensive way Hieronymus' method and achievement as a historian.[16] Our evidence is defective, but does not preclude such an attempt. One may with justice challenge the assumption that Hieronymus is merely another phantom figure of the third century BC.

[12] G. J. Voss, *De Historicis Graecis*, ed. Westermann, Leipzig (1838), pp. 99 ff.
[13] C. A. F. Brückner, *Zeitschrift für die Alterthumswissenschaft* (1842), pp. 252 ff.
[14] F. Reuss, *Hieronymos von Kardia*, Berlin (1876).
[15] See esp. W. Nietzold, *Die Überlieferung der Diadochen-geschichte*, Würzburg (1905); R. Schubert, 'Die Quellen Plutarchs im *Eumenes, Demetrius* und *Pyrrhus*', *Jahrb. f. kl. Phil.* Suppl. ix (1877–8), and *Quellen zur Geschichte der Diadochenzeit*, Leipzig, 1914; H. Kallenberg, *Philologus* xxxvi–xxxvii (1877–8). For a recent analysis see M. J. Fontana, *Le lotte per la successione di Alessandro Magno*, Palermo, 1960, pp. 151 ff.
[16] The best short study of Hieronymus remains Jacoby's article in Pauly–Wissowa, *Real-Encyclopaedie*, viii (1913) s.v. 'Hieronymos' no. 10 (henceforth cited as Jacoby *RE* 'Hieronymos'). For Hieronymus' political outlook see also T. S. Brown, 'Hieronymus of Cardia' *Am. Hist. Rev.* liii (1947), pp. 684 ff.

Chapter 1

Hieronymus' Life and Writing

A native of Cardia in the Thracian Chersonese (T1), Hieronymus was
born about the middle of the fourth century BC.[1] The general period of
his *floruit* is not in doubt, for he lived to record the death of Pyrrhus in
272 (F15), and according to Agatharchides, cited by Pseudo-Lucian in
the *Macrobioi*, he was 104 years old when he died (T2).[2] It is usually
assumed that this was *c.*260 (allowing him several years after Pyrrhus'
death to write up this part of his history), and that he was born *c.* 364.
This calculation gains support from the fact that he led an important
diplomatic mission from Eumenes to Antipater in the year 320 (T3),
since it might be expected that the chief ambassador would be a man in
middle age. Furthermore, Hieronymus is described as the 'friend' of
Eumenes, who was forty-five when he was executed in winter 317 to
316.[3]

The calculation is, of course, far from precise. It is likely that
Hieronymus was in fact Eumenes' nephew, which suggests a gap
between their ages.[4] A blood relationship could also explain the choice
of Hieronymus as leader of the envoys, even if he were less than thirty.
Elected state ambassadors in classical Greece were normally men of
standing and maturity;[5] but an independent dynast was able to make a
personal appointment, and from Eumenes' point of view Hieronymus'
most important qualifications would be his trustworthiness, and, as his
own friend or relative, ability to inspire trust: a comparable case would
be the action of Philip in sending Alexander as head of the embassy to
Athens after Chaeronea.[6] The reliability of the *Macrobioi* also is
questionable. In this section of the work Pseudo-Lucian was probably
drawing on an earlier compilation of the same sort as his own, rather

---

[1] The testimonia and fragments of Hieronymus are reproduced in App. I.
[2] He certainly died before Antigonus Gonatas in 239, because Ps.-Lucian cites
Hieronymus for the ages of many other diadochs, but another source for that of Gonatas
at his death: Ps.-Lucian, *Macrob.* ii; cf. Polyb. ii.44.1–2.
[3] Nepos, *Eum.* xiii.1.
[4] See below, p. 8.
[5] Cf. D. J. Mosley, *Historia, Einzelschrift* 22 (1973), ch. 8, p. 46; Adcock and Mosley,
Diplomacy in Ancient Greece, ch. 16, pp. 157 f.
[6] K. J. Beloch, *Gr. Gesch.* iii (2) 1, p. 573, with references. Compare also Luke 20: 9,
16: the 'Lord of the vineyard' sends three servants to the wicked husbandmen, and
finally his beloved son, for 'it may be they will reverence him when they see him.'

than making his own calculations, as he does elsewhere;[7] but, if
Agatharchides is correctly cited, one wonders how Agatharchides
knew. Jacoby suggested that autobiographical details were contained
in the preface to Hieronymus' history (we know that Aristobulus
prefaced his history with a statement of his age at the time when he
began the work).[8] No one can record his own death, however, and to
explain the phrase μέχρι τῆς τελευταίας ἡμέρας, it is preferable to
suppose that a friend or editor appended a biographical note to
Hieronymus' manuscript.[9] The statement could, however, have derived ultimately from the mouth of the historian himself, who was
certainly interested in statistics of this kind.[10] Towards the end of his
long life he may have found a certain gloomy satisfaction in recounting
to a younger generation how he had outlived so many of his famous
contemporaries—and have been guilty, perhaps, as very old people
sometimes are, of a little exaggeration.

If a slight distortion, possibly originating with Hieronymus himself,
is admitted in the traditional figure, Hieronymus' birth may be placed
sometime during the 350s. Thus his childhood fell during a period
when Athens had concluded her struggles against her allies in the east
Mediterranean, and when the new king of Macedon was beginning to
look towards the Chersonese; a period in which his city sought, first of
all, autonomy and independence, and when that was no longer possible, the alliance of Philip. Cardia, founded in the seventh century by
Miletus and Clazomenae and by 342 the greatest city in the Chersonese, had always been exceptional in its politics.[11] Its inhabitants were

[7] F. Rühl, *Rh. Mus.* lxii, pp. 421 ff., accepts the arguments of Hirschfield (*Hermes* xxiv, pp. 156 ff.) for a date in the time of Caracalla, and suggests that Ps.-Lucian and Phlegon used a common source, of uncertain date, for their notices on the ages of historians, and possibly for those on kings and generals: cf. ch. 10, Ps.-Lucian makes the same mistakes as Phlegon on the age of Arganthonius; ch. 17, ἱστορήκασι indicates an earlier compilation deriving ultimately from historical sources.

[8] Ps.-Lucian, *Macrob.* 22; cf. Jacoby, *RE* 'Hieronymos', col. 1542 and *F. Gr. Hist.* IID, p. 545.

[9] Cf. below, p. 15.

[10] Hier. F8,10, 7, 4: Ps.-Lucian cites Hieronymus for the ages of Antigonus Monoph-thalmus, Lysimachus, Mithridates, and Ariarathes, and he may be the authority for the ages of Antipater and Ptolemy, who are mentioned in the same group of octogenarians. Cf. C. F. Edson, *HSCP* xlv (1934), p. 225 n. 2. The suggestion of T. S. Brown, art. cit., p. 685, that the figure 104 has 'mystical' significance is not persuasive.

[11] Foundation of Cardia: G. Busolt, *Gr. Gesch.* i², pp. 463–4; Beloch, *Gr. Gesch.* i², 1, p. 256. Demosth. ix. 35: Χερρονήσσον . . . τὴν μεγίστην πόλιν Καρδίαν. (For the date of this speech see R. Sealey, *REG* lxviii (1955), pp. 101 ff.) The early Ionian foundations of the Chersonese seem to have been small agricultural colonies: Demeter and Persephone on the coins of Cardia and Sestos are crowned with ears of corn. (Compare Plut. *Eum.* vi.5: on the eve of his battle against Craterus at the Hellespont, Eumenes of Cardia dreamed that Demeter wove a wreath of corn for the victor, and he

not all, or not purely Greek, for Herodotus implies that the Dolonci formed a large part of the population, and that the peninsula was hellenized only as a result of Athenian colonization.[12] During the sixth century Cardia had its first taste of tyranny when the elder Miltiades made it the centre of his private empire. In 493 the city medized and the younger Miltiades was expelled: 'As for the Chersonese,' said Herodotus, 'the Phoenicians subdued all the towns in it πλὴν Καρδίης πόλιος', the first use of a phrase familiar in the fourth century.[13] The position of Cardia on the corn route from the Black Sea made it an important possession in the Athenian Empire;[14] and though we have no evidence that the city defected in its payments of tribute, the Cardians of the fourth century did not forget the burdens of the Athenian ἀρχή, and after the Social War stood resolute against renewed attempts by the Athenians to control their city.[15] In 352 Cardian territory was excepted when Cersobleptes handed over the Chersonese to Athens, and for a few years seems to have enjoyed independence; but Cardia was an ally of Philip before 346, according to Philip's own statement, and was enrolled as such in the Peace of Philocrates.[16] Demosthenes tried to insinuate in 341 that Philip was in breach of the peace in defending Cardia against Diopeithes, but such help as he did send was justified by an alliance of more than five years standing.[17] The Cardians preferred the patronage of Macedon to the interference of Chares or the depredations of Diopeithes, and the hostility between Athens and Cardia was deep. When Demosthenes described to the Athenians the atrocity committed by the Cardians against Miltocythes, he said that their behaviour was worse than that of barbarians,

gave 'Demeter and Alexander' as his watchword.) They were not very important places during the 5th century, because the whole of the Chersonese is assessed together at 18 talents in the Athenian Tribute Lists, though it is likely that this sum was paid by Cardia on behalf of itself and the other cities: cf. H. T. Wade-Gery, *JHS* lii (1932), pp. 266–7 = *Essays*, p. 269. We have coins only from about 400 BC, of which the chief types are the heads of Demeter and Persephone, and the lion or lion's head, the emblem of Miletus: cf. J. Brandis, *Münzmass und Gewichtswesen in Vorderasien bis auf Alexander den Grossen*, Berlin (1866), pp. 394 ff.

[12] Herodotus vi.34–40; cf. Busolt, loc. cit.

[13] Herodotus vi.34. He means it did not need to be conquered, because it came over voluntarily: cf. How and Wells, comm. ad loc.; Hdt. vi.58, ix.115.

[14] Cardia may have paid tribute on behalf of the other Chersonesian cities: cf. n. 26.

[15] On 4th-century Cardia see N. G. L. Hammond and G. T. Griffith, *Macedonia*, Oxford (1972 and 1979), vol. ii, pp. 380 f.

[16] Demosth. xvi.34.4; Ps.-Demosth. xii. For the clause in the peace of Philocrates, Demosth. v.25, xix.174. Cf. Hammond and Griffith, op. cit., p. 381: the alliance perhaps went back to 352.

[17] Demosth. viii, *On the Chersonese* (341 BC), esp. paragraphs 64, 66: cf. Schol. Aesch. iii.38. On the truth of Demosthenes' allegations, see G. L. Cawkwell, *CQ* n.s. xiii (1963) p. 200.

and spoke of the Cardians as 'your enemies'—Καρδιανοῖς τοῖς ὑμετέροις ἐχθροῖς.[18] We need not doubt that the sentiment was returned.

The city of Hieronymus' birth, part Thracian, and touched by the lengthening arm of Philip, was not, therefore, a typical Greek city. Hieronymus' elders had rejected alliance with one of the old leaders of Greece and had cast in their lot with the new power to their west; and the Cardian background is of considerable significance when one considers Hieronymus' later career among Macedonians and his attitude to the Greek states under Macedonian suzerainty. Personal links with the Macedonian nobility may have existed at an early stage. Arrian tells us that Eumenes' father was called Hieronymus,[19] and the common custom of Greek nomenclature, by which names were shared by grandparents and grandchildren, suggests that Hieronymus the father of Eumenes may have been the grandfather of Hieronymus the historian, who is described as φίλος καὶ πολίτης of Eumenes.[20] It is both possible and plausible that he was Eumenes' nephew; and it should hardly surprise us if the two most distinguished of all Cardians were members of the same family. According to Nepos (*Eum.* 1.2), Eumenes was 'domestico summo genere'; and Plutarch (in a passage where he is probably following Hieronymus), says that Eumenes owed his advancement under Philip and Alexander to the guest friendship which existed between his father and Philip.[21] Hieronymus the elder was therefore a prominent citizen of Cardia, the friend of Philip, perhaps active in persuading his fellow citizens to accept the alliance of Philip in the 340s; and Hieronymus the younger would have grown up in a Cardian family notable for its Macedonian politics, in which the topics of the Macedonian alliance, Philip's growing empire, and the character of Philip himself, were, no doubt, constantly under discussion. We may speculate whether Hieronymus ever met Philip and was inspired by that great man with lifelong admiration for the Macedonian character. It seems certain, at least, that his early environment inculcated in him attitudes to the future masters of the world which were not shared by his contemporaries in Athens or Thebes.

The Cardia of Hieronymus' early years was a democracy. During the reign of Alexander it was ruled by the tyrant Hecataeus, who had

[18] Demosth. xxiv.169. Cf. also Demosth. xxiii.183: Apollonides the Cardian acts against the interests of Athens.

[19] Arrian, *Ind.*18: the suggestion that the historian was related to Eumenes was first made by U. Köhler, 'Über die Diadochengeschichte Arrians', *Sitz. d. Berl. Akad.* 1890, p. 558 n. 1.

[20] Diod. xviii.50.4 = Hier. T4.

[21] Plut. *Eum.* i.1. Cf. Hammond and Griffith, loc. cit., on Eumenes and Philip.

perhaps seized power in a period of uncertainty following the assassination of Philip, and whose son was thriving at the end of the fourth century.[22] Hecataeus was the political enemy of Eumenes—ἦν γὰρ αὐτοῖς πατρική τις ἐκ πολιτικῶν διαφορῶν ὑποψία πρὸς ἀλλήλους— and we are told that Eumenes frequently denounced Hecataeus and urged Alexander to restore its freedom to Cardia.[23] Their enmity was such that Eumenes feared he might be murdered by Antipater to please Hecateus; and doubtless Eumenes took himself to Philip's court and followed Alexander because his position in Cardia under the tyranny had become impossible. We hear of another Cardian in Alexander's retinue, Xenodochus, who, perhaps for similar reasons, sought his fortune away from his native city.[24] Hieronymus' career during this period is quite unknown. He may have shared Eumenes' exile and taken part in the great expedition to the East; through nothing that we know of his history necessarily suggests personal knowledge of Alexander or of his campaigns.[25]

It was in the period after Alexander's death that he became of real service to Eumenes, who, suffering as he did from the disadvantage of being a non-Macedonian and having, so far, a relatively undistinguished military career, needed to marshal support for the coming struggle.[26] He must have been a member of Eumenes' staff by 322, when Eumenes was confirmed as satrap of Cappadocia after the defeat of Ariarathes, and made a number of administrative appointments in his new satrapy.[27] Some reorganization of the army must also have been necessary after the recent war with Ariarathes;[28] but it is not clear

[22] *IG* iv² 49: 'Ηγησίστρατος 'Εκαταίου Καρδιανός is made proxenos and thearodokos of the Epidaurians. The inscription is to be dated to the late 4th century, and must antedate 309, when Cardia lost its independent identity as a city (Paus. i.9.8). The 'thearodoky' was given to the most prominent citizens of Greek states: hence possibly Hegesistratos succeeded his father as tyrant of Cardia: cf. Chr. Habicht, *Chiron* ii (1972), pp. 105 f.

[23] Plut. *Eum*. iii.4.

[24] Plut. *Alex*. li. H. Berve, *Das Alexanderreich*, München (1926), ii, no. 575 infers from Xenodochus' position with Alexander that he was 'vornehmen Standes'. Samian honorary decrees from the years 314–306 mention a Cardian who performed services to Samians in exile before 322 and then entered the service of Antigonus and Demetrius; the name is unfortunately lost, though in lines 2–3 ['Ιερώνυμο]ς would fit. See E. Buschor, *Misc. Acad. Berol.* ii.2, 1950, 27; cf. Habicht, art. cit., p. 106 n.10. Naturally a Cardian would wish to help Samians against Athens.

[25] Jacoby, *RE* 'Hieronymos', col. 1540, thinks Hieronymus was probably with Eumenes already at the time of Alexander's death.

[26] Arr. *Anab*. v.24.6: Eumenes was made hipparch under Alexander.

[27] Plut. *Eum*. iii.7; καὶ τὰς μὲν πόλεις τοῖς ἑαυτοῦ φίλοις παρέδωκε, καὶ φρουράρχους ἐγκατέστησε καὶ δικαστὰς ἀπέλιπε καὶ διοικητὰς οὓς ἐβούλετο. Cf. P. Briant, *REA* lxxiv (1972), pp. 32 ff. for discussion of these arrangements.

[28] Briant, *Antigone le Borgne*, Paris, 1973, pp. 147 f. infers from Plut. *Eum*. iii.5 that Eumenes had been given part of the royal army by Perdiccas.

whether Hieronymus began on the civil or on the military side. Jacoby saw him as a non-military man, but the sharp distinction implied is hardly tenable.[29] Eumenes and Antigonus used him as envoy and diplomat; Demetrius made him harmost of Thebes—an office with military powers; the expedition which he led to the Dead Sea was possibly more scientific than military, since it could not defend itself against the attacks of hostile Arabs, but his title on this occasion, *epimeletes*, does have military implications.[30] Possibly his main functions in his early career were those of a *grammateus*: in this capacity Eumenes had served Alexander, and it was a job for which an educated Greek was needed.[31] The sources speak frequently of letters and other documents to which a member of the chancellery would have had ready access, including letters written 'in Syrian characters'— Συρίοις γράμμασιν—i.e. Aramaic, the common language of the Achaemenid empire.[32] Few of Alexander's generals bothered to learn Persian:[33] the task of reading, writing, and translating therefore fell largely on the Greek staff and their interpreters, who would have been exceptionally well informed about the affairs of empire. Hieronymus is described as *philos* of Eumenes, which possibly has a technical as well as personal sense. The *philoi* of the Macedonian kings and generals normally formed a military advisory council; but in the settled kingdoms of the Diadochi the functions of the king's *philoi* became divided between the military and the civil, and Hieronymus should perhaps be seen as a forerunner of the class of civil servants which grew up under the Seleucids and Ptolemies.[34]

Hieronymus emerges at last into the light of history in 320, when he accompanied Eumenes, now formally outlawed by the Macedonians as a former adherent of Perdiccas, to the Phrygian hill fortress of Nora. Here they were besieged by the forces of Antigonus, and Hieronymus is mentioned by Diodorus and Plutarch as leader of the embassy sent by Eumenes to Antipater to discuss terms for Eumenes' surrender

---

[29] Cf. Jacoby, *RE* 'Hieronymos', col. 1541; and see below, n. 43.

[30] Hier. T3, 4, 8, 6.

[31] Cf. Jacoby *RE* 'Hieronymos', col. 1541; Berve i, pp. 42–55; M. Rostovtzeff, *RE* vi. s.v. *Epistula* no. 2 (*ab epistulis*), on the position of *grammateis* in the Hellenistic period.

[32] Diod. xix.23.3; 96.1.

[33] Peucestas: Arr. *Anab*. vi.30.3, vii.6.3; cf. Berve ii, no. 634. Cf. Arr. *Anab*. iii.6.6, Laomedon was said to be δίγλωσσος ἐς τὰ βαρβαρικὰ γράμματα. But at iv.3.7 a Lycian interpreter, Pharnouches, is used.

[34] E. H. Bevan, *The House of Seleucus*, London, 1902, ii, pp. 280 ff.: the title *philos* signified status rather than office, but the body of *philoi* inevitably tended to include the chief ministers and military officers, such as the Minister of Finance (ὁ ἐπὶ τῶν προσόδων: App. *Syr*. 45), Secretary of State (ἐπιστολαγράφος: Polyb. xxx.25.16).

(T3, 4). We are not told whether the embassy achieved its purpose. Antipater died about this time, and affairs in Macedon were thrown into confusion by the disagreement between Cassander and Polyperchon. Hieronymus may have received assurances of assistance, however, because after his return Eumenes continued to hold out at Nora, and Polyperchon later wrote to him with offers of money and the office of *strategos autokrator* in Asia.[35] On his return to Nora, Hieronymus was approached by Antigonus, whose permission must have been needed before the envoys could re-enter the fortress. Antigonus asked him to deliver to Eumenes a proposal of alliance and partnership, terms which were, in effect, a counter to those which Hieronymus had brought back from Macedon. He also offered Hieronymus μεγάλαι δωρεαί. Whether these were accepted, our sources do not relate: Hieronymus perhaps mentioned them in order to enhance his own importance in the transaction.

In winter 317–316, after the defeat at Gabiene and Eumenes' execution by Antigonus, Hieronymus was brought in among the wounded prisoners of war, and won the trust and kindness of Antigonus, whose service he is now entered (T5). The transfer of troops from the camp of the defeated to that of the victor was common practice during the wars of the Successors—often there was probably no alternative.[36] His acquaintance with Antigonus formed during the negotiations at Nora doubtless made the change easier, and our sources preserve echoes of the propaganda, possibly transmitted through Hieronymus himself, by which Antigonus tried to exonerate himself from responsibility for Eumenes' death and mitigate the blow to Eumenes' followers. Diodorus asserts that Antigonus was unwilling to kill Eumenes—which seems unlikely, since he had fought for four years to eliminate him—and was forced to do so by the demands of the Macedonian soldiers, from whose leaders he later exacted a just retribution.[37] It is said also that he treated Eumenes with kindness during his last days and allowed his ashes to be sent home to his relatives; and Plutarch records that Nearchus the Cretan and the eighteen-year-old Demetrius pleaded with Antigonus for Eumenes' life.[38] This was perhaps the

[35] Diod. xviii.57–8. For the result of Hieronymus' mission cf. Justin xiv.2.4.

[36] Rostovtzeff, *SEHHW* i, p. 148, iii, p. 1345 n. 17; Griffith, *Mercenaries of the Hellenistic World*, Cambridge (1935), pp. 261 f. Cf. also Diod. xviii.41.4, Antigonus takes over many of Eumenes' troops after the battle of Orkynia; Plut. *Eum.* v.5, the defeated troops of Neoptolemus join up with Eumenes (and cf. the Arrian fragment *PSI* xii.1284); Diod. xviii.32.2, Eumenes hoped for the same result by his concessions to the defeated army of Craterus in 321; Diod. xix.73.10, Lysimachus absorbs part of Pausanias's army.

[37] Diod. xix.44.2–3; cf. 48.3–4. Cf. Engel, *Athenaeum* n.s. l (1972), p. 122.

[38] Diod. xix.44.2; Plut. *Eum.* xix.2, xviii.3.

beginning of Hieronymus' friendship with Demetrius. Our sources are well informed about incidents like the battle of Gaza, the battle of Salamis, and the siege of Rhodes, involving Demetrius alone, and again about those such as the Arabian expedition, on which both Demetrius and his father were present, but have little to say about Antigonus in the periods when he was apart from Demetrius— Diodorus is completely silent on the struggle between Antigonus and Seleucus after 312—and this suggests that Hieronymus was attached to the staff of Demetrius after winter 317 to 316, perhaps to spare him the embarrassment of direct subordination to his former enemy. References to Demetrius at the battles of Paraetacene and Gabiene (Diod. xix.29.4; 40.1), where he held his first commands in battle, introduce us to the young prince in whom Hieronymus may have thought at first he saw a second Alexander: the portrait of Demetrius at the time of Gaza, and the description of his prowess at Salamis, seem to reflect this early period of optimism, when it looked as though Antigonus and Demetrius would conquer Asia and establish themselves as Alexander's heirs. The four special councillors assigned to Demetrius by Antigonus before Gaza included two Greeks, Andronicus of Olynthus and Nearchus the Cretan (already associated with Demetrius on the occasion of Eumenes' execution); and it is not unlikely that Hieronymus, too, was among the *philoi* who advised Demetrius not to fight Ptolemy in 312 and whose advice was ignored.[39]

Diodorus mentions the historian once more on Antigonus' Arabian expedition in 312 (T6), when Hieronymus is named as leader of a party ordered to collect bitumen from the Dead Sea. He is described as 'overseer (ἐπιμελητής) of the revenue'—a vague title, but it is not impossible that Antigonus envisaged an office of a permanent nature. The administration of his Asian possessions was a major concern to Antigonus: directly after his victory over Eumenes the people of Asia began to call him *basileus*, and he began to treat the conquered territory as a kingdom, establishing a communications system like that of the Achaemenid rulers, appointing his own nominees as satraps, and inquiring into the financial accounts of the satraps; later he set up a mint at Tyre, and founded cities: when in 302 he was called to Ipsus it was from the festival celebrating the founding of his new capital at Antigoneia. Territorial aggrandizement does not seem to have been an end in itself for Antigonus, as it was for Alexander: his main object was the secure establishment of his dynasty, as modern writers have

---

[39] Diod. xix.69.1; 81.1.

stressed.[40] The discovery of the 'asphalt lake' pleased him because he thought it would be a source of revenue for the kingdom—δοκεῖν εὑρηκέναι τινα τῇ βασιλείᾳ πρόσοδον (xix.100.1): bitumen was exported to Egypt for use in the embalming process.[41] Nor was this the only commercial advantage of the region: the Nabataeans asked disingenuously what Antigonus hoped to gain by conquering a nomad people of the desert; but they did not mention the great caravan route which passed through Petra, carrying the spices of Arabia to Egypt and the Syrian coast. The importance of this route was certainly appreciated by the Ptolemies, and suggests that Hieronymus' expedition was not merely a raiding party.[42] Antigonus' exact methods of government are unknown, but Hieronymus' appointment could have been seen in the wider perspective of a settled and prosperous kingdom, in which he was intended as military governor of one of the southern regions.[43] On this view we might explain Josephus' statement that Hieronymus 'governed Syria': τὴν Συρίαν ἐπετρόπευεν.[44]

Hereafter Hieronymus' fortunes must have run parallel to those of Demetrius. A notice in the *Macrobioi* cities him for the age of Antigonus at Ipsus, and describes him as ὁ συστρατευόμενος αὐτῶι (sc. Ἀντιγόνωι):[45] the sense is ambiguous, but we have no reason to doubt that Hieronymus was present at the 'battle of the kings', and witnessed the sudden ruin of Antigonus' great hopes. In 293 he held another post of importance when Demetrius made him governor of Thebes after the Boeotian revolt: ὁ δὲ ταῖς πόλεσιν ἐμβαλὼν φρουρὰν καὶ πραξάμενος πολλὰ χρήματα καὶ καταλιπὼν αὐτοῖς ἐπιμελητὴν καὶ ἁρμοστὴν Ἱερώνυμον τὸν ἱστορικόν, ἔδοξεν ἠπίως κεχρῆσθαι (Plut. *Demetr.* xxxix.3–7 = T8). Boeotia now became, like Athens, a subject state, and Demetrius departed from the policy of Cassander and

[40] For this aspect of Antigonus' achievement see esp. C. Wehrli, *Antigone et Démétrios*, Geneva, 1968, pp. 75–102.
[41] Diod. xix.99.3; but see below, ch. 4, pp. 149 ff.
[42] P. M. Fraser, *Ptolemaic Alexandria*, Oxford, 1972, i, pp. 176 f., ii, pp. 300 f. n. 350. Cf. Rostovtzeff, *SEHHW* i, pp. 387 f.
[43] Diod. xix.100.1 calls Hieronymus ἐπιμελητής, which in Hellenistic histories regularly implies military functions: cf. F. W. Walbank, *HCP* i, pp. 533 f.; W. S. Ferguson, *Hellenistic Athens*, London, 1911, p. 47 n. 3 (comparing Diod. xviii.74.3, xx.45.3 etc., where Demetrius of Phaleron is called ἐπιμελητής); *Syll.*³ 318 = IG II² 1201, line 11, Wilhelm supplements ἐπιμελητής (of Demetrius of Phaleron). The trilingual inscription from Xanthos gives a new instance of the word in this sense: see H. Metzger, *CRAI* 1974, pp. 82 ff., and *Fouilles de Xanthos* vi, Paris, 1979. Cf. also *Syll.*³ 534, line 6 with Pomtow, n. 3; Durrbach, *Choix d'Inscriptions de Délos*, no. 95. Hieronymus held the same office at Thebes under Demetrius (Plut. *Demetr.* xxxix.3–7 = Hier. T8), where he must, in the circumstances, have had military competence.
[44] Joseph. *c. Apion.* i.213–14 = Hier. F6.
[45] Ps.-Lucian, *Macrobioi* 11 = Hier. T7.

Philip, which might be called the traditional Macedonian policy, hated by the Greeks, of controlling the Greek cities by means of local tyrants and factions, in favour of direct rule through his own governors.[46] The 'Macedonizing' of Greeks from the peripheries of the Greek world is nowhere better illustrated than in the appointment of the Cardian Hieronymus to govern Thebes, champion of Greek liberty, in the name of the Macedonian suzerain. His task was not an easy one: while Demetrius was absent in Thessaly, the Thebans organized a second insurrection; though there is no evidence that the governor had shown incompetence.[47]

The duration of his governorship is unknown, but the second subjugation of Thebes must have brought Hieronymus in close contact with Antigonus Gonatas, who defeated the Thebans in battle during his father's absence. He was perhaps between sixty-five and seventy years old in 287—not too old for Demetrius' expedition into Asia; but the king may have preferred to leave his trusted servant as friend and counsellor to his son, as Antigonus the elder had left him with Demetrius at the time of Demetrius' first independent command. He may be imagined among the 'friends and commanders' at Athens and Corinth, to whom Demetrius sent word after his capture that they should regard him as dead and take orders in future only from Antigonus: this notice in Plutarch (*Demetr.* li.i) probably comes from Hieronymus' history. He then shared with Antigonus the period of watching and waiting. By 279, Antigonus' possessions in Greece were limited to Demetrias, Corinth, and Piraeus, and like Demetrius, he sailed for Asia to seek better fortune.[48] At Lysimacheia his luck changed; and the prestige of his Gallic victory carried him into Macedon.[49] In 309 Lysimachus had ruined or eclipsed the town of Cardia by the foundation of his own capital city, and if Hieronymus was with Antigonus in 277 he would, by a curious irony, have marched with the victorious Macedonian army from the site of Cardia to the royal court at Pella. There was by this time nothing at Cardia to make him return: 'the greatest city of the Chersonese' had become a village, and the political background of Hieronymus' youth—the feud between the factions of Hecataeus and Eumenes, and the issue of the alliance with Macedon—had disap-

---

[46] For Demetrius' policy towards Boeotia see P. Treves, 'Jeronimo di Cardia e la politica di Demetrio Poliorcete', *Riv. Fil.* x (1932), pp. 194 ff. J. Briscoe, *The Antigonids and the Greek States* in *Imperialism in the Ancient World*, ed. Garnsey and Whittaker, Cambridge, 1978, p. 146 regards Demetrius' policy as no less severe than Cassander's. On *epimeletes* see above, n. 43.

[47] So T. S. Brown, art. cit., p. 690.

[48] Tarn, *Antigonos Gonatas*, p. 137.

[49] Ibid., pp. 165 f. Gonatas struck the first coins of his reign at Lysimacheia: cf. F. Heichelheim, *AJP* lxiv (1943), pp. 332 f.

peared along with the city itself.[50] One must suppose, therefore, that Hieronymus, already a Macedonian by adoption, finally found a home in the country of his master. He may have gone to the Peloponnese with Antigonus for the final campaign against Pyrrhus, for he seems to have recorded this episode in detail (F14, 15), though by the time of Pyrrhus' death in 272 he must have been an old man of over eighty. We may assume that the evening of his life was passed in comfortable retirement in Macedon, pensioned and rewarded as his forty years of service to the family of Antigonus deserved.

Our last testimony on Hieronymus' life comes from a *Life of Aratus*, in which it is said that Antigonus wrote either to or about Hieronymus.[51] Either reading is evidence of a close relationship between Antigonus and Hieronymus, confirmed by Pausanias' comment that Hieronymus wrote ἐς ἡδονὴν Ἀντιγόνου and praised him immoderately.[52] 'About Hieronymus' suggests a biography or an obituary notice written by Antigonus, and it is tempting to connect such a work with *Testimonium* 2, which contains information about Hieronymus' age and his state of health in his last days which can only have come from an editor or biographer. Perhaps the reading πρὸς Ἱερώνυμον is more likely, however, since Antigonus is said to have mentioned a number of the philosophers and men of letters who formed a cultural circle at his court: Aratus, Persaeus, Antagoras, and Alexander the Aetolian. Jacoby's suggestion that this was an invitation to Hieronymus to join Antigonus and his friends at court is an attractive one, which incidentally depicts Hieronymus living in retirement away from Pella, no doubt on a country estate bestowed on him by the king.[53] Here, probably, he ended his long life, remaining, according to Agatharchides' statement, sound in mind and body until his last day;[54] and here he would have completed his history, the fruit of a life which can scarcely be paralleled among historians of any

---

[50] Foundation of Lysimacheia: Justin xvii.1; Strabo vii, p. 331, frgs. 52, 54; cf. Paus. i.9.8. Cardia was not totally destroyed, or else it later revived, because Appian, *B.C.* iv.88, says that at the time of the civil wars Lysimacheia and Cardia occupied between them, like gates, the isthmus of the Thracian Chersonese; and Pausanias, i.10.5, speaks of Cardia as a village still existing in his own time. In c.230 BC a proxenos of Coroneia in Boeotia could be described as Καρδιανός: *SEG* xxiii.289. On the site of Lysimacheia see Walbank, *HCP* ii, p. 478, with references.

[51] Theon, *Vit. Arat.* p. 147, 18M = Hier. T9. The reading is either ἐν τοῖς πρὸς Ἱερώνυμον, or ἐν τοῖς περὶ Ἱερωνύμου. Cf. F. Susemihl, *Gesch. d. gr. Lit.* i, p. 3.

[52] Paus. i.13.9, i.9.7 = Hier. F15, F9.

[53] Jacoby, *RE* 'Hieronymos', col. 1542. For Antigonus' circle cf. Tarn, *Antigonos Gonatas*, ch.vii, *passim*. Susemihl, loc. cit., thinks that 'to Hieronymus' would indicate Hieronymus of Rhodes as the addressee: cf. below, App. I, p. 253.

[54] On the importance of health in old age at this period see W. S. Ferguson, *Hell. Athens*, p. 86.

period in its range of experience and in the momentous changes of the times it encompassed.[55]

The best histories, according to Polybius' maxim, are written by men who have practical knowledge of affairs. In this Hieronymus represented the antithesis to that other great historian of the third century, his younger contemporary Timaeus, who supposedly hardly left his library. It was the historian of the West who attracted the doubtful honour of Polybius' attention; to the historian of the East he might have been more amiable. A Greek, of standing in his native city, but for most of his active life an exile; a diplomat and man of action, who came to admire the power that eclipsed his own nation, winning the friendship and patronage of its leading statesmen, and writing a history of his times which favoured his foreign masters: in many respects Hieronymus invites comparison with Polybius himself. The comparison extends, according to some commentators, to their writings. But here we confront the unavoidable obstacle, that not a word of Hieronymus is directly attested.

None of the fragments of Hieronymus is a direct quotation, and the total number in Jacoby's collection, eighteen, and a doubtful nineteenth, is far smaller than the number for Timaeus, Duris, or Phylarchus. The citations are in general helpful ones, however, from which one may determine the approximate scope of the work and some of its characteristics.[56] The earliest fragment that is exactly datable deals with events in Cappadocia of the year 322 (F3), the latest with the death of Pyrrhus in 272 (F15): the history thus covered a span of at least fifty years, and may have been prefaced by a survey of the earlier history of Macedon (F1). No book numbers are cited, but the work was of considerable length, because Hieronymus gave details on the casualties in Pyrrhus' battles in Italy (F11, 12), and these cannot have been central to the history. There seem also to have been numerous digressions: on the funeral carriage of Alexander (F2), on the Dead Sea (F5), on the early history of Rome (F13), the topography of Corinth (F16), the ancient history of Thessaly (F17), the geography of Crete (F18). Moreover, Josephus' complaint that Hieronymus failed to write about the Jews (F6) suggests that he did write about other foreign peoples. These examples of discursive writing—six out of the eighteen fragments—in which Hieronymus filled in the background to places and events mentioned in his history, show us a historian with the wide-ranging antiquarian and ethnographical interests of his Ionian

---

[55] S. Mazzarino, *Il Pensiero Storico* ii, Bari (1966), p. 334, compares Hieronymus to the mediaeval French historian and diplomat, Philippe de Commynes.

[56] See App. I for a detailed commentary on the fragments of Hieronymus.

forefathers from Miletus. At the same time, his history was characterized by a remarkable precision in statistical details: he is cited for
the ages of Ariarathes, Mithridates, Antigonus Monophthalmus, and
Lysimachus (F4, 7, 8, 10) at the time of their deaths; for the measurement of the ditch which the Spartans dug as a defence against Pyrrhus
(F14); for the casualty figures at Heraclea and Asculum (F11, 12); for
the size of the island of Crete (F18); and wherever his evidence
conflicts with that of another writer, it is almost always the more
conservative estimate, a fact which encourages faith in his accuracy.
That Hieronymus was reliable in his treatment of historical personalities is less certain. Pausanias alleges that he slandered Lysimachus
because he had a grudge against him for destroying the town of Cardia,
and claims that he was hostile to 'all the kings except Antigonus'
(F9)—Antigonus Gonatas, that is, as becomes clear from a later
passage (F15), where he implies that Hieronymus was unfair in his
treatment of Pyrrhus because he wrote to please Antigonus.

The fragments show, at least, that this was a serious historian. By
themselves, however, they take us no further, except to serve as
criteria in tracing the use of Hieronymus by later writers; and it is in the
latter that there lies the real hope of reconstructing some substantial
portion of his work. All ancient accounts of the Diadochi, there is
general agreement, derive in some degree from Hieronymus. But
most writers are reticent in acknowledging their sources, and they
often used several authors simultaneously, rewriting according to their
own interpretation and for their own purposes. Diodorus of Agyrrhium is an exception:[57] he did not draw on Hieronymus casually for
biography, regional history, or strategic *exempla*, but swallowed
whole slices of his work into his own vast compendium of the history of
the world. It will be argued that his narrative of the years 323 to 302
provides a continuous text which can be used, despite many qualifications, to estimate Hieronymus' writing, and which acts as a vital
supplement to the small collection of fragments in which Hieronymus
is cited by name.

---

[57] The library-list discovered in 1969 on fragments of a *pinax* from Tauromenium in
Sicily, only fifty miles from Agyrrhium, shows that Diodorus, even in this provincial
setting, had access to such historians as Callisthenes, Philistus, and Fabius Pictor: he did
not necessarily have to go to Rome (though he claims to have worked there: i.4.2) to
read a copy of Hieronymus. See G. Manganaro, *Parola del Passato* xxix (1974),
pp. 389 ff., for text and discussion: the Tauromenium library may have specialized in
historiography.

were first translated from Greek into Latin by Lehan Lascary, then from Latin into French by Claude de Seyssel in 1530; and from the French into English by Thomas Stocker in 1569; and each of these editions included a translation of Plutarch's *Life of Demetrius* as an epilogue to the story of the Diadochi.[6] One copy of Seyssel's French edition, which had originally been dedicated to Louis XII, bears the autograph monogram of Henry VIII on the title page.[7] Interest in Diodorus in England was not confined to intellectual royalty. Henry Cogan translated the first six books into English in 1653; and in 1700 George Booth of Chester testified to his continuing popularity by 'making English' the first fifteen books of the *Bibliotheke*.[8]

But already some scholars had looked beyond Diodorus' entertainment value. In 1670, J. H. Boecler included in his *Lectiones Polybianae* an essay entitled 'Diodori Siculi Imitatio Polybiana'; and in his great edition of 1746 Wesseling suggested that parts of Diodorus' preface were dependent on Polybius and remarked that he often seemed to imitate the spirit of Polybius in a general way. Since that time faith in Diodorus' value as an independent historian has gradually been eroded, and nineteenth-century German scholarship made his work one of the most eligible subjects for the operations of *Quellenforschung*. Niebuhr described him as 'naïve, unlearned, totally spiritless, without judgement, silly, incompetent even as an epitomiser', one of the 'worst historians who has come down to us in either of the languages of antiquity from any period'; and Mommsen, equally damning, spoke of the 'incredible foolishness and even more incredible unscrupulousness of this most miserable of all writers'.[9] These sweeping judgements were qualified, but rarely contradicted in later years; and Schwartz's analysis of Diodorus' sources in his Pauly–Wissowa article of 1905 summed up the prevailing mood of scepticism.[10] Since then it has been usual to regard the *Bibliotheke* as

---

[6] 'L'histoire des successeurs de Alexandre le Grand, extraicte de Diodore Sicilien: et quelque peu de vies éscriptes par Plutarque, etc.'; Translatée de Grec en Latin par messire Lehan Lascary. Et de Latin en Francoys par messire Claude de Seyssel. Paris, 1530. Thomas Stocker: 'A righte noble and pleasant History of the Successors of Alexander surnamed the Great, taken out of Diodorus Siculus; and some of their lives written by the wise Plutarch.' London, 1569.

[7] HR: BM General Catalogue, loc. cit. No. C45g4.

[8] Cogan: 'The History of Diodorus Siculus. Containing all that is most memorable and of greatest antiquity in the first ages of the world until the war of Troy. Done into English by H. C. Gent.' London, 1653. Booth: 'The Historical Library of Diodorus the Sicilien. In 15 books . . . Made English, by G. Booth, of the City of Chester, Esq.' London, 1700.

[9] Cf. L. O. Bröcker, *Untersuchungen über Diodor*, Gütersloh, 1879, p. 5.

[10] Schwartz, *RE* v (1905), s.v. 'Diodorus' No. 38, cols. 663 ff.; see esp. col. 669: 'Die Frage nach den Gewährsmännern ist bei D. noch cardinaler als bei anderen secundären

derivative in the most damaging sense of that word. The sources Diodorus is thought to have used include a number of very important or interesting historians whose works are otherwise lost: Schwartz's list includes Hecataeus of Abdera, Ctesias, Posidonius, Agatharchides, Megasthenes, Ephorus, Cleitarchus, Duris, and Hieronymus. The crucial question is the manner in which Diodorus derives from these authors.

Diodorus does not tell us that he is a compiler. He cites a number of authors, especially in the early books on prehistory and foreign lands, where he may have felt that there was less discredit in admitting his debt;[11] but the citations are embedded in the surrounding text in such a way that it is often unclear exactly where they begin and end. In Books xviii–xx he twice cites Timaeus for Western history (xx.79.5, 89.5), but for the narrative of Greek and Asian affairs no authorities are named. Certainty about what sources are being used, and how, could only be reached if we possessed original histories of the period; but we do not have one of the works which Diodorus cites or is suspected of having used—except Polybius, and the part of the *Bibliotheke* which seems to follow Polybius itself survives only in fragments. As so often happened with ancient epitomes, Diodorus' *Bibliotheke* helped to drive the original works off the market. His dependence on earlier literature in a general way is not in doubt, but unless this is the dependence of a true epitomizer, drawing on one author at a time over long sections, little can be learned from Diodorus about the lost Hellenistic historians. If, on the other hand, his work is the product of critical research into earlier historians, independent of those historians in attitudes and historical interpretation, Diodorus becomes a far more significant author in his own right than he has usually been supposed, but his value as a repository of lost works is greatly diminished. Whereas the 'fragments' of a historian represent the selection made by particular authors for their own purposes, and can be misleading as to the character of the original, an epitome tends to preserve the general assumptions and attitudes of the source:[12] hence characterizations of Hecataeus, Ephorus, Timaeus, or Hieronymus are largely dependent on what are taken to be abbreviations of their works in various parts of the *Bibliotheke*. However, even if these historians are Diodorus' chief

---

Historikern. Denn sein Bibliothek ist und will thatsachlich nichts anderes sein als ein Serie von Excerpten.'

[11] At iii.52.3, for example, Diodorus states his dependence on Dionysius Scytobrachion. Cf. Fraser, *Ptol. Alex.* i, pp. 297–7.

[12] Cf. Brunt, 'On Historical Fragments and Epitomes', *CQ* n.s. xxx (1980), pp. 477 ff., for a general discussion of this problem.

authorities for a period, the characterizations attempted by modern scholars are not valid unless it can be shown that these sections are genuine extracts, not pieces of original writing by Diodorus, dependent on his predecessors for the facts alone.

It was at one time thought that Diodorus was entirely unoriginal, copying out long extracts from a single source at a time, with little or no alteration, and changing sources as infrequently as possible. In 1882 L. O. Bröcker launched a general attack on this view: reviewing all recent work on Diodorus, he argued that inconsistencies in the narrative and the repetition of the same material in different books of Diodorus made the so-called *Einquellen–theorie* untenable.[13] Bröcker had a number of followers, and although the idea of a multiplicity of sources for any one section was never universal, probably no one since that time was wanted to maintain the single-source theory in its extreme form. However, many of Bröcker's arguments were based on trivial discrepancies in the narrative, and were not enough to damage seriously the belief that Diodorus followed a single *main* source, supplemented by additions which could, in principle, be distinguished. This modified view, as set out by Schwartz, found general acceptance until quite recently, when detailed research on Book i has produced fresh scepticism. The arguments of W. Spoerri show that the philosophical thought of Diod. i.7–13 cannot belong to the time of Hectaeus of Abdera, who had always been considered the main source for Book i; and in a new commentary on Book i, A. Burton declares that the single-source theory is no more than an assumption which cannot be demonstrated conclusively.[14] Burton questions the validity of the 'snowballing' process used by Schneider and Jacoby to build up a picture of Hecataeus as the main source for Egyptian affairs; and it is dangerous, she claims, to assume at the outset that Diodorus epitomized in a straightforward way, following one author for many chapters at a time and abandoning him only when absolutely necessary. Her own conclusion is that Diodorus undoubtedly made some use of Hecataeus, but at the same time incorporated material from widely different authors into 'the framework of his own construction'. Whether or not this is the right view of Book i—a book which is not necessarily typical—it is an important challenge to the whole theory of single sources. If Diodorus has spliced his sources together in the way

---

[13] Bröcker, *Moderne Quellenforscher und antike Geschichtsschreiber*, Innsbruck, 1882.
[14] W. Spoerri, *Späthellenistische Berichte über Welt, Kultur, und Götter*, Basel, 1959. A. Burton, *Diodorus Siculus, Book I, A Commentary*, Leiden, 1972; cf. the review by O. Murray, *JHS* xcv (1975), pp. 214 f.

Chapter 2

Diodorus and Hieronymus

Diodorus could claim a certain popularity in antiquity. His books were in such demand at the time of composition that some were pirated for publication before he had had time to revise them: so he tells us himself, apparently with a touch of pride.[1] He is not cited by pagan authors, apart from Pliny, and there are no papyrus fragments of his work: this suggests that in Egypt, at any rate, older and more famous historians were preferred.[2] However, he suited Christian taste. Writers like Eusebius and Julius Africanus valued Diodorus not only for the high moral tone of his history (he constantly awards praise and blame to famous men), but especially for his chronological organization. Unlike the majority of pagan historians, who took a cyclical view of history, Diodorus traced the history of mankind from a fixed point in time at which life was created, and saw man's development through the ages as a process guided by divine *pronoia*. Hence Christian authors describe him as wise and illustrious.[3]

From the fifteenth to the seventeenth centuries he was again highly valued as a historian. The Latin scholar Rhodoman was ecstatic when he first received Stephanus' edition of Diodorus: 'Quem ubi primum legere coepi, dicere non possum, quantos in animo statim meo hic scriptor amores excitarit! in quantam sui admirationem me rapuerit! adeo, ut ex illo tempore illum amare et magnifacere, praedicare etiam, ubi occasio daretur, nunquam destiterim.'[4] We have many Renaissance editions of his work; and the translations into French, German, Italian, and English, as well as Latin, together with selections and extracts in these languages, are an indication of his general popularity.[5] Books xviii–xx seem to have had especial appeal: they

---

[1] Diod. xl.8. Cf. Wachsmuth, *Über das Geschichtswerk des Sikelioten Diodors*, Leipzig, 1892, pp. 7 and 8 n. 1.

[2] Pliny, NH, *Praef.*25.

[3] Eusebius, *Praep. Evang.* 1.6: ὁ Σικελιώτης Διόδωρος γνωριμώτατος ἀνήρ; Justin, *Cohort.* 9 (p. 44, Otto): ὁ ἐνδοξότατος δὲ παρ' ὑμῖν τῶν ἱστοριογράφων Διόδωρος; John Malalas of Antioch, *Chronographia*, Bonn Corpus, p. 54, line 13: περὶ οὗ συνεγράψατο Διόδωρος ὁ σοφώτατος χρονογράφος; and p. 68, line 10: καθὼς καὶ Διόδωρος ὁ σοφώτατος συνεγράψατο.

[4] Rhodoman's preface is included in vol. i of Wesseling's edition of Diodorus.

[5] See B. M. Catalogue of Printed Books, vol. 53 (1960), s.v. *Diodorus*, for a list of translations and extracts made between the 15th and 18th centuries.

here suggested, he may still not be an original historian, but he becomes a very difficult historian to deal with. There are some inconsistencies and anachronisms in Books xviii–xx which make it clear at the outset that Diodorus here used a supplementary source at least occasionally. Accordingly, the sceptical position has to be answered before a single source on the Diadochi can be assumed.

The problem may be approached first, by a general consideration of the nature of the *Bibliotheke*; second, by comparing the few texts which may be regarded as 'controls'; third, by identifying distinguishing characteristics in a given section of Diodorus, of a kind which suggest one source.

THE 'BIBLIOTHEKE'

There are several peculiarities about the *Bibliotheke* which give a clue to its real nature. The title, first of all, is a strange title for a history.[15] *Bibliotheke* normally means a place to put books—a book-case or a library—and there seem to be only two other instances in which it is used as a book title.[16]

Photius' most celebrated work was the review of classical and Byzantine writers called *Bibliotheke tou Photiou* or *Photiou Myriobiblion e Bibliotheke*. The provenance of this collection is unknown, and it is possible that the title refers to an actual rather than a metaphorical library.[17] But the choice of contents is clearly personal, including writers on many different topics; and it is Photius' whole object to acknowledge the authors and the titles of their works. *Bibliotheke* is also the title of a work on the mythical age of Greece attributed to Apollodorus of Athens, the famous grammarian of the second century BC, and this shows greater similarity to Diodorus' book, since the

---

[15] Cf. B. Farrington, *Diodorus Siculus*, Inaug. Lect. Swansea, 1936, p. 5.

[16] For *Bibliotheke* in its normal sense, cf. Polyb. xii.27.4; Strabo xiii.1.54. In Christian writers it regularly means the Bible: Alc. Alvit. *c. Eutych.* i, p. 209; Isid. *Orig.* vi. 3.2.; cf. Du Cange, *Gloss.* I.

[17] The prefatory address to Photius' book shows that he undertook the work at the request of his brother Tarasius, who grieved at their separation when Photius was sent on an embassy to the Arab government; and it has often been thought that *Bibliotheke* refers to the contents of a travelling library that Photius took with him. Other portable libraries are known from this period. Constantine Porphyrogenitus recommended that a small library of mainly strategical works should be included in τὰ βασίλικα ταξείδια, to be taken on his eastern campaigns: *De Ceremoniis* App. i, pp. 444 ff. Cf. A. Toynbee, *Constantine Porphyrogenitus and his World*, p.197. L. Reynolds and N. G. Wilson, *Scribes and Scholars*, Oxford, 1974, p. 55, suggest that Photius organized ' a kind of private literary club', and before setting off on the Arabian mission wrote, as an offering and a consolation to Tarasius, a summary of the books read or discussed at gatherings of their circle. This would account for the wide variety of writers in the collection, which includes historians, secular as well as ecclesiastical, medical writers, philosophers, orators, poets, and romance writers.

subject matter is quasi-historical, not a mixture of genres like Photius' collection.[18] It is clear that the attribution to Apollodorus is wrong, since the work is anachronistic for the second century BC, and, following the judgement of Schwartz, it should be regarded as a later compilation which cannot be assigned to any one author.[19] Schwartz argued that the date of such compilations in general is more important than their authorship: Diodorus himself seems to have used a similar compilation in Book iv, and they must have been indispensable to poets like Calvus and Catullus whose works were full of mythological allusions. It seems likely, therefore, that the *Bibliotheke* of Pseudo-Apollodorus or others like it were in circulation in the first century BC and known to Diodorus.[20] The natural inference is that Diodorus' historical *Bibliotheke*, like the mythographic *Bibliotheke*, was intended as a handbook for a general reading public—a sort of manual of what everyone needs to know about history.[21]

Pliny's discussion of book titles in the preface to his *Natural History* supports this interpretation.[22] After mocking the ridiculous titles the Greeks have given their books he concludes, 'apud Graecos desiit nugari Diodorus et *Bibliothekas* historiam suam inscripsit.' Diodorus' book must have been the same in kind as the other works mentioned, or the point would be lost; and all the others are compilations, like Pliny's own. Diodorus is being classed, therefore, among the compilers of handbooks.[23] Furthermore, he is the only historian in the list: Pliny therefore recognized something about his work which made it different from other histories. The title he thought modest compared

[18] In *Mythographi Graeci*, ed. R. Wagner, vol. i, Leipzig, 1894.

[19] C. Robert, *De Apollodori Bibliotheca*, Berlin, 1873; Schwartz, *RE* s.v. 'Apollodorus', no. 61, col. 2875 ff. We do not know how early the work was fathered on Apollodorus. Diodorus founded the chronological framework of his history on the *Chronika* of Apollodorus, which covered the history of 1,040 years from the sack of Troy to the late second century. The mythographic *Bibliotheke*, which covered the pre-Trojan period, may have been known to Diodorus as the work of the same author, and perhaps suggested a title for his own work.

[20] M. Galdi, *L'epitome nella letteratura latina*, Naples, 1922, p. 8, puts it in the 1st century AD but gives no reasons for this date.

[21] This is in accordance with what Diodorus says in his preface about the need for an up-to-date universal history (i.3); and the pirating of some of his books before their final revision shows the demand for such a work (see above, n. 1). The *Bibliotheke* belongs to a general background of encyclopaedic writing in Rome of the 1st century BC: see below.

[22] Pliny, *NH, Praef.* 24 ff.

[23] Cf. T. Janson, *Latin Prose Prefaces*, Stockholm, 1964, p. 29. It was the Roman convention to present a literary work as an impromptu effort, engaging no more than a small part of one's time and personality. Diodorus, who resided at Rome for some of the period of his researches, may have been influenced by this convention. Justin wrote that he only epitomized Trogus to while away his leisure (*Praef.* 4–5): epitome was the occupation of a dilettante.

with *Violets* or *Talks by Lamplight*; but it still belongs within the context of compilation titles, and is remarkable as a title for a history.[24] It looks, then, as though Diodorus could not only be recognized as a compiler by ancient readers, but actually was advertising himself as such by his title.

The claims he makes in his preface, however, are much more ambitious. Here he stresses the utility of history in general as an incentive to the noblest actions and as an education for the highest offices of state; he associates universal history with the Stoic doctrine of *pronoia* which guides all men through all eternity; and he cites the prestige of history as his own motive for undertaking his subject, and criticizes the efforts of his predecessors. The labour of a work on universal history must be immense, yet it will be of the utmost value to those who are studiously inclined. 'For from such a treatise everyone will be able readily to take what is of use for his special purpose, drawing as it were from a great fountain.' These flattering remarks are clearly intended to apply to his own book, and they raise the highest expectations of a weighty work of scholarship. He goes on to describe his qualifications as a historian: he has been engaged in research for thirty years, and has visited a large part of both Asia and Europe, 'with much hardship and danger', in order to examine historical sites; he mentions his long residence in Rome and the facilities for research there, and his familiarity with both Latin and Greek. Finally he expresses the hope that his work will never be mutilated at the hands of future compilers.

The proem, then, far from advertising Diodorus' dependence on his predecessors, creates the expectation of a history in the grand manner, aimed at a discriminating audience—τοῖς φιλαναγνωστοῦσιν.[25] Turn-

---

[24] Trogus called his work *Historiae Philippicae*. Nicolaus' universal history is cited as ἱστορίαι or ἱστορία καθολική (*F. Gr. Hist.* 90 T1). The oddity of Diodorus' title is reflected in the confusion it caused among later writers. In three cases we find a nonsensical genitive form: Athenaeus xii.541E, *Διόδωρος . . . ἐν τοῖς περὶ Βιβλιοθήκης*; Hier. *in Dan.* ii.36, p. 718, 'Polybius et Diodorus, qui bibliothecarum scribunt historias'; Pliny, *NH, Praef.* 25, 'Diodorus *βιβλιοθήκης* historiam suam inscripsit.' These passages must be either textually corrupt or based on a curious misunderstanding. Stephanus, *De Diodoro Brevis Tractatus* (included in P. Wesseling, vol. i), wanted to emend the MS tradition of Pliny to *βιβλιοθήκας* which would at least bring this passage into line with others which speak of *βιβλιοθῆκαι* in the plural: cf. Justin, *Cohort.* p. 10: Euseb., *Praep. Ev.* x.10.488C, cf. ii.i, p. 52 (i.114), and ii.2, p. 52 (i.125); *Chron.*1.284. Eusebius once speaks of *historike bibliotheke*, not as Diodorus' title, but when describing his trouble in collecting material (*Praep. Ev.* i.6); and Büdinger, *Die Universalhistorie im Altertum*, 1895, p. 113 n. 2, considered this passage as the probable basis for the MS tradition which gives *Bibliotheke Historike* as Diodorus' title. However, it is certain that Diodorus used the word in some form as his title, because Pliny, writing only a century later, expressly says so. Cf. also Suidas, sv. *Διόδωρος*. (Δ115 Adler) Σικελιώτης, ἱστορικός· ἔγραψε βιβλιοθήκην.   [25] Diod. i.3.6.

ing to the narrative itself, the banality of Diodorus' moral and philosophical sentiments and his errors of fact and chronology are at once a
disappointment; but it is more serious that his statements about his
method of work appear to be untrue. The claim that he travelled
widely in order to avoid the mistakes of 'common historians' is certainly false, for there is no evidence for first-hand knowledge of any
country except Egypt; and some basic mistakes suggest that he never
travelled in Asia.[26] Similar claims in the proem therefore become
suspect; and a comparison with other historical proems makes it clear
that almost every item in it is a conventional proem topos.[27] Justifica-
tion of one's own historical theme or approach goes back to Herodotus
and Thucydides, and praise of historical writing in general to before
the time of Polybius, for Polybius states his intention of avoiding this
theme. The theme of universal history and the utility of history are
characteristically Polybian, and there is a general imitation of Polybius
in spirit.[28] Polemic against one's predecessors is a constant motif in
Greek prefaces from Hecataeus of Miletus onwards. The claim to have
travelled widely in order to avoid the mistakes of other historians is
made by Polybius; and the theme of long years spent in research and
preparation, which appears in several other historians, seems also to
be only a rhetorical motif in this case.[29] The conventional nature of
Diodorus' preface has long been recognized: Arthur Darby Nock

[26] At i.44.1 Diodorus says that he visited Egypt in the reign of Ptolemy Auletes
(60 to 56 BC: the Macedonians have controlled Egypt for 276 years since Alexander,
i.e. 331 BC; cf. xvii.49); and later he refers to an incident he had witnessed there in which
a Roman ambassador was mobbed for accidentally killing a cat. Cf. i.61.4, 22.2, 10.6–7.
For his ignorance of Asian geography, cf. ii.3.2, where Nineveh is placed on the
Euphrates.

[27] For ancient proems in general, see G. Engel, *De antiquorum epicorum didacticor-
um historicorum proemiis*, Marburg, 1910; Lieberich, *Studien zu den Prooemien in der
gr. Geschichtsschreibung*, München, 1899; D. Earl, 'Prologue Form in Ancient Historiography', *Aufstieg u. Niedergang der röm. Welt*, ii (1972), pp. 842 ff. Lucian, *Hist.* 53
summarizes the best of previous practice with regard to historical prologues. For
Diodorus' proems see M. Kunz, *Die Prooemien in Diodors Bibliothek*, Zurich, 1935.

[28] Compare Diod. i.1.1 f.—Polyb. i.35.6 f; D.i.1.4—P. i.35.7; D.i.1.4—p. xxx.6.4,
xii.25b.3; D.i.1.5—P.xxxii.16.1; D.i.1.5—P.i.1.2; D.i.1.5—P.ix.9.9; D.i.1.5, i.2.2—
P.ii.61.3; D.i.2.2—P.i.14.6; D.i.3.2–P.i.4.2 f.; D.i.3.8—p.iii.32.2; D.i.4.1—P.iii.59.7;
D.i.5.2—p. xviii.20.8.

[29] Dion. Hal. *Ant. Rom.* i.27 (22 years of research); Cass. Dio. lxxii.23.5 (10 years
gathering material plus 12 years writing, i.e. 22 in all); cf. ibid., frag.i.2. Dionysius'
remarks on Theopompus in the *Letter to Pompeius* (vi.783) imply that Theopompus,
too, had enlarged on the length and the carefulness of his research; and in the *Peri
Thoukididou* he says that Thucydides spent 27 years composing his history (i.115 ff.):
Thucydides himself said nothing on the matter, and Dionysius evidently computed this
figure from the number of years spanned by the history, because it was customary for a
historian of his own day to provide such information. Nicolaus of Damascus took only
ten years to write the 144 books of his universal history (cf. Wachsmuth, *Einleitung*,
p. 105).

called it 'the proem style of a small man with pretensions'.[30] Only two items are novel: Diodorus is the first known Greek historian to conclude the proem with a *captatio benevolentiae*, an appeal for a favourable audience;[31] and he is unique in expressing the fear that his work may be mutilated at the hands of future compilers (*diaskeuastai*)—a fear which perhaps tells us something about his own practice and his guilty conscience.[32] The most remarkable feature of the proem is the absence of any discussion of the historian's handling of his sources and his methods of composition. This was the one topic which a serious student of history would really want to hear about, and the one proem convention that Diodorus did not choose to imitate. He put into his preface only those items which he considered the hallmark of a stylish history, and which were designed to announce him as heir to the great historians of the past. He was untroubled about the relevance of the proem to the history itself, and did not scruple to make a claim which was demonstrably false; and most of his statements about the way he approached his work cannot be taken as sincere. The proem, which presents the author as a serious historian, is therefore in conflict with the title of the book, which seems to announce a compilation; and it is Diodorus' own ambivalence on the matter which has made it especially difficult to assess his originality.

A degree of deliberate concealment cannot be ruled out; but there was perhaps a real difficulty for Diodorus in trying to classify his work. It does not seem to belong with other World histories of the period— Trogus' *Philippica* or Nicolaus' *Historia Katholike*; on the other hand it is too large to be a handbook like the *Bibliotheke* of Pseudo-Apollodorus. There is a stylistic peculiarity in Diodorus' work, namely, the isolation of individual books by means of extended book proems which introduce the subject of the book. This associates it on the one hand with Ephorus, the historian whom Diodorus most admired, and in general with the epideictic school of Isocrates which favoured book proems.[33] But book proems are also characteristic of contemporary didactic works like those of Varro and Vitruvius, and Diodorus may have felt the influence of this 'encyclopaedic' genre. By convention, the books of a didactic work were short, so that the reader should not be wearied by the difficulty of the contents, and this encouraged the author to add a proem containing matter extraneous to the real subject of the treatise, which provided an elegant introduction

---

[30] A. D. Nock, *JRS* xlix (1959), p. 5.
[31] Cf. Polyb. xvi.20.8, however.
[32] Diod. i.5.2.
[33] See R. Laqueur, *Hermes* xlvi (1911), pp. 161 ff.

to the argument.[34] Diodorus' *Bibliotheke* is often called an encyclopaedia, but without a clear account of what this means. Considered
against its contemporary literary background, however, it appears not
so much as true historiography, but as an encyclopaedic compilation,
like the compilations on linguistics, strategy, agriculture, architecture,
and other branches of knowledge which characterized this period. The
best practice in making up a compendium, as enunciated by Vitruvius
in the proem to his seventh book, was to name one's predecessors in the
field and to indicate the extent of one's debt to them: criticism was
tasteless and plagiarism despicable.[35] Thus Diodorus, as will become
apparent, succeeded neither as an original historian nor as a conscien-
tious compiler.

PARALLEL TEXTS

None of Diodorus' sources survives in a complete form, but the
fragments of some authors can be used to check his method over
limited sections. The longest of these is a section of Photius' epitome of
Agatharchides' book on the Red Sea, which can be compared with
Diodorus iii.12–48.[36] The scale of the epitome is approximately the
same in each case, so that the two texts can be set out side by side; and
the similarities between them are remarkable; Diodorus has rewritten
Agatharchides in his own words, watering down the lively style of the
original, but for both facts and opinions he is totally indebted to his
source. The agreement extends to verbatim repetitions of remarks
made in the first person by Agatharchides: at iii.41 Diodorus refers to
an earlier account of the voyage from Ptolemais to the Tauri promon-
tories—τὸν . . . παραπλοῦν . . . προειρήκαμεν—although there is
no such description earlier in his own work; and at iii.38 he claims that
in describing the Arabian Gulf he is drawing 'in part upon the royal
records preserved in Alexandria, and in part upon what we have
learned from men who have seen it with their own eyes'—the very
words used in testimony by Agatharchides.

Posidonius seems to have been used in the same way. The citations
of Posidonius in Strabo and Athenaeus show a close correspondence
with sections in Diodorus Book V describing the Gauls and the Etrus-
cans, and here too Diodorus has taken over remarks made by Posidonius which were in some cases inappropriate to Diodorus' own day. At
v.35, for example, he says: 'In the preceding books which told of the

---

[34] Cf. Engel, op. cit., p. 15.
[35] Vitruvius, *De Architectura*, vii, *Praef.* 3 ff.
[36] C. Müller, *Geographi Graeci Minores*, pp. 123–94 sets out the parallel texts side by
side.

achievements of Heracles we have mentioned the mountains in Iberia which are known as the Pyrenees.' But the Pyrenees are not mentioned in his earlier books: he must have copied this pointlessly from his source. He repeats a famous riddle of Demetrius of Phaleron which Posidonius had incidentally preserved; and he has no scruples in echoing Posidonius' criticisms of his predecessors for their accounts of tin-mining in Spain.[37] Again in Book iv Diodorus has appropriated a story about the hardihood of Ligurian women which, as we know from Strabo, was told to Posidonius by a friend.[38]

This slavish dependence on his sources was not confined to the early books on foreign lands. For his account of classical Greek history we are able to compare Diodorus with a papyrus fragment taken probably from Ephorus, Diodorus' main source for the classical period, or at least from a very good epitome of Ephorus.[39] The fragment concerns the operations of Cimon off Caria and Cyprus and the battle of the Eurymedon, the plot of Artabanus against Xerxes, and the character of Themistocles. The estimate of Themistocles (frg.3) shows the most striking resemblances to Diodorus (xi.59 ff.). Diodorus' version is slightly shorter; part of it is paraphrased, part repeated verbatim—in one place no less than thirteen consecutive words are identical; and the opinion of his source about Themistocles and the treatment he received from the Athenians is appropriated wholesale. Fragments 8, 9, 10, and 53 of the papyrus, which deal with the fighting around Caria and Cyprus, show many verbal similarities to Diodorus' account of the same events, and in the case of fragment 8, the differences between the two texts are minimal. The long fragments 12 and 13, on the battle of the Eurymedon, again show many general resemblances to Diodorus; and fragment 16—Artabanus' plot—is almost verbally identical with Diodorus. Overall, Diodorus' text is rather shorter than that of the papyrus; but this comes about not so much through abbreviation of the original, as through the omission of whole episodes, e.g. Cimon's recovery of the bones of Theseus (frgs. 47–51), the capture of a Persian admiral (frgs. 75–6), etc. He appears to be *extracting* rather than systematically condensing his source in the way that, for example, Photius does. In a few places Diodorus' manner of expression is

---

[37] Diod. v.37.1; cf. Posidonius *F. Gr. Hist.* 87 F47, 48; Diod. v.38.4.

[38] Diod. iv.20.2–3: ἴδιόν τι καὶ παράδοξον καθ' ἡμᾶς συνέβη περὶ μίαν γυναῖκα γένεσθαι. Cf. Strabo iii.4.17. Diodorus also fails to modernize his chronology in Book i: cf. O. Murray, *JEA* lvi (1970), p. 145 n. 3. Again, his remarks about the strategic importance of Chalcis at xix.78.2 are appropriate to the early Hellenistic period, but not to his own day, and the present ἔστιν shows that he is here reproducing his source literally: cf. J. G. Droysen, *Hell.* ii.3, pp. 33–4 n. 3.

[39] P. Oxy. xiii.1610 = *F. Gr. Hist.* 70 F191.

slightly fuller than that of the papyrus, but his additions contain nothing substantial: the same method of 'padding' his source can be seen in the case of Agatharchides. Grenfell and Hunt in their commentary on the papyrus conclude: 'Evidently Diodorus was a writer of very slight originality, and a future editor of Ephorus' fragments will be able to include most of Diodorus XI with confidence . . . the effect of 1610 on the criticism of other books of Diodorus . . . is . . . likely to be considerable.'[40]

For his account of the period 220 to 146 it is clear that Diodorus relied heavily on Polybius, the standard Greek historian of the period and a writer who appealed to him as being a 'universal' historian. The comparison here is not straightforward, since we have Diodorus only in fragments (mainly the Constantinian excerpts), and Polybius often likewise. In many passages, however, there is sufficient general resemblance to show that Diodorus was at least paraphrasing Polybius; and sometimes he has adopted the attitudes and reflections of his source in the way that has been noted in other cases.[41] The relation between Diodorus xxxi.10 and Polybius xxix.21, discussing the 'prophecy' of Demetrius of Phaleron in his treatise $Περὶ Τύχης$, is very striking: Diodorus is partly paraphrasing, partly repeating word for word (the actual citation of Demetrius is more or less verbatim); and he finally excels himself by echoing Polybius' $ἐγὼ$ . . . $ἔκρινον$ with $καὶ$ $ἡμεῖς ἐκρίναμεν$.[42] These pointless and naïve repetitions make it clear that, so far from reinterpreting his sources, Diodorus has preserved their attitudes with some precision and appears to have done so in every case. Wherever he *can* be checked, he turns out to be following one source very closely indeed, and for many chapters at a time; and it is significant that these check points occur in widely differing parts of the *Bibliotheke*—in the early books on foreign lands and ethnography, in the Ephoran narrative discussing the personality of Themistocles,

---

[40] Grenfell and Hunt, comm. ad loc., p. 111. T. W. Africa, *AJP* lxxxiii (1962), pp. 86 ff., minimizes the correspondences unduly.

[41] Compare Diod. xxviii.5—Polyb.xvi.I (Philip ravages the territory of Pergamum); Diod. xxviii.6—Polyb. xvi.34 (Aemilius Lepidus meets Philip at Abydos); Diod. xxix.2—Polyb. xx.8 (Antiochus becomes demoralized after his marriage); Diod. xxx.1—Polyb. xxvii.6 (Perseus' last embassy to Rome; declaration of war); Diod. xx.2—Polyb. xxviii.1, cf. xxvii.19, 13 (dispute between Ptolemy and Antiochus over Coele Syria); Diod. xxx.5—Polyb. xxvii.15 (character of Charops); Diod. xxx.17–Polyb. xxviii.21 (character of Ptolemy); Diod. xxx.18—Polyb. xxviii.18 (character of Anticochus); Diod xxix.27, cf. 2 (Popilius Laenas meets Antiochus); Diod. xxxi.5—Polyb. xxx.4 (Rhodian envoys try to exculpate themselves before the Senate). Cf. H. Nissen, *Kritische Untersuchungen über die Quellen der vierten und fünften Dekade des Livius*, Berlin, 1863, ch. vi, pp. 110 f.

[42] Arrian, too, could give as a personal judgement one that others had made: compare, e.g., *Anab*. iii.10 with Plut. *Alex*. xxxi.7 f.

and in the political and military narrative based on Polybius in the later parts of the work.

Another control source can be added which has a direct bearing on Diodorus' method in his account of the Diadochi.[43] In 1918 Hiller von Gaertringen published a papyrus found in Middle Egypt which concerns Demetrius' siege of Rhodes in 305 to 304.[44] The siege is described by Plutarch in his *Life of Demetrius*, and in greater detail by Diodorus in Book xx,[45] and it was at once clear to the transcribers of the papyrus that the fragment bore a remarkably close resemblance to the account in Diodorus, so much so, that the two texts could be used to restore and correct one another. The fragment consists of two columns of writing in Ionic dialect, and the form of the handwriting dates it to the second century AD; but we do not know the author, nor the purpose of the composition. It is not an ordinary historical composition, because it has been corrected by erasures in a different coloured ink, and a more concise version written in, by the first hand, above the line in a darker colour. The author therefore cannot be a copyist, nor a man extracting for his own use, who knew in advance what he wanted to write. On the other hand, the form of the writing and the difficulty of the subject seem to exclude the idea of a school exercise. Hiller regarded it as the work of a man sketching a presentation for a high official, for the Ionic dialect shows some literary aspiration.

The historian whom he is abbreviating is undoubtedly the same as Diodorus' source at xx. 93–4; and the main interest of the fragment is the light it sheds on Diodorus' method of composition for this part of the *Bibliotheke*. Each author contains information not included by the other, so that Diodorus cannot be the source of P, nor can P be a copy

---

[43] The fragment of Arrian describing Eumenes' negotiations with a defeated army seemed to earlier commentators to derive from the same source as Diod. xviii.30–2 (*PSI* xii.2, 1284, ed. Bartoletti; cf. K. Latte, *Nach. d. Akad. d. Wiss. in Göttingen, phil.-hist. Kl.* 1950, pp. 23–7; A. Rostagni, *Riv. Fil.* xxix (1951), pp. 186 f.; Wirth, *Klio* xlvi (1965), pp. 283 ff.). The opportunities for direct comparison are limited, but in col. 1 of the papyrus (πα lines 20–1) the letters]γνυ and]σσφα seemed to correspond to ἰγνὺν . . . σφαλείσης at Diod. xviii.31.4 (cf. Plut. *Eum.* vii.6, ἰγνύαν), describing Eumenes' duel with Neoptolemus during the battle against Craterus at the Hellespont in 321. A. B. Bosworth, *GRBS* xix (1978), pp. 227 ff. argues convincingly, however, that the fragment refers not to the great battle in which Craterus fell, but to the preliminary encounter, in an unknown part of Asia Minor, in which Eumenes defeated Neoptolemus and his phalanx and for which Plutarch is our only source (*Eum.* v.2–3). The letters]γνυ could be, e.g., a part of the verb ῥήγνυμι.

[44] P. Berl. 11632 = Pack² 2207; F. Hiller von Gaertringen, *S. B. d. preuss. Akad.*, 1918, pp. 752 ff.; G. Vitale, *Aegyptus* ii (1921), pp. 207 ff.; F. Bilabel, *Kleine Texte*, no. 8, pp. 20 ff.; Jacoby, *F. Gr. Hist.* IIIB 533 (Rhodos, Anhang); E. M. Walker, in J. U. Powell and E. A. Barber, *New Chapters in Greek Literature*, ii, pp. 66 ff. Cf. below, App. II, pp. 274 ff.

[45] Plut. *Demetr.* xxi–xxii; Diod. xx.81–8, 91–9.

of Diodorus' source: both are drawing on a single common source. The texts printed side by side in Hiller's edition show how remarkable the coincidences are, extending even to trivial details (cf. App. II, below). The passage opens with the capture by the Rhodians of the ship bearing royal robes to Demetrius from his wife Phila: the first words in the papyrus refer to this incident. It continues wth the capture of other ships, containing engineers—*katapeltaphetai*—destined to construct siege engines for Demetrius, but kidnapped by the Rhodians to work for themselves. The word *katapeltaphetai* is found only in the Florentine manuscript of Diodorus, and is otherwise extremely rare.[46] The manuscript reading had previously been considered corrupt, and even the most recent editions of Diodorus print Fischer's emendation, *kai katapeltas*. The papyrus shows that the reading of the Florentine manuscript ought to be restored, and we here have an instance of Diodorus taking over even a rare technical word from his source. (This was not his invariable practice, however: at xx. 94.2 he has μεταλλεία instead of P's μεταλλωρύχος—a *hapax legomenon*; and in Book iii he avoids Agatharchides' technical terms on gold-mining.) At this point the papyrus contains information not included by Diodorus, about Demetrius' attempt to ransom his engineers: this extra paragraph illustrates the general tendency of P to concentrate on personal details rather than factual matters. Diodorus shows the opposite tendency: he omits the quarrel over the ransom agreement, but he here includes the politically important account of a Rhodian proposal to pull down the statues of Antigonus and Demetrius, which P omits. Both continue with the story of Demetrius' attempt to undermine the city walls, and the construction of the Rhodian counter-tunnel. This culminates in the

---

[46] *Katapeltaphetai*. See the following: IG xii. 5.30 (Ceos, early 3rd century = *Syll.*[3] 958; discussed by A. H. M. Jones, *The Greek City*, p. 224). Philon, *Bel.* 82.13 (Philon, *Bel.* 51.10 ff., says he derived information on artillery from personal association with artificers in the arsenals at Rhodes and Alexandria: cf. E. Marsden, *Greek and Roman Artillery*, Oxford, 1971. ii, p. 8). Rostovtzeff, *REA* xxxiii (1931), pp. 16 f., the treaty between Eupolemus of Caria and Theangela, lines 14–15: ἀποδοθῆναι δὲ καὶ τοῖς καταπελταφέταις ὀψώνια μηνῶν τεσσάρων (= L. Robert, *Collection Froehner*, i, 1936, no. 52); cf. W. H. Buckler, *JHS* lv (1935), pp. 75 ff., an inscription mentioning two companies of Ptolemaic ἀφέται at Paphos in *c*. 150–100 BC (lines 10 ff.). *Clara Rhodos*, ii (1932), p. 169, a Rhodian inscription from *c*. 300 BC, lines 7 ff.: Πολέμαρχος Τιμακράτεος Κασαρεὺς καταπελταφέτας (Κασαρεύς is a Rhodian demotic). *Syll.*[3] 502, a decree of the inhabitants of Samothrace for Hippomedon, the Ptolemaic governor, 228–225 BC, lines 8 ff., refers to βέλη καὶ καταπάλτα[ς καὶ] τοὺς χρησομένους τούτοις. *Syll.*[3] 1249, the funerary inscription, set up at Piraeus, of a *katapeltaphetes* from Mysia. The latter must have been an expert imported from Greek Asia Minor, the centre of military technology, to be a trainer of the ephebes; likewise Mnesitheos of *Syll.*[3] 385, lines 25 ff. (*c*. 282–281 BC): such men had the expertise to manage the *katapaltai* mentioned e.g. in *Syll.*[3] 329, lines 15–16 (honouring Euxenides of Phaselis, *c*. 306–305 BC). Cf. below, ch. 5, p. 201.

episode centred on Athenagoras, the Rhodian mercenary commander, and the capture of Demetrius' captain, Alexander, and an
account of the decree rewarding Athenagoras for his loyalty to the
Rhodians. Once more the papyrus is fuller than Diodorus on the
personal aspects of these events: P narrates the ambushing of Alexander at length, where Diodorus has only a summary; he mentions the
oaths exchanged between Athenagoras and Demetrius' soldiers: and
he concludes with something about the fate of Alexander—the Rhodians were going to kill him, but they changed their minds when a
herald came from Demetrius . . . and here the papyrus breaks off.

The original length of this composition cannot be estimated: only
two columns are preserved, 49 lines in all, and the corresponding
section of Diodorus is less than two chapters. However, there are
references within the surviving portion which presuppose the earlier
stages of Diodorus' narrative. The opening lines of the papyrus clearly
refer to the incident of Demetrius' clothes: and the mention of λύτρων
τῶν τεταγμένων refers to the ransom agreement made between Demetrius and the Rhodians in the previous year of the siege, which
Diodorus records some nine chapters earlier. Undoubtedly further
concordances would be observable if more of the papyrus were
preserved. Brief as it is, the significance of this fragment is nevertheless considerable. It provides a check point for Diodorus' method
within a section of his work for which no sources are acknowledged,
and it confirms the evidence of comparisons between Diodorus and
Agatharchides, Posidonius, Ephorus, and Polybius, that Diodorus
adhered very faithfully to his sources at least over limited sections: the
longest of these is in Book iii, where the comparison with Agatharchides extends over 36 chapters. He did not copy them word for word:
an analysis of Diodorus' style shows that it is consistent throughout the
Bibliotheke (the problem of language is discussed below, App. II). He
seems, however, to be a reliable vehicle for the subject-matter of the
histories he used, taking over both facts and the inbuilt attitudes and
assumptions, and his language frequently echoes, even when it does
not actually repeat, the language of the original.

THE HOMOGENEITY OF BOOKS XVIII–XX

It is a natural assumption that Diodorus followed the same method of
composition in all parts of the *Bibliotheke*: the passages in which he
can be checked are entirely random, but all point to the same conclusion. Whether he followed one author exclusively for a whole period
or a whole book at a time is a further question. The case for the
'single-source theory' must rest on the homogeneity of extended sec-

tions, and on differences, other than stylistic, between one section and another.[47]

Several structural features isolate Book xviii from the narrative which has gone before. Chronologically there is a new beginning. In ch. 2 Diodorus opens with the archon year of Cephisodorus and proceeds to give an account of the struggle for the succession on Alexander's death: but Alexander died on 10 June 323, and the succession was settled within the next seven days; the new Athenian archon year did not begin till July. Diodorus, on the face of it, has tried to match a new year with a new phase of his narrative, which suggests a break from the source for Book xvii.[48] The first four chapters of Book xviii are a bridge passage, containing material of more than one origin;[49] then with Chapters 5 to 6 there are again signs of a new author. These chapters contain a geographical survey of Asia, designed to help the reader follow the Asian campaigns of the Diadochi; and if Diodorus had been using one source for Books xvii and xviii, this survey ought to have preceded the account of Alexander's expedition. It looks instead like the opening of a new history.[50] Furthermore, during the early part of xviii there is a large number of references back to the period of Alexander—no less than 15 within the first 22 chapters—many of which were unnecessary, because adequate information had been provided in Book xvii.[51] In some instances Diodorus himself,

[47] Cf. the remarks of Hammond, *CQ* n.s. xxxi (1937), pp. 79 ff. on the source problem of Diodorus xvi.

[48] Cf. F. Schachermeyr, *Alexander in Babylon*, Wien, 1970, p. 114; and below, ch. 3, p. 88.

[49] See ch. 3, pp. 87 ff.   [50] Ibid., pp. 80 ff.

[51] xviii.3.1 (Alexander and Cappadocia): recalls Hier. F3; cf. pp. 61 f. xviii.3.2 (Taxiles and Porus): cf. xvii.86.7, 89.6. xviii.4.1 (Craterus in Cilicia): cf. xvii.109.1. xviii.4.2–6: for Alexander's 'Last Plans' see ch. 3, pp. 131 ff. xviii.7.1 (revolt of Bactrian Greeks): cf. xvii.99.5–6, with Curtius ix.7.1–11. (Apparently two different rebellions are described, since Curtius says in 326–325 the rebels got safely home, whereas in 323 they were all massacred by the Macedonians; also the names of the Greek leaders are different in Curtius and Diodorus xviii: cf. E. Badian, *JHS* lxxxi (1961), p. 27 n. 76; Beloch, *Gr. Gesch.*, iv² 1, p. 93, for the older view that Diodorus has confused the two rebellions. At xvii.99.6, ὕστερον κ.τ.λ., he is, however, thinking ahead to his source for xviii.) xviii.8.1–5 (causes of the Lamian War): Alexander's 'exiles' decree' was mentioned briefly at xvii.109.1, though without documentary support. xviii.9.1 (Harpalus' money): cf. xvii.108.4–8, the detailed account of Harpalus' defection, to which Diodorus himself here refers. xviii.9.2–3 (Leosthenes' preparations for war): cf. xvii.111.1–3, where τὸ δὲ τελευταῖον κ.τ.λ. suggests that Diodorus here anticipates the account in xviii. xviii.11.3–4 (Boeotia and Athens): cf. xviii.10.4 for the 'famous misfortunes' of the Thebans (i.e. Alexander's sack of Thebes). xviii.12.1 (Craterus in Cilicia): Diodorus here repeats himself—cf. xviii.4.1, 16.4.xviii.12.1 (shortage of manpower in Macedonia). xviii.13.6 (Demosthenes and Harpalus): cf. xvii.108.8. xviii.16.1: see above on xviii.3.1. xviii.19.1–2 (murder of Harpalus): cf. xvii.108.4–8, to which Diodorus here refers (the sentence ἐκεῖθεν δὲ πλεύσας κ.τ.λ. possibly anticipates the account in xviii). xviii.22.1 (execution of Balacrus).

possibly, is responsible for anticipating or repeating material; but the overwhelming impression is the use of a historian who is near the beginning of his history and wanting to explain the background to events such as the Lamian War and the murder of Harpalus. With chapter 25 we encounter another new feature: a chronological framework which is unique to this part of the *Bibliotheke*. Throughout Books xviii–xx events are classified year by year, and the turn of the year is marked by reference to the winter quarters of the armies.[52] The resulting clarity in historical sequence at once distinguishes these books from, for example, the books on the Peloponnesian War, where Diodorus has tried to reconcile a *kata genos* with his own archon and consul system and produced hopeless chronological confusion, or from the vague sequence of the Alexander narrative, with its many erroneous archon dates. A new terminology for the principals also presents itself in Book xviii. In xvii Diodorus refers to Alexander's companions *passim* as *philoi*, in place of the correct contemporary term *hetairoi*, which Arrian took from Ptolemy. *Philoi* might be Cleitarchus' usage; more likely it is Diodorus' own, reflecting general Hellenistic practice. In xviii the council of officers of each diadoch are his *philoi*; but the dynasts themselves are regularly called the *hetairoi* of Alexander, or, where this was the case, his *somatophylakes*, in xviii and the early part of xix. (Thereafter a gradual progression can be traced, via the neutral *hegemones*, to *dynastai* and finally *basileis*.) Thus Diodorus' language was influenced by his new source, who knew the technical military terms of Alexander's time.[53] Another instance is the word *synedrion*, denoting the council of the king or general. The sources on Philip and Alexander fall back on periphrasis such as 'he

---

[52] Diod. xviii.25.1 (322/321); 40.1 (321/320); xix.12.1, 15.6 (318/317); 34.8, 37.1, 39.1, 44.4, 46.1 (317/316); 56.5 (316/315); 69.2, cf. 68.5–6 (314/313); 77.7, 80.5 (313/312); 89.2 (312/311); xx.28.4 (309/308); 109.2, 109.4, iii.2, 112.4, 113.5 (302/301).

[53] *Hetairoi*: xviii.2.2, 3.4; xix.22.2, cf. 82.3 (Demetrius imitating Alexander's terminology?). *Somatophylakes*: xviii.2.2, 2.4, ibid., 7.3; xix.14.4. *Dynastai*: xx.19.2, 51.1, 81.2 (and thereafter all are *basileis*). Elsewhere, οἱ ἡγεμόνες, οἱ Ἀλεξάνδρῳ συστρατευόμενοι, οἱ ἐν ἐξουσίαις ὄντες, etc. In Book xvii, *philoi* occurs at least 30 times of Alexander's companions, and some half dozen times of the Persian or Indian nobles. For other terms cf. 37,2, ἡ ἑταιρικὴ ἵππος; 65.1, υἱοὶ . . . πρὸς τὴν σωματοφυλακίαν ἀπεσταλμένοι; 99.4, Πευκέστης, εἷς τῶν ὑπασπιστῶν; 100.2, ἐν . . . τοῖς ἑταίροις παραληφθείς τις Μακεδών, ὄνομα Κόραγος, κ.τ.λ. (the same incident at Curtius ix.7.17 ff., Aelian, *VH* x.22, but Coragus is not otherwise known: cf. Berve, ii, no. 445); 110.1, οἱ περὶ τὴν αὐλὴν ὑπασπισταί (cf. Arrian, *Anab.* vii.6.3); 114.2, τις τῶν ἑταίρων is cited for the *logos* that Craterus was 'king-loving' etc. Diodorus xviii–xx shows some inconsistency in describing the Macedonian monarchy—sometimes βασιλεύς, sometimes βασιλεῖς; but this confusion is common to our other sources for the period, both literary and epigraphic: cf. Habicht, 'Literarische und epigraphische überlieferung zur Geschichte Alexanders und seiner ersten Nachfolger', *Akten des VI Internationalen Kongresses für gr. und lat. Epigraphik*, 1972, pp. 367 ff.

called his friends together': only after Alexander's death does this meeting acquire a name.[54] And the source of xviii–xx shows a general fondness for technical vocabularly: the *katapeltaphetai* at the siege of Rhodes are one example; another is *asthippoi*, 'townsmen-cavalry'; not to mention the famous corps of *argyraspides*, 'Silver Shields'.[55]

Not only do specific items isolate Books xviii–xx from the preceding narrative; the tone, also, is wholly different when one passes from xvii to xviii. The Alexander narrative is vague, full of silly stories, and has no sort of political insight; with Book xviii the reader at once feels that he is in the hands of a serious historian. The characteristics of this narrative will be the subject of detailed study in later chapters, but the most distinctive may be mentioned here.

There are no gods in Diodorus' narrative of the Diadochi, and no talk of sacrilege or piety: occasional references to prophecies and oracles do not imply a personal belief, but only a recognition of superstitious belief in others.[56] By contrast, there are numerous naïve allusions to miraculous happenings and divine omens in Book xvii; again, in Book xvi the plunder of the Delphic oracle is recounted in a tone of outrage.[57] The homily on Tyche at xviii.59.5–6 is probably the work of Diodorus himself (the language compares with the language of his proem to Book i); but Tyche may have played some part in the account given by his source, because some references can be paralleled in Nepos' *Life of Eumenes*.[58] The supernatural background to the history of Agathocles, in the same books of Diodorus, has a slightly different emphasis: the word *tyche* appears, but is less prominent than *to daimonion* or *to theion*. By contrast, then, to his Sicilian narrative, Diodorus' account of the Diadochi is essentially secular. The dynamic forces of this narrative are on the one hand the personalities of the generals, on the other the collective will of the armies under their command.

The narrative focuses on the careers of individuals; not all the Successors, however, are given equal attention. Book xviii and the first half of xix concentrate on the history of Eumenes: the wealth of personal detail in this section points to an eye-witness—someone who had travelled with Eumenes' army; and the praise of Eumenes'

[54] Cf. Hammond and Griffith, *Macedonia*, ii, p. 397.
[55] For *katapeltaphetai* see above, p. 31 and n. 46. For *asthippoi*, cf. Diod. xix.29.2; Hammond, *CQ* xxviii (1978), pp. 128 ff. On *argyraspides* see below, ch. 5, pp. 190 ff. Cf. also Diod. xx.93.2, ναῦς τὰς καλουμένας παρὰ Ῥοδίοις φυλακίδας, and below, App. II, p. 277 and n. 15.
[56] Cf. Jacoby, *RE* 'Hieronymos', col.1553.
[57] Diod. xvi.56–7, 61, 64; xvii.10. 2–6, 17.6–7, 41.5–6, 49.4–6, 114.5, 116.1–7.
[58] Nepos, *Eum.* vi.5, cf.i.1.

character and intelligence, together with an intimate knowledge of his thoughts and plans, suggest that this was a friend and admirer of Eumenes. The rest of Book xix and Book xx show a similar imbalance: after the death of Eumenes, Diodorus concentrates on the history of Antigonus Monophthalmus and Demetrius, and again shows a pre-occupation with their character and ambitions, though we miss the eulogistic tone of the section dealing with Eumenes. The other Diadochi appear, in general, only when their history coincides with that of Eumenes, Antigonus, or Demetrius. They are judged in terms of personal ability: questions of personal morality play no part, except perhaps in the case of Eumenes' rival Peucestas, who is depicted as a coward and a traitor.[59] There is a fundamental distinction, therefore, between the values of Diodorus' source on the Diadochi and the values of his sources in Books xi–xvii: one may contrast the standardized panegyrics on Gelon or Epaminondas, which serve an exemplary purpose, or the tediously repeated characterization of Alexander in xvii as a model of *epieikeia*.[60] Women as well as men are treated seriously in Books xviii–xx: Olympias, for example, is criticized for her generalship during the siege of Pydna; Phila and Cratesipolis are praised for their σύνεσις.[61] Furthermore, the characterization of individuals is absolutely consistent throughout the books in question, and this is true not only of the main characters: Polyperchon and Cassander are recognizably the same personalities at the time of their conflict in 318 (Diod. xviii.68 ff.), and during the negotiations over the pretender Heracles, nine years later (xx.28).[62]

A consistent political attitude is less easy to define. Eumenes is repeatedly praised for his loyalty to the house of Alexander, and, during the period when he was at war with Eumenes, Antigonus is described as *apostates*; but it is not clear that this reflects the historian's personal attitude to the issue of legitimacy and the unity of the empire, rather than his desire to present Eumenes as a man of honour and champion of legality. After Eumenes' death, Antigonus declared himself protector of the Argead house; and after the murder of Alexander IV and the naval victory at Salamis, Antigonus and Demetrius proclaimed themselves *basileis*, laying claim, as is usually supposed, to the whole of Alexander's empire. Repeated references in Diodorus to Antigonus' great ambitions nevertheless leave the tone of the discus-

---

[59] Cf. below, ch. 4, p. 155.
[60] Gelon, xi.21.3, 22.5, 23.3, 38.5, 67.2–3; Epaminondas, xi.1.2; xv.39.2–3, 88; xvi.2.3; Alexander, xvii.24. 2–3, 38.3–7, 66.6–7, 69.9, 76.1, 79.1, 91.7, etc.
[61] Cf. below, ch. 5, pp. 225 ff.
[62] Ibid., pp. 224 f.

sion ambiguous: that Diodorus' source thought these ambitions either impossible or undesirable—as is often asserted—is by no means a clear inference: rather, the idea of possession of the whole empire—in Diodorus, represented by the vague expression, τὰ ὅλα—appears as an obsessive preoccupation, as the idea of ἀρχή was for Thucydides. Diodorus' source perhaps felt that Antigonus' failure was chiefly a failure of leadership: world dominion was not in principle an impossibility, but those who aspired to Alexander's empire lacked Alexander's charisma.[63] There is ambiguity again in attitudes to the Greek desire for *eleutheria*: Diodorus' narrative of the fighting in the Lamian War shows admiration for the courage of the Greek and Thessalian leaders; but he takes a Macedonian view of Antipater's settlement and of the installation of Demetrius of Phaleron; and Cassander's governor in Megalopolis, Damis, is praised for his intelligence and skill. He is sceptical about the rival professions of Antigonus and Ptolemy towards the Greek cities in 315 (Diod. xix.62.1–2); but later comments that Antigonus was trying to liberate the Greeks 'in very truth'—πρὸς ἀλήθειαν (xix.78.2). This has sometimes been taken as a sign of more than one source; but other explanations are possible. The attitude is essentially a pragmatic one: the Greek revolt of 323 failed because of disunity among the Greek allies and insufficient preparation; after its suppression, the question was one of finding an acceptable formula for living under the Macedonian suzerain; the situation was different in Asia and the islands, and the liberal policy adopted by Antigonus would not necessarily have worked had he become king of Macedon—ultimately this was Demetrius' experience.[64]

Consistency in the political narrative is more readily illustrated by the persistent use of political documents: a recent study counts over sixty citations of documents in Diodorus xviii–xx, a feature which sharply distinguishes this part of the *Bibliotheke* from earlier books (there are none in Book xvii).[65] The source is evidently one who valued primary evidence and whose authority is therefore to be respected.

Finally, the most impressive feature of these books is the military narrative. Diodorus gives regular statistics on the strength of armies and fleets, casualties in battle, and prisoners of war; he notes the financial resources of the generals and satraps, the times and distances of marches, the relation of terrain to battles and campaigns; he describes the equipment and provisioning of armies. This is rare in any

[63] Cf. ch. 4, p. 170.
[64] Ibid., pp. 171 ff.
[65] K. Rosen, 'Political Documents in Hieronymus of Cardia', *Acta Classica* x (1967), pp. 41 ff. Cf. ch. 4, pp. 131 ff.

ancient author, and almost unknown elsewhere in Diodorus. The source has a good understanding of strategy: he states the objectives and plans of the generals, and reports discussions at councils of war. His descriptions of battles are unmistakably superior to those in earlier books of Diodorus. The battles of the Persian War and the earlier fourth century follow a standardized rhetorical pattern: the trumpets sound and the troops send up a war cry; the fighting is stubborn and there is gallantry on both sides; the issue is doubtful until some lucky turn gives an advantage; one side flees, pursued by the victors.[66] Diodorus may have found this scheme in Ephorus, but it is applied also in Books xvi and xvii. The topoi are couched in nearly identical language, and are punctuated by eulogies on the bravery and prowess of the combatants, at the expense of any real information about strengths, dispositions, terrain, or tactics. This description of the battle of Issus is typical: 'Many were killed as the battle raged indecisively because of the evenly matched fighting qualities of the two sides. The scales inclined now one way, now another, as the two sides swayed alternately backward and forward'; this is accompanied by comments on the inspiring example of the officers, the prowess of individuals, the pathetic state of the female prisoners of war.[67] By contrast, most of what we know about early Hellenistic warfare is derived from the accounts of battles in Books xviii–xx. At Paraetacene, Gabiene, and Gaza, it is apparent that Diodorus' source had given strengths and dispositions in full. The nature of the terrain is related to the course of the battle: at Gabiene, for example, Antigonus captures the enemy baggage under cover of the dust which arose from the salt plain. The corporate spirit of groups of professional soldiers, like the Macedonian 'Silver Shields', is given more emphasis than the prowess of individuals. Tactical novelties are noted. At Paraetacene (the most detailed account of a battle in these books), it appears that both Eumenes and Antigonus started off at the extreme ends of their lines in order to take up any position subsequently without disturbing their original dispositions, and throughout the battle they seem to know what is going on elsewhere on the field: Tarn observed that this is virtually the first instance of generals acting as directors of a battle rather than merely as leaders of the fighting.[68] Paraetacene also provides the first example of a true reserve: Philippus with 300 horse

---

[66] Cf. Wachsmuth, *Über das Geschichtswerk des Sik. Diodors*, p. 7; G. L. Barber, *The Historian Ephorus*, Cambridge, 1935, pp. 140 ff.

[67] Diod. xvii. 33.6 ff. There are, in xvii, scraps of the type of 'good' military writing found in xviii–xx (e.g. the dust at Arbela is rightly mentioned), but in xviii–xx it is incomparably greater and more systematic.

[68] Tarn, *Hellenistic Military and Naval Developments*, Cambridge, 1930, pp. 34–5.

picked from all the cavalry contingents was stationed behind Eumenes on the extreme right.[69] It would be impossible to derive information of this kind from the military writing of Diodorus' other books. Considerable attention is also paid to military technology. Diodorus' source went out of his way to describe Eumenes' device for exercising his horses, the elephant traps at the siege of Megalopolis, forms of telegraphing in the Persian empire, the use of dromedary camels for communication over long distances; his account of the battle of Gaza is interrupted by a short lecture on the correct use of the elephant in warfare.[70] He gives a detailed account of the sieges of Megalopolis, Pydna, Salamis, and Rhodes, mentioning the use of *helepoleis* and other engines, and, in contrast to the majority of ancient historians, avoids dwelling on the emotions of the besieged. Diodorus' description of naval warfare in these books—for example at the battle of Salamis—is similarly of a high quality, and must come from the same source as other military items.

The features here isolated are to be found in each of Books xviii, xix, and xx; and between them they link up the greater part of all the narrative of Greek and Asian affairs. Hence one should not doubt the direct use of a single main source in this section of the *Bibliotheke*: it is internally consistent in structure, attitudes, and factual detail, and it differs in several respects from the earlier part of Diodorus' work. In particular, a single source for Alexander and for the Diadochi is absolutely excluded.[71] There may be special reasons for excepting a particular passage, but one cannot object to *many* passages of the same type, ignoring the existence of the group which they form, because the whole case for homogeneity is cumulative. The implication is, that in these books of Diodorus we have an extensive epitome of (or more precisely, a series of extracts from), a Hellenistic historian; and on the assumption that Diodorus' method of paraphrasing was similar here to his method of paraphrasing Ephorus, Agatharchides, *et al.*, the epitome is close enough to justify conclusions about the character and method of the original. It is perhaps more important to isolate a source in this way than to establish his identity; but there can in fact be no reasonable doubt that the historian in question is Hieronymus of Cardia.

THE CASE FOR HIERONYMUS

Although Diodorus characteristically nowhere acknowledges a source

---

[69] Ibid., p. 34. [70] Diod. xviii.42.3–4; 71.2–4; xix.17.6–7; 37.6; 84.3.
[71] Fontana, *Le lotte*, believes that Duris was used both for xvii and the early chapters of xviii, a thesis which has not found general acceptance.

for his history of the Diadochi, on four occasions he mentions Hieronymus as a historical figure. No other minor character is so prominent in the account, and it is reasonable to suppose that these notices come from Hieronymus himself; in the same way Thucydides sometimes referred to himself in the third person.[72] The object was perhaps more to guarantee the reliability of his account than to underline his own importance. Everything we know about Hieronymus' life is compatible with the historiographical approach in these books: his friendship with Eumenes, his connection with Antigonus and Demetrius, the fact that he was a Greek serving Macedonian masters. Hence the apologia for Eumenes, the many signs of eye-witness observation, the concentration on the affairs of Antigonus and his son. Hieronymus ended his life under Antigonus Gonatas, and if he was writing or revising his history in his old age, his ambivalent attitude towards Greek independence in 323 could have been influenced by the events of the Chremonidean War.

To the biographical argument may be added the evidence of some of the fragments of Hieronymus: fragments 2, 3, 4, 5, and 16 correspond to some degree with passages of Diodorus, and this strengthens the case. None of the fragments, however, contains a direct quotation from Hieronymus: hence the argument from verbal resemblance is very limited, and the agreement of subject-matter alone does not, of course, prove the use of Hieronymus. Thus the fragments serve as corroborative evidence, not as a starting point; indeed, each of them raises problems of its own which demand discussion in detail.

FIVE HIERONYMUS FRAGMENTS AND THEIR RELATION TO DIODORUS

Fragment 2

The citation is from Athenaeus, listing writers who had described spectacular objects. Diocleides of Abdera described the *helepolis* built for Demetrius at the siege of Rhodes; Timaeus described the pyre of Dionysius; Hieronymus the funeral carriage of Alexander; Polycleitus the lamp made for a Persian king. Diodorus xviii.26–8 gives an elaborate description of Alexander's funeral carriage as it looked on completion in 321 BC, and *prima facie* this was the account he found in Hieronymus.

The difficulty of attribution arises from peculiarities in Diodorus' following chapters. The panegyric of Ptolemy in chapter 28, and again in chapters 33 ff., describing Ptolemy's prowess at the Fort of Camels,

---

[72] Diod. xviii.42.1; 50.4; xix.44.3; 100.1; Plut. *Eum.* xii.1. Cf. Thuc. iv.104.4.

is out of character with the restrained and realistic portraits of individuals we find elsewhere in these books. Diodorus' references to Ptolemy are consistently favourable, but nowhere else, in the history of the Diadochi, at least, does he lapse into obsequious flattery; hence a supplementary Ptolemaic source is indicated. Exactly where the use of this source begins is unclear, but some items in chapter 28, preceding the eulogy of Ptolemy, are suspect.

With the sentence Πτολεμαῖος δὲ τιμῶν τὸν Ἀλέξανδρον κ.τ.λ. (28.3), Diodorus implies that the funeral cortège was destined for Alexandria in Egypt. But we know from Pausanias and Arrian that Perdiccas' original plan had been to send it to Aegae in Macedon, the traditional burial place of the Macedonian kings, and that in fact the body was hijacked by Ptolemy when it reached Damascus and rushed off to Egypt pursued by Perdiccas' lieutenant Polemon.[73] The opening sentence of 28.3 accordingly suggests a writer who sought to justify the theft of Alexander's body by Ptolemy I. Furthermore, Ptolemy did not, as Diodorus says, take the body straight to Alexandria: the evidence of Pausanias, Pseudo–Callisthenes, and Curtius, confirmed by the Parian Marble, shows that it was first buried at Memphis, and later transferred to Alexandria—by Philadelphus, as Pausanias says, but according to Curtius, 'paucis post annis'.[74] Pseudo–Callisthenes also implies that the body did not stay long at Memphis, and it is likely that Ptolemy kept it there merely for the duration of the war with Perdiccas, thinking that it would be vulnerable at Alexandria, which was still without walls.[75] Strabo's version supports this view. He mentions first Ptolemy's seizure of Alexander's body when Perdiccas was bringing it down from Babylon; then Perdiccas' invasion of Egypt, the murder of Perdiccas, and the departure of the kings for Macedon; finally he says that Ptolemy took Alexander's body to be buried at Alexandria.[76] Probably the outbreak of war with Perdiccas gave Ptolemy no time to make proper arrangements for the burial, and accordingly the body was left at Memphis for safe-keeping. After the settlement at Triparadeisos he was confirmed in his possession of Egypt, and with the departure of Antipater and the kings he was able to return to the unfinished business of the burial.

Diodorus' allusion to the establishment of a cult of Alexander also seems to be anachronistic in this context. Our earliest evidence for a

---

[73] Paus. i.6.3; Arr. *Succ.* F9.25.

[74] Paus. i.7.1; Ps.-Callisth. iii.35; Curtius x.10.20; *Marmor Parium, F. Gr. Hist.* 239 F Bll. Cf. Jacoby, 'Die Beisetzungen Alexanders des Grossen', *Rh. Mus.* lviii (1903), pp. 461 f.

[75] Ps.-Callisth., loc. cit.; cf. Fraser, *Ptol. Alex.* i, pp. 11–18.

[76] Strabo xvii.1.8 (794C).

priest of the dynastic cult of Alexander comes from 285 to 284, and there was no such priest even as late as 311. It is possible that a cult of Alexander the Founder existed from an early date, perhaps even in Alexander's lifetime, but it is unlikely that there was attached to it the pomp and status indicated by Diodorus' description, which more naturally suggests the later dynastic cult.[77] His reference to the burial at Alexandria and the institutions of games and sacrifices are therefore highly elliptical: none of this took place until a later date, and it is difficult to suppose that his main source disturbed chronological order to this extent.

The allusion to Ammon as the destination of Alexander's body in 28.3 apparently gives the pretext for taking Alexander's body to Egypt: the vulgate tradition on Alexander alleged that it was Alexander's dying wish to be buried at Ammon, and Ptolemy and Arrhidaeus might represent themselves as the executors of Alexander's last orders. For later Ptolemaic writers the Ammon story would help to account for the presence of Alexander's tomb at Alexandria. Here again, then, is an indication of a pro-Ptolemaic source.

The identity or date of this source cannot be established with certainty.[78] One chronological indication is the description of Alexandria in 28.3 as πόλιν ἐπιφανεστάτην οὖσαν σχεδόν τι τῶν κατὰ τὴν οἰκουμένην. Alexandria in 321 could hardly be described as the most illustrious city of the world. The remark may be Diodorus' own, for he had visited Alexandria himself, and had commented on its size and wealth in a digression in Book xvii, in connection with Alexander's founding of the city.[79] It would be a curious remark, nevertheless, for an author writing in first-century Rome.[80] An earlier Alexandrian source seems very probable; and it is in any case difficult to attribute an encomium on Alexandria to Hieronymus, writing in the Macedon of Antigonus Gonatas. The nearest parallel for the praise of Alexandria as the greatest city of the *oikoumene* is the encomium of Alexandria found in a papyrus fragment of the first century BC to first century AD: αἱ μὲν γὰρ ἄλλαι πόλε[ις] τῆς ὑποκειμέ[νης χώ]ρας πόλεις εἰσίν, Ἀλεξανδρείας δὲ κῶμαι· τῆς γὰρ οἰκουμένης Ἀλ[ε]ξανδρεία πόλις ἐστιν.[81] This fragment should perhaps be associated with the local histories, or *patria*, which we know from the imperial period, and whose titles refer to Alexandria, Heliopolis, Hermoupolis, and the

[77] See Fraser, op. cit., i, pp. 212 and 215 f.
[78] Cf. ch. 3, pp. 92 ff., where it is argued that Cleitarchus is the most likely candidate.
[79] Diod. xvii.52.
[80] Cf. Diod. i.4.3.
[81] P. Berl. 13045. Cf. Fraser, op. cit., ii, pp. 702 n. 58, 740 n. 160; cf. i, p. 513.

Great Oasis. It may, however, come from a work rather earlier than other members of this genre. A date as early as the third century has been suggested, and the encomium may have been delivered at the victory celebration of Ptolemy Philadelphus which was described by Callixeinus of Rhodes.[82] If this is right, Diodorus' Alexandrian source is perhaps to be dated to the same period; and this date is appropriate to the whole tone of the passage, which seeks to justify and applaud the behaviour of Ptolemy I, particularly with reference to the burial of Alexander. Soon after 280 Ptolemy II officially instituted the cult of Soter and Berenice, and at such a moment it would be appropriate for an Alexandrian historian to assert the legitimacy of the original burial of Alexander and the establishment of the dynastic cult by the founder of the dynasty.[83]

Diodorus' use of this source in xviii.28 must affect our view of the preceding chapters. At the end of chapter 25 Diodorus had outlined Perdiccas' plans for the invasion of Egypt and the defence of the Hellespont. In chapters 26–8.2 he describes the funeral carriage; and at 28.2–6 he is using the Alexandrian source. At 29.1–3 he recapitulates the account of Perdiccas' strategy given at 25.6. Thus the description of the funeral car and the Ptolemaic passage are 'sandwiched' between two accounts of Perdiccas' strategic plans, and the repetition is a further sign that Diodorus has been using a supplementary source.[84] Whether the Alexandrian author is responsible not only for the encomium of Ptolemy, but also for the description of the funeral car, remains unclear.

There is nothing intrinsically improbable in the attribution of this description to Hieronymus. Their capacity for being astonished at beautiful and strange things is an appealing characteristic of early Hellenistic writers. In the first instance this was a legacy from Herodotus, who came into his own—despite attempts by imitators to impugn his accuracy—in the period of expanding horizons which came with Alexander's conquests. Theopompus, whose admiration of Herodotus took the form of epitomizing his work, filled his own history of

---

[82] J. H. Oliver, 'The Ruling Power', *TAPS* 1953, pp. 882 f.; cf. Fraser, op. cit., ii, p. 702 n. 58.

[83] Cf. *Syll.*³ 390.

[84] Briant, *Antigone le Borgne*, pp. 192 ff., distiguishes the 'Pisidian' war council of Perdiccas from the (later) 'Cilician' council; but cf. H. Hauben, 'The First War of the Successors (321 BC): Chronological and Historical Problems', *Ancient Society*, viii (1977), p. 107, questioning whether the latter was actually a council as such. That Diodorus has at any rate conflated two episodes at xviii.29.1–3 by looking back to the information of 25.6, Briant admits (op. cit., p. 196). Comparison with Arrian shows that Diodorus must have omitted a number of important events at this point: cf. Goukowsky, *Diodore xviii*, note compl. à 29.3.

Philip with digressions, one of them on *thaumasia*; and for the writers who had gazed at the wonders of India there was a strong incentive to follow his example. As a form of writing it became typical of the period: authors like Euhemerus and Iambulus departed further from reality and wrote accounts of Utopian lands full of marvels, invested with a strong philosophical content; the tidy minds of the Alexandrians, led by Callimachus, set them compiling lists of *thaumasia*. Hieronymus' digression on the funeral carriage therefore looked to the fashion of his own age: works of art and architecture were 'wonders' which appealed typically to contemporary taste. Athenaeus mentions three authors apart from Hieronymus who included *ekphraseis* in their works: Diocleides, Timaeus, and Polycleitus; and we have also the description of Hephaestion's funeral pyre at the end of Diodorus xvii, which perhaps comes ultimately from Cleitarchus.[85] There are other brief allusions to works of art in Diodorus xvii–xx: the ornaments worn by the wife of Ceteus the Indian; the golden vine of the Persian kings which Antigonus found in the treasure at Susa.[86] Accordingly, a detailed account of the funeral car, such as Diodorus gives, would not have been out of place in Hieronymus' history.

There are other candidates, however. Droysen suggested Ephippos of Olynthus as the source.[87] Athenaeus records as the title of Ephippos' work both Περὶ τῆς Ἀλεξάνδρου καὶ Ἡφαιστίωνος τελευτῆς, and Περὶ τῆς Ἀλεξάνδρου καὶ Ἡφαιστίωνος ταφῆς. However, it is easy to see that the latter title might arise because the funeral of Hephaestion, though not that of Alexander, was mentioned. Furthermore, the fragments of Ephippos, which refer only to the later part of Alexander's lifetime, show a certain hostility to the King, whereas the account of the magnificent funeral procession in Diodorus is evidently designed to promote the glory of Alexander.

A more serious possibility is a Hellenistic rhetorical or periegetic writer. The account as it stands is cast in narrative form: 'First they prepared a coffin . . . the space about the body they filled with spices . . . Upon the chest there had been placed a cover of gold . . . Over this was laid a magnificent purple robe . . .'; and the account concludes with information about the progress of the carriage and the mechanics

---

[85] Athen. v.40, p. 206DE (= Hier. F2); Diod. xvii.115. Cf. also Aristobulus, *F. Gr. Hist.* 139 F51 (= Arr. *Anab.* vi.29.4–11), on the tomb of Cyrus. For the general tendency, cf. Eratosthenes' strictures on the Alexander historians and Megasthenes: Strabo ii.70 and Arr. *Anab.* v.3.

[86] Diod. xix.34.4; 48.7; cf. Hdt. vii.27.2 for the golden vine.

[87] Droysen, *Hell.* ii.1, p. 126 n. 2; cf. B. Niese, *Geschichte der griechischen und makedonischen Staaten*, Gotha, 1893–1903, i, p. 217 n. 2; J. Kaerst, *Rh. Mus.* lii (1897), pp. 54 f. On Ephippus, see E. Schwartz, *Hermes* (1900), p. 127.

and roadmenders who accompanied it. Although this at first suggests a historian's account, and some circumstantial details even give the impression of eye-witness observation, we have other examples from the third or second centuries of rhetorical *ekphraseis* set out as historical narratives. The most famous of these are the descriptions of the *Pompe* of Philadelphus and the barge of Ptolemy Philopator by Callixeinus of Rhodes.[88] Callixeinus was writing not earlier than 221, when Philopator succeeded to the throne, and perhaps as late as the second century, since Moschion, the contemporary of Hieron of Syracuse, did not mention him in the list of his predecessors. Jacoby thought that Callixeinus' use of the past tense indicated the use of an earlier literary account, not only for the description of the *Pompe* of Philadelphus, but even for that of the barge of Philopator.[89] However, even if there were special reasons for using narrative style in Callixeinus' case, this must have been an acceptable form for an *ekphrasis* because Moschion described the ship built by Hieron in narrative form.[90]

The ultimate fate of Alexander's funeral carriage is unknown: the tomb of Alexander could be seen at Alexandria until the time of Caracalla,[91] but the carriage, after leaving Damascus in 321, is never mentioned again. We may guess that it was used to transport the body of the King from Memphis to Alexandria in or after 321, and that ultimately it shared the fate of the gold sarcophagus which was plundered by Ptolemy Cocces;[92] but how long it escaped the melting-pot of the Ptolemaic mint, and who saw it in the meantime, are matters of speculation. Certainly an object so huge and so striking could not have escaped the notice of ancient tourists, and it is just the sort of thing Callixeinus would have included in his *Peri Alexandreias*, a guide which described the architecture and famous sights of the city.[93] But

---

[88] *F. Gr. Hist.* 627 F1, F2; cf. F5 (= Pliny, *NH* xxxvi.67–8), on the obelisk erected by Philadelphus in front of the Arsinoeion and the elaborate machinery needed to move it. Cf. Fraser, op. cit., i, pp. 512 f.

[89] Jacoby, *RE* x.2 s.v. 'Kallixeinos', cols. 1752 f.

[90] Athen. v.40, p. 206DE.

[91] Herodian iv.8.9.

[92] Cf. Strabo xvii.1.8 (749C). S. Weinstock, *Divus Julius*, Oxford, 1971, pp. 362 ff., concludes that the funeral carriage of Alexander was the model for Julius Caesar's open shrine. Its existence in Caesar's time is not thereby implied: no doubt literary descriptions and architectural tradition sufficed. (Weinstock, loc. cit., supposes Alexander's successors to have been buried in similar style.)

[93] Cf. Fraser, op. cit., i, p. 513. For a reconstruction of the funeral carriage see Quatremère de Quincy, *Monuments et ouvrages d'art antiques*, ii, Paris, 1829; K. F. Müller, *Der Leichenwagen Alexanders des Grossen*, Leipzig, 1905; E. Petersen, *Der Leichenwagen Alex. d. Gr.*, Leipzig, 1905; H. Bulle, 'Der Leichenwagen Alexanders', *Jahrb. d. Deut. Arch. Inst.* xxi (1906), pp. 53–73 (correcting Müller); cf. D. Kurtz and

46 *Diodorus and Hieronymus*

whether the account in Diodorus represents that of Hieronymus himself, or of someone who used Hieronymus, or of a later 'ekphrastic' writer who had seen the vehicle at Alexandria, cannot be ascertained. The fact that such writers seem to have drawn on one another makes the picture more complex.

The coincidence between Hieronymus fragment 2 and this passage of Diodorus tends to create an overwhelming prejudice in favour of the derivation of Diodorus (here) from Hieronymus; and this is reinforced by the impression of a general change of tone at xviii.28.2–3 (the antithesis between Ἀρριδαῖος μέν and Πτολεμαῖος δέ is artificial).[94] One is nevertheless obliged still to talk in terms of likelihood rather than of proof.

Fragments 3 and 4

The fragments concern the campaign of Eumenes and Perdiccas against Ariarathes of Cappadocia in summer 322, and the earlier condition of Cappadocia. Appian, *Mith.* 8 (= Hier. F3) gives two versions of Alexander's dealings with the Cappadocians. It is his own opinion (μοι δοκεῖ) that Alexander imposed tribute on the rulers of Cappadocia before he hurried on against Darius (ἐπειγόμενος ἐπὶ Δαρεῖον); but Hieronymus says that Alexander 'did not touch the Cappadocians at all', but marched against Darius by another route.

Two passages of Diodorus come in question. The first is xviii.16.1, where Diodorus opens his account of Perdiccas' attack by explaining the *casus belli*; οὗτος γὰρ (sc. Ariarathes) οὐ προσέχων τοῖς Μακεδόσιν ὑπὸ μὲν Ἀλεξάνδρου παρεωράθη διὰ τοὺς περὶ Δαρεῖον ἀγῶνας καὶ περισπασμούς. This is at least consistent with Hieronymus' statement: nothing is said about tribute; and the vague demand for recognition of Macedonian suzerainty (οὐ προσέχων τοῖς Μακεδόσιν) is not precluded by Hieronymus' version.

In the second passage, at xviii.3.1, Diodorus states that at Babylon Eumenes was assigned Cappadocia and Paphlagonia, ἃς Ἀλέξανδρος οὐκ ἐπῆλθεν ἐκκλεισθεὶς ὑπὸ τῶν καιρῶν, ὅτε διεπολέμει πρὸς Δαρεῖον. Here there is a more distinct resonance of F3, with its theme of Alexander's haste. The historical note on Cappadocia at xviii.3.1 singles out

J. Boardman, *Greek Burial Customs*, London, 1971, pp. 304 ff., and fig. 76 (p. 305), following Bulle. See now C. Picard, *Man. Archéol. gr., La Sculpture*, ive s., ii, 1963, pp. 1284–7, figs. 503–4. The funeral carriage of the Duke of Wellington—a sombre and splendid vehicle in black and gold, now housed in the crypt of St. Paul's Cathedral—suggests the impression which must have been produced by Alexander's *harmamaxa*.
[94] Müller, op. cit., pp. 32–3, argues that the use of the word ἁρμάμαξα at Diod. xviii.26 ff. indicates Hieronymus as the source, on the grounds that 'the West Greek Diodorus otherwise avoids this Persian expression'. Compare, however, Diod. xiv.22.4.

Eumenes' satrapy for especial mention: few in Diodorus' list attract a comment of this kind. This is not Diodorus' addition, however, because Plutarch glossed Eumenes' appointment in the same way: Εὐμένης λαμβάνει Καππαδοκίαν . . . οὔπω τότε Μακεδόνων οὖσαν, Ἀριαράθης γὰρ αὐτῆς ἐβασίλευεν. Diodorus and Plutarch therefore seem to share a source which particularly noted the state of Eumenes' satrapy; and this interest in Eumenes naturally suggests Hieronymus. Appian's condensed survey of Cappadocian history from the time of Alexander until the founding of the Pontic kingdom by Mithridates follows the same sequence as the scattered references to Cappadocian affairs in Diodorus. It may be guessed, then, that Appian worked through Hieronymus systematically, taking his first extract (and here citing Hieronymus) from Hieronymus' satrapy list, at a point corresponding to Diodorus xviii.3.1 and Plutarch, *Eum.* iii.2; and that he went on, without further acknowledgement, to summarize later allusions to Pontic history in this author, which are represented, more nearly in their proper context, by Diodorus xviii.16.1 ff.

Hieronymus fragment 4 (= Ps.-Lucian, *Macrob.* 13) mentions the death of Ariarathes: ἐν τῆι πρὸς Περδίκκαν μάχηι ξωγρηθεὶς ἀνεσκολοπίσθη. The same fact is recorded by Appian, *Mith.* 8, by Diodorus xviii.16.3, and again by Arrian, F1.11. There are minor variations of language; nevertheless fragment 4 and fragment 3, taken together, present a strong cumulative case for the derivation of Appian and Diodorus, in these passages, from Hieronymus. (Diodorus gives a real variant in his later discussion of the kings of Cappadocia, at xxxi.19, where he states that Ariarathes died in battle: here his ultimate source, perhaps via Polybius, was probably a local patriotic historian of the Pontic house.)

Fragment 5

The paradoxographer cites Hieronymus for a description of the 'bitter lake' in the country of the Nabataean Arabs: no fish or other water creature can live in this lake, and the local peoples take from it blocks of asphalt. The fragment is naturally associated with Diodorus' digression on the 'asphalt lake' at xix.98 ff., where the same features are described at length. In the preceding chapters (xix.94 ff.) he has described the land of the Nabataean Arabs, also mentioned in fragment 5; and at the end of the excursus he has a biographical notice on Hieronymus—the historian was sent as leader of an expedition to gather asphalt from the lake (xix.100.1). The *prima facie* case for deriving these chapters from Hieronymus is therefore very strong.

It has been considered, however, that Diodorus' use of the phrase τὴν σατραπείαν τῆς Ἰδυμαίας in this context is problematic (xix.98). Beloch asserted that such a satrapy could not have existed until Coele Syria became Seleucid after the battle of Paneion at the beginning of the second century: there was no satrapy of Idumaea under Alexander, and no satrapies anyway in the Ptolemaic empire.[95] At xix.95.2 Diodorus talks of the 'eparchy' of Idumaea—a common word in the Roman period meaning district or *provincia*;[96] but Beloch claimed that while Diodorus could have substituted the colourless ἐπαρχία for the technical word σατραπεία, he could not have done the reverse. This seeming anachronism has been used to argue that Diodorus did not draw directly on Hieronymus, but knew him only through a historian of the second century, possibly Agatharchides.[97]

The obstacle here is actually minimal. The manuscripts R and X of Diodorus omit the phrase τῆς Ἰδυμαίας altogether, and it is highly probable that the identification of the satrapy as Idumaea is nothing but a later gloss on the text. The satrapy in question is probably Συρία καὶ Φοινίκη mentioned at 94.1, at the beginning of the excursus on Nabataean Arabia.[98] The name Idumaea did not become usual before the first century BC (although the Edomites had inhabited the region to which they gave their name from approximately the sixth century), and probably under the Seleucids it was regarded as an 'eparchy', or subdivision of a satrapy.[99] However, the words 'satrap' and 'satrapy' continued to be used colloquially by Greek writers of provincial governors in Asia until the Parthian period:[100] hence the copyists of

[95] Beloch, *Gr. Gesch.* iv.2.², p. 5 with n. 2.
[96] *Eparchia*: cf. Polyb. ii.19.2; Diod. xxxvii.10; xxxviii.8; xix.44.4.
[97] See below, pp. 62 f.
[98] This suggestion was made by H. Bengtson, *Die Strategie in d. hell. Zeit.* ii, München, 1944, pp. 34 ff. The reference to the 'eparchy of Idumaea' at xix. 95.2 perhaps comes from Diodorus himself, using the terminology of his own day: the text however, is corrupt at this point, the figure 2,200 stades being impossible in the context and inconsistent with xix.98.1. Cf. ch. 4, n. 176.
[99] Idumaea: cf. Beer, *RE* ix s.v. 'Idumaea', col. 913. For the suggestion that the eparchy was a μέρις of a satrapy, see Bengtson, loc. cit.
[100] Cf. Welles, *RC*, p. 361; Rostovtzeff, *Yale Class. Stud.* ii, pp. 46 f. In the Hellenistic kingdoms the term *satrapes* was in most cases replace by *strategos*; but Greek writers continue to refer to the Seleucid governors as 'satraps', and Rostovtzeff suggests that the official name for a province of the Seleucid empire was not 'strategy' but 'satrapy'. Diodorus himself sometimes uses 'satrapy' (*pace* Beloch, loc. cit.), as a general, not a technical term. At ii.24.3 he speaks of the 'satrapy' of Babylonia when the context is the Assyrian, not the Achaemenid empire. At xviii.5.4 he calls Armenia a satrapy, although its ruler, Orontes, had long been independent in all but name, and it had not been included in the list of satrapies and satraps drawn up by Perdiccas in 323. Armenia is again excluded from the list of appointments of 321, recorded by Diodorus at xviii.39.5–7; but four years later he is still describing Orontes as 'satrap' of Armenia (xix.23.3). Geographical districts which had not at any time been governed by their own satraps are also defined as *satrapeiai*: cf. xviii.5.4, 6.3 (Lycaonia and Sittacine). Cf. below, ch. 3, p. 84.

Diodorus would find no difficulty in describing Idumaea as a satrapy. This phrase should not, therefore, cast serious doubts on the natural inference that Hieronymus was Diodorus' direct source for his excursus on the Asphalt Lake and on Nabataean Arabia as a whole.

Fragment 16

Hieronymus is cited with several other writers for Strabo's description of Corinth. Strabo had also seen the site for himself: it is not easy, therefore, to identify the contribution of each of his sources. Diodorus, however, in describing Demetrius' siege of Corinth in 303 (xx. 103) refers to the place called Sisyphium and to the Acrocorinth, both of which are mentioned by Strabo, and Jacoby concluded that it was at this point in his narrative that Hieronymus described the topography of the city.[101] The resemblance is slight, but adds to a cumulative picture. Five of the named Hieronymus fragments seem to match passages in this part of the *Bibliotheke*, and these passages range from the early chapters of Book xviii to the later chapters of Book xx.

SUPPLEMENTARY SOURCES IN DIODORUS XVIII–XX

The general picture of Hieronymus as Diodorus' source on the Diadochi needs certain qualifications. It can be shown from 'parallel' texts that Diodorus followed his sources very closely; but it would be wrong to assume that he is a purely mechanical copyist. At the least, his sources for the history of the West must have been different from those on mainland Greece, since no Greek historian before Polybius was able to cover both areas in detail.[102] For his account of Agathocles in Books xix and xx he seems to have drawn chiefly on Duris, and in the later stages he twice cites Timaeus;[103] and the tone of the sections on Western affairs is highly coloured and romantic, in contrast to the sober style of his narrative of the Successors. These sections, then, may be left out of account altogether in a consideration of Hieronymus.[104] Problems arise with episodes which are not, like the

---

[101] Jacoby, *F. Gr. Hist.* 11D, p. 547.

[102] The Sicilian sections are missing from Book xviii. At xix.3.3 and 10.3 Diodorus refers to the Syracusans Heracleides and Sosistratus, whom he claims to have mentioned in the preceding book; but nothing has been said about Italy and Sicily since Book xvii. This gap perhaps resulted from the hasty publication of this part of the work: cf. F. Bizière, *Diodore XIX*, pp. ix f. n. 3.

[103] Schwartz, *RE* s.v. 'Diodoros', no. 38, cols. 687–8.

[104] For the 3rd century, Diodorus did have Hieronymus' history of Pyrrhus in Italy and Sicily, though the extent to which Hieronymus was used in the fragmentary books must remain uncertain. In Book xxi, Hieronymus must have been the source for the battle of Ipsus and its aftermath. xxi.2, the other dynasts, united in fear of Antigonus, ὥρμησαν

Western sections, obviously external to the main history of the Diadochi, but where there is a detectable change of tone and manner.

The opening of Book xviii contains a number of oddities which can only be explained on the assumption that Diodorus had two sources in front of him; and Chapters 2–4 ought to be regarded as a bridge passage in which the transition was made, not without difficulty, from Diodorus' old source on Alexander to his new source, Hieronymus. In particular, the description of the so-called 'Last Plans' comes from an author who was interested principally in the spectacular; and the use in this context of the term *diadochi*, rather than *hetairoi* or *somatophylakes*, as elsewhere at the start of Diodorus' account of the Successors, indicates an author less meticulous than his main source. Detailed discussion of this section is reserved for a later chapter: the conclusion there reached is that Diodorus' source on Alexander—Cleitarchus, or a writer who used him—had taken his history down to the burial of Alexander, and that Diodorus continued to make use of this tradition, alongside Hieronymus, until it ran out.[105]

It is possibly this Alexandrian source which is used at xviii.28.3–6 for the pro-Ptolemaic account of how Alexander's body came to Egypt, and again at xviii.34.2–5, where Diodorus describes the per-

---

ἑτοίμως πρὸς τὴν τῶν ὅλων κοινοπραγίαν: for the language, cf. below, ch. 4, pp. 167 ff. xxi.5, letters between Ptolemy and Seleucus are mentioned, and συνθῆκαι, suggesting Hieronymus' habitual use of documents (cf. below, ch. 4, pp. 131 ff.); and the word δορίκτητος, perhaps Hieronymus' own, appears (and again at xxi.2.2: cf. below, p. 53). Constant reference to πλεονεξία (the theme of the introduction, xx.1.1) indicates one of the motifs of Hieronymus' work. The chapters dealing with Agathocles in Sicily (chs. 3–8) seem to depend on Duris, who is cited at 6.1 (cf. Schwartz, *RE* s.v. 'Diodoros', no. 38, cols. 687 f.); and the anecdotal tone of ch. 12 (Dromichaetes makes Lysimachus see sense) seems unlike Hieronymus. The latter was certainly used, however, for the Theban revolt at xxi.14 (cf. προσηνέχθη τοῖς Βοιωτοῖς μεγαλοψύχως with Hier. T8, ἔδοξεν ἠπίως κεχρῆσθαι). The story of Agathocles' end (xxi.15–16) is evidently from the source of xxi.3–8 and of the Agathocles sections of Book xx (cf. xx.101, where allusion is made to his death), and the authorities mentioned for Agathocles' age at his death are Timaeus, Callias, and Antander: cf. Schwartz, loc. cit. At xxi.17, the attack on Timaeus seems to imitate Polybius (xii.15, 26b 4). The account of Demetrius' captivity in Syria and Lysimachus' plots against this πλεονέκτην ἄνδρα, may derive from Hieronymus (xxi.20); and ch. 21, a series of moralizing precepts, could have been inspired by the career of Pyrrhus (mentioned at 21.12; cf. Plut. *Pyrrh.* xiii–xiv, on Pyrrhus' ambitions). In Book xxii, Hieronymus could have supplied information on Apollodorus of Cassandreia (ch. 5, though the tone is rather dramatic), on the Gallic invasion (ch. 9: cf. below, pp. 73 f., for Pausanias' treatment), Pyrrhus' victory over Gonatas' Gallic mercenaries (ch. 11: the inscription recording the dedication of their shields to Athena Itomis is quoted), and Pyrrhus' sack of Aegae (ch. 12). Much of the Sicilian history of this book is perhaps derived from Timaeus and othes; but the rare section of good, coherent, narrative, in ch. 8, with its detailed naval specifications, recalls the military information on Pyrrhus' Italian campaigns for which Hieronymus is cited (F11, F12).

[105] See below, ch. 3, pp. 92 ff.

sonal prowess of Ptolemy in battle against Perdiccas: the tone of flattery in these passages is foreign to Diodorus' general treatment of the Diadochi. Some, therefore, but perhaps not all, of Perdiccas' campaign in Egypt can be attributed to this source.[106] At xviii.33.1 Diodorus makes an error of chronology, placing the news of Eumenes' victory over Craterus before the start of Perdiccas' campaign. This is nonsense, because it was the apparent military failure of Perdiccas and his allies which led to Perdiccas' assassination: at 37.1 Diodorus states that news of Eumenes' victory arrived in Egypt directly after Perdiccas' death, and that had it been known two days earlier, 'no one would have dared raise a hand against him.' Plutarch gives exactly the same version (*Eum.* viii.2); and this must have been what Hieronymus said. Diodorus' inconsistency shows that he was here unsuccessfully trying to combine Hieronymus with his second source. xviii.38.1 is a further indication: after the departure of Antipater for Asia, says Diodorus, the Aetolians made a campaign into Thessaly for the purpose of diverting Antipater κατὰ τὰς πρὸς Περδίκκαν συνθήκας—a treaty which has not been mentioned before. The proper place was either at 29.1, where Perdiccas' other preparations for the invasion of Egypt are described, or at 33.1, where Antipater leaves the Hellespont and sets out for Asia to help Ptolemy. Diodorus takes up his Ptolemaic source, with its muddled order of events, at 33.1, and it is perhaps at this point that the Aetolian treaty has dropped out.

A Ptolemaic source has also been claimed for the section on Cyrene at xviii. 19–21, at the end of which Ptolemy is wrongly called 'basileus'; the use of titles and of terminology elsewhere in Diodorus' history of the Diadochi is without exception accurate.[107] This idea is developed in a recent study by E. Will of the position of Cyrene at this period.[108] The thesis advanced is that Cyrene did not become a province of Egypt in 322 to 321, as stated at Diod. xviii.21.9, (οἱ . . . Κυρηναῖοι . . . ὑπὸ τὴν Πτολεμαϊκὴν βασιλείαν ἐτάχθησαν), and as implied by Arrian F9.34, where Ptolemy, in the division at Tripar-

[106] Cf. J. Seibert, *Untersuchungen zur Geschichte des Ptolemaios I*, München, 1969, pp. 69 ff. Polyaenus, who drew on Hieronymus elsewhere in Book iv (doubtless not directly: cf. below, p. 74 f.), relates the story of Perdiccas' Nile crossing (iv.19); cf. Strabo xvii.1.8, mentioning the blockade of Perdiccas by Ptolemy on an island (cf. Diod. xviii.34.6). Diodorus differs from Arrian in the details of events surrounding Perdiccas' murder and the conduct of Ptolemy: cf. P. Goukowsky, *Diodore XVIII*, note compl. à 36.6. (Diodorus stresses Ptolemy's public appearances before the Macedonian assembly; though it is not clear that his account is actually 'irreconcilable' with that of Arrian.)

[107] Cf. Jacoby, *RE* 'Hieronymos', col. 1554.

[108] Ed. E. Will, 'La Cyrénaïque et les partages successifs de l'empire d'Alexandre', *Antiquité Classique* xxix (1960), pp. 369 ff.; reviewed by Bizière, *REG* lxxxvii (1974), pp. 369 ff.

adeisos, is given Αἴγυπτον . . . καὶ Λιβύην καὶ τὴν ἐπέκεινα ταύτης τὴν πολλὴν καὶ ὅ τι περ ἂν πρὸς τούτοις δόριον ἐπικτήσηται πρὸς δυομένου ἡλίου. Will thinks that both Arrian and Diodorus have combined Hieronymus with another author who misinterpreted the events of 322 to 321 in the knowledge that Cyrene did, at a later period, become a province of Egypt. He reconstructs Hieronymus' text, regarding the lands allotted to Ptolemy in 321, as follows: Αἴγυπτον <καὶ ᾿Αραβίαν> καὶ Λιβύην καὶ ὅτι περ ἂν πρὸς τούτοις δορὶ ἐπικτήσηται πρὸς δυομένου ἡλίου Πτολεμαίου εἶναι. The second source added, it is argued, after Libya, the words καὶ τὴν ἐπέκεινα ταύτης γῆν πολλήν, referring to Cyrene:[109] Diodorus, unable to make sense of δορὶ ἐπικτήσηται (the phrase which *actually* gave Ptolemy *carte blanche* to annex Cyrene), changed it to δορίκτητος, (xviii. 39.5), making it refer to the whole satrapy and explaining it by Ptolemy's success over Perdiccas.

Two items come into question here. First, Diodorus' reference to *basileus* and *basileia* at xviii.21.9, at a period long before Ptolemy in fact became king. More than one explanation could be devised: a) Diodorus wished to distinguish Ptolemy 'the king' from other Ptolemies who frequented his narrative; b) he was under the general influence of the Ptolemaic source he used elsewhere, which habitually referred to Ptolemy as 'king'; c) his source, in relating the capture of Cyrene in 322/1 (itself a perfectly genuine event, as the Parian Marble shows), looked forward to the later annexation of the country, and Diodorus has failed to make it clear that this is an anticipation of later events. These remain possibilities. On the face of it, nevertheless, allusions to a Ptolemaic 'kingdom' do suggest a source who is not Hieronymus and who could be the Ptolemaic source of Diod. xviii.28.2 ff.[110] If this is the case, it is very unclear how far the interpolation extends. The Cyrene digression as a whole is paralleled by Arrian (*Succ.* F9.16–19), and within the same sequence of events as Diodorus xviii; and to deny that their common source here was Hieronymus involves the assumption that both authors used a re-working of his history—an assumption which has far-reaching consequences and which is for many reasons unsatisfactory. No doubt it is not inconceivable that only the last paragraph of this excursus was imported from the second source—the foregoing narrative shows none of the muddle or the extravagance which mark Diodorus' narrative of Perdiccas in

---

[109] Will, art. cit., p. 377, emends τήν to γῆν.

[110] The suggestion of Bizière, art. cit., p. 372, that *basileia* here means 'sovereignty' is special pleading, and does not meet the problem of *basileus*. Seibert's idea of a separate 'Cyrenian' source is not convincing: op. cit., p. 65.

Egypt. On the other hand, his combination of sources may simply have been more successful here (though the general tone of the Thibron narrative, with its emphasis on the constant ups and downs of *tyche*, is subtly different from Diodorus' regular manner in xviii–xx).

If interpolation is uncertain here, it is still more so in the list of satrapal appointments at Triparadeisos. In the case of Arrian, the phrase τὴν ἐπέκεινα ταύτης γῆν πολλήν is too vague to support the argument Will proposes. If the source were pro-Ptolemaic, and, either misinformed about or wishing to exaggerate Ptolemy's achievements, were trying to say that he had already annexed Cyrene, why did he not specify Cyrene? Compare Diod. xviii.3.1: Εὐμενεῖ δὲ Παφλαγονίαν καὶ Καππαδοκίαν καὶ πάσας τὰς συνοριζούσας ταύταις χώρας. Such phraseology was needed for areas on the peripheries of the *oikoumene* where the exact extent of central control was hard to specify. At Diod. xviii.39.5 the text does not, at this point in the list, offer an exact parallel to Arrian, hence no conclusion can be reached about the precise wording of his source. All that Diodorus says of Ptolemy is this: Μετὰ δὲ ταῦτα τὰς σατραπείας ἐξ ἀρχῆς ἐμερίσατο καὶ Πτολεμαίῳ μὲν τὴν προϋπάρχουσαν προσώρισεν· ἀδύνατον γὰρ ἦν τοῦτον μεταθεῖναι διὰ τὸ δοκεῖν τὴν Αἴγυπτον διὰ τῆς ἰδίας ἀνδρείας ἔχειν οἱονεὶ δορίκτητον. Wishing merely to convey an impression of Ptolemy's impregnability in Egypt, he is thoroughly vague on the extent of his territories. The one word which seems to carry a resonance of the Arrian fragment, δορίκτητος, is used three times elsewhere in Diodorus xviii–xx and three times in the fragmentary books on the Successors, xxi and xxii, not to mention the famous instance at xvii.17.2, where Alexander casts his spear into the land of Asia.[111] The antique idea of 'spear-won' land had been revived by Alexander and was used by his successors in the newly conquered lands of the empire to shore up their claims to personal dominion.[112] There is no reason to doubt that Diodorus found this word in Hieronymus and that it represents a slogan familiar from the early years of the Diadochi. At xviii.39.5 it might, indeed, show the influence of δορὶ ἐπικτήσηται—if such was what Hieronymus wrote; but the supposition that Diodorus was trying to make sense of conflicting traditions is quite unnecessary.

Another passage that is candidate for derivation from an Alexandrian source is Diod. xx.21. The account of the death of 'Nicocles of

[111] Diod. xviii. 43.1; xix.105.4; xx.76.7; xxi.1.5 (twice); 2.2; xxii.1.3.
[112] See W. Schmitthenner, 'Über eine Formveränderung der Monarchie seit Alexander d. Gr.', *Saeculum* xix (1968), pp. 31 ff. For another view, Walbank, *JHS* lxx (1950), p. 80, comparing the symbolism of the hurled spear with Roman fetial practice described in Livy.

Paphos' and his family is rather dramatic in tone, and can be read as seeking to excuse the severity of Ptolemy's action towards the Cypriots; the name 'Nicocles', also, is here a mistake for 'Nicocreon'.[113] This alone, however, is insufficient evidence for a change of source. That Diodorus has confused the famous Nicocreon of Salamis, descendant of Evagoras and viceroy of all Cyprus under Ptolemy I, with the lesser ruler, Nicocles of Paphos, has been generally accepted since the discovery of the Parian Marble, which places Nicocreon's death in the year 311 to 310.[114] Arrian, too, clearly distinguishes the two, and shows that Nicocreon was the principal of those Cypriot kings who made an alliance with Ptolemy after Alexander's death. In the list of contents to Diodorus Book xx the identification is half-right (Ὡς. . .Πτολεμαῖος δὲ Νικοκρέοντα τὸν βασιλέα τῶν Παφίων ἐπανείλατο); and similarly Polyaenus, recounting the heroic end of Axiothea, while making her, as Diodorus does, the wife of Nicocles, describes the latter as 'King of the Cyprians', a title more plausibly indicating Nicocreon, the Ptolemaic *strategos* of Cyprus and scion of the island's most illustrious house.[115] It is surely the house of the kings of Salamis, whose ancestry was flatteringly traced by the Argives in an honorific decree to Nicocreon, to which Diodorus refers when he speaks of the *oikia* of the kings. Confusion of dissimilar, let alone similar names, is sufficiently common in Diodorus to necessitate no special explanation, but it may have been assisted in this case by the fact that Nicocreon's grandfather was Nicocles, son of Evagoras, and, like his father, subject of a historical portrait and addressee of a letter from the pen of Isocrates. It is also possible that more was said in Diodorus' source about the kings of Paphos. At xix.79, several of the Cypriot kings are apprehended by Ptolemy on suspicion of collaborating with Antigonus, and among other measures, the inhabitants of Marion are transported to Paphos: the position of Paphos was surely mentioned in the original; and if its ruler remained loyal to Ptolemy at this time, along with Nicocreon, then

---

[113] Jacoby, *RE* 'Hieronymos', col. 1555.
[114] *Marmor Parium, F. Gr. Hist.* 239 B17. On Nicocreon (= Berve ii, no. 568) see Plut. *Alex.* xxix.2 (cf. J. R. Hamilton, comm. ad loc. pp. 75 f.); Arr. *Anab* ii.20.6, 22.2 (he was with Alexander at the siege of Tyre, and apparently succeeded his father Pnytagoras directly afterwards); Arr. *Succ.* F10.6 (after Alexander's death Nicocreon, along with Nicocles of Paphos *et al.*, supports Ptolemy against Perdiccas); Diod. xix.59.1, 62.5, 79.5 (Nicocreon works for Ptolemy and is made his *strategos* on Cyprus); Tod ii, 194—Argos honours Nicocreon for gifts for the Heraea (see M. N. Tod, comm. ad loc. for Nicocreon's gifts to Delphi and Delos); cf. S. F. Miller, *Hesperia* xviii (1979), p. 79, for a new *thearodokoi* list from Nemea, which mentions Ἐγ Κύπρωι, Ἐν Σαλαμι / Νικοκρέων Πνυταγόρα. Cf. F. Stähelin, *RE* xvii s.v. 'Nikokreon', no. 2, cols. 357 ff., and s.v. 'Nikokles'; G. F. Hill, *History of Cyprus*, i, pp. 158 ff.
[115] Polyaen. viii.48.

shared the latter's downfall two years later (the two kings are closely associated by Arrian, *Succ.* F10.6), the chances of confusion by the epitomator would be greatly increased. To suppose that Diodorus' misidentification in itself indicates a change of source would therefore be unjustified. The fate of Nicocreon of Salamis forms the natural conclusion to the sequence of notices about his career in Book xix, and is a logical prelude to the events of the siege of Salamis at xx.47 ff.; and the well-established connections of his house with mainland Greece would make this episode especially interesting to Greek readers— hence, no doubt, Diodorus' emphasis on the tragic nature of the family's extinction.

As far as the supposedly 'Ptolemaic' tone of this passage is concerned, it is common to a series of notices in Diodorus xviii–xx dealing with Ptolemy, which stress his *epieikeia* and *philanthropia*—though the pronounced tone of encomium appears only at xviii.28.[116] Probably Hieronymus' comments on Ptolemy were not unfavourable—he recognized the personal ability of all the Successors—but it can hardly be supposed that he went out of his way to praise the founder of the dynasty most consistently hostile to the Antigonids. The distortion can be explained in a general way in terms of Diodorus' special interest in Egypt, the only foreign country he had visited, and hence in the founder of the Ptolemaic dynasty.[117] He may also have been particularly under the influence of Hecataeus of Abdera, whom he had used for his account of Egypt in Book i. The attributes ἐπιείκεια, φιλανθρωπία, χρηστότης, and εὐεργεσία—the virtues of a model Hellenistic king—which are associated with Ptolemy I in Books xviii– xx are also prominent in Book i as qualities of Osiris, Sabacon, or other ancient kings. Diodorus' source for Book i projected on to the legendary rulers of Egypt the virtues advertised by the Hellenistic kings of his own time (the virtue χρηστότης was associated with the Ptolemies in particular).[118] However, in most cases it is unnecessary to seek a specific source. If Diodorus had used an Alexandrian source for Book xvii, a favourable picture of Ptolemy would be in his mind, and he

[116] Diod. xviii.14.1; xix.55.5 and 56.1; xix.86.2–4; etc.
[117] *Contra*, Jacoby, *RE* 'Hieronymos', col. 1555.
[118] Diod. i.13.5, 17.2, 18.5, 21.8: Osiris is consistently *euergetikos*; also Isis (i.22.1, 25.3), Aegyptus (i.51.4), Sesoosis (i.54.2, 55.10), and Psammetichus (i.67.9). Sesoosis, Actisanes, Mycerinus, Sabacon, and Amasis showed *epieikeia* in their rule of Egypt; Sabacon excelled his predecessors in *chrēstotēs*. At i.90.2 Diodorus has a digression on the importance attached to *euergesia* by the Egyptians. For χρηστότης, cf. *Letter of Aristeas* 290: ἦθος χρηστὸν καὶ παιδείας κεκοινωνηκὸς δυνατὸν ἄρχειν ἐστί. Herondas, *Mimes* i.30: ὁ βασιλεὺς χρηστός, referring to Ptolemy Philadelphus (cf. J. A. Nairn, comm. ad loc.: the phrase seems to be an 'indivisible compound', suggesting that it was commonly used of Ptolemy).

would use his own, conventional, language to convey this, wherever Ptolemy's actions lent themselves to a favourable interpretation.

In addition to the Alexandrian source of Book xviii, Diodorus certainly made use of a Rhodian author, both for his account of the 'third inundation' of Rhodes at xix.45, and in Book xx for his account of Demetrius' siege of Rhodes. The Rhodian flood, at first sight irrelevant to the narrative of Antigonus' campaigns in which it is embedded, gains more point on Hiller's hypothesis that it was the disastrous consequences of this inundation that impelled the Rhodians to bow to Antigonus' diplomatic pressure at a time when he did not even possess a fleet, and actually to fight on his behalf in the years 315 to 311: in 306 to 304 they resisted him, although he was by then much stronger. Diodorus has obscured the connection with Antigonus' policies—if, indeed, it was made explicit by his source—preferring to dwell on the drama of the flood itself.[119] But although the existence of this passage can be rationalized, our view of its origin must be influenced by the extended 'Rhodian' section in Book xx, where the chapters 81–8 and 91–110.4 fall under suspicion in the first instance because of the reference at 81.3 to the 'Will' of Alexander: 'Alexander, the most powerful of men known to memory, honouring Rhodes above all cities, both deposited there the testament disposing of his whole realm and in other ways showed admiration for her and promoted her to a commanding position.' This is the fiction of a Rhodian patriot: the entire history of the Diadochi makes sense only on the assumption that Alexander left no will.[120]

The account of the siege in the following chapters is a piece of good historical writing (unlike the historically muddled account of Ptolemy in Book xviii), and it differs only slightly in manner from the narrative of Diodorus/Hieronymus. The differences are important, however. The account is generally favourable to the Rhodians, who are treated as innocent victims of Antigonus' aggression, and it is very well informed about events within Rhodes: the measures taken as preparation for the war (emancipation of slaves, provision for public burial of the fallen and for widows and orphans, etc.); the discussion in the Rhodian assembly of a proposal to pull down the statues of Antigonus and Demetrius, and the honorary decree voted to the mercenary captain Athenagoras, are all items which indicate knowledge of affairs from the Rhodian side.[121] The general interest in siege machinery

---

[119] R. Hiller, *RE* Supp. v (1931), s.v. 'Rhodos', cols. 778–9. Cf. H. Hauben, 'Rhodes, Alexander and the Diadochi from 333/332 to 304 B.C.', *Historia* xxvi (1977), p. 335.
[120] On Alexander's 'Will' see R. Merkelbach, *Die Quellen des griechischen Alexander-romans*, München, 1954, pp. 124 ff., 151.   [121] Diod. xx.84.2–6, 93.6–7, 94.5.

might be thought a Rhodian interest, Rhodes and Alexandria being the centres of Hellenistic military technology; and there is some evidence of Rhodian terminology. The rare word *katapeltaphetai* at 93.5, now supported by the parallel text of Hiller's papyrus; the phrase ἐπὶ νήσων in the same paragraph, without the definite article; and the *hapax legomenon* μεταλλωρύχος of the papyrus, which Diodorus has converted to the more usual μεταλλεία and μεταλλεύς, are all very Rhodian expressions.[122]

In this section Diodorus seems also to adopt a new style of military writing. There is a dramatic note in the picture of the anxious Rhodians gazing down at the enemy fleet (83.2), in the hand-to-hand battle at 87.3, in the appeal of the Rhodian 'prytaneis' to the patriotic citizens (88.3), and again in the fears and weeping of the women and children during Demetrius' final assault on Rhodes (98.8–9). This dramatic manner is not characteristic of other siege descriptions in Diodorus xviii–xx (contrast, for example, his account of the siege of Megalopolis at xviii.70 ff.);[123] although Thucydides' picture of the final sea-battle at Syracuse should be a warning that 'serious' historians did not necessarily deny themselves opportunities to bring colour and excitement into their writing.

One passage in the 'Rhodian' section needs special comment. This is the elaborate description of the great *helepolis* built by Demetrius in the second year of the siege (xx.91). The technicality of this description has given rise to the suggestion that it derives from a writer on military technology—a theory which has serious implications for Diodorus' method of composition, since it implies that in this passage he wove together material of various origins, rather than making a simple addition from a single author to his main source. Marsden compared Diodorus' account of the *helepolis* with the description by the third-century technical writer, Biton, of the *helepolis* built for Alexander by the engineer Posidonius.[124] He concluded that the striking similarity both in details of subject-matter and in the order in which they are discussed postulate a technical writer like Biton as the ultimate source of Diodorus: this writer could have been Diocleides of Abdera, who was famous for his description of the Rhodian *helepolis*;[125] and Diodorus' direct source might have been a collection of engineering excerpts. However, this supposition overlooks the fact that

[122] Hiller, *S. B. d. preuss. Akad.* 1918, pp. 757 f., and above, n. 46. On the expression ἐκκαλεῖσθαι see below, App. II, p. 276. Cf. also Diod. xx. 93.2: ναῦς . . . φυλακίδας.
[123] Cf. Jacoby, *RE* 'Hieronymos', col. 1554.
[124] E. Marsden, *Greek and Roman Artillery*, ii, p. 85.
[125] Athen. v.40, p. 206DE.

the narrative following the description of the *helepolis* contains repeated allusions to items in its construction which are not only consistent with the original description but actually presuppose it. The references to the pent-houses, the iron plates which covered the machine, and the men assigned to move it, would be unintelligible unless they referred back to a complete description of the *helepolis*.[126] Moreover, the fact that Diocleides, of whom nothing else is known, wrote a famous description of the Rhodian *helepolis*, does not guarantee that this was the one used by Diodorus: a man who won fame for describing a *helepolis* was surely a rhetorical, not a technical writer. We know from Plutarch that Demetrius' machines were objects of wonder to all his contemporaries, and they may have inspired a number of *ekphraseis*.[127] A historian who embarked on a description of this sort must have had access to technical expertise, but the expert most naturally associated with the Rhodian *helepolis* is Epimachus of Athens, the engineer who built the machine.[128] A contemporary historian could have drawn on Epimachus' engineering notes, just as Biton used the *hypomnemata* of Posidonius; likewise Philon and Heron used the *hypomnemata* of Ctesibius.[129] This hypothesis would explain the similarities between the accounts of *helepoleis* in Biton and in Diodorus, for Greek engineers presumably learned from one another and passed on traditions of design and construction, and after Posidonius doubtless other *helepoleis* were based on the pattern he had established. There are good reasons, therefore, for associating Diodorus' description of the Rhodian *helepolis* with the rest of the Rhodian section and attributing the entire passage to a single subsidiary source.

The general problem remains, of the ultimate origins of Diodorus' whole account of the siege of Rhodes. The publication of Hiller's papyrus, with its parallel account, inspired a number of guesses. The Ionic dialect of the papyrus does not necessarily point to Duris of Samos, still less to Diyllus of Athens;[130] for there is sufficient evidence for the popularity of Ionic for historical compositions in the second century AD, at the time the papyrus was written: Arrian's *Indike* is the best-known example.[131] The dialect is therefore likely to be the affectation of the writer of the papyrus. The most likely candidate is Zeno of Rhodes, whom Diodorus had cited in Book v for the legendary history

---

[126] Compare xx.95.1 and 91.8 (penthouses); xx.96.7 τῶν ἀπὸ τῆς μηχανῆς λεπίδων τινές, and 91.3; xx.96.7, τοὺς τεταγμένους ἐπὶ τῆς κινήσεως, and 91.7.
[127] Plut. *Demetr.* xx.3–5.
[128] Vitruvius x.16.4 (281), Athenaeus, *Peri Mechanematon* 27 (ed. Wescher).
[129] Marsden, op. cit., pp. 1–2, 5–6, 8–9.
[130] So E. Cavaignac, *Mél. Glotz*, 1932, pp. 160 f.
[131] Cf. Hiller, art. cit., p. 760, for examples of the vogue for writing in Ionic.

of Rhodes, including the great *kataklysmos* which inundated the island in early times.[132] There is no difficulty in attributing to Zeno the detailed and intelligent narrative, with its use of Rhodian documents and its Rhodian bias, which forms the basis of the papyrus fragment and of Diodorus xx.81 ff. In particular, the introductory section in chapter 81 contains resonances of conditions of the later third to early second century BC: the author's comments on flourishing commerce with Alexandria and on the state of the Rhodian navy could be true of the late fourth century, but sound slightly exaggerated for that period. In the same section, the foreign policy of Rhodes during the period directly preceding the siege is outlined as one of universal friendship and neutrality, and here the general tenor is in agreement with a passage of Polybius recounting early relations between Rhodes and Rome (the Rhodians wish for a general friendly agreement—presumably on commerce, suppression of pirates, etc.—without being committed to a full military 'symmachy' which would circumscribe their foreign policy), and which is probably based on Zeno.[133]

If Diodorus here combined Hieronymus with Zeno, he did so with skill; though it is not impossible that Zeno himself, living a century after the event, had drawn on Hieronymus' account of the great siege, as being the standard literary version. That Hieronymus described in detail this episode, which demonstrated all the brilliance and the futility of Demetrius' achievements, can hardly be doubted; and in Diodorus the knowledge of affairs on the Macedonian, as well as the Rhodian side, is most naturally attributed to a Macedonian source. The description of Demetrius' *helepolis* can be ascribed ultimately to Hieronymus (with the collaboration of the engineer Epimachus), and linked to other examples of technological interest in this narrative, especially the account of the Salaminian *helepolis* at xx.48. The chapter on the Rhodian *helepolis* passes naturally into the portrait of Demetrius 'Poliorcetes', the builder of the machine (xx.92), and this is to be compared with character portraits of other diadochs in Diodorus. Furthermore, the parallel at this point with Plutarch, who sketches Demetrius' character in terms similar to Diodorus and in the same context, is most easily explained on the assumption that Plutarch and Diodorus have a common source, directly or ultimately, in Hieronymus, whom each used in the non-Rhodian parts of their works. Diodorus must have turned to the Rhodian history at this point

---

[132] Diod. v.56.7 = *F. Gr. Hist.* 523 T2 and F1.

[133] See K. Abel, *RE* Suppl. x (1972), s.v. 'Zenon', no. 6, col. 139, for Zeno as Diodorus' source; Walbank, *HCP* i, Introd. pp. 29 f. for Zeno as a source of Polybius, cf. Polyb. xvi.15.8 and Walbank, op. cit. pp. 31 f. Cf. Hauben, art. cit., pp. 318 ff., 334 f.

because it offered more material—the Macedonian version was balanced by a Rhodian point of view—and treated it in a generally more vivid manner. In the same way he had looked at events in Egypt through an Alexandrian source, although Hieronymus also had recounted them. And in both cases it is extremely probable that he turned to a historian already familiar to him: Cleitarchus, his main source on Alexander, and Zeno, his main source for the local history of Rhodes.

The theory of two, and only two, identifiable supplements has an attractive economy. Diodorus' method was the same when he reused Hecataeus in Book xl, and anticipated Hieronymus in Book ii (see below). Other disruptions in the Diadochi narrative have been suspected, but are not easily proved. The supposed correspondence with a Duris fragment in the description of Rhagae at xix.44.4–5 is not convincing.[134] Strabo's citation of Duris agrees with Diodorus in content only, not in words, and he attributes the same information elsewhere to Posidonius.[135] Rhagae was a famous place in antiquity (it figures also in the Book of Tobit);[136] and it is perverse to deny that Hieronymus, who had been there, could have described it. Diodorus was, indeed, familiar with Duris' history of Agathocles; but that he used Duris' *Macedonica* is speculation. The argument for a different source for Greek affairs in Book xviii must also remain very uncertain. Information on the Lamian War is duplicated in Books xvii and xviii; but that Diodorus used the same source in each book, rather than anticipating or repeating, or finding the same facts recounted by two different historians, cannot be demonstrated. No extended passage on Greek events in Book xvii is given a different and inconsistent treatment in xviii;[137] but the account of the Lamian War in xviii reveals a distinctly Macedonian slant, pointing, it might be thought, to Hieronymus. The only anomaly, which is one of tone, rather than fact or political outlook, is the description of Phocion's trial and death (Diod. xviii.66.4–67.6). The apologia for Phocion might derive from a local historian who shared Phocion's views—perhaps Philochorus;[138]

---

[134] Duris, *F. Gr. Hist.* 76 F54 = Strabo i.3.19. Cf. Jacoby, *RE* 'Hieronymos', col. 1549. The passage was taken as evidence for an extensive use of Duris in Diodorus' history of the Diadochi by older commentators.

[135] Strabo xi.9, p. 514. = *F. Gr. Hist.* 87 F87a.

[136] Book of Tobit, 4:1, 4:20, 5:6: Tobit's son Tobias goes to Rhagae to collect his father's silver, accompanied by the angel Raphael.

[137] In xvii Leosthenes negotiates with the Aetolians during Alexander's lifetime, in xviii only after his death; see also above, p. 33 n. 51.

[138] See Jacoby, *Atthis*, pp. 78 f. for Philochorus' conservative sympathies, and p. 74 for his relation to that well-known conservative, Androtion; cf. *F. Gr. Hist.* 328 F117 and comm. ad loc., IIIB, p. 461. It is perhaps significant that Diodorus makes no mention of

but such a source could well have been used by Hieronymus himself, who had to rely on second-hand evidence for most of his Greek history until after Ipsus, and who is far more likely to have sought such testimony than Diodorus himself, with his preference for general and universal historians (the comments on the instability of Fortune may have been Diodorus' own, however: cf. xviii.59.5–6, and below). The same consideration argues against the use of a local Pontic historian at xx.22 ff., where disproportionate space is given to the affairs of the Bosporan royal house.[139] Diodorus' reasons for choosing to dwell on the history of Eumelus and his brothers must in any case be a mystery; but the fact that the excursus seems long and irrelevant is not necessarily an argument against derivation from his main source, in whom the connection with the central narrative could have been made clear enough. Indeed, remarks in chapter 25 suggest that this may have been attached to the history of Lysimachus' activities, for the allusion to the siege of Callantia picks up the story of xix.73, and Eumelus is praised as benefactor of the Greek states on the Pontus when they were hard pressed by Lysimachus, and gave to many, Diodorus recounts, a new city in which to live.[140] Not only might the Cardian historian wish to express fellow feeling for the Greek cities oppressed by Lysimachus (cf. Hier. F9); he also had an interest in the Pontic region, where Eumenes had fought Ariarathes, and where Demetrius' friend Mithridates was to found a powerful kingdom (cf. below, App. I, pp. 243 ff.), and this he may have developed in his history by incorporating local accounts. Alternatively, it may be conjectured that Polybius included such an excursus in a lost portion of his work (cf. below, p. 236 and n. 6), which Diodorus extracted for use in advance of his main Polybian narrative. The use of this major historian in an unexpected context would be in keeping with Diodorus' practice in the case of Hecataeus and others, and is more plausible than the supposition that Diodorus himself had looked so far afield in his researches.

Diodorus' own additions to Hieronymus are mostly brief and unimportant passages which tie together the various sections of his unwieldy narrative, and which can be paralleled in other books of the *Bibliotheke*. Chapter i of Book xviii, for instance, is Diodorus' own introduction to his new theme; likewise at xviii.75.3 he writes his own conclusion to the book, and regularly he marks the change from one

Phocion's part in allaying Athenian suspicions (justified, in the event) about Nicanor's designs: Diod. xviii.64; cf. Plut. *Phoc.* xxxiii.3 ff., Nep. *Phoc.* ii.4. For the view that Diodorus used Diyllus as a source for Athenian affairs, see below, ch. 4, p. 177 and n. 302.

[139] Cf. Jacoby, *RE* 'Hieronymos', col. 1554.

[140] For the accuracy of the Callantia narrative, cf. below, ch. 4, pp. 117 f.

theatre of events to another in his own words. Philosophical reflections also often represent Diodorus' own thought; for example, those on the workings of Tyche at xviii.59, where the language is resonant of his *Hauptproem*.[141] Such additions are easily identified. Neither the supplements from Diodorus' other sources, nor his own reflections on the nature of history, affect our view of Hieronymus as his single main source in the history of the Diadochi, a narrative which shows the consistency of detail and of general outlook already described; and it is here taken as a principle of argument that there need be special grounds for doubting the derivation of any passage from Hieronymus.

INTERMEDIARY SOURCES

To resolve the problem of 'supplements' in Diodorus by positing the use of an intermediary source is tempting but facile. A second-century historian, specifically Agatharchides, has been the most popular candidate.[142] The idea of an intermediary originated in a belief that Diodorus was a mindless copyist of his sources and used only a single author at a time, while at the same time was recognized the need to account for obvious anomalies: hence the theory of a proto-Diodorus who had already combined material of different origins. This ghost-figure, however, fails to explain major repetitions in the *Bibliotheke*. Diodorus took Hecataeus of Abdera as his principal source for his description of Egypt in Book i; but he omitted Hecataeus' account of the Jews at this point, to introduce it forty books later as a digression in the narrative of Pompey's Jewish War.[143] A description of the Dead Sea is given in Book xix, in connection with Antigonus' Arabian campaign; but the same description occurs in Book ii, as part of a geographical excursus on Arabia.[144] The two passages agree almost word for word. This might represent a chance use of a common author by Diodorus and his source in Book ii; but it is altogether more credible that Diodorus had read a number of authors before he started

---

[141] Diod. xviii.59.6, πάντα τὸν αἰῶνα: cf. i.1.3, 2.3; xviii.59.6, ὁ κοινὸς βίος: cf. i.1.1, 2.1, 8.8, 9.2; cf. App. II, p. 271.

[142] Cf. Beloch, *Gr. Gesch.* iv.2², pp. 3 ff.; Schwartz, *RE* s.v. 'Diodoros', no. 38, col. 685; A. Vezin, *Eumenes von Kardia*, pp. 4, 6 f.; C. Bottin, *Rev. Belge de Phil.* vii (1928), p. 1326.

[143] Cf. O. Murray, 'Hecataeus of Abdera and Pharaonic Kingship', *JEA* lvi (1970), pp. 145 f.

[144] Diod. xix.98; ii.48.6–9. At ii.7.3 Diodorus refers to Cleitarchus, his main source on Alexander in Book xvii; cf. ii.29–31, where in an excursus on the Chaldaean astrologers Diodorus refers to their predictions about Alexander and Antigonus, to be treated in later parts of his work. P. Krumbholz, 'Wiederholungen bei Diodor', *Rh. Mus.* xliv (1889), pp. 286 ff., rightly regards these repetitions as equivalent to cross-references in a modern publication.

to write, and tried to make use of them not only where they provided the standard account of a period, but also where they had something to contribute in a specialized area. Thus he seems to have used Cleitarchus and Zeno, possibly Polybius, in xviii–xx; and the repetition or anticipation of material in different books of the *Bibliotheke* shows that Diodorus' method, unsophisticated as it was, yet was not entirely mechanical.

The specific arguments in favour of Agatharchides or some other re-working of Hieronymus are not compelling.[145] The reference to the 'satrapy of Idumaea', supposedly indicating a date after 198 BC, has been discussed. The geographical description of Asia at xviii.5–6, with its horizontal division along the line of the Taurus–Caucasus, has sometimes been thought to presuppose the scheme of Eratosthenes; but our ignorance of the state of Greek geography directly before Eratosthenes hardly allows this conclusion. It is entirely possible that the north–south division of Asia is an idea which goes back to Alexander's geographers; and there are in any case references in this passage to the political conditions of Alexander's time which could not have survived a general renovation in the light of Eratosthenes' work.[146] The passages of Book xviii which show sympathy for Ptolemy are admittedly not derived from Hieronymus; but it is no compliment to Agatharchides to suppose that it was he who made these clumsy additions. The Ptolemaic passages are so clearly different in manner from the central narrative that it makes little difference to a final estimate of Hieronymus whether they are additions of Diodorus or of 'proto-Diodorus'; but it is in fact arbitrary and pointless to insist that they could not have been made by the author of the *Bibliotheke* himself. That Agatharchides knew Hieronymus' history is a natural inference from Hieronymus T2, but there is nothing to show whether this was a casual allusion, or whether it indicates a more extensive use of his predecessor. It is in any case highly improbable that Agatharchides merely copied out long extracts from Hieronymus' work.

The theory of an intermediary cannot actually be substantiated, and it solves no problems relating to the source criticism of Diodorus xviii–xx. In the following chapters it is assumed that Diodorus drew on Hieronymus directly in his history of the Diadochi, and that, with the exceptions noted above, he drew on Hieronymus alone.

THE OTHER SECONDARY AUTHORS

All the surviving accounts of the Diadochi derive to a greater or lesser

---

[145] Cf. the arguments of Fontana, *Le lotte*, pp. 161 ff.
[146] See below, ch. 3, pp. 80 f.

degree from Hieronymus; though few writers of the imperial period seem to have used him both directly and extensively. For this reason it is essential to take Diodorus as a starting-point: we do not know in advance what sort of history Hieronymus wrote, since the fragments tell us so little; and it is only from Diodorus, thanks to his unique method of composition, that an idea of its characteristics can be formed. Generally speaking, the other accounts add little to our knowledge, and close comparison of the texts tends to reveal more about the methods of the secondary authors than about Hieronymus himself. Accordingly, for detailed analysis of the historiographical tradition, reference is here made to earlier studies, and only a resumé is offered in the present chapter.[147]

Among writers of the Roman period who used Hieronymus, our greatest loss is undoubtedly Arrian's τὰ μετὰ ᾽Αλέξανδρον. Photius' epitome of this work shows that it included the same items as Diodorus for the years 323 to 321, and in the same order; and the similarity of subject-matter alone is such, in this case, as to suggest a common source.[148] Where Photius goes into more detail, for example in his account of the settlement at Triparadeisos (F9.34), he agrees with Diodorus almost word for word. Arrian diverges from Diodorus in recounting how Alexander's body was brought to Egypt (F9.25): here, as we have seen, Diodorus was using an Alexandrian source, and it may be supposed that Arrian preserves Hieronymus' version. On the other hand, where Arrian and Diodorus differ in their accounts of the murder of Demades, Arrian is probably using not Hieronymus but an Athenian source.[149] He relates the incident in connection with the fate of the other Athenian democrats in the context of the year 322, and makes Cassander responsible for the murder, whereas Diodorus puts it in 318, shortly before Antipater's death, and says nothing about the deaths of Demosthenes, Hypereides, and the other Athenians:[150] an

---

[147] See above, p. 4, n. 15, for references. The tradition on events in Babylon after Alexander's death is discussed in greater detail in ch. 3.

[148] Cf. F. Grimmig, *Arrians Diadochengeschichte*, Diss. Halle, 1914; U. Köhler, 'Über die Diadochengeschichte Arrians', *S. B. d. Berl. Akad.*, 1890, ii, pp. 557 ff; Fontana, *Le lotte*, pp. 213 ff.

[149] Arr. *Succ.* F9.14, cf. Plut. *Phoc.* xxx, *Demosth.* xxi; Diod. xviii.48.1–4. This is especially plausible if Arrian was living at Athens by the time of writing his work on the successors, as Brunt supposes: Introd. to Loeb edn. of Arrian, vol. i, p. xii. *Contra*, G. Wirth, *Historia* xiii (1964), pp. 227 f., suggesting that the *Successors* was published before the *Anabasis*.

[150] Diodorus' reference to Demosthenes and Hypereides at xviii.13.5–6 is perhaps his own addition. The statement that Demosthenes was still in exile at this time appears to be an error: cf. A. Schäfer, *Demosthenes und seine Zeit*,[2] Leipzig, 1885, iii, p. 341. Diodorus sometimes comments on famous orators elsewhere in the *Bibliotheke*, e.g. xvii.4.8, Aeschines, xiv. 109.3, Lysias; cf. xvi.84–5, taken from Demosthenes, *De*

Athenian author therefore probably lies behind Arrian F9.13–15. Furthermore, the description of Antipater as σαπρὸς καὶ παλαιὸς στήμων occurs in Arrian and in Plutarch, but not in Diodorus, and the offensive phrase must derive from an Athenian democratic source, not from a historian writing from a Macedonian point of view.[151] It seems likely, therefore, that Arrian's method in his history of the Successors was similar to his method in his history of Alexander, where he says that he took the best original accounts of the period—Ptolemy and Aristobulus, (though many would argue that in fact it is Ptolemy's version which predominates in the *Anabasis*) and supplemented them with the lesser histories and *legomena*. The fragments of the τὰ μετὰ Ἀλέξανδρον do not otherwise conflict with Diodorus, but in many places they add substantially to Diodorus' information. This is true particularly of F10 (cf. F9.25–6), dealing with the outbreak of the war in 321 between Perdiccas and Eumenes on the one hand and Antipater's coalition on the other; also of the papyrus fragment which concerns Eumenes' negotiations with a defeated phalanx.[152] These appear to be true fragments of Arrian, as distinct from the abbreviated version of Photius, and they give an idea of the scale on which Hieronymus must have written, for the treatment of the material is exhaustive.

Trogus, also, we have only in epitome. His *Historiae Philippicae* seems to have been written as serious history, though with a certain moralizing and anecdotal tendency, and in his method of work he differed significantly from Diodorus, weaving together different historiographical traditions on any one period.[153] For the period of the Diadochi the account of Trogus/Justin in many places corresponds closely with that of the Hieronyman tradition in Diodorus, particularly at xiii.6, discussing Perdiccas' conquests in Cappadocia and Pisidia and his marriage plans, and at xiii.8, describing Perdiccas' harsh character.[154] The account of Eumenes' battle with Neoptolemus and his exile on Perdiccas' death also parallels that in Diodorus.[155] Again in Book xiv, where he narrates the later fortunes of Eumenes, Justin follows the tradition of Diodorus/Hieronymus, though he fails to

---

Corona xviii.169–78. These notices, like his notices on historians and poets, were apparently an attempt to bring cultural history within the scope of κοινὴ ἱστορία.

[151] Cf. Plut. *Demosth.* xxxi.5; *Phoc.* xxx.9. Cf. ch. 4, pp. 171 ff.

[152] Cf. p. 30, n. 43 above.

[153] Amm. Marc. xv.9.2, Trogus collected material 'ex multiplicibus libris'. Cf. Justin, *Praef.* i: 'quae historici Graecorum . . . segregatim occupaverant'.

[154] Cf. Diod. xviii.22–3 (it is presumably Justin himself who has conflated the Cappadocian with the Pisidian campaign); Diod. xviii.33.3, Arrian, *Succ.* F9. 28.

[155] Justin xiii.8.4–10; cf. Diod. xviii.30 ff.

mention Hieronymus at Nora.[156] For the final battle at Gabiene, however, this tradition is abandoned, and Justin gives an account recalling that of Plutarch, referring to Eumenes' attempt to flee from the army. This unflattering account of Eumenes' behaviour possibly derived from Duris, likewise the theatrical last speech of Eumenes, recorded by Justin and Plutarch.

The excursus on the history of Cyrene at xiii.7 is certainly from a source other than Hieronymus, and seems to replace the narrative of Thibron's fortunes in Cyrene given by Diodorus and Arrian. Justin also differs from Diodorus in his narrative of the Lamian War, which is written from a Greek, not a Macedonian point of view, and suggests an author who tried to minimize the final catastrophe of the Greeks.[157] Again, his account of reactions in Babylon to Alexander's death differs considerably from that of Diodorus and resembles the last chapters of Curtius' history, both in its dramatic tone and in the record of the generals' speeches; like Diodorus, on the other hand, Justin refers to the decision to send Alexander's body to Ammon—an item which occurs in these two authors alone.[158]

It is possible that Trogus' account of events at Babylon, like that of Curtius, had elements deriving ultimately from Duris; but unlikely that he used either Duris or Hieronymus direct.[159] His knowledge of Hieronymus might have come from Diodorus, since Justin has no factual details, in the Hieronyman parts of the narrative, which are not also in Diodorus, and such a relation would explain the reference to Ammon in each. However, Diodorus does not seem to have been used generally by other historians before the Christian chroniclers, and the relative dates of writing of Trogus and Diodorus are very uncertain.[160] It has often been thought that Trogus drew extensively on Timagenes

---

[156] Cf. Diod. xviii. 40 ff. For Justin xiv.5–6, Olympias' return to Macedon and her death, cf. Diod. xix.11; 35–6; 49–51.

[157] Justin xii.5.15–17; n.b. 5.17, 'Graecorum quoque copiae finibus Graeciae hoste pulso in urbes dilapsae.'

[158] Diod. xviii.3.5, Justin xii.4.6; cf. below, ch. 3, pp. 90 f.

[159] As suggested by Fontana, *Le lotte*, pp. 187–200.

[160] Diodorus was at work on his history by 56 BC (i.44.1–4, with xii.49), and was perhaps revising it in 36 BC (xxi.7.1, the refounding of Tauromenium: for the date, see Beloch, *Die Bevölkerung der gr.-röm. Welt*, Leipzig, 1886, p. 337). He had probably finished by 30 BC, since the Macedonians, not the Romans, are said to be the last alien rulers of Egypt (i.44.4). Trogus' floruit is uncertain, depending on whether the 'Pompeius' of Justin xliii.5.11 is his father or his grandfather: the latest event mentioned is the ending of the Spanish War by Augustus in 19 BC, but Trogus wrote when the greater part of Livy's history was completed (Justin xxxviii.3.1). The suggestion of Welles, Introd. to Loeb edn. of Diodorus, vol. viii, that Trogus was Diodorus' source for Book xvii, can hardly be substantiated, since the dates of both authors are so uncertain; the use of a common source on Alexander is more likely. Cf. Brunt, op. cit., p. lxxxiv.

for his history of Alexander, and it may be that a common use of this author by Trogus and Diodorus accounts for the detail about Ammon at the beginning of their narratives of the Diadochi, where the old source on Alexander had not yet altogether been laid aside.[161]

The biographers Nepos and Plutarch have detailed accounts of the careers of Eumenes, Demetrius, and Pyrrhus, which undoubtedly derive in part from Hieronymus; though it remains uncertain whether either knew his work at first hand, and in the case of Plutarch, especially, the biographical form makes it difficult to isolate his sources.[162]

Nepos in his *Life of Eumenes* is very similar in a general way to Diodorus. His account of Eumenes' high birth and his important position under Philip and Alexander (ch. 1) is probably from Hieronymus (contrast Duris *ap*. Plutarch *Eumenes* i.1); likewise his narrative of Eumenes' campaigns in Asia (chs. 3–10), which corresponds closely with Diodorus, although much briefer. The allusion in chapter 2 to Alexander's ring was a story which appeared in the vulgate tradition on Alexander; whether Hieronymus also recorded it must remain uncertain. The final chapters of the *Life* (11–12), which contain *dicta* and other material found in Plutarch but not in Diodorus, also suggest a more popular type of historical writing. Chapter 13 contains mostly Nepos' own conclusions, though in the final paragraph (13.4) he seems to return to the Hieronyman tradition for his account of Eumenes' burial (cf. Diod. xix.44.2).

As our most important source after Diodorus and Arrian, the methods used by Plutarch demand a general comment. The view that he used only secondary sources found its extreme expression with Meyer (who believed he had not even read Thucydides and Herodotus in the original), and was prevalent in the earlier part of this century. This was very much an *a priori* assumption, however, and detailed analysis of individual *Lives* has increasingly shown that Plutarch actually possessed a deep interest in history and antiquities and had read extensively among the Greek historians (his knowledge of Roman writers is a more disputed matter). To prove direct acquaintance is in most cases impossible, but the practice, for example, of citing a

[161] Trogus and Timagenes: cf. A. von Gutschmid, *Rh. Mus.* xxxvii (1882), pp. 548 ff., = *Kl. Schr.* v, pp. 218 ff.; modified by Wachsmuth, *Rh. Mus.* xlvi (1891), pp. 465 ff., cf. *Einleitung*, pp. 114 f.; Jacoby, *F. Gr. Hist.* IIC, pp. 220–2, 227 f.; Laqueur, *RE* s.v. 'Timagenes', no. 2, cols. 1065 ff.; Klotz, *RE* s.v. 'Pompeius', no. 142, cols. 2307 ff.; Schwartz, *RE* s.v. 'Curtius', no. 30, cols. 1887 ff.; Fraser, *Ptol. Alex.*, ii, p. 748 n. 214. Cf. below, ch. 3, pp. 138 f.: Timagenes' own source on Alexander was probably Cleitarchus.

[162] For Nepos' knowledge of the older historians whom he cites cf. E. Jenkinson, 'Nepos', in *Latin Biography*, ed. T. A. Dorey, London, 1967, p. 6.

work by book numbers is suggestive of first-hand knowledge (this he does not, in fact, do for Hieronymus), and not uncommonly he admits knowing an author at second hand only: he makes no such confession when he cites Hieronymus. Attempts have been made to estimate the extent of Plutarch's direct access to sources, using as a criterion the number and spread of his citations; but this method ignores the scope of an author's work: Hieronymus, mentioned five times altogether in the *Lives* of Demetrius and Pyrrhus, was an obvious authority for their period, but Plutarch would have had small occasion to consult him elsewhere. (He is clearly a source or ultimate source in the *Eumenes*, but is not actually cited there.) Plutarch certainly had opportunity to read Hieronymus in the original. In a rare comment on method (*Demosthenes* ii.1) he says that a historian needs to live in a large city, devoted to the arts, where he will have books of all kinds in abundance. He goes on to remark that he himself lives in a small city; but this is in the context of an apology for not knowing Latin well: from Chaeronea he had access to the library resources of Athens, where Arrian, not long after, apparently found a copy of Hieronymus. The abundance of personal detail preserved, especially at the end of the *Pyrrhus*, which is found in no other source, strongly suggests knowledge of the original authority; and this possibility enhances the value of Plutarch in reconstructing the later part of Hieronymus' work, where Diodorus' account survives only in brief excerpts.[163]

Plutarch mentions Hieronymus in each of his three biographies of the early Hellenistic princes. In the *Eumenes* and the *Demetrius* he is named as a historical character, and the fact that, like Diodorus, he speaks of the 'historian' Hieronymus (*Demetr.* xxxix.2) suggests that the latter was one of his principal sources. In the *Pyrrhus* he is cited three times as a source.[164] For Plutarch, however, Hieronymus was only one of many authorities. At the beginning of the *Eumenes* he cites Duris for the view that Eumenes' father was a waggoner: the alternative version, that Eumenes owed his advancement to the guest-

---

[163] On Plutarch's method, see E. Meyer, *Forschungen zur alten Geschichte*, ii (1899), pp. 65 ff., for the older view. K. Ziegler, *RE* xxi s.v. 'Plutarchos', no. 2, cols., 636 ff., tries to distinguish those authors Plutarch had certainly read, those he had probably read, and those he knew only through an intermediary. For a modern estimate of the problem, see C. P. Jones, *Plutarch and Rome*, 1971, pp. 81 ff., and Hamilton, *Plutarch, 'Alexander'*, 1969, pp. xliii-xlix. C. Pelling, *JRS* xcix (1979), pp. 74 ff., arguing that Plutarch composed a group of *Lives* simultaneously, believes that he drew on a wide range of material, but failed to 'weave items from all these sources into a composite and independent narrative' (p. 91): i.e. Plutarch, like Diodorus, tends to reproduce his source for any individual episode with little contamination.

[164] Plut. *Eum.* xii, cf. Hier. T4; *Demetr.* xxxix.3–7 = Hier. T8; *Pyrrh.* xvii.7, xxi.7, xxvii.8 = Hier. F11, 12, 14.

friendship between his father and Philip of Macedon, presumably comes from Eumenes' admirer Hieronymus. The hostile account of Eumenes' career under Alexander in chapter 2 again suggests Duris, and there are signs of this author at the end of the *Life*, where it is imputed that Eumenes showed cowardice before the final battle against Antigonus, and in the dramatic account of Eumenes' capture and execution. The main narrative of Eumenes' adventures in Asia is based on Hieronymus, but has been worked over, whether by earlier writers or by Plutarch himself, so as to put character and moral issues into high relief. Thus Eumenes' battle with Neoptolemus, the death of Craterus, the demagogic behaviour of the Eastern satraps to the soldiers, the battle with Antigonus, and the account of Eumenes' illness, all show an exaggeration for the sake of effect which is absent from the parallel sections of Diodorus. Some of these episodes may be influenced by the tradition from Duris;[165] but in general the more colourful elements can be sufficiently explained in terms of Plutarch's own method of composition.[166]

In the *Demetrius*, at least three principal strands are woven together.[167] Hieronymus or a version of Hieronymus was clearly used for the main part of the historical narrative: thus chapters v–vii and xii.1 can be paralleled in Diodorus, also the characterization of Demetrius at ii.2–3 and at xix.6–xx.1; and to these sections should probably be added chapter iv (Demetrius and Mithridates), xxviii–xxix (character of Antigonus and battle of Ipsus), and the narrative of Demetrius' later fortunes in Greece and Asia in Chapter xxx–xxxvii, xxxiv–xl (reference to Hieronymus at xxxix.2), xliii–xliv.2, xlv–lii.[168] This narrative is on the whole favourable to Demetrius, though it does not minimize the weaknesses of his character (for example, ch. xl, Demetrius' retort to his son), or the magnitude of his final catastrophe (cf. li.1, ὥσπερ τεθνηκότος ᾿Αντιγόνῳ τὰς πόλεις κ.τ.λ.).

Plutarch's account of the battle of Salamis diverges in some details from that of Diodorus; the figures for the fleets of Ptolemy and Demetrius are different, and so are the losses; and the colourful

---

[165] So Fontana, op. cit., pp. 231 f.

[166] Cf. Jacoby, *RE* 'Hieronymos', cols. 1559 f. for the distortions in Plutarch's account.

[167] Cf. W. Sweet, *Classical Weekly* 44, no. 12, March 1951, pp. 177 ff.; E. Manni, Introd. to edn. of Plutarch's *Vita Demetrii*, Florence, 1953. R. Flacelière, Budé edn. of the *Demetrius*, 1977, pp. 10 ff., sees Hieronymus and Phylarchus as the basis of Plutarch's account, and the other sources used, in decreasing order of importance, as Duris, Demochares of Leuconoe, Philochorus, Lynceus, and Demochares of Soli.

[168] In ch. xxxii the casual reference to the treasury of Cynda suggests that Plutarch is excerpting from an extensive work in which Cynda was often mentioned: cf. Diod. xviii.62.2; xix.56.5; xx.108.2; F. Reuss, *Hieronymos*, p. 137.

picture of Ptolemy and Demetrius exchanging κομπωδεῖς λόγοι is missing from Diodorus.[169] There was a contingent of forty Athenian ships on Demetrius' side at Salamis (Diod. xx.50.3), and it is possible that Plutarch here used an Athenian author. An Athenian source seems certain, at least, for the hostile account of Demetrius' invasion of Attica and his misbehaviour in Athens: the most likely candidate is Philochorus, the atthidographer who believed in the ideals of the old democracy; and in a number of places there is a correspondence between Plutarch's account and fragments of Philochorus.[170]

Some of the more scurrilous anecdotes perhaps derive from the comic poets or from the popular historian Duris. It is probably Duris who lies behind the frequent references to Demetrius' love of finery and theatrical show,[171] and Plutarch's general interpretation of the life of Demetrius as a tragic play (see especially chapter liii) may owe much to Duris' 'mimetic' style of historiography.[172] To what extent the Peripatetic view of a change in Demetrius' character was generally accepted by contemporaries must remain in doubt; but there are some indications that Hieronymus, despite his personal association with the prince, recognized in him the development of the harsh traits of his father Antigonus, and passages of the *Life* which imply a criticism of its subject should not invariably be attributed to the tradition hostile to the Antigonids.

For the sources of Plutarch's *Pyrrhus*, the picture is more complicated.[173] Hieronymus is cited three times, but on each occasion in conjunction with either Dionysius or with Phylarchus, and Plutarch doubtless knew him via these authors as well as directly for the events here related.[174] Either the original or a version of his work was probably used, however, for most of the historical narrative treating Pyrrhus' campaigns in Macedon before and after the Western expedition, and again for the Peloponnesian campaign at the end of Pyrrhus' life. The history of Pyrrhus was deeply involved with that of Demetrius

[169] Plut. *Demetr.* xvi. 1–2; Diod. xx.50.1–4, cf. 52.6.
[170] Compare Plut. *Demetr.* x, Philoc. *F. Gr. Hist.* 328 F66; *Demetr.* xii (the month Munychion took the name Demetrion), Philoc. F166; *Demetr.* xxiv, Philoc. F67; *Demetr.* xxvi (the Eleusinian mysteries), Philoc. F69–70 (contrast the account at Diodorus xx.100.1—from Hieronymus?). At *Demetr.* xi–xii the record of Athenian psephismata recalls Philochorus' collection of Athenian documents—ἐπιγράμματα Ἀττικά. At ch. viii events are dated by the Attic calendar month Thargelion. Cf. Reuss, *Hieronymos*, pp. 132 ff. and above, p. 60 and n. 138.
[171] Compare *Demetr.* xli and Duris, *F. Gr. Hist.* 76 F14 = Athen. xii, p. 535E.
[172] Cf. P. de Lacey, 'Biography and Tragedy in Plutarch', *AJP* lxxiii (1952), pp. 159–71.
[173] For a detailed study, cf. Lévêque, *Pyrrhos*, Paris, 1957, pp. 22–6; 61–6.
[174] Hier. F11, 12, 14.

and Antigonus Gonatas, and Hieronymus necessarily treated in some detail the career and character of the enemy who had posed the greatest threat to the establishment of the Antigonid dynasty in Macedon. His account evidently showed little sympathy for Pyrrhus, and perhaps failed to do justice to his grand visions of empire. The contrast in the personalities of Pyrrhus and Antigonus Gonatas is clearly drawn in the later chapters of the *Life*, and here the authorship of Gonatas' faithful servant cannot be in doubt. The *dicta* of Antigonus, recorded at xxxi.2 and xxxiv.5, together with the topographical and personal details of the last campaign at Argos suggest an author who had been present on the Macedonian side or at least had first-hand information; and the omission of any reference to Pyrrhus' victory over Antigonus outside Argos might indicate that bias in favour of his master which Pausanias attributes to Hieronymus.[175] The closing scene, in which Antigonus weeps over his fallen rival, possibly represents the finale to Hieronymus' own history.[176]

Hieronymus did not confine himself, however, to relating those parts of Pyrrhus' history which brought him in contact with the Antigonids. Plutarch cites him for the losses incurred at the battles of Heraclea and Asculum, and it seems probable that he was used in conjunction with Proxenus, Timaeus, and Roman annalistic sources, for much of Plutarch's account of the Italian expedition (though not for Pyrrhus' activities in Sicily).[177] Interpretation of his attitude on the basis of Plutarch's narrative is problematic; but it seems unlikely that Hieronymus, viewing Pyrrhus' Western expedition as an episode in the war of Greeks against barbarians, was disposed to treat Pyrrhus more sympathetically in his role as representative of Hellenic aspirations.[178] More probably the attack on Rome was, for Hieronymus, the supreme folly of the king's career, and the Romans, to whom he devoted a special excursus, were seen as embodying an ideal of barbaric courage and independence, like the Nabataeans who resisted the imperialistic expansion of Antigonus Monophthalmus.[179]

Among the minor sources on the Successors, Dionysius appears to have read Hieronymus in the original, because he comments unfavourably on his style (Hier. T12). He also cited him as author of the first Greek treatment of early Roman history (*Ant. Rom.* i.5.4 = Hier. F13), and this excursus must have fallen in the section of Hieronymus' work dealing with Pyrrhus in Italy (ἐν τῇ Περὶ τῶν Ἐπιγόνων πραγματείᾳ,

[175] Paus, i.13.9 = Hier. F15; cf. App. I, p. 248.
[176] See below, ch. 3, pp. 102 ff.
[177] Hier. F11, 12; Lévêque, locc. citt.
[178] So Lévêque, op. cit., p. 25.   [179] See below, ch. 4, pp. 177 ff.

Dion. Hal., loc. cit.). Taking this with the evidence of Plutarch, who twice cites Dionysius and Hieronymus together on Pyrrhus' battles against the Romans, it appears that Hieronymus was one of the sources of Dionysius in his *Antiquities*, Books xix–xx, where he treated Pyrrhus' invasion. These books survive only in excerpts, but we know from the citation of Proxenus at xx.10.2 that Greek sources were used, and among these Hieronymus was probably the principal authority for the military narrative. Dionysius' descriptions of the battles at Asculum and at Beneventum show a competence which at once recalls the excellent military writing of Diodorus xviii–xx, and certain details about the equipment and fighting methods of the Roman army, which are anachronistic for Dionysius' own time, suggest a Greek author writing for a Greek audience, who can only be Hieronymus.[180] Thus despite his complaints about Hieronymus, Dionysius evidently found him useful for these episodes.

Pausanias twice cites Hieronymus, but almost certainly had no direct knowledge of his work. The allusion at the beginning of Paus. i.6 to οἱ συγγενομένοι τοῖς βασιλεῦσιν ἐπὶ συγγραφῇ τῶν ἔργων might include Hieronymus; but it is improbable that Pausanias conducted serious research into writers who were by then, as he himself indicates, both ancient and obscure, and his immediate sources for the historical episodes introduced into his *Periegesis* were probably compilations or abstracts of the imperial period. The criticism of Hieronymus' reliability implied in both Pausanias' citations perhaps suggests that Hieronymus has been filtered through that notorious fault-finder, Timaeus;[181] other intermediaries are a matter of guesswork. Probably Hieronymus is the ultimate source for a series of sketches in Pausanias Book i, describing the careers of the Successors;[182] and he is named explicitly in connection with the summary of Pyrrhus' career at i.11–13.[183] The passage describing Pyrrhus' ambition to conquer the Romans—notorious as a result of Perret's thesis about the legend of the Trojan foundation of Rome—may, as Perret claimed, derive from Hieronymus' account of Pyrrhus;[184] he is also probably the source for some

[180] Dion. Hal. *Ant. Rom.* xx.1 (Asculum: the Greek dispositions are given in detail); xx.11.1 (Beneventum: cf. Lévêque, op. cit., p. 522). Cf. E. Rawson, *PBSR* n.s. xxvi (1971), pp. 24–6; and below, ch. 4, p. 142.

[181] Cf. M. Segre, *Historia* ii (1928), pp. 217–37.

[182] Paus, i.6.2–8, Ptolemy; i.9.5–10.5, Lysimachus; i.11–13, Pyrrhus; i.16.3, Seleucus. Cf. O. Pfundtner, 'Die Historischen Quellen des Pausanias', *Neue Jahrb. f. Philol. u Paedagogik*, xcix (1869), pp. 452–4; R. Daebritz, *RE* s.v. 'Pausanias', col. 1560.

[183] Paus, i.13.9 = Hier. F15; cf. i.9.8 = Hier. F9.

[184] Paus. i.12.1; J. Perret, *Les Origines*, p. 414 n. 1. Cf. App. I, p. 250. The reference at i.12.1 to the *hypomnemata* recalls Plut. *Pyrrh.* xxi.12, where it is implied that Hieronymus drew on Pyrrhus' *Memoirs*: see below, ch. 4, p. 128.

details on the Western expedition, for example, the provenance of the elephants which Pyrrhus took to Italy.[185]

Pausanias' long account in Book x of the Gallic invasion of Greece is more problematic.[186] It is substantially the same as the more compressed versions of Justin and Diodorus, and not incompatible with his own summary of the same episode in Book i.[187] The detail of the narrative makes it unlikely that he has omitted much of his source, and though the elaborate comparisons with Xerxes' invasion of Greece, taken from Herodotus, likewise the allusions to Homer and Pindar, are probably the additions of Pausanias or his immediate source, this section must represent a considerable extract ultimately from a Hellenistic historian.[188] Some features do suggest Hieronymus: the narrative is clear and circumstantial, with good strategical detail; the account at xix.9–12 of the organization called *trimarcisia* is consistent with the interest Hieronymus showed in foreign customs and military institutions. It is, on the other hand, much more highly coloured than Diodorus/Hieronymus, with its account of furious fighting (21.3–4), cannibalism (22.3–4), pathetic or heroic women (ibid.; 22.5–6), oracles and miracles (23.1–2), etc. There is also a distinct tone of Greek patriotism, not only in the comparison with the Persian invasion (19.5; 20.1), but in the account of fighting at Thermopylae, where the *Attic* Greeks outshine all the others in valour (21.5), and Telesarchus and Aleximachus show outstanding zeal ἐς τὰ Ἑλλήνων (22.1, cf. 23.3); and the panic which eventually falls on the Celtic army takes the form of a delusion that their own people are Greek, bearing Greek arms, and speaking Greek. The briefer account in Pausanias' first book is similarly pro-Greek and especially pro-Athenian (cf. esp. i.4.1–2). Clearly, then, there is much here that is not from Hieronymus.

[185] Paus. i.12.3.

[186] See J. G. Frazer, *Commentary on Pausanias*, vol. v, pp. 341 ff. for views on the ultimate source. Hieronymus was suggested by Segre, *Historia*, 1927, pp. 18 ff.; cf. Tarn, *Antigonos Gonatas*, pp. 439 ff.; Walbank, *HCP*, i, at p. 213, n. on ii.35.7.

[187] Paus. x.19.7, Brennus and Acichorius: cf. Diod. xxii.9.2, Brennus and Cichorius (the same mistake, since 'Brennus' was probably a title, 'king'). Paus x.19.7, Bolgius: cf. Justin xxiv.5.1, Belgius. Paus. x.19.9, invading army has 152,000 foot, 20,400 horse (61,200 including grooms' horses): cf. Diod., 150,000 foot, 10,000 horse (plus hordes of camp followers including 2,000 waggons), and Justin, 150,000 foot, 15,000 horse. Paus. x.23.12, Brennus puts an end to himself by drinking neat wine: cf. Diod. xxii.9.2, Brennus killed himself with his sword after drinking much neat wine; Justin xxiv.8.11, Brennus killed himself with a dagger because unable to bear the pain of his wounds. Paus. x.23.13, not a man returned home: *sic* Diod. xxii.8.11, Justin xxiv.8.16; at i.4.5 Pausanias says most crossed over to Asia (as at Polyb. iv.46 and in other writers), but this is not necessarily incompatible with x.23.14, viz., an allusion to the body of Celts who had not invaded Greece.

[188] Paus. x.20.1–2, 22.8; 22.7; 22.9. Cf. Frazer, op. cit., vol. i, pp. lxxii ff., for Pausanias' knowledge of poets and historians, especially Homer and Herodotus.

Naturally he must have described the Gallic incursion and Gonatas' victory in the later part of his work, but if his account was indeed the basis of that in Pausanias it must have been extensively rewritten.

Pausanias probably has only a garbled version of what Hieronymus said about Lysimachus and the tombs of the Epirot kings (Hier. F9); and Hieronymus' own version of Pyrrhus' death apparently was different from those Pausanias recounts.[189] Pausanias, then, while he preserves some valuable details absent from other sources, is not always a reliable vehicle for the transmission of Hieronymus.

Appian in the *Mithridateios* also cites Hieronymus by name (Hier. F3 = *Mith*. 8–9); and the similarities between his summary of Cappadocian history and the references to Cappadocia and Mithridates in Diodorus and Plutarch suggest that Hieronymus, perhaps indirectly, was his principal source throughout the excursus. Hieronymus seems to be an ultimate source again in the *Syriaca* for the history of Seleucus I, and here Appian is a valuable authority for items such as the partition of Antigonus' empire after Ipsus (ch. 55) and Seleucus' war against Lysimachus (ch. 62), which may represent those later parts of Hieronymus' history missing from Diodorus. It is unlikely, however, that Hieronymus was also responsible for the list of Seleucid oracles mentioned in connection with the battle of Ipsus.[190] No doubt the Chaldaean seers' prophecy to Antigonus and the claims to divine patronage made by Seleucus when he returned to Babylon go back to Hieronymus: these were historical events, and the psychological effect of such prophecies made them historically important;[191] but it is not obvious what purpose would have been served, in a work which focused principally on the Antigonids, by a collection of pro-Seleucid stories current at the time of Ipsus—as far as can be judged from Diodorus, Hieronymus was not a writer who recorded religious phenomena for their own sake. Appian's source in chapter 56 was more plausibly Duris, for the story about Lysimachus' dog at chapter 64 recalls Duris F55.[192]

Polyaenus is another author who drew on Hieronymus only selectively, using Hieronymus' evidence for the military skill of the diadochs to illustrate his *strategemata* of the Macedonians in Book iv. Polyaenus states at vi.18.21 and 60.5 that he compiled his work from many historical writings, and, according to the general opinion, he is as

[189] *Contra*, Reuss, *Hieronymos*, p. 147. Cf. below, App. I, p. 248.
[190] So R. A. Hadley, *Historia* xviii (1969), pp. 142 ff.
[191] Diod. xix.55.6–8; 90.3–4. Cf. Jacoby, *RE* 'Hieronymos', col. 1553.
[192] Duris, *F. Gr. Hist.* 76 F55 = Pliny, *NH* viii.143.

reliable in any instance as his sources.[193] In Book iv, parallels with Diodorus' account of Eumenes and Antigonus show that Hieronymus is certainly the ultimate source;[194] and it may be supposed that he was also the authority for stratagems omitted by other authors—for example, Antigonus' moral victory over Eumenes' fleet in Phoenicia (iv.6.8), an incident which explains Eumenes' withdrawal from Phoenicia into Mesopotamia after 318 (compare Diod. xviii.73.2: *καταχούμενος δ' ὑπὸ τῶν καιρῶν ἀνέζευξεν ἐκ τῆς Φοινίκης κ.τ.λ.*). Polyaenus claimed to be of Macedonian descent, and so had a special interest in Macedonian history (Bk. iv, *Praef. τῶν ἡμετέρων προγόνων*). However, it is improbable that Hieronymus' history was known to him in the original, especially as he compiled his work in a hurry, so that the emperors Marcus Aurelius and Lucius Verus might take it with them as an *ἐφόδιον* on their Parthian campaign. The close similarities with Diodorus perhaps can be explained by the lively and even anecdotal manner of the original, which ensured their preservation down to imperial times (some of the same stratagems are preserved by Plutarch and Nepos). Moreover, not all Polyaenus' stratagems of the Diadochi can derive from Hieronymus: for example, the story of Eumenes hiding from some pursuing Gauls (iv.8.1) perhaps comes from Duris' uncomplimentary portrait; and like many writers of this period, he may have made use of an already existing compilation which took material from a range of Hellenistic authors.

A little can be added to our knowledge of Hieronymus from writers of the first and second century AD. The majority, perhaps, of ancient historians and biographers who were not writing contemporary history had a tendency to transmit their immediate sources with little alteration;[195] none the less in many cases Hieronymus can only have been known indirectly, and was used only incidentally, by authors whose main purpose was not to re-tell the history of the Diadochi, but to write biography, *strategemata*, or Roman history. Arrian had the luck, or the instinct, to hit upon sources of exceptional quality. But among those whose works on the Successors survive, only Diodorus used Hieronymus both directly and for an extended piece of writing; and the peculiar nature of the *Bibliotheke* allows us to reconstruct from it the character of Hieronymus' lost history in a way which would otherwise be impossible.

[193] See J. Melber, 'Über die Quellen u. den Wert der Strategemensammlung des Polyaen', *Jahrb. f. klass. Phil.* 14 Suppl. Bd., Leipzig, 1885, pp. 415–685. Cf. F. Lammert, *RE* xxi.2, s.v. 'Polyainos', col. 1434; Droysen, *Hell.* i, p. 685.
[194] Cf. H. Kallenberg, *Philologus* xxxvi (1877), pp. 644 ff.
[195] Cf. Pelling, art. cit., p. 91.

Chapter 3

Hieronymus' Book

Possibly no ancient authority cites the title to Hieronymus' work. Suidas' τὰ ἐπ' Ἀλεξάνδρῳ πραχθέντα seems only to describe the content;[1] for it is not to be reconciled with the evidence of Diodorus— ὁ τὰς τῶν διαδόχων ἱστορίας γεγραφώς, of Josephus—ὁ τὴν περὶ τῶν διαδόχων ἱστορίαν συγγεγραφώς, or of Dionysius—ἡ περὶ τῶν ἐπιγόνων πραγματεία.[2] The terms Diadochi and Epigoni are used regularly by writers of the first century BC to refer to the first and second generations respectively of Alexander's Successors. Appian, describing the power and wealth of the 'satraps' who succeeded Alexander, concludes: ἀλλὰ πάντα ἐς τοὺς ἐπιγόνους αὐτῶν συνετρίφθη. Similarly Strabo: εἰς πλείους τοὺς διαδεξαμένους καὶ τοὺς ἐπιγόνους τούτων μερισθεῖσα ἡ ἡγεμονία τῆς Ἀσίας διελύθη. Diodorus, too, in his main proem, says that among previous historians, some have closed their accounts with the deeds of Philip and Alexander, some with the Diadochi or Epigoni: τινες δ' εἰς τοὺς διαδόχους ἢ τοὺς ἐπιγόνους κατέστρεψαν τὰς συντάξεις.[3]

Nothing is to be inferred from these passages, however, about Hieronymus' title. Diodorus in Book xviii once speaks of οἱ διάδοχοι in the relevant sense; but this is in the context of the 'Last Plans', a notoriously controversial passage which can hardly be used to adduce anything about Hieronymus' language.[4] In the main narrative of xviii–xx Diodorus uses the contemporary terminology *hetairoi*, or, where appropriate, *somatophylakes*, as Arrian does;[5] these were evidently

---

[1] Suidas, *I* 201 Adler, = Hier. T1. For this use of ἐπί, cf. Appian, *Syr.* i.1: Λυσίμαχος μὲν ὁ Θρᾳκης ἐπ' Ἀλεξάνδρῳ βασιλεύσας.

[2] Diod. xviii.42.1, = Hier. T3; Joseph. *c.Apion.* i.213, = Hier. F6; Dion. Hal. *Ant. Rom.* i.5.4, = Hier. F13. Cf. Diod. xviii.50.4, xix.44.3, 100.1, where Hieronymus is described simply as 'the writer of the histories'.

[3] Appian, *Praef.* 10; Strabo xv, p. 736; Diod. i.3.3. Cf. also Suidas, *E* 360 Adler: Hecataeus of Abdera lived ἐπὶ τῶν Ἀλεξάνδρου διαδόχων; and ibid., *A* 2704, s.v. Ἀντίπατρος: στρατηγὸς Φιλίππου, εἶτα Ἀλεξάνδρου καὶ διάδοχος βασιλείας. Antisthenes of Rhodes (*c.*200 BC) wrote a Φιλοσόφων Διαδοχαί: *F. Gr. Hist.* 508 F10. Cf. Diod. xviii.9.1; xix.52.4.

[4] Diod. xviii.4.1.

[5] Cf. ch. 2, p. 34 with n. 53.

the terms habitual with Hieronymus, though the more portentous *diadochoi* is not necessarily precluded as part of his title. Polybius does not use 'Diadochi' when he speaks of the Successors as a group;[6] but it is likely that the term already had this specific meaning in his day. By the second century, *diadochoi*, along with *philoi* and *protoi philoi*, have become a class or order at the Hellenistic courts: our evidence suggests that members of these orders were never referred to in the singular, but always as belonging to the class τῶν διαδόχων, τῶν πρώτων φίλων, etc., and also that the orders were honorary and did not imply real office;[7] and the term 'successors' is scarcely intelligible in this context unless, at an earlier stage, it had been applied to Alexander's generals and acquired a sense parallel to that of *philoi* or *hetairoi*.[8] Third-century historians may well represent this intermediate stage.

The early Hellenistic period offers a few examples of the use of 'epigoni'. This was the name given by Alexander to the contingent of 30,000 Persian boys brought to Susa in 324 and trained in Macedonian fashion. It appears also on Ptolemaic papyri of the third and second centuries referring to the first generation of the descendants of mercenaries settled in Egypt, the *katoikoi*.[9] Laqueur tried to establish a connection between these two uses of *epigonoi* and the famous Epigoni of the third century, the sons of Alexander's generals, arguing that *epigonoi* was the name given by Alexander to the sons of his Macedonian veterans at the end of his life, that it was extended to include the sons of his officers and generals, and that the expression is a mark of a time before the unity of the empire became a dead letter.[10] It is true that the idea of kinship was a motif of the last year of Alexander's life; but Justin is alone among our sources in stating that Alexander called the sons of his veterans *epigonoi*, and it is possible that he has confused them with the Persian boys (Justin xii.4.11). Arrian clearly distinguishes the 30,000 Persian παῖδες ἡβάσκοντες from the half-oriental children who were left behind in Alexander's care when their fathers returned to Macedon.[11] Whether the *epigonoi* of the Ptolemaic papyri are to be explained in terms of Alexander's policy of fusion is also uncertain; but a connection between the Persian *epigonoi*

[6] Polyb. viii.10, ix.29.1.
[7] See M. L. Strack, *Rh. Mus.* lv (1900), pp. 168 ff. and 189 f., with examples from papyri and inscriptions of the period 191 to 117 BC.
[8] Cf. also Welles, *RC*, p. 368, on *somatophylakes*.
[9] Arr. *Anab.* vii.6.1, cf. vii.8.2. *PSI* vi.588.7; U. Wilcken, *Urkunden der Ptolemäerzeit*, Berlin, 1927–57, xiv.70.
[10] Laqueur, *RE* xvii s.v. 'Nymphis', col. 1609.
[11] Arr. *Anab.* vii.12.2.

at Susa—30,000 of them—and the small group of early Hellenistic kings who were called the Epigoni, does not seem likely. Arrian is clear that it was Alexander himself who gave this name to the Persian boys, and the use is highly individual.[12] As applied to the sons of his generals, it is more plausibly a reference to the seven heroic Epigoni of legend, who fought against Thebes in the quarrel between the sons of Oedipus, and, as such, its origins are probably literary. Hieronymus' interest in Theban legend, presumably a consequence of the period he spent as governor of Thebes, is apparent in the 'archaeology' of Thebes at Diod. xix.53.4 ff., in which the heroic Epigoni are mentioned, and this might have inspired an imaginative application of the title to those would-be heroes, Pyrrhus and Demetrius. It is perhaps true that Demetrius and the rest would not have thought of themselves as a group with a collective name at the time when they held power and were at war with one another; but writers who had a view over the whole period of the Successors could have applied the name in retrospect. The evidence that these men were ever known colloquially as *epigonoi* is extremely tenuous:[13] unlike *diadochoi*, the word does not seem to have found its way into the terminology of the Hellenistic courts.

Some support for 'Diadochi' and 'Epigoni' in Hieronymus' title is to be found in the title cited for his contemporary, Nymphis of Heraclea. According to Suidas, Nymphis wrote a work Περὶ Ἀλεξάνδρου καὶ τῶν Διαδόχων καὶ Ἐπιγόνων in twenty-four books; and in describing Nymphis' history of Heraclea, Suidas uses also the phrase τὰ μετὰ τοὺς Ἐπιγόνους, suggesting that his terminology for the whole period which he treated was sharply defined.[14] Nymphis must have been born before 310 at the latest, and died after Ptolemy Euergetes took the throne, probably in the 240s; and he began to write after 281, when he returned from exile to his native city: he was thus a much younger

[12] H. Droysen, *RE* vi s.v. 'Epigonoi', col. 68 takes the view that Arrian has misapplied the name: but Arrian's explicit statement οὓς Ἐπιγόνους ἐκάλει Ἀλέξανδρος must be taken from Ptolemy.

[13] Usener's theory that 'Epigonos, father of Antigonos', mentioned in an epigram from Cnidus (Kaibel 781), is the 'Epigonos' Demetrius Poliorcetes, father of Antigonus Gonatas, has been definitely refuted by the discovery of an inscription from Miletus honouring the Cnidian Ἀντίγονος Ἐπιγόνου (*Milet*, 1.3, 'Das Delphinion', Berlin, 1914, no. 138, line 73. For bibliography on this controversy see C. Habicht, *Gottmenschentum u. gr. Städte*, München, 1970, p. 79). 'Epigonos' here is thus a personal name. M. Holleaux suggested Πτολεμαῖον ἐπίγ[ονο]ν as a possible supplement to a decree from Telmessos of 240 BC (*OGIS* 55, line 22), referring it to Ptolemy son of Lysimachus (*Études*, iii, pp. 373 ff., 382 ff.); but this has not gone unchallenged: see A. Bouché-Leclerq, *Histoire des Lagides*, iv.312; E. Kalinka, *Tit. Asiae Min.*, ii.1.4 f. The reading of the fourth letter is very uncertain: it may be *T* or *Γ* or *Π*.

[14] *F. Gr. Hist.* 432 T1.

contemporary of Hieronymus, writing at approximately the same time.[15] The relative order of writing is unknown, but we might assume that it was Hieronymus, the elder and more celebrated historian, who inspired imitation.[16] The parallel between their supposed titles suggests in any case that their works were arranged along similar lines, and it led Jacoby to claim that 'die termini Διαδόχοι und Ἐπίγονοι sind für ihn (sc. Hieronymus) gesichert.' A comparable case is Anaximenes, who divided his work into Πρῶται Ἱστορίαι, Αἱ περὶ Φίλιππον Ἱστορίαι and Τὰ περὶ Ἀλέξανδρον.[17] The degree to which the parts of Anaximenes' work were self-contained is indicated by the fact that each had its own system of book numbers, and it is likely that Nymphis, also, numbered the books to the three parts of his work separately.[18] No book numbers are mentioned in our citations of Hieronymus' work. The evidence suggests, however, that it was not uncommon for a historian to bring out his work in instalments with separate titles;[19] and it is possible that Hieronymus made a structural break in his work, probably after Ipsus and the death of the 'diadoch' Antigonus Monophthalmus.[20]

Thus there are indications that Hieronymus followed the example of Theopompus, Anaximenes, and the Alexander historians in placing the individual at the centre of his history: to call it *Macedonica* would have been to obscure its personal element. The idea of grouping Alexander' successors into a first and second generation is one which could have originated with Hieronymus himself: as the servant of three successive members of Antigonus' dynasty he must have been

---

[15] Jacoby, *F. Gr. Hist.* IIIB p. 259.

[16] So Laqueur, *RE* s.v. 'Nymphis', col. 1608.

[17] Cf. *F. Gr. Hist.* IIIB, Noten, p. 169 n. 12 and n. 14; *F. Gr. Hist.* 72 F3, 4, 15, etc.

[18] *F. Gr. Hist.* 432 F17: Aelian mentions the 9th book of a work Περὶ Πτολεμαῖον (i.e. Philadelphus), which is usually identified with the Περὶ τῶν Ἐπιγόνων. If the numbering were continuous throughout, one would expect a higher book number for events of the 3rd century.

[19] See T. S. Brown, *AJP* lxxi (1950), p. 141 with n. 53, on the practice among ancient authors of bringing out their works in instalments.

[20] Wachsmuth, *Einleitung*, p. 581, wanted to combine the evidence of Diodorus and Josephus, to make Hieronymus' title Ἱστορίαι τῶν διαδόχων καὶ ἐπιγόνων. Most commentators have seen the work as consisting of two parts: cf. Susemihl, i, p. 562. (This does not, of course, imply that a long period of time elapsed between the publication of each part: see below, ch. 4, pp. 174 f.) Recently Fontana, *Le lotte*, p. 257, has revived the idea, which goes back to Sévin, of an independent treatment of Pyrrhus. However, Dionysius mentions a work on the Epigoni in connection with Pyrrhus' Western expedition, not a history of Pyrrhus; and Hieronymus seems, in any case, to have had little admiration for Pyrrhus: it would be astonishing if he had selected him as the subject of a historical biography in preference to either Antigonus Gonatas or Eumenes. Cf. the scepticism of O. Müller, *Antigonos Monophthalmos und das Jahr der Könige*, Bonn, 1973, p. 7 n. 31.

peculiarly conscious of the continuity of history from one generation to another. Nymphis probably imitated him, and late Hellenistic authors took over his convenient terminology, which we still use: Hieronymus' selection of his theme has so dominated the tradition that even now it is difficult to think of this period except as the period of the Successors.

THE OPENING OF THE HISTORY

1 The Geography of Asia

With the exception of Xenophon, who took his role as Thucydides' continuator rather literally, it was normal practice among Greek historians to begin with a statement of aims and methods and perhaps a few autobiographical details; but since Hieronymus' epitomators were only interested in the content of his history, such information as Hieronymus gave in a general preface about himself, the nature of his work, and the circumstances in which it was composed, cannot be recovered.[21] There is, however, some evidence for an introductory section dealing with the history of Macedon down to the time of Alexander's death, suggesting that Hieronymus began in the manner of Thucydides and Polybius, with a survey of the historical background, which explained the situation at Babylon in summer 323 and set the tone of the work as a whole.[22] A *terminus ante quem* for the opening of the main narrative is offered by Diod. xviii.16.1–3, which coincides with Hier. F3, concerning events of 322. Signs of Hieronymus' starting-point are therefore to be sought in the first fifteen chapters of Book xviii.

One passage in this section stands out: this is the geographical survey of Asia at xviii.5–6, a self-contained section which falls between the account of the Succession in chapters 2–4 and the narrative of Pithon's campaign against the Bactrian Greeks in chapter 7, and which is clearly designed to stand as an introduction to events in Asia. It is closely linked to Diodorus' account of the Bactrian revolt, and its object, he states, is to make the narrative easier to follow by setting forth both the causes of the revolt and the disposition and character of the satrapies. It occurs in no other author; hence it has sometimes been regarded as an interpolation from a subsidiary, possibly a non-literary source. The North–South division of Asia, which forms the main structure of the geography, recalls the scheme adopted by Eratosthenes, and there is at 6.1–2, in the description of India, a reminiscence

[21] On the origin of T2 see ch. 1, pp. 6 and 15.
[22] Cf. App. i, pp. 238 f.

of a passage of Strabo which draws on Eratosthenes.[23] The verbal resemblance between Diodorus and Strabo is not, however, extensive nor especially remarkable. As for the scheme of the geography, it is possible and even likely that the horizontal division of Asia along the line of the Taurus–Caucasus did not originate with Eratosthenes, but was an idea at least implicit in the studies made by Alexander's bematists, which were known to Eratosthenes and frequently used by him.[24] Diodorus' geography does not mention the *sphragides* which were a striking characteristic of Eratosthenes' own system.[25] There are, finally, positive grounds for dating the geography earlier than Eratosthenes, because it contains traces of the political conditions of the time of Alexander, which could not have appeared in a third-century geographer presenting an up-to-date world picture.

The indications of the date were analysed in detail by Tarn, who described the geography as a political gazetteer of Alexander's empire, and believed that it was based on a document compiled in the last year of Alexander's life.[26] His arguments can be summarized as follows. The gazetteer includes the Indian provinces and is therefore later than Alexander's return from India in 324. The Hyrcanian and Caspian Seas are still two separate lakes; it is therefore earlier than the report made by Patrocles in *c.*280, which spoke of only one sea, and belongs to the brief period in the fourth century when Aristotle and Alexander knew the truth about the Caspian and the Aral. Chandragupta is apparently unknown; it is therefore earlier than Megasthenes. Porus is still alive; it is therefore earlier than 317. Media is still undivided, so it is earlier than the partition at Babylon when the fiction of an Armenian satrapy was abolished and never revived. It is earlier than the partition at Triparadeisos, because there are three instances of the verb συμβαίνειν, signifying a temporary political arrangement known to have existed in 324 to 323, but which was terminated by the new political dispositions of 321. The gazetteer, Tarn concluded, can be dated precisely: it was compiled between summer 324 and June 323, in the last year of Alexander's life.

[23] Strabo xv.1.13: Ἄπασα δ᾽ἐστὶ κατάρρυτος ποταμοῖς ἡ Ἰνδική. Diod. xviii.6.2: ἡ λοιπὴ τῆς Ἰνδικῆς . . . παραποταμίοις ὕδασι κατάρρυτος. (The corrupt παραποταμίοις is emended to ποταμίοις by Reiske; P. Goukowsky, *Diodore XVIII* ad loc., plausibly suggests πέντε ποταμῶν, alluding to the five rivers of the Punjab.)
[24] See E. Thonke, *Die Weltkarte des Eratosthenes und die Feldzüge Alexanders*, Diss. Strasburg, 1914, esp. pp. 45–9, 52–4, 56. Bematists: *F. Gr. Hist.* 119–123. Curtius vii.3.19 and Arr. *Anab.* v.5.4–5 describe the river system of Asia in similar terms. Cf. Aristobulus, *F. Gr. Hist.* 138 F23 (= Arr. *Anab.* iii.28.5) who described the East-West line of the mountains of Asia.
[25] Cf. Jacoby, *RE* 'Hieronymos', cols. 1555–6. Sphragides: Strabo ii.1.22; xi.12.5.
[26] Tarn, *JHS* xliii (1923), p. 93; *Alex. Gt.* ii, App. 17.

Not all Tarn's arguments are equally compelling, but his general conclusion on the date must be accepted.[27] The question then arises, how Diodorus came by the document, if such it is. He had access, it seems, to a certain amount of pseudo-documentary material purporting to date from the end of Alexander's life: the 'Will' of Alexander, and, in the opinion of many, the 'Last Plans' of Alexander belong to this category, and the gazetteer, like these, appears in no other source. However, the gazetteer must, for two reasons, be considered genuine: it has no politically tendentious content, like the Will; and it is not 'thaumasion', like the Last Plans. In addition, there are echoes of the thought and language of the gazetteer later in Books xviii and xix which show that it must have come from Diodorus' main source. Thus at xix.17.3 the Pasitigris (here mistakenly called the Tigris) is described as flowing down from the mountains into the Erythraean Sea in a way which apparently applies the principle, set out in the gazetteer, that the rivers of Asia flow north and south from either side of the central mountain range: τὸν Τίγριν ποταμόν, ἀπέχοντα Σούσων ὁδὸν ἡμέρας, ἣ τῆς ὀρεινῆς ἐκχεῖται . . . καὶ φερόμενος . . . ἀπὸ τῆς ὀρεινῆς . . . εἰς τὴν Ἐρυθρὰν ἐξερεύγεται θάλασσαν. Compare xviii.5.3: ἀκολούθως δὲ τούτοις τοῖς κλίμασι τῶν ποταμῶν τὰς ῥύσεις ἐχόντων ἀντιπροσώπους . . . οἱ μὲν εἰς τὸν κατὰ τὴν Ἰνδικήν . . . ἐνίοι δ᾽ εἰς τὴν καλουμένην Ἐρύθραν θάλατταν καταφέρονται. Again, at xviii.39.6, in the list of satrapal appointments made at Triparadeisos, reference is made to, τῶν . . . πρὸς τὴν ἄρκτον κεκλιμένων (sc. σατραπειῶν), and under this category are included Cappadocia, Great Phrygia, Lycia, Caria, Lydia, and Hellespontine Phrygia. In the gazetteer we are told that the satrapies are divided like the rivers, to north and south of the mountains: ὁμοίως δὲ τούτοις διελημμένων τῶν σατραπειῶν αἱ μὲν ἐπὶ τὴν ἄρκτον, αἱ δ᾽ ἐπὶ τὴν μεσημβρίαν ἔχουσι τὰς κλίσεις. καὶ . . . τῶν πρὸς τὴν ἄρκτον ἐστραμμένων κεῖται . . . Καππαδοκία . . . ἥ τε μεγάλη Φρυγία καὶ ἡ ἐφ᾽ Ἑλλησπόντῳ

[27] Periphrasis with verbs like συμβαίνειν, χρῆσθαι, τυγχάνειν, is so common among Greek writers of the later Hellenistic period that the 3 uses of συμβαίνειν in this passage (xviii.5.4, 6.2, 6.3) hardly call for special explanation. J. Palm (*Über Sprache und Stil*, pp. 97 f.), discussing Diodorus' use of this verb, accepts a special category which he dignifies with the name 'chorographic', and of which the three instances in question are supposedly a paradigm; but it is more probable that Diodorus uses συμβαίνειν here, as frequently, to avoid hiatus: the words Ἰνδος and Ὑρκανία presented problems in this respect. For Media, see below. Tarn's general conclusion is reinforced by the demonstration of Bosworth, *CQ* n.s. xxiv (1974), pp. 49 f., that Diodorus uses the early Hellenistic nomenclature for the divisions of Syria, both in the 'gazetteer' and elsewhere in Books xviii–xx, viz., 'Coele Syria' for the area from Egypt to Phoenicia, and ἡ ἄνω Συρία for the northern district next to Cilicia. This is in contrast to the usage of both Appian and Arrian, who describe the division of the Levant into three sectors from north to south, as it was in their own day.

κειμένη, ἐκ δὲ τῶν πλαγίων . . . Λυδία καὶ Καρία, ὑπερδέξιος δὲ τῆς Φρυγίας καὶ παράλληλος ἡ Πισιδικὴ καὶ ταύτης ἐχομένη Λυκία. Such consistency in the geographical assumptions of his narrative was not the fruit of Diodorus' efforts, because Arrian's version of the Triparadeisos arrangements agrees with Diodorus almost verbatim, and the final section of Arrian's list is introduced with the words, τῶν δὲ ἀπὸ τοῦ Ταύρου ὄρους ὡς ἐπὶ τὴν ἄρκτον φερόντων Καππαδόκας μὲν Νικάνορι ἐπέτρεψεν κ.τ.λ. The view of Asia presented to us in the gazetteer was therefore maintained consistently by Hieronymus, the common historical source of Arrian and Diodorus, and Hieronymus must be the source of the gazetteer itself.

The nature and purpose of the excursus then come in question. Tarn argued that πᾶσα Ἀσία or ὅλη Ἀσία (as at xviii.5.1 and 2) in the latter part of the fourth century regularly meant the Persian empire which Alexander claimed to rule, i.e. a political rather than a geographical entity, and he regarded the gazetteer as primarily a list of political divisions rather than a geography.[28] 'Asia', however, although frequently in Arrian's *Anabasis* and elsewhere signifying the Persian empire, is on three occasions given a wider scope, including India beyond the limits of Persian rule even as Alexander might have imagined it; and it is Asia in this extended, geographical sense that is certainly meant in Diodorus' description.[29] Indeed, if the gazetteer were political, it would be a singular sort of document. Alexander did not need a reminder of the names and number of the provinces he claimed to rule, and there is no correlate, such as a tribute quota or military levy. It could, perhaps, have been something like the list of tribute-paying peoples which was drawn up for Darius: if so, it has been radically modified.[30] As it stands in Diodorus, it is plainly intended just as a geographical aid. Diodorus describes it as a *topothesia* which will make the narrative easier to follow—εὐπαρακολούθητος— and when he states in the introductory paragraph that he is going to set out τῶν σατραπειῶν τὰ μεγέθη καὶ τὰς ἰδιότητας, he reveals something about the character of the original, for this promise is not fulfilled in the excursus as he gives it: it must be inferred that Hieronymus had included those details about the size and nature of the satrapies which he omits.[31]

Further indications that this excursus is physical geography are the term 'Indike' (6.1, 6.3), meaning the land of India as a whole, in which various political units, such as the kingdoms of Taxiles and Porus, were

[28] Tarn, art. cit., p. 93 n. 2; cf. *The Greeks in Bactria and India*, p. 153 n. 1.
[29] Cf. Brunt, Loeb edn. of Arrian, i, p. liii n. 64, and App. XV.
[30] Cf. Herodotus iii. 89 ff.   [31] Cf. Goukowsky, *Diodore xviii*, note compl. à 5.1.

contained; also the category of ἄνω σατραπεῖαι, an expression not unique to this part of Diodorus, but one to which the Diadochi narrative made frequent reference, and for which Hieronymus' readers might need an explanation (the account of the Bactrian revolt, beginning in chapter 7, makes immediate use of it; and 'Upper Satrapies' are alluded to in the Triparadeisos appointments). Though the word 'satrapy' is used everywhere, this may be the fault of Diodorus, and the term cannot be pressed too hard. The 'satrapy' of Armenia, and the undivided Media, may be intended as geographical entities to which the historian knew he was going to refer in the course of his narrative.[32] Some satrapies, like Parapamisadae, are missing; other names— Lycaonia, Indike, Sittacine—are not those of satrapies at all. Possibly Hieronymus also had given the names of the 'cities of the Greeks', which Diodorus passes over. The real 'satrapy lists' are those which recorded the political divisions of the empire at Babylon and Triparadeisos. This excursus, by contrast, serves the function of the map which would be essential in a modern history of the Successors; for few of Hieronymus' readers would know the journey 'up country' from their own experience. (The remark at 6.3, ἐκ δὲ θατέρου μέρους, ἀφ' οὗ ποιούμεθα τὴν ἀνάβασιν, may represent Hieronymus' own recollection of his travels with Eumenes and Antigonus, described so vividly in Diodorus xviii and xix.) Hence the idea of a documentary source should be abandoned: familiarity with the work of Alexander's chancellery could have supplied Hieronymus with a bematist's view of Asia, in addition to his own memories.[33] In the course of his history he was careful to note changes in the administration of the satrapies; and the indications in the Geography of a date before 321 suggest the deliberate avoidance of political anachronisms.[34]

This conclusion has a consequence, *inter alia*, for the notorious mention at xviii.6.1 of Alexander and the Ganges. If the Geography is not a document of 324, no argument about Alexander's knowledge of the Ganges and his ultimate intentions can be based on it.[35] The close cultural unity of India at this time, and the fact that Alexander was

---

[32] Diod. xix.23.3: Orontes is described as holding the 'satrapy' of Armenia in 317. Diod. xix.20.2–3: Pithon's Media is described as 'the land of Media', *tout court*, a country famous for its τετράποδα.

[33] Goukowsky, loc. cit., suggests that the description was based on a *pinax* engraved by the bematists.

[34] See Diod. xviii.3 and xviii.39.6 ff. for the reorganization of the empire in 323 and 321; cf. xix.48.1–5; xix.56.4.

[35] Tarn, art. cit., pp. 93 ff.; *Alex. Gt.* ii, App. 14. Cf. E. Meyer, *Klio* xxi (1927), pp. 183 ff.; Schachermeyr, *Natalicium C. Jax Sept. Obl.*, I, Innsbr. Beitr. z. Kulturgeschichte, 3 (1955), pp. 123 ff. = Griffith, *Main Problems*, pp. 137 ff.; Hamilton, *Plutarch, 'Alexander', A Commentary*, Oxford, 1969, p. 171.

only two hundred miles from the Ganges when he reached the Hyphasis, make it more likely than not that he did know of another great river system beyond that of the Indus;[36] but Diodorus offers no documentary evidence. Detailed knowledge, of course, was only achieved in the early Seleucid period and made general with Megasthenes and Daimachus. Hieronymus would certainly have known of the Ganges, both through their writings and through his own campaigning experience in the Eastern satrapies;[37] and it was relevant for him, in his Geography, to refer not only to those parts of India which were (at least nominally) parts of the Macedonian empire, but also to point out that much was not, especially as he must later have had occasion to speak of Chandragupta and his deal with Seleucus. The word $<\Gamma\acute{\alpha}\gamma\gamma\eta\varsigma>$, rightly restored by Fischer at xviii.6.1 (cf. Diod. ii.37.2 and xvii.93.2), therefore marks the start of Hieronymus' *topothesia* of the 'southern regions', in which he works from east to west (the Indus comes next in paragraph 2), and is not (*pace* Tarn) the interpolation of Diodorus, echoing his source for Book ii or Book xvii, where similar information is given.[38] Diodorus may, however, be responsible for other items here, since 'Indike' occupies a disproportionate amount of space in the Geography (two out of nine paragraphs), and, like Egypt, but unlike every other satrapy, is awarded more than a merely factual comment. India and Egypt were countries to which Diodorus had devoted the first two books of his *Bibliotheke*, giving a detailed account of the great rivers which brought fertility and life to these lands; and having a sense of their importance as cradles of civilization, he may have been anxious to remind readers of Book xviii of his main treatment in i and ii. Hence the phrases ποταμίοις ὕδασι κατάρρυτος καὶ κατὰ τὴν εὐδαιμονίαν ἐπιφανεστάτη (6.2), and σατραπεία πασῶν ἀρίστη καὶ προσόδους ἔχουσα μεγάλας (6.3), which single out India and Egypt, may represent an expansion of the original by Diodorus himself, in the interests of the unity of the *Bibliotheke*.[39] He had also spoken of both countries at length in Book

---

[36] Schachermeyr, loc. cit.; Hamilton, loc. cit.
[37] Cf. D. Kienast, *Historia* xiv (1965), p. 188.
[38] Tarn, *Alex. Gt.*, ii, p. 14. At Diod. xviii.6.1 the Gandaridae are located only vaguely in the Ganges plain, perhaps on the wrong side of the river; but vagueness or error on the part of Hieronymus is not impossible on such a point, and anyway Diodorus might not be accurately reporting what Hieronymus had said. The order is apparently meant to be, i) Gandaridae, whose frontier was perhaps made out to be the Ganges, and who were not subject to the Macedonians; ii) the Punjab, which Alexander did conquer and which in 323 was actually in the hands of Porus and Taxiles, where the Indus runs; iii) lands to the west of India. (Professor Brunt's suggestions on this matter have been of great assistance).
[39] Cf. Tarn, loc. cit., pp. 277 f.: the excisions he proposed are too drastic, however.

xvii.[40] The mention, too, of Alexander's projected campaign against the Gandaridae at xviii.6.1, which he called off because of the number of their elephants, does not strictly count as *topothesia* (unlike the Ganges, which is part of the Geography's essential structure); and here Diodorus possibly recalls the story at xvii.93–4—a story also found in Curtius.[41] There can, of course, be no guarantee that Hieronymus did not lend his support to some traditions of the Vulgate (according to Arrian's criteria in the *Anabasis*, Hieronymus too would count as *legomena*); but there is a case for thinking, as will be argued below, that in the early chapters of Book xviii Diodorus was still influenced by his source for Alexander, and the allusion to the numerous elephants of the Gandaridae may be one example of such contamination.

Once the Geography is seen as Hieronymus' own composition, designed to accompany the narrative at least down to Ipsus, and in particular to set the scene for the first episode, the revolt in Bactria, it is a natural conclusion that this was the introduction to the whole historical narrative.[42] A geography, as a basic historical aid, was an obvious way to open a history. Among Hieronymus' contemporaries, Hecataeus of Abdera included a formalized geography of Egypt in his work on the Egyptians, and Timaeus used probably his first five books for a προκατασκευή on the geography and early legends of the West.[43] These Hellenistic writers found their ultimate model in Herodotus, though it is possible that Timaeus, at any rate, was influenced by the arrangement which Ephorus had adopted: Ephorus' fourth and fifth books were taken up with a geographical introduction to Europe and Asia respectively, in which he rambled from place to place in periegetic style, discussing city foundations, rivers and harbours, and other such details of topography. A universal history demanded some account of geography: Polybius, too, included one such book, and both Polybius and Diodorus stressed the importance of travel to the historian. It appears that Hieronymus' Geography did not follow the most typical pattern, for it is a survey of regions rather than a detailed

[40] Diod. xvii.52, *passim*: an excursus on Alexandria written by Diodorus in his own person, in which he stresses the pre-eminence and wealth of Ptolemaic Egypt (as at xviii.6.3 and 28.3). Alexander's journey through India occupies most of the later part of Book xvii.

[41] Curtius ix.2. Arr. *Anab.* v.25.1 says that reports of many war elephants ahead was one reason for the soldiers' refusal to go on beyond the Beas; he does not name the Gandaridae or mention the Ganges, except in Alexander's speech.

[42] Cf. Reuss, *Rh. Mus.* lvii (1902), p. 586 n. 1.

[43] On Hecataeus, see O. Murray, *JEA* lvi (1970), pp. 141 ff.: Hecataeus showed little interest in serious geography, since he failed to mention Egypt's most striking physical feature, the Nile. For Timaeus, see L. Pearson, *YCS* xxiv (1975), p. 185.

description of lands and peoples, a map rather than a *periegesis*. In particular, the East-West dividing line, derived, perhaps, from Alexander's bematists, was novel as a historian's device. The old Ionian geographers, followed by Ephorus, had divided the world into four parts, each occupied in its extremities by one of the famous barbarian peoples—Scythians, Ethiopians, Indians, and Celts. Timaeus and Polybius followed the Herodotean tradition of a threefold division into continents—Asia, Libya, and Europe.[44] Indeed, closer in spirit is that romantic military writer, Xenophon, who, in the preface to the *Cyropaedia*, 'gives a clear and magnificent idea of the extent of the empire of Cyrus'.[45] Other parallels are to be found in Roman, rather than Greek historians: the simple geographical proposition of Caesar at the beginning of his *Gallic War*—the product of a military mind; or the brilliant survey of provinces which opens Tacitus' *Histories*. With such an introduction, a historian could 'plunge into the stream of events, stripped for action and unencumbered by the paraphernalia of explanation'.[46]

II. The Struggle for the Successsion and Alexander's Last Plans

Hieronymus' main historical narrative took its starting-point from the *staseis* that broke out everywhere in the Greek world on Alexander's death. But Diodorus begins his eighteenth book with an account of events in Babylon: could he have used Hieronymus for this introduction? We have several accounts of the Succession, which show a fair degree of unanimity in the facts they relate, though they differ greatly in scale. This unanimity does not in itself show that Hieronymus is their common source: the versions of Diodorus, Arrian, and the biographers are so abbreviated, and those of Curtius and Justin so overlaid with rhetoric and obviously later elaboration that the identifying marks of their sources are almost obscured. There are indications, nevertheless, that Hieronymus did treat the Succession and that Diodorus made some use of his account.

Plutarch and Nepos both allude briefly to events in Babylon in their biographies of Eumenes, and there must be a presumption that each was here using the historian who was his main source for the rest of the

---

[44] Polyb. xii.25, iii.37; cf. Hdt. ii.16–17, iv.45.5; Walbank, *HCP* i, pp. 368 f.

[45] Gibbon, *Decline and Fall of the Roman Empire*, ch. viii (ed. Bury, vol. i, 1900, p. 208 n. 57). Cf. Xen. *Cyrop.* i.1.4.

[46] R. Syme, *Tacitus*, pp. 146 f. G. E. F. Chilver, *A Historical Commentary on Tacitus' Histories I and II*, p. 45, note on i.4, states of Tacitus' survey of the empire that it 'has no known precedent in ancient historiography'. But this ignores Hieronymus, who, like Tacitus, was describing the struggles of great armies and their leaders for the supreme power which had previously been in the hands of one man.

Life.[47] Plutarch underlines the part which Eumenes played in reconciling the hostile factions of the Macedonians; Diodorus, however, does not name the negotiators (οἱ χαριέστατοι τῶν ἄνδρων ἔπεισαν αὐτοὺς ὁμονοῆσαι, xviii.24), and *prima facie* this argues Hieronymus as the source of the biographers but not of Diodorus.[48] One may perhaps appeal to the extreme compression of Diodorus' account: Curtius names Pasias of Thessaly and 'Damyllus' of Megalopolis as the envoys sent by the cavalry, and it is possible that Hieronymus mentioned several names, or more than one embassy.[49] The biographer would ignore everyone except Eumenes, in order to put his subject into high relief; Diodorus, writing general history, disposed of the ambassadors as a group. However, in Diodorus xviii.3, Eumenes' satrapy is one of the few to which a historical note is appended— it had not previously been conquered by Alexander—and this comment may be intended to enhance Eumenes' glory as the conqueror of Cappadocia (cf. Diod. xviii.16). There is also a coincidence between this passage and Hieronymus fragment 3.[50] Brief and colourless as it is otherwise, there is thus a case for thinking that the account of xviii.2–3 owes something to Hieronymus. Diodorus' chronological organization lends support to this idea, since he wrongly puts his narrative of the Succession under the archon year of Cephisodorus, i.e. July 323 to 322. The new archon year should open with the revolt in Bactria at xviii.7.1, where Hieronymus' main narrative began; and this suggests that Diodorus tried to relate his archon system to the break between one source and another.[51]

Hieronymus probably began, then, where a history of Alexander would naturally break off. He reviewed the disturbances which followed immediately upon Alexander's death and which produced the nominal successors of Alexander: Philip the idiot, and Roxane's unborn son. Doubtless his account was more complete and coherent than that of Diodorus; though whether it contained the sort of detail we find in Curtius is questionable: it is unlikely that Hieronymus was the

---

[47] Plut. *Eum*. iii.1–2; Nep. *Eum*. ii.1–5.

[48] Cf. Tarn, *JHS* xli (1921), p. 8.

[49] Damyllus is possibly to be identified with Damis of Megalopolis: cf. Diod. xviii.71.2, and below, ch. 4, pp. 172 f.

[50] See ch.2, pp. 46 f., and App. I, pp. 239 ff.

[51] For the date on which Alexander died A. E. Samuel, *Ptolemaic Chronology*, München, 1962, pp. 46 f.; cf. Curtius x.10.9. On the misplacement of Cephisodorus' archonship, Schachermeyr, *Alexander in Babylon*, p. 108, and above, ch. 2, p. 33. There are, of course, many erroneous archon dates in Book xvii, hence the explanation here suggested is not strictly necessitated; cf., however, Goukowsky, *Diodore XVIII*, p. xxxviii for the suggestion that each of the four archon dates in Book xviii were made by Diodorus to coincide with a book division in his source (and below, n. 91).

latter's sole source at the end of Book x.[52] One item does seem to have been set out at length: this was the list of provinces and governors, which named the real 'heirs' of Alexander, and which forms a complement to the list of satrapies at xviii.5–6, taking us from events in Babylon to events in the empire at large: places and individuals are ranged before us for future reference. The account of the *stasis* at Babylon thus was introductory and forward-looking, focusing attention on the problem of succession to Alexander's empire, which was to be the chief preoccupation of Hieronymus' history: the contestants were lined up, the prize—the empire—set on display. All this is a prelude to the main action. When the satraps had taken up position in their satrapies, the narrative could advance: ἤρξαντο ὑπερβάθμιον τείνειν πόδα ὡς ἠδύναντο ἕκαστος.[53] Pithon was the first to move, characteristically: he was by nature κινητικός.[54] So we progress to the *staseis* outside Babylon and the *aitiai* of the Greek revolts.

It is *a priori* unlikely that Hieronymus burdened his introduction with irrelevant details about Alexander. Brief allusions to Alexander's lifetime were often necessary; even discussion of the exiles' decree was strictly germane to his purpose in analysing the causes of the Lamian War. The 'Hypomnemata' of Alexander, which occupy such a prominent place in the opening of Diodorus xviii, are, on the contrary, a piece of clutter which a political historian would avoid. Modern scholarship has connected the Plans with a plot of the generals at Babylon against the absent Craterus, seeing them as part of the history of the Successors rather than the history of Alexander.[55] The story of Perdiccas bringing the Plans before the Macedonians and having them cancelled is not, indeed, incredible, whether or not it were part of a conspiracy; and it is not the object here to estimate whether the Plans are in any sense genuine. Rather, the hope is to exclude Hieronymus' name from the discussion. The argument, 'The Plans are from Hieronymus, therefore they are probably genuine', should be seen to be unsupported. Equally invalid, of course, would be the proposition, 'The Plans are incredible, therefore they cannot come from the excellent Hieronymus.' The argument must centre on the style and structure

---

[52] The following discussion is confined to Diodorus' use of Hieronymus. The latter's account of the Succession was certainly used also by Arrian; but the debt of Curtius and other writers remains highly uncertain. For detailed analysis (and widely differing conclusions), see Fontana, *Le lotte*, pp. 151 ff.; Schachermeyr, op. cit., pp. 81 ff.; R. M. Errington, *JHS* xc (1970), pp. 72 ff.

[53] Heidelberg Epitome, *F. Gr. Hist.* 155, 3.

[54] Diod. xix.14.2.

[55] Badian, *HSCP* lxxii (1967), pp. 183 ff. This view is now accepted by Errington, *JHS* xc (1970), p. 59 n. 75, Schachermeyr, *Alexander in Babylon*, p. 187, and Bosworth, *CQ* n.s. xxi (1971), pp. 127 ff.

of these chapters of Diodorus. Most of Tarn's original arguments, by which he tried to discredit the narrative leading up to the *hypomnemata* in Diodorus xviii.4, have by now been refuted, and many oddities in Diodorus' account can be attributed to its compression.[56] Tarn's instinct that there was something odd about the opening of Diodorus xviii was, nevertheless, essentially sound; and a cumulative case can be made for the interweaving of at any rate two sources.

Diodorus xviii.1 is a Diodoran proem of the same type as the proem to Book xix, which passes from a general maxim to the particular illustration: dying souls foreknow the future; this is shown in the case of Alexander of Macedon. Diodorus was not incapable of constructing this simple opening device himself (compare xxxvi.19.3), and one need not seek specific sources behind 1.1–3.[57] Chapter 1.4 contains the dying words of Alexander, which Arrian mentions among the things that are recorded by οἱ δέ , and the latter certainly included Cleitarchus, because the same story appears both in Curtius and at the end of Diodorus xvii.[58] Whether or not this *logos* had any truth in it, it made a suitable introduction to the μεγάλοι ἀγῶνες of the Successors, and undoubtedly Diodorus here repeats it from the end of his previous book. There must be a presumption that the story of Alexander's ring (xviii.2.4) is likewise repeated from Book xvii, where it is given along with Alexander's prophecy; though since Nepos, who drew extensively on Hieronymus, also mentions it, this is not a certain conclusion.[59] The last two paragraphs of chapter 1 continue the theme of a prophecy fulfilled, and conclude with a statement of the scope of the book, such as Diodorus gave in other book proems.[60] The whole of chapter 1 is therefore a proem of Diodorus' own composition, in which he was picking up motifs from Book xvii.

Another repetition from the Alexander historian may be suspected at xviii.3.5, where Diodorus says that Arrhidaeus was appointed to supervise the transport of Alexander's body for burial at Ammon in Egypt. Curtius records that it was Alexander's dying wish to be buried at Ammon, and he links this with the story of the ring and the dying prophecy. Diodorus does not have the Ammon story along with its

---

[56] Tarn, *JHS* xli (1921), pp. 4 ff., *Alex. Gt.*, ii, App. 24; cf. Schachermeyr, 'Die Letzte Pläne Alexanders des Grossen', *Jahreshefte des österreichischen arch. Inst.* 41 (1954), pp. 118 ff. = Griffith, *Main Problems*, pp. 322 ff; Ed. Meyer, *Blüte und Niedergang des Hellenismus in Asien*, Berlin, 1925, p. 12, n. 1 to p. 11.

[57] *Contra*, M. Kunz, *Zur Beurteilung der Proemien in Diodors historischer Bibliothek*, Zurich, 1935, pp. 89 f., who conjectures a source like Posidonius (following Gramann, *Quaestiones Diodoreae*, Göttingen, 1907, pp. 6 ff.).

[58] Arr. *Anab.* vii.26.3, Curtius x.55, Diod. xvii.117.4; cf. Justin xii.15.6–8.

[59] Nep. *Eum.* ii.1.

[60] Cf. ch. 2, p. 25 n. 27.

fellows in Book xvii, no doubt because he consistently reproduces their common source (? Cleitarchus) in less detail than Curtius; but Justin, generally held to reflect the same common source, does include this tradition.[61] There is a conflicting tradition, however, for Pausanias says the body was supposed to go to Aegae in Macedon, and Arrian implies that when Arrhidaeus took it to Egypt in 321, he did so against the orders of Perdiccas.[62] Attempts have been made to reconcile the evidence. To Perdiccas in 323, it has been argued, 'Ptolemy was an ally, and the ruler of Macedon . . . a potential enemy': it would have been at this time unthinkable to send the precious body to Aegae, whereas Ammon would be not only safe, but in accordance with the last wishes—as it was popularly believed—of Alexander. By 321 the situation had changed: Ptolemy was now an enemy and Antipater a friend, therefore for a while Perdiccas wished the body to be buried at Aegae—hence Pausanias' statement. But by the time the cortège was ready to depart, Perdiccas' alliance with Antipater had also collapsed, and now he wished to keep the body under his own control, in Babylon: hence Arrian says, without mentioning Aegae, that Arrhidaeus took the funeral carriage ἀπὸ Βαβυλῶνος against Perdiccas' will.[63]

Arguments from probability can often, however, be reversed. It can equally be maintained that in 323 Perdiccas and Ptolemy were obliged merely to strike a bargain: Perdiccas was confirmed as chiliarch only by conceding to Ptolemy the important province of Egypt. This was compromise, not alliance, and, so far from trusting one another, Arrian says explicitly of Perdiccas at the time when the satrapies were distributed, ὕποπτος ἐς πάντας ἦν καὶ αὐτὸς ὑπώπτευεν.[64] It may be that there was actually no agreement among the generals on the last resting place of Alexander, and that the building of the elaborate funeral carriage was one way of putting off the contentious day of decision. The one certainty is that, as a matter of historical fact, the

---

[61] Justin xiii.4.6. Justin has muddled Arrhidaeus the noble with Arrhidaeus the king, and has this notice in the wrong place.

[62] Paus. i.6.3; Arr. *Succ.* F9.25.

[63] Badian, art. cit., pp. 187 ff.

[64] Arr. *Succ.* F1.5. Negotiations between Ptolemy and Antipater, with the object of safe-guarding the former from Perdiccas, are placed as early as 323 by Diodorus (xviii.14.2): it was perhaps at this time that Ptolemy married Antipater's daughter Eurydice (Paus. i.6.8; App. *Syr.* 62; cf. J. Seibert, *Dynastische Verbindungen*, pp. 16 f.). In 322, at the time when Antipater and Craterus make overtures to Ptolemy, after the disclosure of Perdiccas' marriage intrigues, Ptolemy is already known to be τοῦ . . . Περδίκκου παντελῶς ἀλλότριον, ἑαυτοῖς δὲ φίλον (Diod. xviii.25.4). Cf. also xviii.25.5: Antipater and Craterus make a *dogma* embodying their plans for the Aetolians, i.e. even *they* did not trust each other.

body ended up in Egypt, and if we apply to the statement that it was *meant* to go there the simple test of *cui bono?*, the conclusion is inescapable, that this is Ptolemaic propaganda.

Possibly the Ammon story goes back to Ptolemy himself. We know that he actually buried the body at Memphis, and later transferred it to Alexandria, but he may have named Ammon as his ultimate destination in 321 in order to confer a semblance of legitimacy on the body-snatching, for Alexander's attitude to Ammon was, of course, well known.[65] By leaving it temporarily at Memphis, for safe-keeping during the war with Perdiccas, he shrewdly avoided a final decision on the place of burial until, after Perdiccas' defeat, his unassailable position enabled him to put the body exactly where he wanted it, at Alexandria, the political centre of his kingdom. That the Ammon story was later used by his apologists in Alexandria seems certain, for it appears not only at Diod. xviii.3.5, but also in the passage at xviii.28, containing a panegyric of Ptolemy and an allusion to Alexandria as the greatest city of the world, items which cannot come from Hieronymus. The source, as most commentators have recognized, must be an Alexandrian flatterer of the Ptolemies; and since there is no compelling reason to accept the Ammon story on its own merits, it is a natural assumption that the references to Ammon, both at xviii.28.3 and at xviii.3.5, are taken from the same source, which sought to justify Ptolemy's theft of the royal body by claiming that he had acted in accordance with the wishes of Alexander and the decision of the Diadochi. The *logos* that Alexander expressed a last wish to be buried at Ammon evidently comes from the same, or the same sort of source.

At several points, then, in his opening chapters to Book xviii, Diodorus has casual reminiscences of his history of Alexander: xviii.1.4 (Alexander's prophecy); 2.4 (Perdiccas and Alexander's ring); 6.1 (Alexander in India); 6.3 (Egypt is the best satrapy); 28.3 (the praise of Alexandria); and besides allusions back to his own previous book, he has incorporated some material from a source which is not Hieronymus and which favoured Ptolemy—this is evident at xviii.3.5, 28.2 ff., and again in parts of the account of Perdiccas' Egyptian campaign, where Ptolemy's prowess is written up in heroic style. A connection between these sporadic intrusions is not far to seek. By general consent, Diodorus' ultimate main source for his seventeenth book was Cleitarchus, the Alexandrian historian who established the vulgate tradition on Alexander, and who is known to

---

[65] For the burial of Alexander, see Curtius x.10.20, Ps.-Callisth. iii.34; cf. above, ch. 2, pp. 40 ff.

have flattered Ptolemy.[66] When Diodorus recapitulated passages from Book xvii, therefore, he still had his Cleitarchan source in mind. But the debt of Book xviii to the Alexander historian may go further than this.

We do not know where Cleitarchus ended his history. It is cited as Περὶ Ἀλεξάνδρου or τὰ περὶ Ἀλεξάνδρου;[67] but on one view the history of Alexander ended not with his death but with his burial. Curtius, who also used the Cleitarchan tradition for the main part of his Alexander history, concludes it with an account of the Succession, and ends the whole work by relating how Ptolemy took the body of the king to Memphis and later to Alexandria, 'where every honour was paid to his memory and his name' (x.10.20: cf. Diod. xviii.28.4). A good case can be made for thinking that Curtius was still drawing on his Cleitarchan source for events after Alexander's death;[68] and it has been argued, independently of any considerations of source criticism, that Cleitarchus himself was in Babylon at the time of Alexander's death.[69] If Cleitarchus took his history down to the burial of Alexander, there are clear implications for the problem of Diodorus' sources at the beginning of Book xviii. Diodorus, it seems, like Curtius, though to a more limited extent, continued to draw on the tradition he had used for his book on Alexander even after Alexander's death, when he had already taken up his new source on the Diadochi. Hieronymus he may have found a more difficult author at first than he had anticipated, hence the extreme brevity of his account of the Succession, an episode of a complexity for which Diodorus was not prepared after the lively narrative of Alexander in India; and some thirty chapters later he could still lapse into the easier manner of the alternative source.[70]

---

[66] Pearson, *Lost Histories*, pp. 217 ff., following Schwartz's view that Cleitarchus was the common source of Diodorus and Curtius on Alexander. Cleitarchus, *F. Gr. Hist* 137 F4 = Curtius ix.5.21: Cleitarchus said that Ptolemy saved Alexander's life in the city of the Malli; Arr. *Anab*. vii.11.8 names Peucestas. Curtius ix.8.22 ff. and Diod. xvii.103.6–8: Alexander is especially anxious for Ptolemy during his illness in India (cf. Strabo xv.2.7, p. 723). Cf. Jacoby, *RE* s.v. 'Cleitarchos' no. 2, cols. 622 f.; Pearson, op. cit., p. 214. For Cleitarchus as a native of Alexandria, cf. Philod. *De Rhet*. iv.1, col. xxi; Fraser, *Ptol. Alex*. i, p. 496, ii, p. 717 n. 3.

[67] *F. Gr. Hist*. 137 F1, 2, 3, etc.

[68] Schachermeyr, *Alexander in Babylon*, pp. 92 ff.

[69] Badian, *PACA* viii (1965), pp. 5 ff.

[70] Diodorus need not have read Cleitarchus direct: J. Kaerst, *Philologus* lvi (1897), pp. 627 ff. suggested Timagenes' work *On Kings* as an intermediate source (cf. Quint. *Inst. Or*. x.1.75), and the tone of eulogy in Diodorus' description of Ptolemy in Book xviii is easier to understand if successive Alexandrian historians had embroidered on it. Jacoby, however (art. cit.), held that Diodorus did read Cleitarchus, and he was, indeed, much read in the first century BC (e.g. by Sisenna, *F. Gr. Hist*. 137 T13. For Sisenna's use of Cleitarchus see now E. Rawson, *CQ* n.s. xxix (1979), pp. 327 ff.).

The opening of Diodorus xviii should be characterized, then, not as the epitome of a single source, nor, strictly speaking, as 'patchwork'. Two sources, the old and the new, formed a bridge passage between xvii and xviii, in which the more austere history of Hieronymus was enriched by supplements from the Alexander vulgate.[71] The 'Last Plans' fall under suspicion of being another instance, not because they are themselves unbelievable, but because of the entire manner and the setting of this passage.[72] In chapters 2 and 3 Diodorus' narrative is concise and clear and confined to the facts: at 4.2 the train of thought suddenly becomes obscure, the style is clumsy and long-winded, and in his specification of the Plans Diodorus becomes involved in parentheses and repetitions.[73] The space taken up by the Plans is disproportionate to the rest of Diodorus' account of events in Babylon: they occupy four out of a total of seventeen paragraphs, although the projects themselves, whatever one believes about Perdiccas' machinations, were not relevant to the history of the Successors; and they are included at the expense of far more important items, notably, the earlier stages of the *stasis* and settlement. The points Diodorus tries to stress are the expense, the magnitude, and the importance of the projects: τάς τε λοιπὰς αὐτοῦ ἐπιβολὰς πολλὰς καὶ μεγάλας οὔσας . . . καὶ δαπάνας ἀνυπερβλήτους ἔχουσας κ.τ.λ. The Hypomnemata are, in fact, a *thauma*, and as such belong most naturally in vulgate writing. A comparable *thauma* is Hephaestion's pyre, described at xvii. 115, with emphasis on the great size and expense of the construction: here the ultimate source was certainly Cleitarchus, and the fact that the completion of the pyre is the first of the memoranda named possibly indicates a connection between the two passages.[74]

The setting displays further anomalies, since Diodorus' description of the Plans has displaced other material and disrupted the order of the narrative. Other authorities are unanimous in placing Perdiccas' lustration of the army and the execution of Meleager's following after the reconciliation of the phalanx and cavalry and before Perdiccas' distribution of the satrapies. Diodorus' order is: reconciliation, distribu-

---

[71] Again at xix.33 Diodorus looks back to xvii.91.2 for his description of *suttee* among the Indians (probably from Onesicritus via Cleitarchus: cf. Pearson, op. cit., p. 225). The account of the παλαιὸς νόμος is added to the historical account (from Hieronymus) of the death of Ceteus' wife.

[72] No reliance can be placed on Dionysius' very unspecific criticism of Hieronymus' style (Hier. T12). The clumsiness of these chapters is not characteristic of the narrative (from Hieronymus) later in xviii–xx.

[73] A detailed analysis in K. Rosen, *AC* x (1967), pp. 49 ff.

[74] Hieronymus described the wonderful funeral carriage of Alexander (F2); but the description of this real, tangible work of art has no implications for that of the fantastic schemes attributed to Alexander, which were *thaumasia* in quite a different way.

tion of the satrapies, Last Plans, execution of Meleager and company.[75] It appears from Arrian's account that Meleager was killed later than the other rebels (*Succ.* F1.4, 'not long afterwards'), and possibly Diodorus telescoped events so as to have all the executions coincide. It remains a notable fact, nevertheless, that Diodorus is the only author who has the wrong order of events, and also the only author who has the Hypomnemata. Major disruption is apparent again in the narrative which introduces the Plans and speaks of Craterus' return to Europe. There is no obvious connection between Alexander's instructions to Craterus, as they are reported by Arrian (*Anab.* vii.12.4) and by Diodorus in a later chapter (xviii.12.2), and the Hypomnemata of Alexander, except that both were cancelled after Alexander died. Diodorus has made a clumsy attempt to link the two items by the connective γάϱ, and has produced a *non-sequitur* which seems to indicate a change of source.[76] An especial indication that Diodorus abandoned Hieronymus at this point are the words τοῖς διαδόχοις ἔδοξε κ.τ.λ.: nowhere else, except conceivably in his title, does Hieronymus seem to have described Alexander's generals as *diadochoi*, and this may be Diodorus' own term (as used in his *Hauptproem*), indicating a bridge of his own construction between two sources. The allusion to Craterus in this context is most naturally explained in terms of what has gone before, rather than what follows, because Diodorus has failed to mention him in his satrapy list in chapter 3. There were several stages to the settlement at Babylon, and Diodorus gives only the final arrangements. At the time of the compromise which ended the conflict between cavalry and phalanx, Craterus had been appointed *prostates* of the empire, an office which remains mysterious, but which in any case seems to have been abandoned after the execution of the thirty rebels; and in the final settlement the nobles reverted to a much earlier plan, mentioned by Curtius, according to which Craterus was to share the administration of Macedon and Greece with Antipater; this, at least, is the implication of our best source, Arrian.[77] Craterus' final instructions, therefore, were to *join* Antipater in Macedon, instead of *replacing* him, as

[75] Cf. Errington, art. cit., p. 57 n. 59.

[76] Cf. Tarn, *JHS* xli (1921), p. 8.

[77] Curtius x.7.8–9; Arrian *Succ.* F1.7. Errington, art. cit., analyses the stages of the settlement. Dexippus, *F. Gr. Hist.* 100 F.8.4, whose account was based on Arrian's, mentioned Craterus' *prostasia* in the final settlement, but this is hardly independent evidence: Photius' version of Dexippus is the epitome of an epitome of a work that was itself derived perhaps only in part from Hieronymus. Curtius and Justin do not mention Craterus at all in the final settlement, but in any case their sources may be multiple. The omission of his name from Diodorus' list is more surprising, because the latter is otherwise very close to Arrian's: Beloch, *Gr. Gesch.* iv² 2, p. 309 sets out the parallel lists.

Alexander had ordered. The allusion to Alexander's orders at 4.1 must have been meant to explain this alteration, and recalls other references in the satrapy list to the situation in Alexander's lifetime (Eumenes' satrapy, the Eastern satrapies of Taxiles and Porus). The satrapy list in chapter 3 is therefore the context to which the mention of Craterus properly belongs: Diodorus may have reserved his case for separate discussion because of its special complications: though it is also possible that he lost Craterus accidentally in chapter 3 as a result of rearranging the original order of the satrapy list.[78]

There are other signs of a muddle at the junction between chapters 3 and 4. At the end of chapter 3, after giving Seleucus' appointment as hipparch, the manuscripts of Diodorus go on to mention the kingdoms of Taxiles and Porus. Editors usually adjust the text here, but it is at least arguable that all the Eastern satrapies were listed at this point in the original, and that Diodorus tried to get a more rational order by transposing them to an earlier position; he then absent-mindedly, or because he had omitted them, started to detail the Indian kingdoms in their proper place.[79] This confusion in the text immediately precedes the appointment of Arrhidaeus and the reference to Ammon, which should be attributed to Diodorus' Alexandrian source. At the beginning of chapter 4 we return to Craterus, whom Diodorus has failed to mention earlier (he ought to appear at 3.2, after Antipater); and an association of ideas distracts Diodorus into an elaborate description of the 'Last Plans'. Finally in chapter 4.7, we are offered more left-overs from the Hieronyman narrative in the account of the executions. The hypothesis that most economically explains this confusion is that Diodorus here had recourse to the Alexandrian author whom he used in his narrative of 321 and for the reference to Ammon at 3.5.[80] The Plans themselves are not pro-Ptolemaic, but this is hardly a serious objection: it would be unreasonable to expect Cleitarchus to identify himself by flattering Ptolemy on every page of his history. The intention of their author was rather to describe *thaumasia*, and this, equally, is a characteristic of the Cleitarchan tradition. The fact also that, whether true or false, they are not obviously anachronistic, points to an early Hellenistic author: a later writer fabricating the Plans could

[78] Rosen, art. cit., pp. 47 ff. analyses the *diagrammata* from which he supposes this list was compiled.

[79] Ibid.

[80] F. Hampl would excise only the section xviii.4.4–6, leaving the circumstantial account of Perdiccas presenting Alexander's papers to the Macedonians (*Stud. D. M. Robinson* ii, 816 ff., Washington, 1953 = Griffith, *Main Problems*, pp. 322 ff.). The term διάδοχοι and the inappropriate γάρ at 4.1 tend, however, to cast doubt on everything that follows.

hardly have avoided some mistakes which would have given him away.[81]

At the start of his history of the Successors Diodorus had difficulty, it seems, in controlling his material, and this was because he tried to combine his new source, Hieronymus, with a more colourful source which he had used for Book xvii, and which was either Cleitarchus or based ultimately on Cleitarchus' history of Alexander: the Last Plans were taken from the second source, likewise the references to Ammon as the burial place of Alexander, and other pro-Ptolemaic material. Hieronymus had provided an account of the Succession, but it did not appeal to Diodorus, who summarized it in less than three chapters. Indeed, the problems he must have encountered in making his abridgement are apparent when one considers the scale and complexity of Hieronymus' treatment.

SCALE AND BOOK DIVISIONS

If Hieronymus took his history from the death of Alexander to the death of Pyrrhus its scope was a little more than fifty years. The scale on which it was written is not so easily estimated. Each of Diodorus' Books xviii, xix, and xx treats a period of less than ten years, as compared with twenty or thirty years in most earlier books of the *Bibliotheke*;[82] but this in itself does not necessitate the conclusion that Hieronymus was especially difficult to reduce. Books xxi–xl average twelve years each, showing that Diodorus became increasingly detailed for events nearer to his own time, and that the second half of the *Bibliotheke* was less of an epitome than the first. It is evident, however, that within the period of 323 to 302 he failed to make an even abridgement, preferring to treat some events in considerable detail and omit others altogether.[83] Noticeable omissions are Seleucus' activities in India after 312, and the wars between Seleucus and Antigonus during the same period (known to us from Babylonian documents).[84] On the other hand, Diodorus frequently recounts in detail episodes of

---

[81] Although the list of Plans appears in no author but Diodorus, it is a notable fact that the most remarkable item in it, the Western expedition, was known in a slightly different form to Curtius (x.1.17–19), the other author who drew extensively on the Cleitarchan tradition for his history of Alexander. (Arr. *Anab.* vii.8.1 provides some corroboration of this plan.)

[82] Diod. xiii, however, covers only the 10-year period 415–405. Cf. Bizière, *Diodore XIX*, p. x, n. 1.

[83] R. H. Simpson, 'Abbreviation of Hieronymus in Diodorus', *AJP* lxxx (1959), pp. 370 ff.

[84] Seleucus in the East: Strabo xv.689; App. *Syr.* 44; Justin xv.4. 12 ff. War between Antigonus and Seleucus: cf. S. Smith, *Babylonian Historical Texts*, pp. 124 ff., A. T. Olmstead, *CP* xxii (1937), pp. 1 ff.

marginal importance to the historical narrative: at xviii.26 Alexander's funeral bier is the subject of elaborate description, while the account of Perdiccas' campaign in Egypt in following chapters is very inadequate; other examples include the ancient history of Thebes (xix.53.4 ff.), the ritual death of the Indian princess (xix.33 ff.), and the description of Nabataean Arabia (xix.94 ff.); the inclusion of Alexander's Hypomnemata also shows how unevenly Diodorus distributed his material. The same irregularity appears in Book xx. It can be shown that there is a progressive change in scale in Diodorus' treatment of Greek and Asian affairs, and this can be attributed largely to his increasing interest in the history of Agathocles, which begins in Book xix and which diminished his interest in his main theme.[85] By Book xx he is prepared to sacrifice the whole of Hieronymus' account of Antigonus' war with Seleucus—an episode of military history which was not enlivened by Hieronymus' personal observation—but devotes eighteen chapters to the dramatic events of the siege of Rhodes. For the brief passage where comparison can be made with Hiller's papyrus it is clear that Diodorus has not omitted much of the substance of the original.[86] Evidently he picked out set pieces—a siege, a monomachy, an ethnographical study—and transcribed them perhaps at nearly their original length, while giving only a sketchy account, or none at all, of intervening events. Doubtless Hieronymus himself had written more fully on his personal experiences; but the disproportion in Books xviii–xx, apparent also in xvii and xvi, is certainly the fault of the epitomator, whose object was to write arrangements of historical lollipops: it does not represent the economy of the original.

Arrian possibly gives a better idea of the scale. Fragments 1–9 of his account of the Successors, taken from the Photian epitome, are merely a survey of the contents, and an uneven one at that. Photius summarized separately the first five and last five books, occupying respectively one and a half and three and a half pages of Jacoby's edition, which can hardly represent the proportions of the original; and some incidents are related in disproportionate detail (the satrapy lists of 323 and 321, for example), in the manner characteristic of ancient epitomators.[87] Fragment 10, however—the Vatican palimpsest—is a

---

[85] Cf. Simpson, art. cit., pp. 377 f. Diodorus has 75 chapters on the period 323–318 (xviii.1–75); 54 chs. for years 317–315 (xix.11–64); 32 chs. for years 314–311 (xix.66–105, with interludes on Roman and Sicilian affairs); 47 chs. for years 310–302 (xx.19–113, with interludes on Sicily, Rome, and the history of the kings of Bosphorus).

[86] Cf. ch. 2, pp. 30 ff.

[87] See Brunt, 'On Historical Fragments and Epitomes', *CQ* xxx (1980), p. 487: 'Epitomators in general seem to have aimed not at reproducing faithful resumés but at recording, sometimes at length, what they thought of most interest, and their principles

fragment of the original work, dealing with Eumenes' intrigues with Cleopatra at Sardis and Antigonus' attempts to ambush Eumenes; and it is evident from the more complete portions that the treatment was exhaustive. The same is true of the more recently discovered papyrus fragment of Arrian. If all the events in Photius' summary were treated on this scale by Arrian, it is not surprising that it took him ten books to cover only three years; and if the entire history of Hieronymus, covering more than fifty years, was in proportion, it would have filled some 170 books—a mighty work indeed, surpassing both Theopompus and 'huge Livy'. But nobody called Hieronymus 'Chalcenteros' or 'Scytobrachion', so the length of his work was not a joke. Mechanical calculations on the basis of an epitome are in any case unreliable. Arrian may have used other sources: in the *Anabasis*, while probably omitting many details from Ptolemy, he also supplemented him with a variety of material, including another serious historian, Aristobulus; and though it seems clear that Hieronymus was the main ingredient of the τὰ μετὰ ᾽Αλέξανδρον, the use also of an Athenian historian is likely (cf. ch. 2), and he may have had recourse to alternative accounts of the Diadochi which the brevity of Photius' epitome makes it impossible to detect.

Hieronymus, in any case, probably did not give equal weight to all sections of the work. The space devoted to Eumenes and the Antigonids was considerably greater than that accorded to the other Successors, and episodes in which the historian himself had played a part may have been especially detailed. It is to be expected, too, that the history would concentrate around the great battles—Gabiene, Gaza, Ipsus—and the political landmarks—Triparadeisos, the Peace of 311—with the narrative spread more thinly in between. One of the densest patches would be at the beginning of the history. Thucydides had spent many chapters of his first book talking about prehistoric Greece, summarizing the Pentacontaetia, discussing historiographical method; Polybius filled two books with preliminaries of the same kind. Xenophon's *Hellenica* was also more solid at its beginning: if we had only the first two books, it might be imagined that we had lost an exhaustive political analysis of the early fourth century. For a historian like Hieronymus, whose work covered such a vista of space and time and revolved around successive protagonists, starting off was not a simple matter. Probably after a preface he traced the earlier history of Macedon and the complexities of the Succession; he supplied satrapy

of selection are at times impenetrable. They do not necessarily offer a faithful miniature of the original as a whole.' On the length of Arrian's *Successors* see. P. A. Stadter, *Arrian of Nicomedia*, Univ. of N. Carolina Press, 1980, pp. 144–52.

lists and a Geography of Asia; then he needed to follow the satraps to Bactria, Egypt, Thrace, Cappadocia, to discuss the causes of the Lamian War, and analyse the first major complex of the history, the *koinopragia* which destroyed Perdiccas; finally all these strands were to be reunited at Triparadeisos. Initial explanations and then the ferment of activity which followed Alexander's death, may well have filled several, if not as many as ten, books. After 321, Hieronymus could settle into the straightforward narrative of Eumenes' campaigns against Antigonus, and probably from this point the history moved more rapidly. If one allows for the relatively concentrated character of the first few years, also for a number of geographical and 'archaeological' digressions, and for the speeches which, like nearly every ancient historian, he certainly included, it may be supposed that Hieronymus' history was comparable in size to the histories of Polybius or of some of his third-century contemporaries.[88] Polybius treated the history of eighty-four years (220 to 146) in forty books, including two books on the historical background, a book on geography, and a book on Roman institutions. Ephorus had written thirty books, and seems to have set the fashion for dividing histories into books.[89] Timaeus wrote thirty-three books, Phylarchus twenty-eight, Diyllos twenty-six, Psaon of Plataea thirty.[90] So that if Hieronymus related the history of fifty-five years in twenty to thirty books, he would have been following contemporary practice. Hellenistic histories were undoubtedly on the long side, compared with the fifth-century classics, and this may have been one reason why someone like Dionysius had little patience with them.

[88] Speeches in Diodorus' original may be conjectured in several places. Speeches of exhortation before a battle: xviii.10.2 (Craterus at the Hellespont); xix.81.6 (Demetrius at Gaza); xix.90.3–5 (Seleucus encourages his companions on the return to Babylon). Diod. xix.41.1, Antigenes' proclamation is in *oratio recta*: Ἐπὶ τοὺς πατέρας ἁμαρτάνετε, ὦ κακαὶ κεφαλαί κ.τ.λ. (cf. Plut. *Eum.* xvi.4). Hieronymus may have recorded important speeches on policy: xviii.10.4 (debate at Athens); xviii.36.6 (Ptolemy's defence of his 'separatist' policy); xix.61.1.2 (Antigonus denounces Cassander before the Macedonians). In the history of Eumenes there are some indications of direct speech: xviii.60.2–6 (§6 MSS οἶμαι, followed by Fischer; Dindorf reads οἴεσθαι); xviii.63.4–5; xix.25.5–7 (25.7, ἐπισημαινομένου . . . τοῦ πλήθους καὶ ''Ὀρθῶς' λέγοντος); xix.38.2. Cf. also xix.97.3 ff, the speech of the Nabataean elder: clearly the method here, and no doubt in many other cases, was to record περὶ τῶν αἰεὶ παρόντων τὰ δέοντα. (It must be supposed that Diodorus included this speech, contrary to his normal practice, because of its philosophical content.)

[89] Cf. Bury, *The Ancient Greek Historians*, pp. 163 f. With Ephorus and Theopompus historians seem to have become more aware of the book form of their works. At the same time as deliberate book divisions, appear the first real titles to histories: cf. Jacoby, *Atthis*, pp. 81 ff. with n. 38 (Theopompus' *Philippica* was probably the model).

[90] *F. Gr. Hist.* 566 T1; 73 T1,3; 78 T1; 81 T1; cf. also Demetrius of Callatis, *F. Gr. Hist.* 85 T1 (20 books).

Hieronymus' book divisions can sometimes be traced. His chronological framework was evidently based on the annual campaigning
season, after the manner of Thucydides, for on ten occasions in
Diodorus' history of the Successors the turn of the year is marked by
the mention of winter quarters. Dionysius claimed that this system
proved so unsuccessful in Thucydides that no later historian adopted
it: in order to follow events in each theatre of war during a single
season Thucydides had to chop up his narrative in a way which, in
Dionysius' judgement, made it impossible to follow.[91] But we can see
from Dionysius' illustration (taken from Thucydides Book iii) that he
is exaggerating to prove his point; and the statement that no one
imitated this system is false. Xenophon had used the annalistic plan of
Thucydides in the early part of the *Hellenica*; and it is clear from
Diodorus that Hieronymus was following the same model. The campaigning season of the Hellenistic period was considerably longer than
that of classical times: Philip and Alexander showed that winter need
be no deterrent to military action, and the armies of the Diadochi did
not go into winter quarters until the late autumn.[92] Accordingly,
Hieronymus had the greater part of a year in which to record the
alternate affairs of Asia and Greece, and his narrative may not have
given the disjointed impression to which Dionysius took exception in
the case of Thucydides.

On the Thucydidean system, it was natural to end a book with the
end of a campaigning year—Thucydides does this at the end of Books
ii, iii, iv, and v; and it is probable that Hieronymus often did the same.
Where Diodorus changes to a supplementary source, not infrequently
the reason may be that he had come to the end of a book in his main
source, and in several instances, a change of source coincides with the
end of a year. At xviii.25.6, the year 322 closes with Antipater and
Craterus postponing their winter campaign against the Aetolians and
Perdiccas sending Eumenes to the Hellespont; in the next chapter,
Diodorus launches into his description of Alexander's funeral car-
riage, which may or may not come from Hieronymus, followed by the
Ptolemaic version of the bringing of Alexander's body to Egypt, which
certainly does not. At xix.44, the campaigning year 317 ends with
Eumenes' defeat at Paraetacene and the transfer of the wounded
Hieronymus into the army of Antigonus—the end of an era in the
personal history of Hieronymus: chapter 45 contains a description of

[91] Dion. Hal. *De Thuc.* 9 (1.837).
[92] M. Launey, *Recherches sur les armées hellénistiques*, ii, Paris, 1950, pp. 740 f.: the
treaty between Eumenes I of Pergamum and his mercenaries (*OGIS* 266) stipulates that
they shall serve a ten-month year.

the flood at Rhodes, again not derived from Hieronymus. Diodorus' reasons for changing source are often puzzling: sometimes the motive seems to be pious fervour or the desire to underline a point inadequately expressed, as he felt, by his main source;[93] at the beginning of Book xviii his use of a pro-Ptolemaic source can perhaps be explained by his own interest in Egypt and the founding of the Ptolemaic dynasty. Practical considerations should not be overlooked, however: a natural break in the main source might encourage him to look at other material, which could then be incorporated into his history by way of an interlude, as at xix.45. The end of a book also made an obvious stopping place when Diodorus wanted to turn to his parallel narrative of affairs in Sicily and Italy: book endings may be suspected at xix.69.2 and xx.28.4 (winter 314 to 313 and 309 to 308). Other references to winter quarters mostly correspond with a change from Asian to Greek affairs or vice versa:[94] not all necessarily mark a book ending, though the assembly at Triparadeisos probably did so—the tenth book of the history, if Arrian is a reliable guide. At Diod. xviii.39.7, Antipater departs from Triparadeisos and crosses back into Macedon with the kings and army; at 40.1, Antigonus opens the year 320 with the assembly of his troops from winter quarters to start the war against Eumenes; and Arrian's History of the Successors ended with Antipater's return to Europe.[95] Diodorus concludes his own twentieth book in the middle of winter 302 (references to winter quarters at xx.109.2, 109.4, 111.3, 112.4, 113.5), with the promise that he will relate the battle of the kings in his following book; and there can be little doubt that here, too, he is following the structure of Hieronymus' work, and that Hieronymus made Ipsus the centre-piece of his last book on the 'Diadochi'.

THE END OF THE HISTORY: ANTIGONUS' TEARS

The economy of Hieronymus' history down to the time of Ipsus is relatively clear. Babylon was to have been the capital of Alexander's

---

[93] Cf. R. Drews, *AJP* lxxxiii (1962), pp. 383 ff.

[94] Diod. xix.12.1 (cf. 15.6); 34.8 (cf. 37.1); 77.7; 89.2; xx.109.4 ff. (cf. 111.3 ff.).

[95] Arr. *Succ.* F11.45. The hypothesis of Goukowsky, *Diodore XVIII*, p. xxxviii, that the four Athenian archon years with which Diodorus punctuates Book xviii (chs. 2, 26, 44, 58) correspond to book divisions in his source, is compatible with the arguments offered here. For the archonship of Cephisodorus (xviii.2) see above, p. 33. The allusion to the archonship of Philocles corresponds with the end of a campaigning year and with a (possible) change of source, at xviii.26. The references to the archon years of Apollodorus and of Archippus also fall at natural breaks in the narrative (xviii. 44, passing from the history of Eumenes and of Ptolemy to that of Antigonus; xviii.58, from Polyperchon in Europe to Eumenes in Asia). However, the view that these were the *first* 4 books of Hieronymus is plausible only on the assumption that Hieronymus' history was much briefer and less detailed than is here supposed.

world empire, and here Hieronymus started: Alexander's body, a symbol of the unity of empire, lay in state within the palace, while outside the army mutinied and his generals divided up his lands. The division of the empire was the item of prime importance in the week following Alexander's death—as Diodorus and Arrian recognized when they carefully reproduced the list of satrapies. Centrifugal forces were at work from the moment Alexander died, and in twenty years resolved his unwieldy kingdom into its component parts. Hieronymus' history of the Diadochi correspondingly moved from the centre outwards, following the generals from Babylon to Alexandria, Cassandreia, and Antigoneia, as the new political map took shape. The battle of Ipsus was the natural point to arrest the first part of the history. Here all the threads converged, and the vision of world empire, now embodied in Antigonus, was dealt its death blow.

After Ipsus, the direction of the narrative seems to have changed. We know little of Hieronymus' account of the Epigoni, and that chiefly from Plutarch, whose decision to write on Demetrius and Pyrrhus creates the impression that interest in Ptolemy and Seleucus diminished once they were established in their new domains, and that the growing power of Lysimachus, chief architect of the strategic victory at Ipsus, and the appearance of new kings in Epirus and Macedon, now centred attention on the West. The geographical focus of the history of the Diadochi is implied in the survey of Asia with which it opened; this focus shifts from Asia to Europe as the Eastern kingdoms consolidate, while the European territories are thrown into confusion by the death of Cassander; finally it narrows down to the struggle between Pyrrhus and Antigonus Gonatas. Macedon itself was the last major Hellenistic kingdom to settle under a single ruler, and Gonatas was the last of Alexander's 'heirs': firmly established in Macedon, he formed the third member of the triumvirate who ruled the Eastern Mediterranean, and completed Hieronymus' picture of the evolution of the new dynasties. The last event Hieronymus is known to have recorded is the death of Pyrrhus at Argos in 272, and it is likely that this episode brought his history to an end.[96] With Pyrrhus' death, the last serious threat to Antigonid Macedon was removed, and both historical and artistic considerations could have suggested this as a fitting conclusion. To the loyal servant of Antigonus' house it was a satisfactory dénouement to the history of his times: before his death he had seen

---

[96] Hier. F15, cf. F14. It is not impossible that he took his history down to the death of Mithridates in 266, as von Gutschmid suggested (*Kl. Schr.* iii, Leipzig, 1892, p. 529 n. 1); but this view rests on the evidence of a corrupt notice in Ps.-Lucian's *Macrobioi* (= Hier. F7) and is very uncertain. Cf. App. I, pp. 244 f.; Jacoby, *RE* 'Hieronymos', col. 1543.

Demetrius' son as unchallenged ruler of the Macedonian homeland, and the wars of the Successors might be considered at an end.

With victory did not come complacency. Pausanias, citing Hieronymus as an authority for the last days of Pyrrhus, says that his account was written ἐς ἡδονὴν Ἀντιγόνου, and probably there was substance to this criticism. If Plutarch is using Hieronymus for the last chapters of his *Life of Pyrrhus*, it appears that Hieronymus minimized the importance of Pyrrhus' victory over Gonatas in battle outside the walls of Argos to such an extent that Plutarch omitted any allusion to it: it was perhaps not easy to concede that Pyrrhus, for all his posturing as a latter-day Achilles, might be the equal of Gonatas in tactical skill.[97] One must suspect the suppression of facts which reflected unfavourably on his master. However, Gonatas' eventual victory over Pyrrhus was not to be represented as the triumph of a haughty conqueror. The note on which he ended is suggested by the chapters of Plutarch which describe Pyrrhus' fortuitous death in the street-fighting at Argos and Antigonus' reaction when Halcyoneus brought him the head of his enemy: 'Antigonus, when he saw and recognized the head, drove his son away, smiting him with his staff and calling him barbarous; then, covering his face with his cloak, he burst into tears, calling to mind Antigonus his grandfather and Demetrius his father, who were examples in his own family of a reversal of fortune.'[98]

The victor weeping over the vanquished is a motif of Hellenistic historiography of which this is apparently the first instance. Antiochus wept over the rebel Achaeus; Scipio shed tears at the sight of burning Carthage; Octavian is said, however implausibly, to have wept at the news of Antony's death. In the same spirit Scipio moralizes over the cowardly Hasdrubal, and Aemilius Paullus over the downfall of Perseus.[99] To ponder, at such a moment, on the mutability of Fortune, showed a 'proper Hellenistic sensibility'.[100] The scene in which Antigonus weeps over the dead Pyrrhus with thoughts of mortality calls for especial comment because, as a scene in the final cadence to

---

[97] Cf. below, App. I, p. 248.

[98] Plut. *Pyrrh.* xxxiv.4. This story, like the story of Pyrrhus' challenge to Antigonus (ibid., xxxi.1–2), is told also of Octavian in Plutarch's *Life of Antony*. The version in the *Pyrrhus* is, however, far more circumstantial, and the story inherently more plausible in this context. Tarn, *JRS* xxi (1931), pp. 179 ff. argued that at the time of Actium Octavian deliberately imitated both Demetrius and Antigonus Gonatas: possibly the writers (Plutarch or his sources) who said that Octavian wept for Antony were enlarging on this theme.

[99] Polyb. viii.20.10; xxxviii.21.1–3, 22; Plut. *Ant.* lxxviii.2; Polyb. xxxviii. 20.1; xxix.20.1–4.

[100] Brink and Walbank, *CQ* n.s. iv (1954), p. 104. Polyb. vi.2.5–6: it is the mark of a great man to have learned moderation in success. Cf. Walbank, *HCP* i, pp. 19 f.

Hieronymus' work, it seems to anticipate the concluding book of Polybius' history. Polybius took his work, in its final form, down to the year 146: the fall of Carthage removed Rome's last major enemy in the Mediterranean, and so ended the period of evolution from first state in Italy to mistress of a world empire, which Polybius had set himself to describe. Scipio's reaction as he watched the flames rise from Carthage put into perspective the history of Rome's rise to power, and the quotation from *Iliad* vi.448 echoes the prophecy of Demetrius of Phaleron which had so impressed Polybius and which had served as a comment on the ending of the *Histories*, according to his original plan, with the destruction of Macedonian power: one day Rome too, would suffer the fate of Persia, Macedon, and Carthage.[101] Hieronymus believed that when Antigonus wept he thought of his father and grandfather, who had once been mighty kings and had perished miserably, implying that in the moment of success he, like Scipio, looked forward gravely to an unknown future.[102] Antigonus' rebuke to Halcyoneus and his kind treatment of Helenus suggest not only the clemency of the victor but the superstitious prudence of a man who had learned not to trust the seeming invulnerability of power.

Polybius never mentions Hieronymus in the surviving parts of his work, and a literary imitation here—though that is not impossible—is not provable. But it is at least a notable coincidence that two major political histories of the Hellenistic period used this motif as a statement of their concluding book. There was a common literary ancestor: in the last book of the *Iliad* Achilles is moved to tears by Priam asking for the body of Hector; and as he weeps he thinks, like Antigonus, of his own father and the unhappy lot of men (xxiv.507 ff.). The pathos of this celebrated passage lies not merely in the magnanimity of the strong to the weak, but in the fact that Achilles is close to his own

---

[101] Scipio at Carthage: Polyb. xxxix.5. Polybius and Demetrius of Phaleron: Polyb. xxxix.21.1–6. Polybius' original plan for a history of the years 220–168 is sketched at iii.1–3; at iii.4–5 he outlines his intention to extend it down to the end of the Achaean War in 146, and 'it may fairly be assumed that Polybius' decision to extend his *Histories* to cover the twenty-two years from 168 to 146 was taken after the catastrophic events of the latter year.' (Walbank, *Polybius*, p. 18.) Thus he was not writing a history of his life and times of indefinite length, but, in both the first and the second programme, working to a conscious plan. (The later history of the Numantine War was a separate monograph.) The incident at Carthage does not, of course, form the ultimate episode of Book xxxix: the destruction of Corinth was a parallel catastrophe which might inspire similar reflections in the reader (Polybius comments on the restraint with which Mummius acted after the Greek defeat; there were no tears, however).

[102] The motive for Scipio's tears has received much attention: see A. Astin, *Scipio Aemilianus*, Oxford, 1967, App. IV, pp. 282 ff., for a summary of views; cf. also A. Momigliano, *Alien Wisdom*, pp. 22 f. The parallel case of Antigonus' tears has not attracted comment.

death: this lies outside the scope of the epic, but Thetis has reminded
him, and even as he speaks to Priam, Achilles looks forward to his
approaching fate. In each of these endings, then, can be traced a
common way of thought about the end of war and the final value of the
victor's achievement when set against the powers of fate, or chance, or
time.[103]

Hieronymus perhaps gave less prominence to the role of Tyche than
Polybius, though we might know little of Tyche in Polybius if we
lacked his *ipsissima verba*: he could not in any case be uninfluenced by
the idea of life's uncertainty and the supreme power of Fortune which
dominated Hellenistic popular philosophy. To a historian, Tyche
presented herself on a grand scale, raising up kings and kingdoms and
casting them down again: Demetrius of Phaleron had expressed the
idea of power succeeding power in his treatise Περὶ Τύχης.[104] The
optimistic mood of the days of Alexander had been quenched in the
seemingly interminable wars of the Diadochi, in which the outcome
often appeared to be determined as much by chance as by virtue:
Pyrrhus' death was a classic example, and there was no guarantee that
Antigonus himself would not one day suffer a similar *peripeteia*. The
aged Hieronymus, who could not prophesy the sequel to the events he
had recorded, preferred, it seems, to end his work on a reflective note,
demonstrating the becoming humility of the king in the hour of victory. As the *envoi* to a history of this period, it is to be contrasted on
the one hand with the abrupt termination of Ptolemy's memoir, which
is to be inferred from Arrian; on the other, with the fanfare with which
Diodorus' Alexandrian historian hailed the triumph of Ptolemy.
Neither a military chronicle, nor a court history, Hieronymus' work
shows the conscious design of an author who gave shape and sense to
the mosaic of events, recognizing the individual ambition which moti-
vates action, and at the same time the obstinate nature of things
which persistently frustrates human aspirations.

[103] Cf. also Xerxes' tears, Hdt. vii.45 f., and J. de Romilly, *The Rise and Fall of Greek
States according to Greek Authors*, Ann Arbor, 1977, p. 8.
[104] *F. Gr. Hist.* 228 F39.

Chapter 4

The Historian's Truthfulness

'History is the prophetess of truth', so Diodorus grandly claimed.[1] We can hardly share his faith. Oracles are often ambiguous; and the assumption underlying Diodorus' *Bibliotheke*, of an uncritical trust in historical sources, is one that is opposed to all scientific historical method. Hieronymus dominates the surviving historiography of a period in much the way that Thucydides does; and because of the form in which his history has come down to us, it is especially hard to check it. The general tone of the history inspires confidence; but apparent precision and factuality can be misleading. Thucydides, for all the impression of dispassionate judgement which his work conveys, is nevertheless sometimes suspect; and there is still more need for caution in the case of a historian who is lost to us in the original and who, even in antiquity, was accused of bias.[2] Wilamowitz, for example, certainly overstated the position in his glowing appraisal of Hieronymus' truthfulness.[3] Limited by the sources available to him, and conditioned by pressure and prejudices of which he may be unaware, a historian even of the greatest integrity can only approach the truth obliquely. It is therefore the object of this chapter first to consider the general credibility of Hieronymus' narrative and his use of his sources; and second to examine the personal and political influences which may have coloured his interpretation of the period.

I. THE PRACTICE OF Ἱστορία

The credibility of Diodorus' account

A general consideration of Hieronymus' work leaves no doubt that he was on the whole, and by ancient standards, a very reliable reporter. Turning from Diodorus' history of Alexander in Book xvii to the account based on Hieronymus in Books xviii–xx, the reader's immediate impression is that he is at last in the hands of a serious and competent historian. The military narrative is excellent, and regularly

---

[1] Diod. i.2.2: τὴν προφῆτιν τῆς ἀληθείας ἱστορίαν.
[2] Hier. F9, F15.
[3] Wilamowitz, *Gr. Lit.*, Leipzig, 1912, pp. 171 ff. See T. S. Brown, *Am. Hist. Rev.* 1947, p. 684 for a corrective.

supported by statistics; major political trends—the dissolution of the empire, the freedom movement among the Greeks—are described with understanding, *aitiai* are analysed, documents are cited; with few exceptions facts are related in a straightforward manner and the account is free from rhetorical and pathetic touches. Hieronymus seems to avoid the malicious gossip and tedious moralizing of Theopompus. He is not tempted to invoke the gods to explain the extraordinary: Tyche makes her appearance, inevitably in a Hellenistic historian, but her responsibilities are circumscribed. Account is take of the religious superstition of others: Seleucus' propaganda has its effects; Eumenes is said to have had success in instituting the cult of Alexander; but the religious commitment of the author is not implied.[4] Diodorus' source for the Diadochi stands in the same relation to contemporary sensationalist writers, like Duris, as Ptolemy does to Cleitarchus: the sober account of the one corrects the literary excesses of the other.[5] Here, then, is a historian who seems to approach the standards set by Thucydides, but met by so few of his successors, and whom the modern historian is predisposed to trust.

Areas of doubt arise chiefly from the deficiencies of the secondary accounts or the brevity of citations. Several of the fragments of Hieronymus record disagreement with another author. This is not in itself an indication that his history was especially controversial, because it is in the nature of ancient citations that they are often given to support or disprove a disputed point, though in two instances the disagreement is a serious matter, because Hieronymus apparently gave a version which cast a favourable light on his masters: these cases are examined separately.[6] Where fragments record differences in figures and measurements we may well prefer Hieronymus to the alternatives.[7] Diodorus' narrative raises its own problems, notably a difficulty of chronology; but this arises from his own attempt to reconcile the Athenian archon year, i.e. summer to summer, with the winter to winter year used by Hieronymus. The device he adopted for most of the Hieronyman narrative was to equate the archon year with the campaign year in which it began, so that the events of the first six months of the calendar year are regularly given under the wrong

---

[4] Seleucus: Diod. xix.90.3–4; cf. xix.55.6–8. Eumenes and the cult of Alexander: Diod. xviii.60.4; xix.15.4; cf. C. Picard, 'Le trône vide d'Alexandre dans la cérémonie de Cyinda et le culte du trône vide à travers le monde gréco-romain', *Cahiers Archéologiques* vii (1964), pp. 1–17; M. Launey, *Recherches* ii, pp. 945 ff. Cf. Jacoby, *RE* 'Hieronymos', cols. 1552–3.

[5] Ibid., col. 1549.

[6] See App. I, fragments 3, 15, cf. 9; and below, pp. 246 ff.

[7] App. I, frs. 1, 11, 12, 14, 18.

archon, namely, the one who took office that summer. In several instances Diodorus departed from this principle and created a deeper confusion: in the first half of Book xviii he was still undecided about his chronological system, and two Athenian archons are lost altogether (for 321/320 and 320/319); again, a special solution is needed to account for his misdating of events which properly belong to the year 317; and the extreme compression in his account of the years 313 to 311 has led to uncertainty about the date of Ptolemaeus' arrival in Greece and the battle of Gaza.[8] These chronological muddles are plainly the work of the epitomator rather than his source: Hieronymus' own system of reference to winter quarters did not allow such mistakes.[9]

Occasional errors or inconsistencies in numbers likewise originate in the carelessness of Diodorus or his copyists, as a few examples suffice to show.[10] Speaking of Eumenes' march to the upper satrapies, Diodorus states that the River Tigris (meaning the Pasitigris) flows for 700 stades from the mountains to the Erythraean Sea, and that it is a day's march from Susa at the point where it flows out from the mountains.[11] In Book xvii, he gives the distance as 600 stades and four days march from Susa; and Curtius also speaks of 'quartis castris'.[12] The difference between 600 and 700 stades perhaps does not signify: Hieronymus and the Alexander historian might have calculated from different points. The one day's journey from Susa (ἀπέχοντα Σούσων ὁδὸν ἡμέρας) is wrong, however, and the four days of the Alexander historian is correct. That the mistake originates with Diodorus is apparent when we compare the passage at xix.18.1, where Antigonus makes the same journey from Susa to the Pasitigris: τὰς πορείας ἠναγκάζοντο νυκτὸς ποιεῖσθαι καὶ στρατοπεδεύεσθαι περὶ τὸν ποταμὸν πρὶν ἥλιον ἀνατέλλειν. The plural πορείας and the imperfect ἠναγκάζοντο show that Hieronymus knew the journey took several days.[13] Another kind of mistake can be detected in the battle

[8] See L. C. Smith, 'The Chronology of Books XVIII–XX of Diodorus Siculus', *AJP* xxxii (1961), pp. 283 ff. Smith's discussion of Diodorus' chronology for the years 313–311 is corrected by S. C. Bakhuizen, *Salganeus and the Fortifications on its Mountains, Chalcidian Studies*, ii, Groningen, 1970, App. VIII, pp. 160 f. On the chronology of Book xviii, see now Goukowsky, *Diodore XVIII*, pp. xxivff.
[9] Cf. ch. 3, p. 101.
[10] Hieronymus' statistics have commanded respect even from his less admiring critics: cf. Beloch, *Die Bevölkerung der gr.-röm. Welt*, Leipzig, 1886, p. 10.
[11] Diod. xix.17.3; cf. Plut. *Eum.* 14, Curtius v.3.1; Droysen, *Hell.* ii.1, p. 266 n. 1.
[12] Diod. xvii.67.2; Curtius, loc. cit.
[13] Droysen, loc. cit.; H. Kallenberg, *Philologus* xxxvii (1878), p. 223 n. 9. Cf. Brunt, Loeb edn. of Arrian, App. VIII, p. 488; information on distances in the Alexander historians probably comes ultimately from the reports (*stathmoi*) of the bematists who accompanied Alexander, and who did give fairly accurate measurements; but there were already manuscript variants due to copyists' errors by Pliny's time (*NH* vi. 62).

dispositions at Paraetacene: as Diodorus gives them, the lists of separate units on each side do not match the totals; and the same is true for
the review of the satraps' forces at xix.14.8.[14] In each case, a paragraph
omitted from the original could be sufficient to explain the missing
numbers. Similarly Diodorus' figures for the Athenian navy during the
Lamian War are to be explained by the compression of his account,
which omitted vital explanations in his source. His 170 ships at
xviii.15.8, apparently inconsistent with the resolution of the Athenians
to commission 240 at xviii.10, should be interpreted as a fleet for
guarding the Hellespont only, on the evidence of the *Tabulae Curator-
um Navalium*.[15]

Other differences could have been the result of careless copying of
the text. Describing the settlement which concluded the Lamian War,
Diodorus says that more than 22,000 Athenians were disfranchised
and emigrated to Thrace; but Plutarch in his *Life of Phocion* gives the
number of disfranchised as 'over 12,000'. A recent study suggests that
the total adult male citizen population in the later part of the fourth
century was not more than about 20,000, and hence that Plutarch's
figure is much nearer the truth.[16] Textual error in Diodorus is probably
the explanation here. Doubts must be entertained, too, about the 480
elephants which appear in Seleucus' army at the end of Diodorus xx.
According to the terms of his treaty with Chandragupta, Seleucus had
acquired 500 elephants from India; Plutarch mentions 400 elephants in
Seleucus' army at Ipsus; Diodorus' 480 accordingly has a specious
precision.[17] But none of these figures is actually credible: the largest

[14] Paraetacene: Diod. xix. 27–9, *passim*. The total for Antigonus' army is some 2,000
less than the sum of the individual contingents. For Eumenes' army the discrepancies are
greater: elephants are 125 separately, 114 in total; infantry are 17,000 in separate units,
35,000 in total; cavalry are 6,250 separately, 6,100 in total. Possibly the first contingent in
the list of Eumenes' dispositions—the 150 horse which accompanied Eudamus and the
elephants—have been omitted in the final calculation. The difference in numbers for the
infantry—18,000—is perhaps the number of light-armed troops which filled the gaps
between the elephants (xix.27.5, 28.1); or there may be a lacuna at the end of ch. 27 in
the list of heavy infantry units: cf. Geer, Loeb edn. of Diodorus, vol. ix, p. 357 n. 1.
Forces of the eastern satraps: Diod. xix.14.8. The total is given as 18,700 infantry, 4,600
cavalry. The numbers listed individually total 18,500 infantry, 4,210 cavalry. The
missing contingent is possibly that of Amphimachus of Mesopotamia, mentioned later in
the dispositions at Paraetacene: xix.27.4, cf. F. Bizière, *Diodore XIX*, note compl. à
p. 26. For difficulties raised by the size of the Greek and allied forces in Thessaly
(xviii.38) see H. D. Westlake, *CR* lxxii (1949), pp. 87 ff.
[15] See N. G. Ashton, 'The *Naumachia* near Amorgos in 322 B.C.', *BSA* lxxii (1977),
pp. 1 ff.
[16] Diod. xviii.18.5; Plut. *Phoc.* xxviii.4; C. Pelekidis, *Histoire de l'éphébie attique*,
Paris, 1962, App. 1, pp. 290 f.; A. W. Gomme, *Population of Athens*, p. 78; Jones,
Athenian Democracy, p. 79. *Contra*, E. Ruschenbusch, *ZPE* xli (1981), p. 104.
[17] Diod. xx.113.4; Plut. *Demetr.* xxviii. The treaty with Chandragupta: Strabo xv.724
(probably from Megasthenes), cf. xvi.752; Plut. *Alex.* lxii.2.

fighting force of elephants otherwise known from the Hellenistic period is that of Antiochus III—150 elephants collected in Bactria and India; at Paraetacene Eumenes had either 114 or 125; 400 to 500 therefore seems much too large.[18] Tarn demonstrated that '500' is a stereotyped expression in Indian literature at this period meaning 'a great many', and decided (arbitrarily) that Seleucus really had 150 elephants, like his successor Antiochus the Great.[19] But Diodorus' and Plutarch's figures are not explained on that hypothesis. Possibly at the end of his twentieth book Diodorus was looking ahead to a part of his work in which he used sources other than Hieronymus; and his 480 elephants could have intruded from such a source. Another possibility is that Chandragupta did indeed hand over a very large number of elephants, but that not all were fighting males: elephants at Apamea are mentioned in the context of the Syrian War of 277, and it may be that this was a stud which Seleucus and Antiochus maintained to keep up supplies.[20] There can be no certain solution to problems of this kind. There were similar exaggerations of the number of Porus' elephants. Statistics in ancient texts, however, are peculiarly liable to corruption and misunderstanding, and these occasional discrepancies or exaggerations in the secondary writers cannot be taken as a reflection of inaccuracies in the original.[21]

Outside Evidence

The chief obstacle to an estimate of Hieronymus' factual accuracy is the absence of a continuous alternative tradition; for Greek accounts of the Diadochi, other than Diodorus', are too brief to illuminate the issue, and raise too many source problems of their own. But not all histories of the period came from the Greek side. Important testimony is offered by a cuneiform text from Babylon which gives a synopsis of historical events between 321 and 307 from the Seleucid point of view. The chronicle was first published, with translation and commentary, by Sidney Smith in 1924: it appears to have been written in *c*.280, and Smith conjectured that it might have been compiled for the use of Berossus in his history of Babylon.[22] The main interest of the text in the

[18] Polyb. xi.34.12; Diod. xix.28.4, cf. n. 12 above.

[19] Tarn, *JHS* lx (1940), pp. 84 ff. Cf. H. H. Scullard, *The Elephant in the Greek and Roman World*, pp. 97 f.

[20] Strabo xvi.752; cf. Tarn, *JHS* xlvi (1926), p. 157; Bayard Dodge, 'Elephants in the Bible Lands', *Bibl. Arch.* xviii (1955), pp. 17 ff.

[21] See also R. Engel, 'Anmerkungen zur Schlacht von Orkynia', *Mus. Helv.* xxviii (1971), pp. 227 ff., on oddities in Diodorus' figures for this battle: the conclusion there reached is nevertheless that Diodorus' is the most accurate of the parallel accounts.

[22] S. Smith, *Babylonian Historical Texts*, London, 1924, pp. 124 ff. Cf. Tarn's review, *JHS* xliv (1924), pp. 187 f.

present connection is that it corresponds at many points with the account of the same period in Diodorus, thereby guaranteeing the reliability of Hieronymus in the part of his work which is best known to us.

Under the year 321 to 320 there is a clear reference to the war of Perdiccas against Ptolemy and the murder of the regent by his troops, followed apparently by a reference to the assembly at Triparadeisos and the entry of the new satrap of Babylon, Seleucus, into his capital. The crossing of Antipater to Europe is mentioned, as in Diodorus and Arrian, and his illness and death. There follows an account of Eumenes' activities in Babylonia in the year 318 to 317; and on the reverse of the tablet, after a long break, the chronicle continues with the war between Antigonus and Seleucus after 312. The system of dating employed by the chronicler, who dates first by Philip Arrhidaeus and later by Alexander and finally by Seleucus, has proved exceptionally controversial. It has become clear, however, since publication of the first edition, that the events recorded on the reverse belong to the period after the battle of Gaza, and not, as Smith originally supposed, to the year 317 to 316 and following years.[23] This removes the major difficulties which Smith encountered in trying to reconcile the chronicle with Diodorus' account of 317 to 316.

There remains a problem in matching the Babylonian account of Eumenes in Babylonia in 318 to 317 with the account of Diodorus.[24] Under this year (Philip's seventh), the chronicle refers to the 'royal troops'—presumably the army of Eumenes, the new representative of the Kings in Asia—and to a capture of the 'palace' of Babylon; then Seleucus employs some stratagem involving a dam made of reeds; and the royal *hanu* corps are moved up—apparently an allusion to the Argyraspids. The year concludes with a bare mention of 'Antigonus the satrap'. This account bears some similarities to Diodorus' story of Seleucus breaking open a dam and flooding Eumenes' camp on the Tigris (xix.13.2, cf. xviii.73.4); but this he puts in spring 317 (xix.12.1, Eumenes in winter quarters). Furthermore, Diodorus makes no mention of a capture of the citadel of Babylon. The most probable solution

---

[23] W. Otto, 'Die Bedeutung der von S. Smith . . . veröffentlichten Diadochenchronik,' *S.B München*, 1925; Smith, *Rev. d'Assyr.* xxii (1925), pp. 179 ff. See esp. Furlani and Momigliano, 'La Cronaca Babilonese sui Diadochi', *Riv. Fil.* x (1932), pp. 462 ff. On the chronology see also Olmstead, *CP* 1937, pp. 1 ff.; Parker and Dubberstein, *Babylonian Chronology 626 B.C.–A.D. 45*, ed. 3, 1956, pp. 20 ff.; E. Bickerman, *Berytus* viii (1944), pp. 74 ff.; D. Sachs and D. J. Wiseman, *Iraq* xvi (1954), pp. 202–12 (edition of a new Babylonian king-list), with the comments of A. Aymard, *REA* lvii (1955), pp. 102–12 = *Études*, Paris, 1967, pp. 263 ff.

[24] Momigliano, art. cit., does not meet this difficulty. Cf. Bizière, *Diodore XIX*, note compl. à p. 23.

is that two different episodes are being related, as the different dates imply, and the fact that a stratagem employing a dam is used on each occasion is not surprising, given that the action takes place in Mesopotamia: Seleucus considers using this device yet again, according to the chronicle, after his return to Babylon in 312, when he is again trying to recapture the citadel (Reverse 7: cf. Diod. xix.100.6). Diodorus has altogether omitted the earlier of the two episodes—the capture of Babylon by Eumenes in autumn 318—and it is easy to understand how it dropped out when one considers that this was the point of Diodorus' transition from Asian to Greek affairs (xviii.73–4) and then from Book xviii to xix: in Book xix he began his history of Agathocles, which from this point became increasingly interesting to him; and when he resumed the Eumenes narrative, he made a fresh start with the new campaigning season of 317. Perhaps Hieronymus had started a new book at this point. Before leaving Eumenes at the end of xviii, however, Diodorus had summarized some of his later activities: marching inland from Phoenicia to the Upper Satrapies, he was attacked περὶ . . . τὸν Τίγριν ποταμόν by the local inhabitants; then in Babylonia, παρὰ τὸν Εὐφράτην ποταμόν, Seleucus flooded his camp, but Eumenes escaped by employing a counter stratagem. This summary may conceal an allusion to the operations at Babylon which the cuneiform text relates. The flooding of Eumenes' camp, as described at length in Diodorus xix, took place by the Tigris, not, as Diodorus here states, by the Euphrates. Not for the first time, he has confused the two rivers of Mesopotamia: in Book ii he places Nineveh on the Euphrates (ii.3.2). If the names at xviii.73.3 are reversed, we have first, operations on the Euphrates (? capture of Babylon, autumn 318), second, the flooding episode on the Tigris (spring 317). This is the logical order, considering the direction of Eumenes' march, and would match the information given in the Babylonian chronicle. It may be not without significance that in spring 317 Eumenes' troops repeatedly resisted the attempts of Seleucus and his party to detach them from their commander (xix.12.2–3; 13.1–2): if at this moment Eumenes had a garrison in the citadel of Babylon, guarding his rear, it might well prove difficult to undermine the loyalty of his army.

Further correspondences with Diodorus are apparent on the reverse side of the chronicle. Seleucus' attempts to capture the citadel of Babylon, which are going on in the month of Ab (late summer) of Alexander IV's sixth year (311 to 310), are the consequence of his return to Babylon the previous year after the battle of Gaza. Diodorus describes his return, and later Demetrius' capture of one of the citadels of Babylon: this must be the 'palace' which Seleucus is besieging in the chronicle.[25] The alliance and friendship sworn in the month of Marcheswan (Reverse 10) must be an alliance made between Seleucus and the troops of Gutium (Reverse 11), i.e. the Cossaei, who had proved fiercely hostile to Antigonus in the campaigns of 317 (cf. Diod. xix. 19), and now support Seleucus in his struggle against Antigonus. Momigliano argued convincingly that this alliance cannot be the Peace of 311: the other participants, Cassander, Lysimachus, and Ptolemy, are not mentioned, and the chronicler does not seem to regard the treaty as an event of the first importance.[26] If the allusion is to a local treaty, it follows that the chronicle does not mention the great Peace of 311 at all (we are here at the very end of events of Alexander's sixth year), and this confirms the evidence of Diodorus and of Antigonus' letter to the Scepsians, that Seleucus was not included in the Peace, but was left to fight it out with Antigonus.[27]

The chronicle goes on to relate the war between Antigonus and Seleucus which continued intermittently throughout the years 310 to 308. Diodorus has nothing to say about these campaigns, and direct comparison of the two texts is impossible after this point.[28] It should be noted, however, that the Babylonian account of Antigonus and Seleucus in general confirms the characterization of these men found in the Greek tradition. Seleucus' popularity in his satrapy, and conversely, the brutality of Antigonus to the wretched Babylonians, is testified by the repeated references to burning and plundering during the period after 311, and to 'weeping and mourning in the land' (Reverse 26–9, 39–40). It is evident that it was Antigonus who was responsible for the destruction of Babylon, and not, as once thought, Seleucus himself, and that it was in consequence of this devastation that Seleucus was forced to build a new capital at Seleuceia.[29] Twice the chronicle records specific actions which must have won Seleucus popularity among the local inhabitants: in the year 319 to 318 he is engaged in lavish building activities (Obverse 9–12); and during the war against Antigonus in 308 to 307 he is trying to supply his subjects with corn from Borsippa (Reverse 35–6). For Hieronymus, Antigonus' τραχύτης was the chief cause of his downfall and a contrast with the *euergesia* of men such as Ptolemy and Seleucus

[25] Diod. xix.90ff.; 100.5–7; Plut. *Demetr.* 7.
[26] Momigliano, art. cit., p. 478.
[27] See Momigliano, *Stud. Ital. Fil. Class*, n.s. viii (1930), pp. 83 ff.; Simpson, *JHS* lxxiv (1954), pp. 25 ff.
[28] Tarn *JHS* lx (1940), 86, assumes Hieronymus gave no account of the war between Antigonus and Seleucus, but cf. ch. 3, pp. 97 f.
[29] Cf. Smith, *Bab. Hist. Texts*, p. 136; *Topography and Architecture of Seleuceia on the Tigris*, ed. C. Hopkins, Michigan, 1972, pp. 4f. (founding of Seleuceia).

towards their subjects is implicit in all our Greek accounts of the Diadochi: the independent statements of the Babylonian chronicler are a striking confirmation of a dominant motif in Hieronymus' history.[30]

The cuneiform chronicle, representing a totally different tradition of history and historiography, is the only independent and continuous text which can be brought into direct connection with the Diodoran narrative; but the parallel evidence of Greek inscriptions and archaeology can be compared at certain points, and does show a general agreement. There is naturally a limit to the non-literary evidence which can usefully be cited in his support, but some striking instances may be mentioned.

The majority are, inevitably, epigraphic. Antigonus Monophthalmus' letter to the Scepsians supports Diodorus on the peace terms in 311; it also refers to earlier events in Diodorus xix and confirms his account of Antigonus' attitude to the Greek states.[31] A Milesian decree, which dates to 313 the restoration of freedom, autonomy, and democracy by Antigonus, similarly refers to events mentioned by Diodorus: the liberation of Miletus, he relates, was carried out by Antigonus' generals Medeius and Docimus in 313.[32] Indeed, the inscriptional evidence for Antigonus' 'eleutheria' propaganda among the Greek cities of Asia Minor is abundant, and examples could be multiplied.[33] Epigraphic support for other episodes in the war after 315 can be found in the Athenian decree of *c*.275 in honour of Phaedrus of Sphettus, which mentions the naval war against Antigonus during 315 to 314, and shows that it was Thymochares who commanded the Athenian fleet sent to help Cassander in 313 to 312;[34] or in an inscription from Aspendus referring to Leonidas, the general sent by Ptolemy to subdue the cities of Cilicia Trachea in 310 to 309, and to the mercenaries he stationed at Aspendus: Leonidas' campaign is summarized at Diodorus xix.19.3–4.[35] Another example, of particular interest, is the fragment of a Hellenistic inscription from Thebes, which lists a series

[30] See ch. 5, p. 218.

[31] *OGIS* 5 = Welles *RC* no. 1 = H. H. Schmitt, *Die Staatsverträge des Altertums,* iii, Munich, 1969, no. 428; Diod. xix.75.6.

[32] *Syll.*[3] 322; cf. Diod. xix.75.3–4.

[33] Other inscriptions referring to Antigonus' liberation campaign are *Syll.*[3] 328 (Chalcis); *Syll.*[3] 344 = Welles *RC* 3 and 4 (Teos and Lebedus); *OGIS* 7 (Cyme); *OGIS* 223 = Welles *RC* 15, lines 21 ff. (Erythrae); cf. Meritt, *AJP* lvi (1935), p. 361 (Colophon); also *Syll.*[3] 330, lines 24 f. (the Ilian cities: discussed by Simpson, *Historia* viii (1959), p. 396).

[34] *IG* II[2] 682 = *Syll.*[3] 409; Diod. xix.75.8, cf. 62; cf. Beloch, *Gr. Gesch.* iv[2] 1, p. 122.

[35] *Monumenti Antichi* xxiii (1914), pp. 116 f., no. 83. Cf. Beloch, *Gr. Gesch.* iv[2] 2, p. 334; Segre, *Aegyptus* xiv (1934), pp. 253 ff; Launey, *Recherches,* i, p. 349.

of donors, both individual kings and cities, who have made financial contributions to the city of Thebes.[36] The order is apparently chronological, since the kings are not given pride of place at the top of the list, and the cities are from all parts of the Greek world. The occasion is clearly an extraordinary one, since the Thebans were generally disliked in antiquity, and it can only be the rebuilding of Thebes by Cassander in 316, an enterprise to which many cities would subscribe for political reasons. The restoration of Thebes is described at Diodorus xix.54.1, and 'many of the Greek cities' (τῶν Ἑλληνίδων πόλεων . . . πολλαί) are said to have played a part, not only those from Greece itself, but also those from Italy and Sicily; the Athenians are specified by name. The stone which recorded the final list of contributors does not mention either the Athenians or any of the Western Greeks; but this is because Diodorus (Hieronymus) has given only the first contributors, in and immediately after 316, and the first part of the inscription, where these would have been recorded, is missing. Written history and epigraphy therefore form a remarkable complement to one another in this instance.

Numismatic evidence similarly confirms parts of Diodorus' account. Describing the satrapal appointments made by Antigonus in 316, he records that the new satrap of Susiane was a native Persian called 'Aspisas', a name apparently equivalent in meaning to the Greek 'Philippos', and which occurs only here in Greek literature.[37] It has turned up again, however, on an issue of the Asiatic Alexander coinage, evidently struck at Susa: the reverse bears the inscription Ἀσπείσου, the genitive of the Persian name Aspeisas; and the mention of this man in Diodorus enables the coin to be dated between 316 and 312.[38] Seleucus reduced Media and Susiane after his return to Bablyon in 312, as a later passage of Diodorus relates, and it is not likely that Aspeisas kept his satrapy after this time.[39]

Another numismatic find, this time from the Peloponnese, can be linked with Diodorus' account of the mission of Aristodemus in 315: Ἀριστόδημον δὲ τὸν Μιλήσιον εἰς Πελοπόννησον ἐξέπεμψεν (sc. ὁ Ἀντίγονος) ἔχοντα χίλια τάλαντα.[40] He was to come to an arrangement with Polyperchon and his son, and to hire mercenaries for the war against Cassander. Some of the 1,000 talents brought by Aristodemus seem to have found their way into a small but well-preserved

[36] *IG* VII 2419 = *Syll.*[3] 337. Cf. Holleaux, *Études* i. 1, pp. 3 ff. Diod. xix.54.1–2.
[37] Diod. xix.55.1.
[38] See E. Robinson, *Num. Chron.* 1921, pp. 37 f.
[39] Diod. xix.92.5.
[40] Diod. xix.57.5.

coin hoard at Andritsaina.[41] The hoard contains a very large proportion of Asiatic issues (43, to 30 European ones), all but one from
before the death of Philip Arrhidaeus, and one Babylonian coin, in
excellent condition, which represents an issue directly after Philip's
death in late 317. The condition of this coin, the latest in the hoard,
shows that it had seen little use, and, allowing time for its journey from
Babylon to the Western Peloponnese, it must have been buried within
about a year after it was struck. Both the composition of the hoard
and the date of its burial thus suggest that the Asiatic issues are to
be identified as part of the money which Antigonus sent with Aristodemus.

Finally some archaeological items may be mentioned. In Books xix
and xx Diodorus records two phases of the siege of Callantia on the
Pontus by Lysimachus, between the years 313 and 310/309, and he
mentions the forces sent by Antigonus by land and sea to the aid of the
Callantians; the fleet had been built for Antigonus in 315 in Phoenicia,
and presumably was partly manned by Phoenicians.[42] The whole
account receives unexpected confirmation from the inscription on a
funerary cup found at Callantia and dating from the late fourth century
BC (the cup itself, an Athenian cantharus, dates from about the mid-
fourth century).[43] The graffito on the neck of the cup runs:
Ναυκασαμαι τοὶ σύσσιτοι τοὶ Τιμώνακτος—'The syssites of Timonax
dedicated me to Naukasamas.' Though some instances are known
which were religious or academic, most *syssitoi* seem, like the famous
Spartan *syssitoi*, to have been military associations, though unlike the
permanent institutions of Sparta and Crete, with their special social
organization, the syssites of Athens or Lindos were formed on a
temporary basis in response to specific military needs, and their existence is known from their collective action in dedicating honorific or
funerary monuments. The syssites of Callantia were evidently just
such a group, centred on the person of Timonax, their captain, and the
problem is to find an occasion when it might have formed. Diodorus
supplies the required literary testimony, showing that Callantia was
under siege at a date which matches the epigraphic evidence. The name
Naukasamas (or Naukosmas) provides yet more striking corroboration,

[41] See E. Newell, *Numismatic Notes and Monographs*, xxi (1923), 'Alexander
Hoards, iii, Andritsaina', esp. pp. 21 ff., for the relation of the date of burial to political
events in the Peloponnese. Cf. G. R. Edwards and M. Thompson, *AJA* lxxiv (1970),
p. 350.
[42] Diod. xix.73, xx.25.1 (cf. above, ch. 2, p. 61 for the continuity of the narrative);
cf. xix.58 f. Strabo vii.5.12 calls the city Callatis.
[43] Published and discussed by A. Stefan, *Epigraphica* (ed. Pippidi and Popescu),
Bucarest, 1977, pp. 25 ff.; cf. Robert, *REG* xci (1978), Bull. Ep. no. 322.

for this name can only derive from a Semitic root (as Kasem, Kosam), and this inscription is the earliest evidence for an oriental name on the west side of Pontus. The honorand was a Levantine, and his presence there, and his friendly relations with the syssites of Callantia, are explained by Diodorus' allusion to the fleet of Antigonus which supported the Callantians when oppressed by Lysimachus. Its admiral was Lycon (Diod. xix.73.6); evidently Naukasamas was a Phoenician captain who fell in battle on behalf of the Greek city.

Among the most recent of excavations which relate to the Diadochi are those at the sanctuary of Nemea.[44] Excavation of the stadium at Nemea has revealed the existence of a well-preserved vaulted tunnel, through which the athletes made their entrance, and which is clearly datable to the fourth century BC. A precise date is not ascertainable stratigraphically, since the original floor of the tunnel had been kept clean during use; but on both sides the surface of the stones is covered with grafitti, which include names of the early Hellenistic period.[45] If, then, the tunnel is to be dated to the last quarter of the fourth century, it is of some importance as an architectural monument, since it seems to be an immediate result of the introduction into Greece of a new architectural form, the arch, as a consequence of Alexander's campaign to the East.[46] The Macedonian influence at Nemea which this implies is illustrated by Diodorus' allusion (xix.64.1) to Cassander presiding at the Nemean Games in the course of his Peloponnesian campaign of 315 BC; and one may fairly speculate whether it was not Cassander himself, rebuilder of Thebes and founder of Cassandreia and Thessalonike, who was responsible for a magnificent building programme at Nemea, incorporating the very latest architectural fashion.[47]

Also worthy of consideration are the military fortifications on Mount Salganeus, on the Boeotian mainland opposite Chalcis. Diodorus records that the diplomatic offensive led by Aristodemus was followed up by the sending of Ptolemaeus, one of Antigonus'

---

[44] S. F. Miller, *Hesperia* xlvii (1979), pp. 73 ff.

[45] The names include that of $AKPOTATO\Sigma/[K]A\Lambda O\Sigma$, followed by the scrawled comment in a different hand, $TOY\ \Gamma PA\Psi ANTO\Sigma$, showing that 'the ancient opinion of Akrotatos was not unanimous' (Miller, art. cit., p. 101). This rare name probably indicates either the Spartan king who reigned c.265–252 BC, or the elder man of the same name mentioned at Diod. xix.70, in one of the Sicilian sections, and said to be the subject of plots and attacks—an unpopularity which might account for the hostile irony of the graffito. The elder Acrotatus is mentioned in the context of 314 BC.

[46] Cf. T. D. Boyd, 'The Arch and the Vault in Greek Architecture', *AJA* lxxxii (1978), pp. 88 f.

[47] Macedonian influence appears to extend from the period shortly after the battle of Chaeronea, but many structures still await excavation. Cf. Miller, art. cit., p. 103.

nephews, at the head of a substantial military force: ὁ δὲ Πτολεμαῖος
. . . καταπλεύσας τῆς Βοιωτίας εἰς τὸν Βαθὺν καλούμενον λιμένα
. . . καὶ τειχίσας τὸν Σαλγανέα συνήγαγεν ἐνταῦθα πᾶσαν τὴν
δύναμιν.[48] A recent study of Salganeus shows that it must have been
Ptolemaeus who was responsible for much of the extensive fortifica-
tion works across the peninsula, of which the remains are still visible:
namely, the Antiforitis wall, which defended the plain of Salganeus
against attacks from inland Boeotia, and the fortress known as the
Kastro, which commands the plain and the roads leading to Chalcis.[49]
During his three years as Antigonus' chief commander in Greece
Ptolemaeus showed the strategic importance of the Salganeus plain
and of Chalcis, and Demetrius probably benefited from this experience when he successfully invaded Thessaly in 304. Salganeus and
its fortifications, it has been said, 'still testify to the energy and military
skill which are so characteristic of the first members of the House of
Antigonus'.[50]

One of Antigonus' first victims in his struggle for supremacy, Alcetas the brother of Perdiccas, has an equally impressive memorial. The
largest and most magnificent of the rock tombs at Termessos in Pisidia,
which is probably the earliest of the many tombs on this site, has long
been identified as the tomb of Alcetas.[51] It is rock-cut, like the Lycian
tombs, but Greek in style, and the interior shows Macedonian features, notably the reliefs depicting a horseman and armour, and,
above the kline at the back of the chamber, an eagle fighting a snake.
The tomb 'seems to reconcile many of the more decorative elements of
Macedonian tombs with the Anatolian tradition of rock-cut facades
and chambers'.[52] It provides graphic confirmation of the conclusion to
Diodorus' story of Alcetas: Antigonus maltreated the body of his
enemy for three days and at last threw it out unburied—ἄταφος; but
the young men of Termessos, maintaining their good will for the dead
man, τὸ . . . σῶμα ἀνείλαντο καὶ λαμπρῶς ἐκήδευσαν.[53] This is the

[48] Diod. xix.77.4.
[49] S. C. Bakhuizen, *Salganeus and the Fortifications on its Mountains,* Chalcidian
Studies, ii, Groningen, 1970, pp. 105 ff.
[50] Ibid., p. 130.
[51] K. Lanckoronski and E. Petersen, *Städte Pamphyliens u. Pisidiens,* ii, Wien, 1892,
pp. 69–72; R. Heberdey, *R E* s.v. 'Termessos', col. 755; G. Kleiner, 'Diadochengräber',
Sitz. Wiss. Gesell. Johann Goethe, Frankfurt–Main, i, 1963, pp. 71 ff.; cf. C. Picard,
'Sépultures des compagnons de guerre ou successeurs macédoniens d'Alexandre',
Journal des Savants, 1964, pp. 298 ff. E. Kalinka, *Tit. Asiae Min.* ii, 1, p. 1 has a good
photograph of the hillside.
[52] Kurtz and Boardman, *Greek Burial Customs,* p. 297.
[53] Diod. xviii.47.3. Provision for a cult has been found in the Termessos tomb: cf.
Lanckoronski–Petersen, loc. cit., Picard, art. cit., p. 222.

only tomb of a companion of Alexander which can be identified with any certainty;[54] and the tomb of Alexander himself has notoriously eluded all attempts at discovery—a fact symbolic of the mystery surrounding the great conqueror and the fantasies which most of his historians spun about him. The splendid tomb of Alcetas marks the pomp and solidity of the period of the Diadochi, qualities which can be seen also to characterize the historiographic tradition from Hieronymus. Examples from cuneiform texts, from epigraphic, numismatic, architectural, and archaeological evidence, show that Alexander's successors found a historian who was securely anchored in reality, and whose work can be seen to represent substantial facts.

Autopsy

The most important part of *historia*, according to Polybius, is autopsy and practical experience,[55] a requirement which Hieronymus met, if anyone. The biographical testimonia show that for long sequences of the history of Eumenes, Antigonus, and the Epigoni he was his own best informant. The history of Eumenes is especially vivid in character: the description of Eumenes' duel with Neoptolemus, of conditions at the siege of Nora, and other scenes of army life are clearly drawn from personal recollection.[56] So also are his picture of the young Demetrius in the army assembly at Gaza, and many episodes in the history of Antigonus Monophthalmus, in which the historian seems to dwell chiefly on the weather: Hieronymus had grim memories of being marched through rain, snow, and sand by this relentless task-master.[57]

Numerous details also testify to Hieronymus' personal observation. The depth of the Pasitigris, for example, is measured by the height of the elephants as they crossed: βάθος δὲ κατὰ μέσον τὸ ῥεῦμα πρὸς τὰ μεγέθη τῶν ἐλεφάντων κ.τ.λ.;[58] and the splendour of Antigonus'

---

[54] See Kleiner, op. cit. pp. 80 ff. For the tomb at Belevi near Ephesus; cf. Picard, art. cit., pp. 225 f.; the original occupant might have been Antiochus II, who died at Ephesus in 246; but the tomb may be of considerably earlier date, and has been attributed to the 4th-century Persian general Memnon of Rhodes. A funerary building at Amphipolis is suggested by Picard (p. 226 n. 22) as the tomb of Nearchus of Crete. A. D. H. Bivar, *JRS* lix (1969), p. 307 (reviewing Colledge, *The Parthians,* London, 1967) suggests that the shrine of Khurha, not far from Isfahan, may commemorate the last battle of Eumenes in Gabiene. The occupants of the tombs at Vergina in Macedon newly excavated by Professor Andronikos cannot be certainly identified: in some respects the burials are consistent with those of Philip Arrhidaeus and Eurydice mentioned at Diod. xix.52.5 (cf. Diyllos, *F. Gr. Hist.* 73 F1), but the weight of evidence still points to Philip II and one of his wives. Cf. Hammond, *GRBS* xix (1978), pp. 337 ff.

[55] Polyb. xii.27.6.　　[56] Cf. ch. 5, pp. 196 ff.　　[57] Cf. ch. 5, pp. 221 ff.
[58] Diod. xix.17.3. Contrast, however, xviii.34.7, where the eye-witness description of the Nile crossing must come from the reports of soldiers who had served under Perdiccas. For xviii.27.2 (ὁρᾶσθαι), 28.1 (διὰ τῆς ὁράσεως) cf. ch. 2, pp. 44 f. Cf. Timaeus, *F. Gr. Hist* 566 F 26a, for a similar method of measurement.

army, in Plutarch's account, is described as though by an observer in
Eumenes' ranks: 'The gleam of their golden armour flashed down
from the heights as they marched along in close formation, and on the
backs of the elephants the towers and purple trappings were seen,
which was their array when going into battle.'[59] The same point of view
is taken in Diodorus, describing how Antigonus' soldiers swam the
river Coprates.[60] In Eumenes' journey through Persis Hieronymus can
be identified among the travellers who enjoyed the scenery—ὥστε
τοὺς ὁδοιπωροῦντας μετὰ πολλῆς τέρψεως ἐνδιατρίβειν τόποις
ἡδίστοις πρὸς ἀνάπαυσιν;[61] and the elaborate detail which depicts
Peucestas' feast originates with one who had taken part in it: Hieronymus would have been among those described as οἱ ἔξω τάξεως φίλοι
καὶ στρατηγοί, in the second circle.[62] At Paraetacene, we have, perhaps, an observer's description of the moments after the battle, when
the armies stood by, expecting a further engagement: τῆς δὲ νυκτὸς
οὔσης αἰθρίου καὶ πανσελήνου καὶ τῶν δυνάμεων ἀντιπαραγουσῶν
ἀλλήλας ὡς ἂν ἐν τέτταρσι πλέθροις ὁ ψόφος τῶν ὅπλων καὶ ἱππέων
ὁ φρυαγμὸς ἐν χερσὶν ἐδόκει πᾶσιν εἶναι τοῖς ἀντιτεταγμένοις.[63] At
Gabiene also, Diodorus conveys the sense of confusion accompanying
a great battle: the armies were enveloped by dust kicked up by the
horses' hooves from the salt plain, ὥστε μηδένα δύνασθαι ῥᾳδίως
συνορᾶν ἐξ ὀλίγου διαστήματος τὸ γινόμενον.[64] After Paraetacene,
in describing the reaction of the Greeks in the army to the suicide of
Ceteus' wife, Hieronymus perhaps intended to express his own attitude: ἔνιοι τῶν Ἑλλήνων ἐπετίμων τοῖς νομίμοις ὡς ἀγρίοις οὖσι καὶ
χαλεποῖς.[65] Again, one may suppose that the historian was among
those who were called to witness Antigonus' public rebuke of those who
were slandering Pithon: τούτοις μὲν πολλῶν ἀκουόντων ἐπετίμησεν
κ.τ.λ.[66]

Allusions to witnesses may sometimes have been included in order
to guarantee the truth of a story: thus Eurydice's dying curse on
Olympias is uttered 'in the presence of the servant'—παρόντος τοῦ
κομίσαντος. The rather dramatic account of Eurydice's death probably derived from court gossip, and Hieronymus no doubt wished to
give weight to a story which was hard to substantiate.[67] The value
which he placed on eye-witness reports is perhaps shown again in the
allusion to αὐτόπται who came from Babylon to Athens with news of

[59] Plut. *Eum.* xiv.4.   [60] Diod. xix.18.4 ff.   [61] Diod. xix.21.3.
[62] Diod. xix.22, *passim* and 22.2. On the terminology, see Holleaux, *Études*, iii
pp. 1 ff.
[63] Diod. xix.31.2.   [64] Diod. xix.42.1.   [65] Diod. xix.34.6.
[66] Diod. xix.46.1. Cf. Polyaen. iv.6.14, recording what Antigonus said.
[67] Diod. xix.11.7. Cf. T. S. Brown, *Am. Hist. Rev.* 1946, p. 689.

Alexander's death.[68] Hieronymus' direct allusions to himself also would have been intended to authenticate his history, like those of Thucydides, and of Ptolemy. Ptolemy was less emphatic in affirming that he had been present on Alexander's campaigns, because it was a fact which everyone knew: Hieronymus needed to remind his readers of his own status as the confidant of Eumenes and trusted servant of the Antigonids.[69] This position brought its own hazards to the writing of truthful history, but it gave Hieronymus' narrative the virtues of direct knowledge and a vivid manner.

Hieronymus' informants

In gathering information about wars and politics outside the range of his own experience, Hieronymus had access to a large body of first-hand material, consisting of the statements not only of the Diadochi who were his friends, but of members of the whole entourage who surrounded them, both European and Iranian, military and civil. Inevitably most of this information was woven together in the history to form a complete account of any episode, and only rarely can specific sources be identified. Those who can be named with some degree of probability are men of Hieronymus' own rank, in the immediate retinue of Eumenes or the Antigonids, who could inform him on campaigns or diplomatic missions in which they had taken a leading part, and who would wish their achievements to receive suitable commemoration in the official history of the times—as contemporaries might regard the writings of a Greek in Antigonus' service.

In addition, the mobile mercenary population of this period provided a channel through which detailed news of events in distant theatres of war might reach the ears of the historian, and the tendency for defeated armies to be absorbed into the ranks of the victor gave him a unique opportunity to hear versions of battles and campaigns from both sides. A stratum of the history representing reports supplied by soldiers can be discerned. The account of Thibron in Cyrene must have come from a mercenary source; the narrative of Perdiccas' war in Egypt also may derive from the reports of soldiers.[70]

[68] Diod. xviii.9.4.

[69] Cf. *F. Gr. Hist.* IID, p. 546. Ptolemy: Arr. *Anab.* iii.29.6–30.5 = F14; v.28.4–5 = F23; cf. iv.23.1–3; v.23.7–24.3; iv.24.1–4. Cf. Pearson, *Lost Histories*, pp. 200 f., 203 f., 209. Ancient historians generally avoided giving biographical details about themselves: as a stylistic principle this had been taken over by Herodotus from epic. It was partially broken by Theopompus' proems, and Hellenistic historians became relatively informative about their lives and persons. Cf. Jacoby, *R E* Suppl. ii s.v. 'Herodotos', cols. 245–6.

[70] Thibron: Diod. xviii.19ff.; cf. xviii.35, *passim* on the horrors of swimming a river full of crocodiles.

Again, Diodorus' military narrative of the Lamian War is written with a good understanding of the strategical issues involved: the disunity of the Greek allies, the importance of the cavalry arm, the state of Athenian financial and military preparation, the timing of Leosthenes' death and Craterus' arrival. The account of the actual fighting, as opposed to that of the settlement afterwards, is written from the Greek point of view; and the special praise accorded to the courage and prowess of Menon and the Thessalian cavalry suggests Thessalian informants: Plutarch, recounting the same events in his *Life of Phocion*, mentions the Thessalian contingent only in passing.[71] Menon of Pharsalus had a later claim to fame as the maternal grandfather of Pyrrhus; but his prominence in Diodorus as architect of the Greek victories of 323 to 322 was perhaps underlined by Thessalian survivors of the Lamian War who had served under his command.[72] An Athenian decree shows Athens receiving fifty Thessalian refugees after the battle of Crannon, who are to be allowed to live in Athens free of the metic tax until they can be restored to their homeland: Hieronymus could have spoken with some of these exiles when he came to Athens with Demetrius, before Demetrius liberated Thessaly.[73]

Other examples of a soldier's view might be in evidence if those sections of the narrative centred on Greece, Thrace, and the West were better preserved. In the existing accounts, however, a marked preference can be discerned for official sources: Hieronymus used documents, especially, when these were available, and he must often have relied on the word of commanding officers in the service of his masters. Mithridates, the later king of Pontus, who claimed descent from one of the seven Persians who slew the Magus, would have been a useful informant on Persian historical background and especially on the affairs of Asia Minor; for Eumenes' position as satrap of Cappadocia gave Hieronymus an especial interest in northern Anatolia. Mithridates served in Eumenes' army (he must have been among the 'high-ranking Iranians' in the innermost circle at Peucestas' feast), and after Gabiene transferred to Antigonus' camp along with Hieronymus and many others from Eumenes' staff: later, like Hieronymus, he became a companion of Demetrius.[74] A more senior officer whose career followed the same pattern was Philippus, mentioned in the new fragment of Arrian as involved in the negotiations with Craterus' troops in

---

[71] Diod. xviii.12.3; 15.2–4; 17.2; 17.4. Plut. *Phoc.* 25.3.
[72] For Menon's city, cf. Diod. xviii.38.5. His relationship to Pyrrhus: Plut. *Pyrrh.* 1.4.
[73] IG II² 545: cf. A. Wilhelm, 'Vier Beschlüsse der Athener,' *Abh. d. Preuss. Akad. d. Wiss. phil.-hist. Kl.* xxii (1939), pp. 17 ff.
[74] Diod. xix.40.2; Plut. *Demetr.* 4.1; cf. Diod. xix.22.2.

322, and not implausibly he was Hieronymus' source for this episode.[75] At Gabiene Philippus is mentioned as commander of a reserve force of cavalry—a novel feature in the military history of this period;[76] and after Eumenes' death he served under Antigonus. It is no doubt the same man who appears as one of the four counsellors assigned to Demetrius in 314, 'men advanced in years who had accompanied Alexander on his whole campaign', and who is still faithfully serving Antigonus in 302 as commander of the acropolis of Sardis: Φίλιππος εἷς τῶν Ἀντιγόνου φίλων βεβαίαν ἐτήρει τὴν εὔνοιαν τὴν πρὸς τὸν πεπιστευκότα. Hieronymus had especial reason thus to single out a contemporary and perhaps a personal friend, whose career had run parallel to his own.[77] The other counsellors of Demetrius were also trusted veterans to whom Hieronymus could turn for funds of knowledge and experience: Nearchus of Crete, the friend and admiral of Alexander, who had served under Antigonus before Hieronymus joined him in 316, and had made his own contribution to the written history of Alexander's expedition;[78] Andronicus of Olynthus, mentioned as Antigonus' general at the siege of Tyre in 315;[79] Pithon son of Agenor, an expert on Indian affairs after his many years as satrap of Lower India, and later Antigonus' satrap in Babylon.[80]

Other officers in the retinue of Antigonus and Demetrius were less reliable. Pithon the bodyguard, later satrap of Media, probably supplied Hieronymus with the account of Antigonus' disastrous crossing into Media in 317, representing that Antigonus' difficulties arose from neglect of Pithon's good advice, and that he, Pithon, had saved the situation. Pithon spent the winter of 317 preparing to revolt from Antigonus, and the former adherents of Eumenes, especially those like Hieronymus who were lying on their sick beds, would certainly have been subjected to his propaganda.[81] Antigonus finally executed Pithon for being too big for his boots, but not, it seems, before he had exercised some influence on the new recruits. Pithon was a malcontent: he is described as κινητικός and μεγαλεπίβολος; he had tried to establish a private empire in the upper satrapies, and had been leader of the group of officers who assassinated Perdiccas.[82] His ambition was

---

[75] Arrian, *PSI* 1284, col. iii.1.14–15. Cf. G. Wirth, *Klio* xlvi (1965), p. 287.
[76] Diod. xix.40.4; cf. Tarn, *HMND*, p. 34.
[77] Diod. xix.69.1; xx.107.5; cf. Wirth, loc. cit.
[78] Diod. xix.19.4; Plut. *Eum.* xviii.3.
[79] Diod. xix.59.2.
[80] Arr. *Anab.* 6.15.4; Diod. xviii.3.3, 39.6; xix.56.4.
[81] Diod. xix.18–20, *passim*, cf. ch. 5, pp. 218 f. Diod. xix.46.1–4; cf. Polyaen. iv.6.14; Griffith, *Mercenaries of the Hellenistic World*, p. 51.
[82] Diod. xviii.7.4; xix.14.2; xviii.36.5.

not satisfied by the temporary regency he shared with Arrhidaeus after
the removal of Perdiccas, and his ultimate aim, as it appears from
events in the winter after Gabiene, was to make himself ruler of Asia in
Antigonus' place: Antigonus saw the danger that he might himself
suffer the fate of Perdiccas. Possibly the hostile portrait of Perdiccas in
Egypt, and the charge that he usurped the authority of the other
commanders—τῶν ἄλλων ἡγεμόνων περιαιρούμενος τὰς ἐξουσίας
—derive (orally) from Pithon; and it is perhaps significant that Diodorus describes Pithon at this point in honorific terms: οὐδενὸς . . . τῶν
Ἀλεξάνδρου λειπόμενος φίλων ἀρετῇ τε καὶ δόξῃ.[83] He might also
have been a source for the revolt ʽof the Bactrian Greeks; but
Diodorus is here very brief and an obvious slant to the narrative is not
detectable.

Docimus, the outlawed follower of Perdiccas and later general of
Antigonus, was also a man who had a past to vindicate. At some time
between 323 and 321 he was sent by Perdiccas to replace Archon as
satrap of Babylon, and must have fallen under sentence of exile after
Perdiccas' death, since Babylonia was allotted to Seleucus in the
partition at Triparadeisos. Docimus evidently offered no resistance to
the new master of Babylon (the Babylonian chronicle on the Diadochi
implies that Seleucus' entry was unopposed), but fled in good time to
join Attalus' party in Pisidia. In 319 the exiles did battle with Antigonus, and upon their defeat and capture, were imprisoned in a
Phrygian stronghold.[84] Two years later, as Diodorus recounts, the
prisoners found an opportunity to overpower their guards, but before
they had decided on a course of action, reinforcements arrived from
Antigonus and laid siege to the fortress. Docimus and one companion
escaped by a secret route, and made their way to Antigonus' wife
Stratonice, who was in the neighbourhood; and Docimus, it is said,
was put under arrest and accorded no confidence—οὐκ ἔτυχε
πίστεως—while his companion turned traitor and showed Antigonus'
troops the secret way into the fortress. The improbability of this story
is manifest when Docimus' later career is considered.[85] In 313 he
reappears as Antigonus' general in the liberation of Miletus; and in
303, when he deserted Antigonus for Lysimachus, he was in a position
to betray Synnada and some royal treasuries. Three epigrams from
'the city of Docimus' show that it was he who founded the town of

[83] Diod. xviii.33.3; 36.5.
[84] Arr. *Succ.* F10.3–5; Diod. xviii.39.6; Smith, *Bab. Hist. Texts*, p. 142 (Obv. 5), cf.
p. 130. Diod. xviii.45.3, cf. Plut. *Eum.* viii; Diod. xix.16, *passim*, for the story.
[85] See Simpson, 'A possible case of misrepresentation in Hieronymus of Cardia',
Historia vi (1957), pp. 504 f.

Docimeion in Phrygia, a centre for the export of marble, and coins of the imperial period bear his portrait and the legend *ΔOKIMOΣ*—an indication of his eventual power and fame.[86] The statement that he was 'distrusted' cannot be accepted. Docimus' position under Antigonus was surely a reward for betraying his companions; but in giving his account to Hieronymus, at a time when he was one of Antigonus' senior commanders, he was careful to conceal the discreditable way in which he had saved his own skin. Attalus and the other outlaws are praised for their *τόλμα* and *εὐχειρία* and *ἀρετή* in resisting Antigonus' forces:[87] it did Docimus no harm to dwell on the courageous last stand of his old associates when there was no longer fear of contradiction on the major issue.

Another man of distinction who could have influenced the slant of the history was Medeius of Larisa, the companion of Alexander famous for his fatal drinking party. Like Docimus, he had been a partisan of Perdiccas, but later turns up as Antigonus' admiral, and served also under Demetrius.[88] In 313 he commanded the naval force which acted with the land army of Docimus in liberating Miletus, and shortly afterwards attacked Cassander's fleet at Oreus in Euboea.[89] Medeius would have been a principal source for these operations; likewise for the battle of Salamis, where he commanded the victorious left wing of Demetrius' fleet.[90] Medeius came from the great family of the Aleuadae of Thessaly, who had their seat at Larisa. Towards the end of the fourth century he was voted honours both by the Athenians and by the town of Gonnoi, near to Larisa.[91] In the same year Athens honoured another Larisan, Oxythemis son of Hippostratus, who was possibly Medeius' nephew, and son of the Hippostratus whom Antigonus appointed *strategos* of Media in 316 to 315.[92] These Thessalian aristocrats, the great men of their native towns, like Eumenes in Cardia, would all be known to Hieronymus. The honours given to Medeius and Oxythemis by the Athenians were the consequence of

[86] Diod. xix.75.3; xx.107.3–4. Cf. Robert, *Rév. de Phil.* viii (1934), pp. 267 f.; Launey, *Recherches,* i.342. J. Kaerst, *RE* s.v. 'Dokimos', col. 1274, nos. 4 and 5, distinguishes the general of Perdiccas from Docimus the general of Antigonus. Cf. also Paus. i.8.1 for Docimus and Lysimachus.

[87] Diod. xix.16.1, 16.5.

[88] Berve, ii, p. 261; B. Helly, *Gonnoi,* i, Amsterdam, 1973, p. 84.

[89] Diod. xix.75.3, 75.7.

[90] Diod. xx.50.3, cf. 52.2.

[91] F. Geyer, *RE* s.v. 'Medeios', cols. 103–4; *Syll.*³ 342; Helly, *Gonnoi,* i, loc. cit. and ii, no. 1.

[92] *Syll.*³ 343; cf. Diod. xix.46.5 and Dittenberger, *Syll.* notes 2–3, ad. loc. Cf. Robert, *Hellenica* ii, 1946, pp. 15 ff. esp. 28 f., on the importance of Oxythemis and Adeimantus as agents of Demetrius in Greece.

Demetrius' second visit to Athens: it was at this time that he conquered Thessaly (Diod. xx.110, Larisa is taken first, but kindly
treated), and following Jacoby's conjecture, it was at this point in his
history that Hieronymus included his archaeology of Thessaly.[93]
Medeius, with his ancestral connections at Larisa and his enormous
prestige in 302 as the companion of Demetrius, now master of Larisa,
would be able to facilitate Hieronymus' researches into Thessalian
history, and it might have been he who inspired and encouraged the
idea of this excursus: the Aleuadae, after all, would play a prominent
part in any history of Thessaly.

Strabo cites the researches of Cyrsilus of Pharsalus and Medeius of
Larisa, 'men who had campaigned with Alexander', for his *archaeo-
logia* of Armenia: the eponymous settler of Armenia was a certain
Armenos, who came from the town of Armenion in Thessaly between
Pherae and Larisa; Armenian costume was really Thessalian costume,
and the same went for their armour, which was also used by the Medes;
Armenian monuments called 'Jasonia' recalled the travels of the hero
Jason; and so on.[94] The patriotic pride of the Thessalians had been
fostered by the distinguished part they had played in Alexander's
expedition, and they maintained their role as the crack cavalry of the
Greek world after 323: the Thessalian force under Menon of Pharsalus
played the chief part on the Greek side in the Lamian War; numerous
Thessalians could be found in Egypt in the Ptolemaic army;[95] and the
founder of the Hellenistic town at Ai Khanum on the Oxus in Bactria
bore the Thessalian name Cineas.[96] It was natural that Thessalian
aristocrats who found their traditional warrior virtues prized by the
Macedonian princes of the fourth century, and who produced in
Lysimachus a king of Macedon, should wish to ascribe Thessalian
origins to some of the new lands of the East which they had helped to
conquer, and to link the resurgent glory of the Thessalians to their
heroic past.[97] Menon's daughter Phthia was the mother of Pyrrhus,
who boasted descent from both Achilles and Priam; and it may be
supposed that his claims to a heroic ancestry were derived partly from
the Thessalian side. The aetiologies invented by Medeius and Cyrsilus

[93] Hier. F17, cf. App. I, p. xxi. Duris also had a history of Thessaly at this point in his
work: cf. *F. Gr. Hist.* 76 F11, with *F. Gr. Hist*, IID, p. 547. For the view that Hieronymus
wrote in reply to Duris, see J. G. Droysen, *Hermes* xi (1876), cf. Jacoby, *RE* 'Hieronymus', cols. 1549–50.

[94] Strabo xi.530 ff.; cf. Robert, *CRAI* 1968, pp. 435 ff.; Walbank, *The Hellenistic
World*, 1981, p. 63.

[95] Launey, *Recherches* i, pp. 215 ff., ii, pp. 1139–43.

[96] Robert, art. cit., pp. 422 ff. Cf. also Plut. *Demetr.* xxix.5, Thorax of Larisa stayed by
Antigonus' body on the battlefield of Ipsus.

[97] On Lysimachus' origins see below, n. 234.

belong to a type of myth-making which flourished in the Hellenistic period and which was inspired by the need felt by the Greeks to bring the newly discovered lands of both East and West into connection with the familiar myths and legends of the old Greek world: the best example of this process is the work of Timaeus, who explored the early history and legends of Italy and Sicily.[98] Exactly how Hieronymus' archaeology of Thessaly may have served the interests of his Thessalian friends cannot be discovered in Strabo's brief citation; but it may be conjectured that it followed this characteristic pattern—as, no doubt, did his archaeology of Rome; and it is not impossible that he drew on the researches of Medeius himself and similar native productions.

For other items, too, Hieronymus made use of material whose reliability seemed guaranteed by the signature of a famous man. For Pyrrhus' wars in the West we know that he drew on the 'royal *hypomnemata*', which were either the actual memoirs of Pyrrhus or at least an official record kept by 'ghost' writers in Pyrrhus' chancellery.[99] From Plutarch's citation of Hieronymus in his *Pyrrhus* it is clear that the Royal Memoirs recorded the losses sustained by each side in Pyrrhus' battles against the Romans, and it may be supposed that they were equally helpful on other military details: Hieronymus perhaps constructed his report of the battle at Asculum in part from these records; and if the ἔργων ὑπομνήματα to which Pausanias refers are the same as Hieronymus' $\text{βασιλικὰ ὑπομνήματα}$, they mentioned the provenance of the elephants which Pyrrhus used at Heraclea.[100]

Hieronymus' choice of royal narrative documents was not always so happy, as Diodorus' account of Seleucus' return to Babylon suggests.[101] Survivors of the expedition of 312 would have remembered it vividly, and doubtless Hieronymus had opportunities to talk to some of Seleucus' 800 companions; but the authority he chose seemingly was not oral, but documentary. Diodorus concludes this narrative with the statement that Seleucus now wrote to Ptolemy and his other friends about his achievements, which had given him the stature of a king; and there is a strong presumption that a copy of this letter—the one sent to Cassander, which Hieronymus could have seen in the archives at Pella—formed the basis of the foregoing chapters. This narrative contains clear traces of early Seleucid propaganda, in its emphasis on the popularity of Seleucus among his subjects and his *philanthropia*,

---

[98] Cf. Pearson, *YCS* xxiv (1975), pp. 192 ff.
[99] Plut. *Pyrrh.* xxi.2 = Hier. F12; cf. Dion. Hal. *Ant. Rom.* xix.11; and Paus, i.12.2; but on the last passage see Segre, *Historia* ii (1928), pp. 223 ff.
[100] Paus. i.12.3–4; cf. Segre, art. cit.
[101] Diod. xix.90 ff.

and especially in its reference to the oracle of Branchidae and Seleucus' dream of Alexander. Hieronymus held no special brief for the Seleucids: the extreme interest of the contemporary letter in which the founder of the dynasty set out his claims, apparently led him to prefer its testimony, and his editorial skill was not up to expunging the royal bias.[102]

The principles which Hieronymus followed in collecting and sifting his material may have been set out in a lost preface; but without an explicit statement it is sometimes hard to see why he preferred one version, or whether he had been unduly credulous. There was, at least, a tendency to prefer official versions of events, and—a closely related practice—to follow the 'best' authorities in terms of rank and distinction. This was not an unnatural procedure, nor was it new: Herodotus had consulted λογίοι ἄνδρες, people who came from circles where knowledge might have been expected: 'they were men from the ruling classes who not only cultivated the tradition of their own families, but, as leading men, had a certain knowledge of the nature of the administration or the history of the state.'[103] Thucydides, it seems, had, like everyone else, fallen under the spell of Alcibiades' personality, and unconsciously relayed Alcibiades' view of the events in which he had played a part.[104] Hieronymus' personal contact with many of his informants made him the more exposed to such distortions. On the one hand were trusted friends like Philippus. There were also the grand personages who surrounded his masters, men like Pithon, Docimus,

---

[102] One may compare Arrian's reasons for preferring Ptolemy as his source: Πτολεμαῖος δὲ πρὸς τῷ ξυστρατεῦσαι ὅτι καὶ αὐτῷ βασιλεῖ ὄντι αἰσχρότερον ἤ τῳ ἄλλῳ ψεύσασθαι ἦν (*Anab.* i.i.i). This curious statement recalls a passage in the questions and answers section of the *Letter of Aristeas* (206): 'How should the king adhere to the truth?' asks Philadelphus; and the Jewish elder replies 'By realising that lying brings great shame on all men, but especially on kings; having the power to do what they like, what reason have they for lying?' Aristeas in this section is probably indebted to *Peri Basileias* literature of an earlier date (for a recent discussion see O. Murray, *J. Th. Stud.* n.s. xviii (1967), pp. 337 ff.). Truth-telling then, was regarded as a Hellenistic royal virtue, and conceivably Arrian accepted a claim made by Ptolemy himself in the preface to his history of Alexander, to the effect that he, being a king, was φιλαλήθης; cf. Pearson, *Lost Histories*, p. 194 n. 27. (This, of course, depends on Ptolemy having written after he became king: for another view see Badian, *Gnomon*, xxxiii (1961), p. 665, = *Studies*, p. 258; cf. Brunt, Loeb edn. of Arrian, vol. i, p. xxi.) Brunt, *JRS* xiv (1974), pp. 8 f., argues that veracity was an old Roman, more than a Greek virtue; but cf. also Wilcken, *S. B. Berlin*, 1923, pp. 168 ff.: in a papyrus of *c.* 100 BC the gymonosophists tell Alexander that a king should not lie.

[103] Jacoby, *Atthis*, 1949, p. 216 (he goes on to compare these men with the 4th-century Atthidographers); cf. *RE* Suppl. ii, cols. 410–12. Cf. B. Mitchell, *JHS* xcv (1975), pp. 75 ff. on Herodotus' aristocratic informants in Samos.

[104] Brunt, *REG* lxv (1952), pp. 59 ff., with the reservations of Andrewes, *Historical Commentary on Thucydides, V*, on Book viii, 1981, *passim*.

Medeius, and others of power and rank who are mentioned only briefly in the literary sources: Phoenix, for example, the general of Antigonus who deserted him in 302 for Lysimachus, possibly the same man as Phoenix of Tenedos, who had formerly served under Eumenes;[105] or another Greek, Aristodemus of Miletus, the flatterer of Antigonus, who seems to have been employed chiefly as envoy and diplomat, and would have been a useful source for affairs in Greece between 315 and the revolt of Ptolemaeus in 310;[106] those, too, who are now known only from chance epigraphical finds, such as Adeimantus, organizer of the new League of Corinth, whom Robert has described as the second man in Greece after Demetrius.[107] Some might be relatives of Antigonus and Demetrius like Marsyas of Pella, eyewitness of the battle of Salamis and a potential source not just for this episode: his *Macedonica*, which apparently went down to 330 BC, would have given information on the background to the Macedonian conquests and could have supplied a literary example to the younger historian.[108] The large number of personalities named is one of the distinctive features of Diodorus' history of the Diadochi, in itself showing that Diodorus' source was a contemporary who knew the people that mattered. These powerful men in the following of Antigonus and Demetrius were individuals with whom Hieronymus rubbed shoulders daily for a period of many years, and their influence on the tone of his history should not be underestimated. To question the statements of such people might be embarrassing at the time they were made, and to verify them difficult or impossible by the time Hieronymus came to write that part of his history; for unless the work were written simply as a diary, some time must have elapsed between events and their final writing up. It must be imagined that in the course of his long career Hieronymus took notes on many conversations which could not be checked later, because those with whom they had originated, along with those who might have known otherwise, were no

---

[105] Diod. xx.107.5; xviii.40.2–3; though it may be Phoenix of Tenedos who followed Ptolemaeus when he revolted from Antigonus in 310 and is described as ἕνα τῶν πιστοτάτων φίλων (i.e. of Ptolemaeus): Diod. xx.19.2.

[106] Diod. xix.57.5, cf. xix.66.2. Antigonus' letter to the Scepsians mentions Prepelaus and Aristodemus as envoys in the matter of the truce between Cassander and 'Ptolemaeus' (Welles, *R C* i, lines 9–12); the latter has plausibly been identified as the general of Antigonus, rather than Ptolemy of Egypt, and on this assumption, the Aristodemus of the inscription is likely to be Aristodemus the Milesian, who would have joined Ptolemaeus' staff after 313: see Bakhuizen, *Salganeus*, p. 118 n. 40. For Aristodemus' later career cf. Plut. *Demetr.* 17 and 9: cf. O. Müller, *Antigonos Monophthalmos und 'das Jahr der Könige'*, Bonn, 1973, p. 81 for the view that the story of Aristodemus' flattery of Antigonus is untrue, and derived from an inferior source.

[107] Robert, *Hellenica* ii, 1946, pp. 15 ff.

[108] Diod. xx.50, *F. Gr. Hist.* 135; cf. Laqueur, *RE* xiv s.v. 'Marsyas' no. 8, cols. 1996 f.

longer alive. The choice, then, was either to omit important episodes altogether if he suspected their veracity—a purist's view which would virtually paralyse the historian's activity—or conscientiously to include information as it had been given to him. It would have become progressively easier to compare accounts and estimate their value as he came to deal with more recent times.[109]

It may be supposed that Hieronymus' ambitions as a historian underwent some evolution in the period which elapsed between his earliest attempts to keep a record of his times and the final completion of a grand work on the Successors. As he convalesced from the trauma of Gabiene there perhaps came to Hieronymus the idea of writing a historical encomium on Eumenes; and it would have been at this time that he talked to Pithon, who was killed the same winter, and perhaps to Docimus, like himself, if by a different route, a recent arrival at Antigonus' headquarters. The stories these men had to tell him, about the shortcomings of Antigonus on the one hand, and on the other the last stand of Eumenes' fellow exiles, would be congenial to such a project.[110] Later, as his perspective on the period lengthened, Hieronymus may have begun to see the nature of his task in a different light: real *historia* called for a more critical attitude, and it had to be admitted that Pithon had always been a trouble-maker, a view which Monophthalmus would endorse, and that Hieronymus himself had been well treated by the latter. The belief that Eumenes could do no wrong was not one to be relinquished so easily, and Hieronymus' original interpretation of Eumenes' career probably remained largely unchanged.

Documents

A recent study identifies no less than seventy-four quotations or citations of documents in the accounts which derive from Hieronymus. They include treaties, city decrees, royal edicts, royal and personal letters. Some were paraphrased, others apparently quoted verbatim in the manner of Thucydides (Alexander's proclamation to the Greek exiles and Polyperchon's edict of 318, as given in Diodorus, purport to be copies of genuine documents, though some clauses may have been omitted).[111] Treaties to which the sources make bare allusion, like the Peace of 311, must have been described in detail by Hieronymus; and

[109] On the date of composition, see below, pp. 173 ff.
[110] For Pithon's view of Antigonus, cf. below, ch. 5, pp. 218 f.
[111] K. Rosen, *AC* x (1967), pp. 41 ff., for a detailed analysis of passages where documentary material is traceable to Hieronymus. Rosen's conclusions are here accepted in a general way, though not all his examples convince; see below, pp. 134 f., for problems in documents connected with Eumenes.

the extensive use of documents is a characteristic of Diodorus xviii–xx which has largely contributed to Hieronymus' reputation for 'scientific' historiography.[112] The idea that historiography was primarily an art rather than a science dominated its evolution throughout the classical and Hellenistic periods, and there are signs that even Thucydides had doubts about the propriety of transcribing his written sources: of the sections of his work which include documentary material, Book v and Book viii are certainly unfinished, and it has been argued that in a final revision he would have abandoned the documents and perhaps filled out the work instead with political speeches.[113] Hellenistic histories, partly through Peripatetic influence, were much more liberal in citing decrees, letters, and similar material, though frequently the fashion led to the inclusion of spurious documents. Hieronymus took unusual pains to collect authentic documentary material, and his inclusion of such documentation makes him for the modern critic superior to historians with greater pretensions to style. Apparently it caused him no embarrassment to report *in extenso* the long edicts and flowery epistles of the Hellenistic chancelleries, although in doing so he sealed the fate of his history: Dionysius' artistic sensibilities were outraged by a narrative which was not only devoid of the normal anodyne of rhetoric, but regularly interrupted by indigestible chunks of foreign matter, that all too starkly declared itself to be ὠφέλιμον.

Hieronymus had easy access to documents. Conceivably he began his career as *grammateus* in the chancellery of Alexander or of Eumenes—though this is partly an inference from the frequency with which documents are mentioned. As the friend of Eumenes, he would anyway have been able to inspect many state papers in the possession of Alexander's former secretary. This is often observed in connection with Alexander's 'Last Plans' and their possible transmission via Hieronymus;[114] but many other papers of at least equal interest to the future historian lay on Eumenes' desk by summer 323. Alexander's chancellery had handled a whole range of business, from personal correspondence with individuals in Macedonia to diplomatic transactions with foreign powers; the reports of satraps and members of the

[112] There are no documents in Book xvii (cf. above, ch. 2, p. 37) and almost none in the Sicilian and Italian sections of Diodorus xix and xx (cf. Rosen, art. cit., p. 42).

[113] Schwartz, *Das Geschichtswerk des Thucydides*, Bonn, 1929, pp. 44 f.; Wade-Gery, *OCD*[2] s.v. 'Thucydides', p. 1068.

[114] Cf. ch. 3, pp. 131 ff. See Lehmann–Haupt, *Hermes* xxxvi (1901), pp. 319 f., for the view that Eumenes sent a copy of the Royal Diary to Hieronymus, who used it in writing his history: it is certain, however, that Hieronymus' history began only after Alexander's death (cf. ch. 3, pp. 76 ff. on the title).

military staff would have been kept here, together with copies of the letters and memoranda of Alexander himself; and in addition to its normal work, the chancellery was given the task of collecting and organizing all the scientific information gathered on the march through the East. The accumulated data on botany and other natural phenomena was later incorporated in the royal archives at Babylon (Theophrastus made use of it in his *History of Plants*), and probably much of the other paperwork of Alexander's lifetime was stored at Babylon and ultimately made available to scholars.[115] This body of information on the military, civil, personal, and scientific business of Alexander's reign, filed under the direction of Eumenes at the time when he was chief secretary, provided Hieronymus with the whole background to the Macedonian conquests: from it he could have drawn documents relating to the opening episodes of his history, recording the administrative and military appointments made at Babylon and Triparadeisos; the scheme of his Geography, too, could have been founded on the observations of Alexander's bematists. The correspondence of the department was kept in Attic Greek, though a number of papers must have come in which were written in Aramaic, the *koine* of the Achaemenid empire. Documents written 'in Syrian letters' are mentioned on more than one occasion in Diodorus/Hieronymus, and we hear that when Eumenes forged a letter to Peucestas in the name of Orontes of Armenia, he made it appear authentic by writing Συρίοις γράμμασιν.[116] One need not suppose, of course, that Eumenes and Hieronymus must have been notable linguists: arguing from the fact that no interpreters are mentioned, one might, it has been said, 'find oneself believing that Alexander the Great spoke and understood some very peculiar languages'.[117]

Documents connected with Eumenes and his later masters Hieronymus might have seen at the time they were drawn up or received: those mentioned in our sources are almost invariably concerned with Eumenes and Antigonus. He knew in detail, for example, the terms of the oath which Eumenes swore to Antigonus to secure his release from Nora, and the contents of the letters which passed between Eumenes

[115] For the work of Alexander's chancellery, see Berve, i, pp. 42–55; Alexander's care in maintaining complete records is illustrated by Plut. *Eum*. ii.3: after a fire in Eumenes' tent, Alexander wrote to the satraps and generals everywhere, ordering them to send Eumenes copies of the documents which had been destroyed. For Theophrastus' use of records at Babylon, see Strabo ii.1.16.

[116] Diod. xix.23.3; cf. Polyaen. iv.8.3.

[117] D. Lewis, *J. Th. Stud.* n.s. xx (1969), p. 584 (review of Sevenster, *Do You Know Greek?*). Cf. ch. i, p. 10 n. 33, for knowledge of Persian among Alexander's staff.

and his correspondents in Macedonia.[118] As Eumenes' personal assistant, he no doubt played a part in the drafting of some of these documents. That the first letter of Polyperchon to Eumenes (Diod. xviii. 57.3–4) was actually a forgery drawn up by Eumenes, with the connivance of Hieronymus, is not, however, a plausible suggestion.[119] According to a recent hypothesis, this letter, which offered Eumenes a co-regency with Polyperchon and hinted at an early return to Macedon for the Macedonian troops, was the deciding factor for Antigonus' officers in allowing Eumenes to leave Nora: the second (genuine) letter of Polyperchon (Diod. xviii.58.1–4), which arrived after the escape from Nora, refers only to Eumenes' appointment as general in Asia. It is true that on another occasion Eumenes is said to have forged a letter (see above), and for reasons similar to those here suggested; another instance of sharp practice was the alteration of Eumenes' oath to Antigonus. In both cases, however, our sources, so far from trying to conceal the deceit, actually parade it as an illustration of Eumenes' cleverness. If Polyperchon's first letter had been a forgery, it ought to have qualified as a stratagem of the same type. At this stage Polyperchon's main object must have been to prevent a coalition between Eumenes and Antigonus.[120] The problem is in fact one of a more general nature, because nearly *all* the documents connected with Eumenes demonstrate either his close links with the Argeads, or his high moral and military qualities. This is true not only of his correspondence with Olympias and Polyperchon, and the forged letter sent to Peucestas, but also of earlier transactions with Perdiccas and Antipater. In a letter of *c.*321 Perdiccas ordered Neoptolemus and Alcetas to obey Eumenes διά τε τὴν στρατηγίαν αὐτοῦ καὶ διὰ τὴν τῆς πίστεως βεβαιότητα. Replying to the offer of alliance made by Antipater and Craterus in 321, Eumenes said that he would always aid the injured party and would rather lose his life than his honour.[121] Again, if, as seems likely, the analysis of Eumenes' political position set out at Diod. xviii.42.1–2 represents the substance of the message which Hieronymus' embassy conveyed to Antipater at this time, Eumenes here also officially advertised himself as excelling in intelligence and

---

[118] Plut. *Eum.* xii.1–2. Diod. xviii.57.2–4, 58.1–4; Plut. *Eum.* xiii.1. Cf. Rosen, art. cit., pp. 69 ff.

[119] P. Briant, *REA* lxxv (1973), pp. 75 ff. For Eumenes as a practised letter writer see Hammond and Griffith, *Macedonia* ii, p. 381 and App. 4, p. 714.

[120] Rosen, loc. cit., treats both letters as genuine, regarding the first as an offer, the second as containing the actual terms of Eumenes' appointment. Cf. Goukowsky, *Diodore XVIII*, note compl. à 57.3, 57.4: Polyperchon himself, rather than Eumenes, might have been bluffing in order to secure the adherence of those at Nora, when he suggested bringing a royal army to Asia.

[121] Diod. xviii.29.2; Plut. *Eum.* v.7–8. Cf. Rosen, art. cit., pp. 60 ff.

loyalty.[122] That such passages should be regarded as authentic clauses is highly questionable:[123] Perdiccas would hardly have cited Eumenes' *strategia* and *pistis* as reasons why Macedonian generals should subordinate themselves to his command. They cannot be dissociated from the tone of eulogy with which Eumenes was consistently depicted by Hieronymus, and it seems very likely that the historian coloured his account of these transactions in shades flattering to his fellow-countryman. To estimate the matter properly, we would need to know whether he quoted the letters verbatim in each case or whether he only paraphrased them (which would make remodelling and interpolation easy), and this can hardly be decided from Diodorus' wording.[124] These documents or, as it may be, pseudo-documents, belong to the early, encomiastic section of the history: there is, at any rate, no reason to suspect falsification in those which concern Antigonus and Demetrius and which belong to the more mature part of Hieronymus' work.

A third fund of documentary material to which Hieronymus had access was the archive at Pella. Diodorus refers to the Macedonian archives in connection with the murder of Demades: Antipater had at first been well disposed to Demades, but after the death of Perdiccas certain letters were found ἐν τοῖς βασιλικοῖς γράμμασιν, in which Demades invited Perdiccas to cross into Europe against Antipater.[125] Perdiccas had died suddenly, with no time to destroy dangerous correspondence, and Demades' letters must have passed with the rest of the former regent's paraphernalia into the care of Antipater at Triparadeisos; thence to Macedon and closer scrutiny.[126] Here Hieronymus could have seen them at a later date. Also available to him at Pella would be Seleucus' letter (see above), and copies of the treaties of 311 and the settlement after Ipsus.[127] There is some evidence for Macedo-

---

[122] Cf. Briant, art. cit., p. 74.   [123] So Rosen, loc. cit., implies.
[124] Apparent traces of original phraseology at e.g. Plut. *Eum.* v.6, v.7–8: cf. Rosen, loc. cit.   [125] Diod. xviii.48.2.
[126] The description of Antipater as an 'old and rotten thread', which caused particular offence, is not mentioned by Diodorus, and may have been tactfully omitted by Hieronymus: Arrian (*Succ.* F9.14) and Plutarch (*Demosth.* xxxi.5, *Phoc.* xxx.9) could have found it in Athenian writers, who would have recorded the phrase with gusto. *Contra*, Rosen, art. cit., p. 63. The destruction of incriminating correspondence at a time of danger was recognized as a duty: cf. Plut. *Eum.* xvi. 2, Eumenes destroys his papers before Gabiene; Polyb. xviii.33.3, Philip V burns his correspondence after Cynoscephalae for the same reasons.
[127] Diod. xviii.10.1, οἷς ποτ' ἔφησεν ὁ Φίλιππος τὸν μὲν πόλεμον εἰρήνην ὑπάρχειν κ.τ.λ. apparently refers to Philip's letter to Athens of 340 (Ps.-Demosth. xii), and Hieronymus might have seen a copy of this letter at Pella: so Rosen, art. cit., p. 53. But the epigrammatic character of the sentence, which is a parenthesis in the narrative, suggests that it may be Diodorus' own addition. For the settlement after Ipsus, cf. Appian, *Syr.* ix.55.

nian royal records of a kind similar to the 'Memoirs' of Pyrrhus: Lucian in his *Encomium of Demosthenes* says that he once read the 'Journal of the Macedonian Kings', which gave an account of Antipater's dealings with Demosthenes: it gave him such pleasure, he reports, that he acquired his own copy of the book.[128] But the authenticity of such a compilation is highly suspect: granted that a work of this kind could have been modelled ultimately on real documents, that authentic copies of the official journal of an early Hellenistic court should be on sale in Lucian's day, and should make 'pleasurable reading', is most improbable. The existence of *hypomnemata*, perhaps not really to be distinguished from *basilika grammata*, is testified by Polyaenus, who records that when Antigonus (? Gonatas) gave audience to foreign embassies, he used to brief himself beforehand from the *hypomnemata*—ἐκ τῶν ὑπομνημάτων—and find out who the envoys were, whether they had visited him before, and what their business was about. Then when the audience took place everyone would be struck with admiration at the king's astonishing memory. (This is regarded as a 'stratagem'!)[129]

Other writings of the same kind are mentioned. According to Suidas, Antipater wrote a history of the Illyrian Wars of King Perdiccas, and published two volumes of his own correspondence.[130] The latter, if genuine, would have offered Hieronymus valuable material, and might have formed part of the 'Royal Memoirs' known to Lucian, which treated Antipater's relations with Demosthenes. Since the work is known only from a single reference, however, one cannot be confident that it was authentic. The common practice of writing, for pleasure or as a literary exercise, letters which were fathered on famous personages of the past, is best illustrated by the histories of Alexander and especially the Alexander Romance, in which the correspondence between the king and his mother and other important people has been swelled out by suitable imitations.[131] It became fashionable to include apocryphal letters even in more reputable histories. Eupolemus, in his work 'On the Kings in Judaea' quoted the letters of Solomon to the rulers of Egypt and Tyre; and it has been argued that the two letters which, according to Dionysius, were exchanged between Pyrrhus and Valerius Laevinus in 280 BC were the invention of the early Roman annalist Acilius, who wrote in Greek for a Greek audience, and naturally followed the vogue of contemporary

---

[128] Lucian, *Enc. Demosth.* 26.
[129] Polyaen. iv.6.2.
[130] Suidas, A270 Adler.
[131] Cf. App. I, pp. 254 f. See also Kaerst, *Gesch. d. Hell.*, i, p. 376 n. 2, on the letters of Alexander in Plutarch and the other sources.

Greek historiography.[132] Rhetorical compositions like these are of course to be distinguished from forgeries which served some political end, like the letter forged by Eumenes. Antipater's letters—many, presumably, addressed to Alexander—might belong to the same genre as the spurious letters of the Alexander 'vulgate' and the Alexander Romance. On the other hand, apocryphal correspondence and other supposedly autobiographical documents were able to gain currency in this period precisely because real ones flourished. The Memoirs of Pyrrhus must be regarded as genuine; and they are characteristic of contemporary political memoir writing. Aratus published memoirs in thirty books, with the object, as it appears from Polybius and Plutarch, of exculpating himself and imputing blame to his enemies; Demetrius of Phaleron wrote a work περὶ τῆς δεκαετίας, which was evidently an apologia for his ten-year government of Athens.[133] The distinction between true autobiography and the official memoir was not a sharp one, and Antipater's letters (real or pseudonymous) belong to this class of writing.

The genre of memoir-writing was characteristic of a scientific and record-conscious age. The collection of historical records was treated in at least one instance as an activity parallel to the collecting of botanical, geographical, or aetiological data, which Aristotle and his followers pursued: Craterus 'the Macedonian' (probably the half-brother of Gonatas) published in at least nine books a collection of Athenian decrees dating mainly from the fifth century and described as Συναγωγὴ τῶν ψηφισμάτων.[134] They were quoted verbatim, and a commentary attached. It was perhaps Craterus' work that inspired Hieronymus to include the Athenian version of Alexander's 'exiles' decree, and to record the decrees relating to the Lamian War and the settlements imposed on Athens by Antipater and Cassander.[135] In Athens the activities of the Peripatetic school and of local historians like Philochorus created a climate which particularly encouraged research of this kind.

Logoi and Archaiologiai

It remains to consider Hieronymus' methods in those parts of his work

[132] Bickerman, *CP* xlii (1947), p. 146.

[133] Diog. Laert. v.80. Cf. G. Misch, *A History of Autobiography in Antiquity*, i, Trans. Dickes, London, 1950, pp. 203 ff.

[134] Craterus, *F. Gr. Hist.* 342, with Jacoby, comm. IIIB, pp. 94 ff., esp. p. 95. In Jacoby's view, Craterus was possibly a pupil of Aristotle himself. Tarn, *Antigonus Gonatas*, pp. 342–4 identifies him with Antigonus' half-brother.

[135] Diod. xviii.8.4: the special provision about the Samian exiles shows that Hieronymus copied the text of the draft addressed specifically to the Athenians; cf. Rosen, art. cit., pp. 53 ff.; Diod. xviii.18.4–6; 74.3.

which discussed ethnography, geography, prehistory, or other matters of general interest. Later authors tended to find these sections more interesting than the political narrative, and six out of the eighteen citations of Hieronymus imply a geographical or other kind of digression. To be considered here are the archaeologies of Thebes, Thessaly, and Rome, and the excursus on Nabataean Arabia and the Asphalt Lake.

The *archaeologia* was a common Hellenistic form, used extensively by Timaeus and an important ingredient in ethnographical studies. Early Hellenistic ethnographers gave a systematic treatment to the 'archaeology' of a country, to its geography and inhabitants, its history, and its laws, customs, society, and religion: with variations in the arrangement of topics, this is the pattern found first in Hecataeus of Abdera, and then, following his example, in Megasthenes, Berossus, and Manetho. It was a development of the less formal method followed by Herodotus in his excursuses.[136] *Archaeologiai* in a political history were naturally more limited in scope than those of ethnographical works, and were tied closely to the historical narrative: the purpose of Hieronymus' description of both Thessaly and Rome was apparently to introduce the enemy of his protagonist in that part of the history—Demetrius and Pyrrhus respectively. The technique of introducing an opponent by giving a sketch of his land and history is one which can be found everywhere in Herodotus; but the paradigm for a political historian like Hieronymus was undoubtedly Thucydides' *archaeologia* of Sicily at the beginning of his sixth book;[137] here Thucydides described, as a prelude to the Athenian attack on Sicily, the size of the island, the earliest settlers, the non-Hellenic peoples, and the numerous Greek foundations. Hieronymus' account of Thessaly apparently followed the same pattern: the plain of Thessaly and Magnesia, he stated, is 3,000 stades in circumference; it was first settled by Pelasgians, but these were driven out by Lapiths; then comes a list of all the towns on the Pelasgian plain; and the citation ends with some explanatory details about the eponymous founder of the town of Mopsion. Possibly he organized his description of Crete along similar lines: we know only that he gave measurements of the island, and the context is quite uncertain.[138] Dionysius gives no details in citing Hieronymus as author of a Roman archaeology, except that this was the first of its kind and was merely on outline.[139] It may be conjectured,

---

[136] See O. Murray, 'Herodotus and Hellenistic Culture', *CQ* n.s. xxii (1972), pp. 207 ff.

[137] Cf. Jacoby, *RE* 'Hieronymus', col. 1548.

[138] Thuc. vi.1–5; Hier. F17, F18.   [139] Hier. F13.

however, that it had the same object as Thucydides' excursus on Sicily, which prefaced the rash attack of the Athenians on Syracuse. Thucydides concludes his account of the island: τοσαῦτα ἔθνη Ἑλλήνων καὶ βαρβάρων Σικελίαν ᾤκει, καὶ ἐπὶ τοσήνδε οὖσαν αὐτὴν οἱ Ἀθηναῖοι στρατεύειν ὥρμηντο, ἐφιέμενοι μὲν τῇ ἀληθεστάτῃ προφάσει τῆς πάσης ἄρξαι, βοηθεῖν δὲ ἅμα εὐπρεπῶς βουλόμενοι τοῖς ἑαυτῶν ξυγγενέσι.[140] Pyrrhus' invasion of Italy and Sicily offered a close parallel: the appeal of the Tarentines, like the appeal of Egesta to Athens, inflamed his passion for conquest—his πλεονεξία, the subject of frequent homilies in Plutarch's account—and despite counsels of restraint, he was unable to renounce his hopes of what he desired: ὧν δὲ ὠρέγετο τὰς ἐλπίδας ἀφεῖναι μὴ δυνάμενον.[141] Six years were wasted in a vain attempt to combat the seemingly inexhaustible reserves of Roman manpower.[142] With varying degrees of moral vehemence, all our sources agree in condemning the folly of Pyrrhus' Western expedition: for Hieronymus it seems to have constituted the ultimate example of that excessive lust for power which had ruined many of the first generation of the Successors. What more effective introduction than to characterize Pyrrhus' dour opponents and outline the true magnitude of their resources? According to Pausanias, who may here be close to Hieronymus, the arrival of the Tarentines, appealing for assistance against Rome's encroachments, at once led Pyrrhus to contemplate glorious victory over the Trojan colony:[143] this would be the natural point for Hieronymus to usher in the Romans and explain, according to current beliefs, who they were and how ill founded were the king's expectations.

If Hieronymus' descriptions of Thessaly and Rome were incidental background, modelled on Thucydides' *Sikelika*, the question arises, to what extent they were pieces of original research. Contemptuous of the meanderings of Herodotus, Thucydides did not waste his own time making detailed inquiries about the Sicilian foundations: we know that he relied heavily on the existing work of the local historian, Antiochus of Syracuse.[144] For his *archaeologiai* of Thebes and Thessaly Hieronymus was probably able to follow a similar procedure. Local histories of Thebes would certainly be available: 'ktisis' literature had been in vogue since the time of Cadmus and Hellanicus, and it may be imagined that the new settlers of Thebes after 316 would be anxious to

[140] Thuc. vi.6.1.

[141] Plut. *Pyrrh*. xii.2–3, xii.5, xiii.1–2, xiv, *passim*, xxvi.1; xiv.8.

[142] Plut. *Pyrrh*. xxi.10: τοῖς δὲ Ῥωμαίοις ὥσπερ ἐκ πηγῆς οἴκοθεν ἐπιρρεούσης ἀναπληρούμενον εὐπόρως καὶ ταχὺ τὸ στρατόπεδον.

[143] Paus. i.11.7 ff; cf. App. I, F13.

[144] A. W. Gomme, A. Andrewes, K. Dover, *Hist. Comm. Thuc.*, vol. iv, pp. 198 ff.

reaffirm the antiquity and prestige of the city.[145] (A certain self-consciousness on the part of another of Cassander's city foundations, Cassandreia, is suggested by the title of Lycophron's historical tragedy, *Cassandreis*.)[146] The foundation legends of Thebes as recorded under the year 316 differ in certain details from the version Diodorus gives in Book iv, where he was probably using the mythographical compilation of Pseudo-Apollodorus; and it differs also from the version in Herodotus.[147] Diodorus may therefore have had access via Hieronymus to an early Hellenistic version of the foundation (which could also have been one of the sources of Pseudo-Apollodorus). The possibility that Hieronymus used written sources for his survey of early Thessalian history has been already suggested: a literary as well as a personal connection with Demetrius' companion Medeius of Larisa, who wrote on Thessalian legends and colonization, is not unlikely.

The archaeology of Rome was a different and altogether more ambitious venture, because Dionysius expressly states that it was the *first* proper Greek account of Rome (Hier. F13). An extensive use of written sources was therefore ruled out, including, it seems, the *Memoirs* of Pyrrhus, since Dionysius, who knew about the *Memoirs*, does not mention them in this connection. The project demanded original research. Almost certainly Hieronymus did not travel in the West. He had access to two channels of detailed information: one through the survivors of Pyrrhus' campaigns; the other through Romans, Italians, or Italian Greeks settled in or visiting Greece. The second category comprised not only the Italian traders who are known to us from inscriptions of Chios and Rhodes, but people of some standing, like Volceius, a man who was given proxeny status by the Aetolians *c.*263 and who called himself Ῥωμαῖος.[148] Volceius' business is not known, but some of the Italians who could be met in Greece at this time may have been representing the commercial interests of Roman families. The crude prosopography which can be reconstructed for the middle Republic suggests, despite its limitations, that senatorial interest in overseas affairs was concentrated in a group of

[145] Jacoby, *Atthis*, p. 184; *F. Gr. Hist.* 4 F66; 489 T1.
[146] Cf. Tarn, *Antigonos Gonatas*, p. 186 with n. 62: the inhabitants regularly styled themselves 'Cassandreis' rather than 'Makedones'; this was because Cassandreia was a *polis*: similarly the inhabitants of Pella are called 'Pellaioi'.
[147] Diod. iv.64–7; cf. Schwartz, *RE* s.v. 'Diodoros', no. 38, cols. 673 ff.; Herodotus v.57–61. R. J. Buck, *A History of Boeotia*, Univ. of Alberta Press, 1979, identifies three distinct traditions about early Boeotia in the work of Greek historians, of which that in Diodorus/Hieronymus is one (pp. 46 f., 50, 77).
[148] Cf. App. I, F13, for early contacts between Rome and Greece and allusions to Rome in Greek writers before Hieronymus.

families, of which the principal were the Manlii, Fulvii, Postumii, Valerii, and Sulpicii. These names, with the notable addition of the Claudii, are prominent in the Macedonian wars of the late third century: they can be traced back as far as the embassy sent to Athens, it is reported, in 454 to contemplate the laws of Solon; and there is evidence that this group guided Rome's relations with the Hellenistic states from the last years of the fourth century.[149] The exact nature of the 'Greek lobby' in the Senate is uncertain, but directly or indirectly it must have been commercial. Commercial relations between Greece and Italy had declined since the sixth century, but with the extension of Roman power over the Italian peninsula during the fourth century more enterprising senatorial families began to look beyond Italy and perhaps to seek a market for the sale of agricultural produce from their estates: the prohibition of the *Lex Claudia* of 218 presupposes such activity. By the mid-third century it must have been possible to encounter the representatives of these energetic and outward looking families in the major Greek ports, and Roman 'expansionists' would perhaps be not unwilling to satisfy the curious about Roman history, in pride or as advertisement. There is said to have been diplomatic contact between Demetrius and Rome: Strabo relates that Demetrius sent an embassy to Rome to complain about the depredations of pirates from Antium; but the story is at least doubtful, since Rome had reduced Antium in 337 and destroyed her naval force.[150]

Whether Hieronymus might have derived 'accurate' knowledge of Rome from Pyrrhus' soldiers or his prisoners of war must be uncertain. Plutarch relates that Pyrrhus' adviser, the Thessalian Cineas, who was sent to Rome to negotiate after the battle of Heraclea, conversed there with the 'best men' and observed the life and manner of the Romans and the excellence of their *politeia*, all of which he reported to Pyrrhus; but Roman patriotic sources have been at work here.[151] However, veterans of Pyrrhus' expedition, as well as the official memoirs of Pyrrhus, would be informative on the course of the Italian campaigns and on the character and composition of the Roman army. Hieronymus was here, as elsewhere on military matters, exceptionally well informed and lucid in his presentation. His casualty figures for the major battles, which were taken from the *Memoirs*, and his account of Asculum, probably from the same source, have been mentioned.[152] It

---

[149] Cf. W. G. G. Forrest, *JRS* xlvi (1956), pp. 169 ff.

[150] Strabo v.232.

[151] Plut. *Pyrrh.* xix.4–5. Cineas himself may not have survived the expedition, since he is not mentioned after his mission to Sicily in 279–8 (ibid., xxii.3).

[152] See above, p. 128.

has, too, been suggested very plausibly that Hieronymus was responsible for certain military details on the Roman armies in Dionysius' history of Pyrrhus. Dionysius gives a clear description of the use of a heavy thrusting spear for hand to hand fighting by 'those whom they call πρίγκιπες' (xx.ii): but *principes* no longer existed at the time when Dionysius wrote, and the whole account suggests a contemporary Greek historian writing for a Greek public: naturally one thinks of Hieronymus. He seems to have understood, without having seen a Roman army in action, the way in which it operated and the reasons for its success. 'No other source explicitly points out, what is nevertheless clearly true, that the *principes* were the mainstay of a battle.'[153] Hieronymus thus perceived, and was one of the first to do so, a distinctive feature of the Roman system which was a source of her future power.

Certain peculiarities of the Roman outlook had been recognized by Greeks early in the third century: Duris had recorded the story of the *devotio* of Decius at Sentinum; and Callimachus commented on the rebuke of a Romam *matrona* to her son; Roman *Fides/Πίστις* is personified on the silver staters of Italian Locri after 277, when Locri placed herself under the protection of Rome—she crowns the figure of Roma seated before her.[154] The ethos which these instances demonstrate, that is, the traits which Greeks were beginning to associate peculiarly with Rome, might well arouse the interest of the historian who had made πίστις one of the cardinal qualities of his friend Eumenes.[155] After Pyrrhus' expedition, there can be traced some awareness among Greeks of the qualities of Roman government: Eratosthenes named the Romans after the Carthaginians in a list of the four best-governed barbarian nations, i.e. those which most nearly approached Greek standards; and Aristos of Cyprian Salamis (if it is right to place him in the mid-third century), could claim that Alexander had prophesied the future greatness of Rome after meeting Roman envoys.[156] Interest in specific Roman institutions first appears in the letter of Philip V to the Larisans: Philip's knowledge of the system of manumission and citizenship is remarkable, but not altogether accurate, and suggests that special studies of the Roman constitution had not so far been made by Greek writers.[157] Polybius first presented to the Greek world an analysis of Rome's political and

[153] E. Rawson, *PBSR* n.s. xxvi (1971), pp. 24–6.
[154] Duris, *F. Gr. Hist.* 76 F56; Callimachus frg. 107 (Pfeiffer); Head, *HN*[2], p. 104, fig. 57.
[155] See below, ch. 5, pp. 204 ff.
[156] Strabo i.4.9; Arr. *Anab.* vii.15.5; cf. Momigliano, *Alien Wisdom*, p. 16.
[157] *IG* IX.2, 517 = *Syll.*[3] 543.

military organization, as it appeared to him. Hieronymus' description of Roman methods of warfare is thus a very early specimen of Greek awareness that the Romans were different in specific and interesting ways from which Greeks might have something to learn.

The methods of fighting by which Rome had successfully resisted Pyrrhus would have had peculiar interest for Pyrrhus' enemies in Greece; and Macedon, with her shortage of native manpower, her dangerous northern borders, and her perennial struggle with Egypt and the discontented Greeks, in any case needed military ideas.[158] Gonatas was inventive: he had employed Gauls in his army with success, he enlisted the aid of pirates, and he was prepared to try out other novelties. During the peace after 255 he made ready for another round in the conflict with Ptolemy by creating a new navy, encouraged, as may be guessed, by reports of the successes which Rome, like Macedon traditionally a land-power, was winning over maritime Carthage.[159] It may be Gonatas, too, who was responsible for reorganizing the Macedonian standing army: an inscription of uncertain date, found in several blocks in the bed of the Strymon at Amphipolis, preserves some of the clauses of what was possibly a general *strategikos nomos* regulating conduct in Macedonian camps and garrisons.[160] The lettering of this inscription is ambiguous: a uniformly flat sigma should indicate the reign of Philip V, but other features could point to a date as early as the reign of Gonatas; and the concern shown for discipline in the camp is certainly consistent with the known preoccupations of a king whose military forces were permanently employed in garrisoning both the northern border and the Greek states under his suzerainty.[161] Whether these provisions owed anything to known Roman practice it is impossible to say. It is at least possible, however, that by the later part of the reign of Philip V, Roman institutions had influenced the organization of the Macedonian army. An inscription from Elymiotis, dated to Philip's forty-second year, i.e. 181 BC, after the second Macedonian War, uses the word πρωτολοχία in an unusual sense:[162] in the classic organization of the Macedonian army, this term would refer to the front rank of the companies of four *lochoi*, composed of sixteen men each;[163] but here there appear to be at least six πρωτολοχίαι. The sense might be that of ἐν τῷ πρώτῳ λόχῳ, that is, a whole company of picked troops. It might imply, on the other hand, that the front line

---

[158] On Macedonian manpower and garrisons cf. Tarn, op. cit., pp. 190, 193 f., 201 f.
[159] Ibid., p. 342.
[160] L. Moretti, *Iscrizione storiche ellenistiche,* ii, Florence, 1975, no. 114.
[161] For garrisons on the northern border, cf. Tarn, op. cit., pp. 201 f.; Polyb. ix.32 ff.
[162] Moretti, op. cit., ii, no. 110, line 13 (= *SEG* XIII.403).
[163] Cf. Asclep. *Tact.* ii.5; Arr. *Tact.* viii.1.

had been reorganized on the model of the Roman *principes*.[164] Earlier
in his reign Philip had been quick to notice the advantages of Roman
practice in maintaining the numbers of the citizen population;[165] and
direct contact with the Roman armies not only would bring home the
fact of their great reserves of manpower, but also provided a graphic
demonstration of the defects of traditional phalanx warfare when
confronted by Roman tactics. If Philip learned nothing from reading
Hieronymus' history of Pyrrhus in Italy, it is not likely that he missed
the lesson of Cynoscephalae.[166]

Hieronymus' description of Nabataean Arabia and the Dead Sea
(the 'asphalt lake') is preserved in some detail at Diodorus xix.94 ff.[167]
In 312 Antigonus had prepared to invade the land of the Nabataeans,
for reasons probably both strategic and commercial.[168] Hieronymus
played a part in the campaign, as leader of the expedition which
Antigonus sent to the Dead Sea, and his description of the country of
Nabataea and its people is at first hand.[169] The Nabataeans are introduced in the manner of the Thessalians and the Romans: after
announcing Antigonus' plan of attack, Diodorus depicts the character
of his barbarian opponents before recounting the actual campaign.
The model here, however, is not the Thucydidean *archaeologia*:
Thucydides did not offer a model for a purely ethnographic excursus,
and in his treatment of the Nabataeans it is clear that Hieronymus, like
Theopompus, looked back directly to Herodotus: 'der Bericht über
Demetrios' arabische Expedition . . . ist ganz so angelegt wie ein
Herodoteischen λόγος—etwa der über die Aithiopen.'[170]

Hieronymus seems to have described neither Nabataean history nor
the size of the country, as he did in his description of Thessaly: both, no
doubt, were difficult to ascertain at the time, and indeed remain
obscure. The Nabataeans were probably a nomad tribe which took

[164] Cf. G. De Sanctis, *Riv. Fil.* xii (1934), pp. 520 f.; Welles, *AJA* xlii (1938), pp. 245 f.
[165] See above, p. 142 and n. 157.
[166] Philopoemen, too, perhaps learnt the idea of making his phalanx more flexible
from the Romans: cf. Walbank, *HCP* ii, p. 286; and cf. Polyb. xviii.28.10 with Walbank,
HCP ii ad loc., for Pyrrhus' adoption of the Roman manipular system.
[167] It is possible, but not certain, that Hieronymus also gave details about the Gauls
who penetrated Greece in the 270's. Pausanias' account, with its dramatic and patriotic
tone, cannot be derived directly or wholly from Hieronymus: see above, ch. 2, pp. 73 f.;
cf. also Regenbogen, *RE* Suppl. viii s.v. 'Pausanias', col. 1076; Momigliano, *Alien
Wisdom*, pp. 63 f.
[168] Rostovtzeff, *Caravan Cities*, Oxford, 1932, p. 55; cf. C. Wehrli, *Antigone et
Démétrios*, pp. 51 f.; Will, *HPMH* i, p. 53.
[169] Diod. xix.100.1 = Hier. T6. Cf. ch. 1, pp. 14 f.
[170] Jacoby, *RE* 'Hieronymos', col. 1559; cf. *RE* Suppl. ii s.v. 'Herodotos', col. 512.
Theopompus, *F. Gr. Hist.* 115 F59–61 (from a general survey of the world?), and
F74–75: cf. Laqueur, *RE* VA s.v. 'Theopompos', no. 9, cols. 2212 f.

advantage of the weaknesses of the Persian empire during the fifth
century, and moved west and north, from the desert lands, gradually
encroaching on cultivated areas which could not be defended.[171]
Hieronymus' description is the first certain evidence of this people,
and shows that, at any rate by the end of the fourth century, they
occupied an area extending from 'Petra' to the shores of the Dead Sea.
The account is concerned chiefly with Nabataean *nomoi*, and shows
how laws and customs were related to the character of the land. The
Nabataeans are a people of the open wilderness; they raise camels and
sheep, and live off meat and milk and certain wild plants—the pepper,
and the so-called wild honey.[172] It is their *nomos* to plant neither trees
nor grain, nor to drink wine, nor to construct any house; and the
penalty for infringement of this law is death. Their way of life is based
on love of freedom: they believe that those who live a settled life pay
for the good things they possess by the sacrifice of their freedom to the
powerful. The desert itself is their fortress: no enemy can cross it for
lack of water. The Arabs themselves have developed great skills in the
conservation of water. They excavate underground chambers lined
with plaster which catch the rain and act as reservoirs: these extend to a
length of 100 feet below ground level, but the openings are small, and
can be sealed off and be made invisible to all but their own people.
Although they number only some 10,000, they are a wealthy people,
because they trade in precious spices brought from Arabia Eudaemon
to the sea. When it is time for their general market, they leave their
women and children and possessions on a strong but unwalled rock,
two days journey from the settled country.[173] They write (as appears
from the later narrative) in 'Syrian letters', i.e. Aramaic.[174]

The customs here described closely resemble those of the Rechabites as set out in the Book of Jeremiah: 'Jonadab the son of Rechab
our father commanded us saying, Ye shall drink no wine, neither ye,
nor your sons for ever: Neither shall ye build house, nor sow seed, nor
plant vineyard, nor have any: but all your days ye shall dwell in tents:
that ye may dwell many days in the land where ye be strangers.'[175] The
Macedonian expedition found the Nabataeans still living a nomad

---

[171] See P. C. Hammond, *The Nabataeans*, Göteborg, 1973, pp. 11 ff.

[172] Cf. Herodotus vii.31: the men of Callatebus, on the route to Sardis, make honey
out of wheat and the fruit of the tamarisk: ἄνδρες δημιοργοὶ μέλι ἐκ μυρίκης τε καὶ
πυροῦ ποιεῦσι.

[173] Diodorus' *petra* was identified by G. and A. Horsfeld with Umm el-Biyarn, a rock
about 200 m. high overlooking the valley of Petra. Some pre-Nabataean cisterns were
found on the summit. Cf. J. Starcky, *Bibl. Arch.* xviii (1955), p. 84. *Contra*, A. Negev,
Auf. u. Nied. d. röm. Welt, ii (8), 1977, pp. 520 ff., who locates the rock in the central Negev.

[174] Diod. xix.96.1.

[175] Jeremiah 35:6–10. Cf. G. Barbieri, *New Catholic Encyclopaedia*, s.v. 'Rechabites'.

existence, with laws, apparently characteristic of other Syrian peoples, which made a virtue of necessity and were aimed at the preservation of an ancestral way of life. The picture which Diodorus draws, of Nabataeans living the simple life of the desert, is a guarantee of an early Hellenistic source, because writers of a later period did not know them as desert nomads. Strabo, drawing on Athenodorus (who was born at Petra), gives a very different impression of Nabataean life in the first century BC. Now they drink wine out of golden cups, they are entertained by singing girls, they import luxury items, and the land produces gold and silver; they have planted gardens at Petra; they are settled and industrious and extremely thrifty.[176] Archaeological evidence confirms Strabo's picture: the Nabataeans of the first century and later lived in permanent urban settlements and their way of life was based on agriculture. On the other hand, the accuracy of the earlier, Hieronyman, account is shown by the fact that many of the characteristics he observed later became more pronounced: the use of literary Aramaic, for example, is attested for later periods, and by the mid-second century an individual Nabataean script had developed;[177] the cunning and independence of the people is illustrated by Agatharchides' account of their piratical attacks on Egyptian shipping in the Red Sea, probably during the reign of Philadelphus.[178] In particular, Hieronymus recognized two features of the Nabataean way of life which proved to be the foundation of the power and prosperity of the later Nabataean kingdom: their control of the caravan route from South Arabia to Palestine, and their skill in water conservation.

The trade route through Petra had been developed at a much earlier period, under the Achaemenid empire, and Petra had relations with Egypt, Syria, and the South Arabian kingdoms: by the time of Antigonus' expedition it was evidently a prosperous caravan city, and Rostovtzeff conjectured that it was the aim of this expedition to divert Petraean trade from Egypt and direct it towards the Phoenician ports.[179] In the third century, Ptolemaic control of the Phoenician cities, together with the development of Alexandria as a great commercial port, made the independence of Petra intolerable to Egypt, and Philadelphus made efforts to develop an alternative route from Arabia by sea: the piracy to which some of our sources refer must have been a reply to the measures of Philadephus. Pliny knew the Nabataeans of his day as traders and caravaners; and the wealth which

[176] Strabo xvi.21–22, p. 779–80.
[177] Hammond, op. cit., p. 10.
[178] Cf. Fraser, *Ptol. Alex.* i, pp. 176 f.; ii, pp. 300 f. n. 350.
[179] Rostovtzeff, *Caravan Cities*, p. 55.

commerce brought to the one-time nomads is attested in Strabo's account.[180] Commerce and agriculture are the means of livelihood which characterize Strabo's Nabataeans. The caravan route must have flourished again after the second century, when Ptolemaic power was declining. Agriculture and a settled way of life developed largely through the indefatigable efforts of the Nabataeans to irrigate the desert. Their skill in hydraulic engineering, which was perhaps based on knowledge of the hydraulic systems of Mesopotamia, at least equalled their success as caravan merchants: the remarkable level of technical skill which was achieved is shown by the fact that some Nabataean water-works have been restored by modern engineers and put to their former use.[181] The system of channels, cisterns, and dams at Petra itself, dating from the Roman period, is the most spectacular of these works; but Nabataean hydraulic installations, particularly cisterns of all shapes and sizes, have been identified throughout the Negev. Some of these cisterns were cut out of natural rock, some built of stone and roofed over. Many others have been found which correspond exactly with Diodorus' description of ἀγγεῖα κατὰ γῆς ὀρυκτὰ κεκονιαμένα. A modern survey of the desert water-works reports that: 'There were also numerous others, whose sides were coated with layers of plaster, firmed with bits of pottery, and sometimes overlaid with stone blocks or pebble facings. Numerous natural caves were enlarged into subterranean reservoirs, with free-standing pillars being left to support the extended roofs.'[182] All along the length of the Wadi Abdah have been found the remains of huge cisterns carved out of the chalk rock which forms the sides of the river bed, and which filled up whenever the Wadi filled with water. One of these, opposite the former Nabataean city of Abdah, was till recently being used by Bedouin to water their flocks. Abdah lies on the direct route from Gaza to the Dead Sea and Petra, and it is possible that some of the cisterns along the Wadi Abdah were discovered by Antigonus' army on its march into Nabataean territory.

Hieronymus' description of the Dead Sea was supplementary to his main account of the Nabataeans.[183] It forms an introduction to the expedition, led by the historian, which was sent to gain control of the bitumen fishery of the Asphalt Lake; and it extends the information given earlier about Nabataean commerce. Here too Hieronymus

---

[180] Pliny *N.H.* vi.162, cf. 144.
[181] Hammond, op. cit., pp. 72 f.
[182] N. Glueck, *Rivers of the Desert*, New York, 1959, p. 223. Some layers of plaster are said to be still visible on the walls of an overground cistern at Qasr Wadi Siq, south-west of Abdah.
[183] Diod. xix.98–9.

achieved a high degree of accuracy.[184] Apart from some general remarks about the buoyancy of the salt water and the absence of aquatic life (well-known and perennial features of the Dead Sea), the report centres on the phenomenon of the asphalt from which the lake took its name. Floating lumps of bitumen (ἄσφαλτος) as big as islands, are ejected from the lake every year, accompanied by evil-smelling gases which affect the neighbourhood for miles around and discolour precious metals. The bitumen is collected by the peoples who live on either side of the lake, and they fight each other for possession of it. Their method is to sail out on rafts made from bundles of reeds, two men to row the raft, a third carrying a bow to fend off attackers; and they hack pieces off the floating asphalt with axes and load it on the raft. The asphalt is exported to Egypt where it is used as an ingredient in the embalming of the dead. Other products of the region around the lake are palm trees and balsam, an important drug which grows here more abundantly than anywhere else in the world.[185]

This is the earliest and most informative of many ancient accounts of Judaean bitumen. Strabo has clearly used Hieronymus; Diodorus in Book ii sets out the account of xix almost verbatim.[186] Vitruvius probably had a different source, because he knows about bitumen quarries and bitumen brought down by streams. Josephus refers to the Dead Sea bitumen fishery in a historical connection, and comments on the beautiful colours which are produced by the reflection of light on the oily surface of the lake. Pliny refers to 'slimy bitumen' of Judaea which

[184] The length of the lake, given as approx. 500 stades (= about 57 miles) is inexact. The present measurement is about 47 miles, and the water level is thought to have risen considerably since antiquity: cf. F. G. Clapp, 'Geology of the Dead Sea Area', *Bull. of Am. Assoc. of Petroleum Geologists*, vol. 20, no. 7 (1936), pp. 885 ff. The distance between Petra and the Dead Sea is also a problem on Diodorus' account. At 98.1 he gives 300 stades (c. 34 miles); at 95.2, Petra is two days journey from 'the settled country'; ibid., Athenaeus and a light-armed force take three days and nights to reach Petra, covering a distance of 2,200 stades (c. 250 miles). The last figure is clearly corrupt: cf. Diod. xviii.44.2, where a journey of 2,500 stades, completed in seven days and nights, is considered a forced march (and even this sounds impossible). Petra is actually about 50 miles due south of the southernmost point of the Dead Sea, at its present level. If, however, A. Negev is right in placing the 4th century nomadic Nabataeans and their 'rock' not on the Transjordanian coast around the famous Petra, but in the NE Negev, this difficulty would be resolved: Negev, loc. cit. esp. p. 529; cf. *Palestine Exploration Quarterly*, 1976, pp. 125 ff.

[185] Balsam: compare the more detailed accounts of Diod. ii.48.9, Strabo xvi.2.41, Theophrastus, *Hist. Plant.* ix.6.1 (all different and apparently independent of one another). See also J. I. Miller, *Spice Trade of the Roman Empire*, 1969, pp. 101–2.

[186] Strabo xvi.42 (he confuses the Asphalt Lake with Lake Sirbonis: cf. xvi.32). Strabo cites no authority for this description, but at the beginning of ch. 43 he contrasts this account with the one given by Posidonius, apparently regarding the former as more reliable. Cf. Diod. ii.48.

solidifies to a dense consistency; similarly Tacitus.[187] The whole of the Near East is, it need hardly be stated, exceptionally rich in deposits of liquid and solid oil, a fact which was appreciated from the earliest times: God had said to Noah, 'Make thee an ark of gopher wood; rooms shalt thou make in the ark, and shalt pitch it within and without with pitch.'[188] Modern exploitation of these deposits has involved extensive surveys of the geology of the region of Judaea, and petroleum geologists have confirmed the description in Diodorus at every point. Although the asphalt now appears less often than in antiquity, masses weighing up to 100 pounds have been reported and photographed.[189] Similar phenomena occur also in Mexico and parts of South America, and the effects of the gas (hydrogen sulphide) emitted by the pitch are said to be those described in Diodorus.[190] Hieronymus' account of the production of bitumen in Judaea was therefore substantially correct. For the method of collection, by armed men on rafts of reed, one may compare an Assyrian relief found in the palace at Nineveh and dating from the reign of Sennacherib or Assurbanipal. The relief depicts a combat taking place in the middle of a marsh: the Assyrians sail in small groups on rafts made from bundles of reeds, and fight each other with bows and arrows.[191] The type of raft seems to correspond to Diodorus' δέσμας καλάμων εὐμεγέθεις with oars lashed on (xix.99.1), and was perhaps a Nabataean legacy from Mesopotamia, like their hydraulic skills.

The only part of Hieronymus' account which has caused scepticism is his statement that bitumen was exported to Egypt for use in the embalming process. This claim, echoed by many modern writers, has not actually been supported by finds of Judaean bitumen in Egyptian mummies. The earlier Egyptologists reported finding bituminous materials in the bodies or the packaging of a number of mummies; but chemical analysis performed on mummies this century showed no trace of Judaean bitumen in human mummies from any period.[192] Herodotus does not mention bitumen in his description of Egyptian methods of embalming, and it seems unlikely that it was used at all during the dynastic period; moreover, there seems to be no known

[187] Vitruv. viii.3.9, Joseph, *Ant.* i.10; xv.4–6; *B.J.* i.13; Pliny *N.H.* xxxv.17.8; Tacitus, *Hist.* v.5. Cf. Aelian *V.H.* xiii.16 (finds of bitumen in Babylonia).

[188] Genesis 6:13–14.

[189] Clapp, art. cit., p. 901; photograph on p. 903 (a man stands on the asphalt 'island').

[190] Cf. R. J. Forbes, *Bitumen and Petroleum in Antiquity*, Leiden, 1936, pp. 16–18.

[191] Photograph in J. Deshayes, *Les Civilisations de l'orient ancien*, Paris, 1962, illustration no. 116, p. 312.

[192] T. J. Pettigrew, *A History of Egyptian Mummies*, London, 1834, pp. 56, 59, 70, 81 f., 87, 101 f.; W. Budge, *The Mummy*, 1893, pp. 207 f., 212. A. Lucas, *Ancient Egyptian Materials and Industries*[4], Harris, London, 1962, pp. 303 ff.

Egyptian term for 'bitumen'.[193] However, the original tests were not exhaustive, and do not preclude the use of bitumen at least in non-human mummies in the Ptolemaic period. Later tests, using the technique of exposing specimens to ultra-violet rays, had rather greater success, and it has been concluded: 'It is impossible to avoid the expectation that the presence of bitumen would become substantiated by further work rather than disproved.'[194] If bitumen were used for cheaper forms of embalming, animal burials, for example, much of the evidence would have been destroyed. In the middle ages, at any rate, bitumen was associated with mummies, because according to the twelfth-century Arab physician, Ibn-al-Beitar, *múmijá*, the Arab word for bitumen, was applied to a popular drug made from bits of pulverized mummy.[195] Bitumen was used in Egypt for a wide variety of purposes other than embalming, and seems not to have been produced in Egypt itself, since we do not hear of *asphaltos* along with other mineral products that were Ptolemaic monopolies.[196] Judaea was therefore probably the chief source of the bitumen used in Egyptian manufactures during the Ptolemaic period; and it is not unlikely that it was the Nabataeans, newcomers to Jordan and the Negev probably sometime during the fifth century, who first fished and sold the Dead Sea bitumen: hence it is not mentioned in Herodotus and was apparently unknown in dynastic Egypt. Whatever the truth about an extensive use of bitumen in mummies of the Ptolemaic period, it is impossible to doubt that the bitumen of the Dead Sea represented an important source of wealth to the Nabataeans. Antigonus regarded the bitumen fishery as 'a source of revenue for the kingdom'—τινα τῇ βασιλείᾳ πρόσοδον—and the Arabs were vigorous in protecting their claims to the industry. In the first century BC it was taken from the Nabataeans by Antony and given to Cleopatra, who then leased it again to the Nabataean king Malchus, for 200 talents a year (no mean sum: in Perseus' day the revenue of Macedonia was 200 talents);[197] and this must have been considerably exceeded by the actual profit which Malchus expected to gain from sale of the bitumen.[198]

[193] Herodotus ii.86–8. Forbes, op. cit., p. 94.

[194] P. E. Spielman, *JEA* xviii (1932), pp. 177 ff. with references to Lucas's earlier work. P. C. Hammond, *Bibl. Arch.* xxii (1959), pp. 40–8, gives a summary of the evidence.

[195] Cf. Forbes, op. cit., 93 f.

[196] For the uses of bitumen, see Forbes, chs. iv–vi; cf. Hammond, art. cit., pp. 43 f. (a summary). Ptolemaic monopolies: C. Préaux, *L'Économie royale des Lagides*, Bruxelles, 1939, pp. 342 ff.

[197] Plut. *Aem.* xxviii.4.

[198] Joseph. *Ant.* xiv.370, cf. *B. J.* 1.277; *Ant.* xv.108. Cf. J. Starcky, *Bibl. Arch.* xviii (1955), pp. 92 ff, for a survey of Nabataean history at this period.

The account of Nabataea and its resources is the most detailed geographical excursus which we know from Hieronymus' work. There appear, however, to have been several more cursory allusions to matters of geographical or ethnographical interest. The timber of Lebanon, the fertility of the lands of Media, Susiane, and Persis, are the subject of miniature digressions in Diodorus' account of Asian affairs: here Hieronymus must have enlarged on the geographical sketch which stood at the head of his historical narrative.[199] He described the ritual death of the wife of Ceteus the Indian, and remarked that these νόμιμα were savage and harsh.[200] His account of the siege of Pydna also showed the self-consciousness of the Greek when confronted with barbarian customs: when people began to die of hunger, some of the *barbaroi* fed themselves by eating the bodies of the dead—τῆς φύσεως κατισχυούσης τὴν εὐλάβειαν.[201] The Cossaean tribes who inhabited the passes into Media were nearly as primitive: they lived in caves, and ate acorns and mushrooms and the smoked flesh of wild animals. Thucydides had reproached the Aetolians for their unintelligible dialect and their nasty habit of eating raw flesh: language and diet at once identified the barbarian.[202] Hieronymus perhaps did not maintain unswervingly the standard of accuracy achieved with the Nabataeans. In one instance he reports a local practice which sounds highly improbable. During the struggle against Antigonus in 317, Eumenes' reluctant ally Peucestas sent for reinforcements of 10,000 Persian archers. These forces, reports Diodorus, received the order on the very same day, even though they were thirty days journey distant, so efficient is the Persian system of communication: for Persis is cut by many narrow valleys, and when the people have an important message to convey across country, men with very loud voices are stationed on the tops of the hills, and shout the message in relays right across the land. It is difficult to take this seriously. Someone from the Persian contingent told Hieronymus a tall story; and it may not be too fanciful to suppose that the culprit was Peucestas himself, who had shown a thoroughly bad temper in the matter of the reinforcements and indeed throughout the campaign. When the historian applied to him, as an expert on Persian affairs, for information on Persian methods of telegraphing, Peucestas saw a chance to repay in kind the tricks which Eumenes and his secretary liked to play on dull Macedonians.[203]

---

[199] Diod. xix.58.3, 20.3, 13.6, 21.2–3; cf. xviii.5.1 and ch. 3, pp. 83 f.

[200] Diod. xix.34.6. Cf. Herodotus v.5, giving an account of a similar custom among the Thracians.   [201] Diod. xix.49.4.

[202] Diod. xix.19.3. Thuc. iii.94 (though note ὡς λέγονται). Cf. Polyb. xviii.5.8 on the barbarian descent of the Aetolians. On the Cossaei, see ch. 5, p. 218.

[203] Diod. xix.17.6–7. Cf. Xen. *Anab.* v.4.31 for a similar absurdity. For Peucestas'

Like all Greek writers on the East, Hieronymus was sometimes at the mercy of local informants. Where he trusted to his own powers of observation, however, he achieved a high standard of accuracy, and he showed a talent for perceiving the dominant aspects in the way of life of a foreign people: this is evident in his account both of the Nabataeans and, so far as we may judge, of the Romans. These ventures into ethnography were a remarkable feature in a political history of the Diadochi. Twenty years campaigning on the Asian continent qualified Hieronymus to write with authority on the peoples and countries of the East; but with these qualifications, he might yet have ignored the geographical setting of his Asian narrative except where it was directly relevant to military affairs: there was a good precedent in Ptolemy's account of Alexander; whereas Alexander histories which had attempted to convey the flavour of the mysterious Orient—that of Onesicritus especially—had notoriously tended to drift into fairyland. Serious treatment of geography and ethnography, on the other hand, was usually confined to specialized studies like those of Megasthenes on India (and even this contained absurdities) or of Hecataeus on Egypt. These works were histories of a kind; their obvious roots in Ionian historiography oblige us to describe them as such. They represent, however, only one aspect of the Herodotean history from which they are derived: the early Hellenistic ethnographers isolated the Herodotean ethnographic study, of which his book on the Egyptians formed the paradigm, and developed it into an independent genre.[204] Hieronymus, while primarily a political historian, followed the practice of Theopompus and Aristobulus in adopting the fusion of geography and politics which had produced the first real history. He had begun his work in the grand Thucydidean manner, analysing *staseis* and *aitiai*,[205] and backing up his case with the unimpeachable evidence of contemporary documents. It may be supposed that some of his 'archaeologies' looked directly to Thucydides' *Sikelika* as a model, and that his comments on certain barbarian peoples, like the Cossaei, did not go beyond the occasional remarks which can be found in Thucydides on the practices of the Aetolians or the Odrysians.[206] However, those historians, like Thucydides and Xenophon, who wrote only *Hellenica*, had no necessity or occasion to

expertise on Persian affairs cf. xix.14.4–5, Arr. *Anab.* vi.30.2–3. Eumenes' deception of Peucestas: Diod. xix.23.

[204] Cf. O. Murray, 'Herodotus and Hellenistic Culture', *CQ* n.s. xxii (1972), pp. 204 ff.

[205] Hieronymus rightly perceived that the Samian question was crucial in causing the war: cf. Errington, 'Samos and the Lamian War', *Chiron* v (1975), pp. 51 ff.

[206] Thuc. iii.94, ii.97. The comments on *barbarika nomima* scattered through Xenophon's *Anabasis* are a better precursor: cf. ch. 5, pp. 209 f. for Xenophon's influence on Hieronymus.

develop the geographical excursus. For Hieronymus, newly explored areas of the *oikoumene*, in both East and West, demanded treatment according to the manner established by Herodotus. The Nabataean excursus was a *logos* which contained at least two of the four traditional elements: *nomoi* and *thaumasia* (the underground cisterns); the Nabataeans had no history to speak of, and geography could be summed up as 'desert'. This excursus was not only Herodotean in form, but had also the virtue of originality, not always a feature of the contemporary ethnographers, who frequently aped Herodotus even while disparaging him; and it was, demonstrably, a serious study: although the Arabs are used to illustrate the principle of *eleutheria*— probably a motif of the history—Hieronymus had originally approached his subject, as Nearchus had, with the traveller's innocent eye.[207] We remain in Nabataea and not in Utopia, looking at the observable details of Nabataean life-style and economy. Here Hieronymus showed the true spirit of ἱστορίη.

II. TWO KINDS OF PROPAGANDA

Few can have been better placed than Hieronymus to record the wars of the Successors. His position made him not only an eye-witness but also a witness of what was said; often, too, an active participant in events; and it gave him access to the original evidence, written as well as oral. Within the limitations imposed by time and memory and by the need to record the sometimes doubtful testimony of men of consequence, he made good use of the resources available to him, and ambitiously took his researches even into the field of ethnographic study. It remains to consider Hieronymus' general interpretation of the evidence. The fact which made him so well qualified to write the history of his times, namely his position as protégé of Macedonian kings, at the same time prohibits uncritical acceptance of the historian's verdict on policies and personalities. Proximity, as well as distance, can distort the vision, and even in the ancient sources there are disturbing charges of partiality. Modern estimates of Hieronymus' truthfulness have centred on two points, first, his treatment of Eumenes, which is rightly regarded as apologetic; second, the idea that the general tone of the history, and specifically its standpoint on the question of empire and the question of Greek liberty, was influenced by the policies and the patronage of Antigonus Gonatas: this is more open to question.

---

[207] Cf. Murray, art. cit., p. 207, contrasting Nearchus with the ethnographers who wrote after him and who tidied up the organization of the Herodotean excursus, at the same time importing into it philosophical theories of the ideal state.

The apologia for Eumenes

Hieronymus' history down to the end of the year 317 centred on the figure of Eumenes. This is evident especially from Diodorus' account, with its lively manner and many personal details; Nepos and Plutarch both chose Eumenes as the subject of a biography, using Hieronymus as their principal source; and it is significant that each of the two fragments of Arrian's τὰ μετὰ Ἀλέξανδρον deal with episodes in which Eumenes was the protagonist.[208] It is likely that the two Cardians were related by blood; Hieronymus' admiration for Eumenes is in any case manifest, and it was the living relationship between the historian and his subject which gave this part of his work its especial appeal. It has been observed that the greatest representations of historical personalities in antiquity—Socrates, Pericles, Tiberius— were not strictly biographical in form, and Hieronymus' portrait of Eumenes belongs to this category. Some elements of biography, such as an account of the subject's birth and education, could, however, have been included. Plutarch's first two chapters of the *Life of Eumenes* mention his birth and upbringing before sketching his early career under Philip and Alexander: Duris is cited for the information that Eumenes was the son of a waggoner, i.e. of humble birth, and probably the stories about his avarice and his quarrel with Hephaestion have the same origin; but Plutarch's δοκοῦσι δὲ εἰκότα λέγειν μᾶλλον οἱ διὰ ξενίαν καὶ φιλίαν πατρῷαν τὸν Εὐμενῆ λέγοντες κ.τ.λ. is naturally taken as an allusion to Hieronymus;[209] and its seems to be this 'more likely' version that Nepos followed in his (laudatory) account of Eumenes' early years. Details about Eumenes' background were perhaps introduced by Hieronymus in a digression, like the digression at Diodorus xviii.59. This survey of Eumenes' career (given a strong philosophical bias in Diodorus) keeps Eumenes in play at a time when he was shut up at Nora and not doing anything, and might have been a convenient point to bring in biographical material which had no place in the ordinary narrative.[210] There is no evidence, however, that

---

[208] Arrian *Succ.* F10.8; *PSI* xii.2, 1284.

[209] Plut. *Eum.* i.2. Cf. Kaerst, *RE* vi s.v. 'Eumenes', no. 4, col. 1083. The idea that great men had sprung from obscure origins was a common theme. See also Justin xiii.4.10, of Ptolemy, 'ex gregario milite Alexander virtutis causa provexerat'; Diod. xxi.1, of Antigonus Monophthalmus, ἐξ ἰδιώτου γενόμενος δυναστής (cf. Briant, *Antigone le Borgne*, pp. 19 ff. on his actual origins); Diod. xix. 2, Agathocles was brought up by a potter, cf. Justin xxii.1.8, 'gregariam militiam sortitus'; Justin xv.4.15, Sandracottus, 'Fuit hic humili quidem genere natus'; and on Lysimachus, see below, n. 234. Cf. Droysen, *Hermes* xi (1876), pp. 458 ff.

[210] Compare Diodorus' proem to Book xvi, summarizing the career of Philip. But for

Hieronymus wrote a separate biography of Eumenes, as Xenophon did of Agesilaus, or Polybius of Philopoemen; and he certainly fell short of Polybius' precept (as did Polybius himself) that praise and blame should be kept out of history proper and reserved for the independent encomium.[211]

The characterization of Eumenes turns on three principal features: his cleverness, his Greek origins, and his loyalty to Alexander's family. His intelligence and personal ability we are not in a position to doubt, and it is argued by the high rank to which he rose in Alexander's service. On the other hand, the contrast between Eumenes' character and the character of his opponents is certainly overdrawn in our sources. The treachery of Neoptolemus, Eumenes' personal enemy, is underlined by the order of Perdiccas that he should obey Eumenes in all things διὰ τὴν τῆς πίστεως βεβαιότητα.[212] The popularity of Craterus is probably exaggerated in order to enhance Eumenes' victory at the Dardanelles.[213] The treatment of Peucestas is almost without exception hostile: he is a coward, he covets the chief command for himself, he thinks first of his own safety.[214] Arrian in the *Anabasis* gives a very different picture of Peucestas: he was a brave soldier (he saved Alexander's life among the Malli), and a good officer who rose high in Alexander's favour: πιστόν τέ οἱ ἐς τὰ μάλιστα τιθέμενος τά τε ἄλλα, κ.τ.λ.[215] Hieronymus referred to this in his introduction of Peucestas (Diod. xix.14.4–5); but in the same way he gave the credentials of all the former friends and bodyguards of Alexander.[216] (The comment on Peucestas' popularity among the Persians was perhaps aimed at Antigonus, one of whose shortcomings was a conspicuous failure to take account of native sentiment.) In the main narrative of 317 Peucestas is a leader of dissension in the allied army and responsible for the defeat at Gabiene. Later he was among those who were removed from their satrapies in Antigonus' purge of Alexander's *philoi*; but he turns up again in the retinue of Demetrius:[217] a man with a galling talent for

---

the digression on Eumenes cf. also Plut. *Eum.* ix.1–2, on the constancy of Eumenes through the vicissitudes of Fortune, suggesting a basis in a common source.

[211] Polyb. viii.8.5–9; x.21.6–8.

[212] Diod. xviii.29.2.

[213] Berve, ii, no. 446, esp. pp. 225 f.; cf. De Sanctis, 'Perdicca', in *Problemi di storia antica*, Bari, 1932, p. 149; Badian, *Studies*, p. 265.

[214] Diod. xix.38.1–2, 42.2, 43.5, cf. Plut. *Eum.* xvi.5; Diod. xix.23.1, 17.6; cf. 21.1; 43.9.

[215] Arr. *Anab.* vi.30.2, cf. vi.28.3 f. (from Aristobulus); cf. Berve, ii, no. 634. It would be interesting to know how Arrian in the *Successors* reconciled Hieronymus' picture of Peucestas with that of the Alexander historians.

[216] Cf. ch. ii, p. 34, n. 53.

[217] Diod. xix. 48.5, cf. 56.1–2; Phylarchus, *F. Gr. Hist.* 81 F12.

survival. This was not one of those friends of Demetrius who succeeded in imposing on the historian their versions of past campaigns.

In different ways, the treatment of all Eumenes' rivals enhances his integrity and qualities of leadership. Plutarch regards Antigenes and Teutamus as the villains of the army—φθόνου δὲ καὶ φιλονεικίας . . . μεστοί (Plut. *Eum.* xiii.2)—and has them plotting against Eumenes' life before Gabiene (ibid., xvi.1). In Diodorus they are, on another occasion, paragons of loyalty who resist the blandishments of Antigonus and his agents (Diod. xviii.62.6, ὁ δ' 'Αντιγένης, συνέσει καὶ πίστεως βεβαιότητι διαφέρων). Both authors evidently exaggerate, but at the same time show traces of a portrait in which the sensitive relations between Eumenes and his army were depicted to the advantage of Eumenes. Again, both Plutarch and Diodorus record with moral satisfaction the destruction of the Silver Shields: here as elsewhere, Hieronymus' history of Eumenes lent itself to a moralistic treatment; and the theme of retribution is implicit in Diodorus' account of Antigonus' measures after Gabiene—Antigenes burned alive, Eudamus the elephant-keeper executed, the Silver Shields sent on death missions, the satraps turned out of their satrapies.[218] Eumenes had predicted it: when the lion has pulled out his claws and his teeth a man may club him to death.[219]

The denigration of Eumenes' opponents and the trumpeting of Eumenes' own virtues represents the cruder side of the apologia. Other aspects are less easy to detect or to test, such as the interpolation of references to Eumenes' *strategia* and *pistis* into his supposed correspondence.[220] Eumenes' Greek origins are a problem of this kind. The careers of Medeius and Nearchus, as well as that of Eumenes himself, demonstrate that Greeks were able to rise to high office under Philip and Alexander. Under Alexander, Stasanor and for a time Nearchus held satrapies, and after Alexander's death several other Greeks—Laomedon, Lysimachus, the Cypriots Stasanor and Stasander of Soli. These were men of very considerable standing; and Eumenes, like Nearchus, Lysimachus, and Laomedon, had lived in Macedon and might be thought a 'naturalized' Macedonian. He could afford to be on bad terms with Hephaestion, and he had held a military command.[221] We hear of no general prejudice of Macedonians against Greeks in Alexander's army, and it is not obvious, on the face of it,

---

[218] Cf. Engel, *Athenaeum* l (1972), p. 122, arguing that both Plutarch and Diodorus took the judgement on the Argyraspids from Hieronymus.

[219] Cf. Diod. xix.25.4–7.

[220] See above, pp. 134 f.

[221] Arr. *Anab.* v.24.6. Cf. Hammond and Griffith, *Macedonia*, ii, p. 404, on Greeks in the aristocratic fraternity of the Macedonian 'Companions'.

why it should be thought such a disadvantage to be Greek.[222] Eumenes' case was different to this extent, that he was the only Greek to command a Macedonian royal army (at a later date Aratus was in direct command of Macedonians, and apparently experienced no trouble, but the time and circumstances were different); and Tarn thought that Eumenes was looked down on personally by the Macedonians because they thought of him as a secretary and not a soldier:[223] Nearchus and Lysimachus, men of greater military experience under Alexander, do not appear to have encountered problems of command; and the account of Eumenes' battle with Neoptolemus in all our sources does suggest that Eumenes hoped by a show of personal bravery at the début of his new career to win the military reputation denied to him in Alexander's lifetime. Yet he was not altogether unsuccessful in gaining the affection of the Macedonian troops. Plutarch relates that on one occasion they gave him a special welcome by greeting him Μακεδονιστὶ τῇ φωνῇ—in the Macedonian dialect, which must have been intended as a compliment to a Greek.[224] In any case prejudice among the soldiers would not account for the hostility of the commanders in Eumenes' army, which was surely ordinary jealousy.

The propaganda used against Eumenes in his lifetime nevertheless seems to have made capital out of the fact that he was not a Macedonian;[225] and Lysimachus used the same argument against Pyrrhus when he turned against his former ally after Demetrius' defeat: γράμμασι καὶ λόγοις διέφθειρε τοὺς πρώτους τῶν Μακεδόνων, ὀνειδίζων εἰ ξένον ἄνδρα καὶ προγόνων ἀεὶ δεδουλευκότων Μακεδόσι δεσπότην ἑλόμενοι τοὺς ᾿Αλεξάνδρου φίλους καὶ συνήθεις ἀπωθοῦσι Μακεδονίας.[226] In a crisis, too, latent fears and prejudices might rise to the surface: at Gabiene, when the loss of the baggage was discovered, the Macedonian soldiers turned on Eumenes with the sneer, Χερρονησίτης ὄλεθρος. The words are possibly authentic, since the speech ᾿Επὶ τοὺς πατέρας κ.τ.λ. is recorded in the same context.[227] The expression was not original. The Samians had replied to Maiandrios, the avaricious successor of Polycrates: ἀλλ᾿

---

[222] Arr. *Anab.* vii.4 could imply that Eumenes and Nearchus were among the top eight at court in 324; but the selection of the names could be Arrian's own. See H. D. Westlake, 'Eumenes of Cardia', pp. 319 ff. for a general discussion.
[223] Tarn, *Antigonos Gonatas*, pp. 182 f.
[224] Plut, *Eum.* xiv.5. Cf. Hammond and Griffith, op. cit., ii, p. 46.
[225] Cf. Diod, xix.13.1; Nep. *Eum.* vii.
[226] Plut. *Pyrrh.* xii.6. Cf. Plut. *Demetr.* xliv.4: ἔπηλον δὲ καὶ ξένον ἄνδρα τὸν Πύρρον.
[227] Plut. *Eum.* xvi.8; cf. Diod. xix.41.1.

οὐδ᾽ ἄξιος εἶς σύ γε ἡμέων ἄρχειν, γεγονώς τε κακῶς καὶ ἐὼν ὄλεθρος.[228] The word ὄλεθρος appears in Aristophanes and frequently in Menander as a term of abuse.[229] It was also a favourite with Demosthenes. He calls Aeschines ὄλεθρος γραμματεύς—'pestilent scribe' (xviii.127); and Philip, an interesting example, was described as οὐ μόνον οὐχ ῞Ελληνος ὄντος οὐδὲ προσήκοντος οὐδὲν τοῖς ῞Ελλησιν, ἀλλ᾽ οὐδὲ βαρβάρου ἐντεῦθεν ὅθεν καλὸν εἰπεῖν, ἀλλ᾽ ὀλέθρου Μακεδόνος.[230] 'Plague from the Chersonese' perhaps embodies a similar thought: Eumenes was not even a proper Greek. Whether it amounts to racial contempt is questionable. Lloyd George was called 'Welsh wizard' and 'Welsh pest', the ethnic being hardly more than a distinguishing tag; and probably it was the 'wizardry' of Eumenes that constituted the chief objection.[231]

However Eumenes' origins were really seen by the rest of his army, there remains one consideration of overriding importance: Greek or Macedonian, he failed in the long run to win decisive and profitable military victories. A recent study of Eumenes' relations with his troops suggests that the real difficulties were financial.[232] After Antipater's return to Macedon in 321 the armies of the Successors were organized increasingly on a mercenary, not a national basis, and the generals could do nothing without pay and victory. The frequent exchanges of oaths between Eumenes and the *hegemones* of the troops, which are taken by our sources as marks of loyalty, in fact took the form of a kind of employment contract, and expressed a deep mistrust of the commander. It may be supposed that birth and character played their part: armies are always sensitive to the personality of their leaders. The dominant part played in Eumenes' history by the fact that he was a Greek seems designed, however, to conceal more serious causes of dissension.

The 'Greek' motif has as one of its chief functions to suggest that Eumenes had no intention of aiming at supreme power. Eumenes may actually have exploited his nationality in order to allay such fears;[233] but here too there was disingenuity. Lysimachus became king of Macedon, and he was said to be the son of a Thessalian peasant.[234] Truth or

[228] Hdt. iii.142.5.
[229] Aristoph. *Lys.* 325; Menander, frags. 70, 182, 188, 612 (Körte).
[230] Demosth. ix.31. Cf. also xxi.209, xxiii.202; Plato, *Rep.* 491b.
[231] Cf. below, ch. 5, pp. 202 f.
[232] Briant, *REA* lxxiv (1972), pp. 32 ff.; *REA* lxxv (1973), pp. 43 ff. Cf. below, ch. 5, pp. 204 f.
[233] Diod. xviii.62.7, 60.3; Plut. *Eum.* iii.3. Cf. Westlake, art. cit., p. 318.
[234] Theopompus, *F. Gr. Hist.* 115 F81 = Athen. vi. 260A, with Porphyry, *F. Gr. Hist.* 280 F3.8. Cf. Berve, ii, no. 480, p. 239.

slander, it cannot be assumed *a priori* that in the changed conditions of the time after Alexander a non-Macedonian might not aspire to part of his empire. In these conditions talk of the Macedonian *basileia* becomes ambiguous. We may take it, no doubt, that Eumenes did not covet the position which Cassander came to occupy, as king of the Macedonian homeland. The question is rather whether Eumenes was one of the ἰδιοπραγοῦντες (cf. Diod. xviii.50.1, 42.2) who aimed at possession of part of the Asian territories. Hieronymus elaborately disclaimed the idea: Eumenes was the champion of the kings— προστῆναι τῶν βασιλέων πρὸς τοὺς καταλύειν αὐτῶν τὴν ἀρχὴν τετολμηκότας (Diod. xviii.53.7); he assured Olympias that he held unwavering loyalty towards the kings and would run every risk— πάντα κίνδυνον—for their safety (xviii.58.4); at Gabiene he thought it shameful to flee from defeat, τὸ δὲ τηροῦντα τὴν δεδομένην ὑπὸ τῶν βασιλέων πίστιν γενναίᾳ προαιρέσει συναποθανεῖν προκρίνας κ.τ.λ. (xix.42.5); Antigonus was obliged to execute him because he knew he could never turn him from his devotion to Olympias and the kings (xix.44.2).

Eumenes' loyalty to the royal house and his struggle to preserve the unity of empire are ideas which have permeated the tradition and which aroused the admiration of earlier commentators;[235] if, however, Eumenes was as indifferent to his own advancement as our sources suggest, it is at least surprising that he consistently refused a subordinate post under one of the other generals. The proposed alliance with Antipater and Craterus at the time of the Dardanelles battle, and the overtures of Antigonus at Nora were both rejected, although in each case compliance might be thought more in the interests of the central government and the unity of empire.[236] The deliberate decision in 322 to 321 to back Perdiccas, whose apparent object was to overthrow the settlement made at Babylon, and in 320 to ignore Antigonus, still the representative of Antipater and the kings in Asia, is hardly to be reconciled with the claim, αὐτὸς δ' ἀεὶ τὴν εὔνοιαν βεβαιοτάτην πρὸς τοὺς βασιλεῖς τετηρηκώς κ.τ.λ. (Diod. xviii.58.4). Eumenes' negotiations with the central government at the time of Nora, although obfuscated by the secondary authors, likewise imply a hard-headed grasp of political manœuvring. In Diodorus, Eumenes' flight to Nora is followed by an analysis of Antigonus' ambitions (now that he had taken over Eumenes' satrapies and his army he decided no longer to

---

[235] Cf. A. Vezin, *Eumenes*, p. 126; Tarn, *CAH*, vi, pp. 479 ff. See also Diod. xviii.57.4, 29.2, 42.4; Plut. *Eum*. i.4, v.8; Nep. *Eum*. vi.5, iii.1; Heidelberg Epitome, *F. Gr. Hist.* 155, III.1–2.

[236] Cf. Westlake, art. cit., pp. 319 ff.

take orders from the kings and regent), and Antigonus' offer of a *koinopragia* with Eumenes (Diod. xviii 41.4–7). Eumenes makes excessive demands—his satrapies to be returned, and clearance of all the charges against him—which Antigonus refers to Antipater; Eumenes then sends his own envoys to Antipater. There follow some reflections on the varied fortune of Eumenes, which led him to hope for better things, and a passage which purports to set out Eumenes' views on the current state of affairs in the empire: ἑώρα γὰρ τοὺς μὲν τῶν Μακεδόνων βασιλεῖς κενὸν ἔχοντας τὸ τῆς βασιλείας πρόσχημα, πολλοὺς δὲ καὶ μεγάλους τοῖς φρονήμασιν ἄνδρας διαδεχομένους. ἤλπιζεν οὖν, ὅπερ ἦν πρὸς ἀλήθειαν, πολλοὺς αὐτοῦ χρείαν ἕξειν διά τε τὴν φρόνησιν καὶ τὴν ἐμπειρίαν τῶν πολεμικῶν, ἔτι δὲ τὴν ὑπερβολὴν τῆς ἐν τῇ πίστει βεβαιότητος. (xviii.42.2). The view that these sentiments represent the substance of Eumenes' message to Antipater (delivered by Hieronymus) is extremely plausible;[237] and possibly the account of Antigonus' plans in chapter 41 is in fact a denunciation which has the same origin. Antigonus actually made no move against the central government until the following year, after Antipater's death; but Eumenes had perhaps learned a lesson from Antigonus' own denunciation of Perdiccas;[238] there was a chance to re-establish his credit at the expense of Perdiccas' successor. At the same time a threat was implied that he might sell his services elsewhere: ἤλπιζεν . . . πολλοὺς αὐτοῦ χρείαν ἕξειν. Antigonus had proposed a *koinopragia*, and unless the regent offered him better terms, Eumenes might be forced to back the 'apostate', as he had once backed Perdiccas.[239] This is not an elevating picture of the supposed champion of Alexander's house, despite its dressing of phrases with the word 'pistis'; and the remark κενόν . . . τὸ τῆς βασιλείας πρόσχημα, reveals for a moment Eumenes' consciousness of realities.

In the period after Antipater's death Eumenes' relation to the new regent and to the royal family is said to have been one of mutual trust and support. Polyperchon may have been persuaded by the representations of Hieronymus and his embassy that Eumenes was a lesser danger than Antigonus: while he attended to Cassander's revolt, the prospect of the two generals safely embroiled in Asia was in any case perhaps not unwelcome; and it may be significant that the sen-

---

[237] Briant, *REA* lxxv (1973), p. 74.

[238] Diod. xviii.25.3. See de Sanctis, art. cit., pp. 137 ff. for the view that Antigonus' charges against Perdiccas were unfounded, and below, p. 166 n. 262.

[239] Cf. E. M. Anson, 'The siege of Nora: a source conflict', *GRBS* xviii (1977), pp. 251 ff., arguing that Plutarch's story of Eumenes' altering his oath to Antigonus is unreliable and probably derives from Duris, and that in fact, for some three months of summer 318, Eumenes owned allegiance to Antigonus.

tence of outlawry hanging over Eumenes was apparently not revoked at this time.[240] Whatever the private misgivings of the regent, the repeated assertion in our sources that Eumenes enjoyed the trust of Olympias is probably correct. This association raises its own questions, however. The existence of two kings had caused a deep division within the royal family: Cassander exploited the hostility between Olympias and Eurydice by supporting Philip Arrhidaeus; Polyperchon and his general in Asia were thereby naturally ranged on the side of Alexander IV. Eumenes wrote to Olympias urging her against action which could only end in a bloodbath, but in the same breath he swore his undying loyalty to the son of Alexander: *basileis* are mentioned for the sake of form and diplomacy, but Olympias' grandson is specified by name (Diod. xviii.58.4). Hence it is misleading to speak of Eumenes as supporter of 'the royal house' or the 'legitimate' line: had the child Alexander survived, Eumenes would have enjoyed a position of supreme influence and power at his court, and at some point a clash with the rival line of Philip and Eurydice must have been inevitable.

The presence of Cleopatra at Sardis during the period 322 to 308 adds a further dimension to the problem. Cleopatra had come to Asia in the first instance to marry Perdiccas on the orders of Olympias;[241] but on the death of Perdiccas she decided to manage her own affairs. Her proposal to Leonnatus shows her consciousness of her own importance at an early stage after Alexander's death;[242] and a return to Macedon after 321, to a position in which, at best, she would be overshadowed by the figures of Antipater, Olympias, and her infant nephew, was not a prospect to relish.[243] By setting up court at Sardis she presented herself as a prize for the victor of the struggle in Asia: she offered to an ambitious general an alternative link with the Argead line, and according to Diodorus, she was courted at one time or another by nearly all the Successors, including Cassander, Lysimachus, Antigonus, and Ptolemy.[244] Eumenes had seen the possibilities at an early stage: he advised Perdiccas to marry her, but Perdiccas, on Alcetas' persuasion, married Nicaea.[245] After the rift with Antipater and divorce from Nicaea, Eumenes courted Cleopatra on Perdiccas' behalf; and during the war against Antipater, Cleopatra gave

---

[240] As Westlake suggests, art. cit., pp. 326 ff. Cf. Diod. xix.12.2: Seleucus gave this as a reason for not joining Eumenes in his war against Antigonus.

[241] Arr. *Succ.* F9.21.

[242] Plut. *Eum.* iii.5.

[243] Beloch, *Gr. Gesch.* iv.² 1, p. 83, suggests bad relations with Antipater as the reason for Cleopatra's remaining at Sardis.

[244] Diod. xx.37.3–6.

[245] Arr. *Succ.* F9.21.

assistance to Eumenes and saved his life.[246] Antipater later harangued her on the subject and accused her of being in cahoots with Perdiccas and Eumenes, and she answered him back, κρεῖσσον ἢ κατὰ γυναῖκα.[247] According to Plutarch, Eumenes had further dealings with Cleopatra after Perdiccas' death and his own condemnation. He wished to give battle on the plain of Sardis, both because of his superiority in cavalry, ἅμα καὶ τῇ Κλεοπάτρᾳ τὴν δύναμιν ἐπιδεῖξαι φιλοτιμούμενος; and it was at this time that his friends received from him 'honours such as kings bestow'—ἃς οἱ φίλοι παρὰ τῶν βασιλέων; 'for he was empowered to distribute purple caps and military cloaks, and this was a special gift of royalty among the Macedonians.'[248] If Plutarch's chronological sequence is correct, and he has not confused this with the episode that took place, according to Arrian, during Perdiccas' lifetime, this is an astonishing statement.[249] In the period of his exile, but before the negotiations with Polyperchon and Olympias, βασιλικαὶ τιμαί could only imply a compact with Cleopatra. Had Eumenes played Tristan to Perdiccas' King Mark? His connection with Cleopatra was perhaps inhibited by the new understanding reached with Olympias in the following year: Olympias seems to have lost interest in her daughter's prospects after the return of the kings to Macedon, and to have pinned all her hopes on the young Alexander. But Cleopatra could have remained Eumenes' second string until Gabiene.

Eumenes' death at Gabiene leaves many questions unanswered. The test of his loyalty would have come only with victory over Antigonus, leaving him as master of Asia; his failure meant that the claims Hieronymus made for him could not easily be disproved. That he was really governed by motives quite different from those of the other generals, is, however, a proposition in itself highly improbable, and which is not borne out by his actions in the period before he was made *strategos autokrator*. The loyalty motif made Eumenes something of a tragic figure in Hieronymus' history, and gave him a significance which he would otherwise have lacked. It imparted a moral tone to this part of the narrative, in which judgements generally turned on questions of expediency. Histories centring on the individual inevitably inclined to moral judgements: this was clearly the case with Theopompus' history of Philip, which was designed to portray a grand embodiment of vice and virtue;[250] and the Peripatetic account of Demetrius which lies

[246] Arr. *Succ.* F9.26; cf. Justin xiv.1.7.
[247] Arr. *Succ.* F10.8–10, cf. F11.40.   [248] Plut. *Eum.* viii.4, viii.7.
[249] Cf. Arr. *Succ.* F10.8–10 with F11.40.
[250] Cf. C. Grayson, in *The Ancient Historian and his Materials*, p. 39.

behind parts of Plutarch's *Life* shows the same concern with moral features. It is likely that Hieronymus' account of Eumenes was based on an early phase of his writing. He may have begun by composing, directly after Eumenes' death, an encomium *in memoriam*, which was later incorporated into his general history of the Successors (this is suggested by his use of certain oral sources in this section);[251] and at this stage he perhaps looked to the established literary forms of the fourth century in which individuals were presented as *paradeigmata*. When re-working this section at a later time, the tone of apologia may have become more pronounced: Duris had perhaps represented Eumenes as tricky and ambitious, and Hieronymus wrote in reply to his hostile criticism.

An interesting parallel is offered by the literary tradition which grew up around the figure of Hermias of Atarneus, the close friend of Aristotle, put to death treacherously by Mentor and the Persian king.[252] Aristotle and Callisthenes appear to have founded the biographical tradition favourable to Hermias when they composed, for a memorial service, a hymn and encomium celebrating him as the upholder of Hellenic honour against barbarian treachery. It was taken up by Hermippus, and later Peripatetics came to idealize him as the type of the philosophic ruler. It was probably Theopompus, whose vitriolic attacks on Hermias are preserved through Didymus' scholia to Demosthenes, who was the source of the continuing hostile tradition, developed by critics of the Peripatetics. Among the points Theopompus stressed in his depiction of the tyrant were his humble origins and his avarice—attributes which Duris attached to Eumenes. The favourable tradition on Eumenes wanted it clear that Eumenes was 'summo genere', and Diodorus stresses that at first Eumenes *refused* the 500 talents sent to him by Polyperchon: Eumenes was at various times in charge of large sums of money, a fact bound to cause malicious gossip.[253]

Denigration of personal opponents and inflation of the subject's virtues were standard tricks of autobiography and commemorative writing (Aratus' memoirs are a good example of the way a Hellenistic statesman and general sought to exculpate himself from the charges of his enemies and render an account of his life): this kind of memoir writing probably had its roots partly in the law courts, where personal

---

[251] Cf. above, pp. 124 f.

[252] See D. Wormell, 'The Literary Tradition Concerning Hermias of Atarneus', *YCS* v (1935), pp. 57 ff.; cf. W. Jaeger, *Aristotle* (trans. Robinson), pp. 117 ff.

[253] Nepos *Eum*. i.3; Diod. xviii.60.2, cf. xix.15.5. For Duris' statements cf. above, p. 154 n. 209.

and autobiographical considerations might enter into even non-political cases.[254] Since Eumenes could not write his own memoirs, his old comrade-in-arms sprang to his defence; and since attacks on Eumenes' memory doubtless cast aspersions also on his former companions, there was perhaps in this part of the history an element of *antidosis* by the historian on his own behalf.

The policies of the Antigonids

Hieronymus' personal commitment to Eumenes prevents any conclusion about his own attitude to the question of legitimacy. It is clear that the posthumous influence of Alexander was in many ways very considerable. The men who had been his companions or served in his army boasted of the fact, and his name was used as a talisman in the battles of the Successors.[255] The attempts of many of the generals to secure an alliance with Cleopatra, and the (unjustified) claim of the Antigonids to a blood relationship with Philip and Alexander, again illustrate the enormous prestige which the Argead name continued to bear, long after the actual extinction of the line;[256] and the younger generation, especially Demetrius and Pyrrhus, hero-worshipped Alexander and imitated the superficial trappings of his charismatic figure.[257] Memories of Alexander as a real personality seem to have faded quickly, however: possibly only Hephaestion had ever known him well, and the King had become a legend even before his death. Instances of real loyalty to his memory are hard to find, if one doubts the sincerity of Eumenes' professions; and there is neither evidence nor probability that Hieronymus felt himself bound by institutional loyalty to Alexander's house. We may take it that a man in Hieronymus' position would tend to be φιλαντίγονος or φιλευμενής, not φιλοβασιλεύς—to adapt Alexander's remark about Craterus.[258]

Whatever one's judgement of Eumenes, then, it is not legitimate to view Hieronymus himself as a sentimental royalist, but only as the

---

[254] Cf. Misch, *History of Autobiography*, i, pp. 203 ff.

[255] See Briant, *Antigone le Borgne*, pp. 129 ff. and J. Seibert, *Untersuchungen zur Geschichte Ptolemaios I*, pp. 152–6, for the main evidence; cf. below, ch. 5, pp. 189 f. See also C. Picard, 'Le trône vide d'Alexandre', *Cahiers Archéologique* vii (1964), pp. 1–17, on the cult of Alexander in Eumenes' army. Visions of Alexander: Diod. xviii.60.4–6; Plut. *Pyrrh.* xi.2; Plut. *Demetr.* xxix.1; Plut. *Eum.* vi.5–6, and cf. vii.3, οὐ καταισχύνας ὁ Κρατερὸς τὸν Ἀλέξανδρον (as though Alexander were watching the battle).

[256] Antigonids and Argeads: C. F. Edson, *HSCP* xlv (1934), pp. 213 ff.; see now Briant, *Antigone le Borgne*, pp. 19 ff. on the probable descent of Monophthalmus. The Lagids, too, asserted blood kinship with Alexander: cf. Brunt, Loeb edn. of Arrian i, App. v, pp. 478 f.

[257] See below, ch. 5, p. 195.

[258] Plut. *Alex.* xlvii.5; cf. Diod. xvii.114.2.

apologist of Eumenes. By praise of Eumenes' character and actions he had sought to redeem and to enshrine the memory of a friend: this was apologia, or historical propaganda.

More insidious distortion could result from the interpretation of past events in terms of present politics—in short, political propaganda. Two political issues were central to Hieronymus' history, the unity of the empire, and the freedom of the Greeks; and on both, it has been argued, the historian's outlook was conditioned by the policies of Antigonus Gonatas. Jacoby concluded that Hieronymus, 'during the incessant battles of Alexander's Successors, gained a conviction of the purposelessness of the struggle after sole dominion . . . He must have recognized the wise restraint of Gonatas as the only possible policy.' A more recent view regards Hieronymus as an able writer of 'court history', and the 'Greek encomiast' of Gonatas, who interpreted the whole period he treated in terms flattering to his royal patron. Hence Eumenes' deferential attitude to the Macedonians, the praise of Ptolemy's policies, which seemed to have anticipated those of Gonatas, and the condemnation of the impractical aspiration of Monophthalmus and Demetrius after a great Asian empire; hence, also, his 'Macedonian' attitude to the Greeks, notably in his account of the Lamian War and of the regime of Demetrius of Phaleron: '. . . whether his interpretation was inspired by Antigonus and his advisors, or whether the wise old Cardian was a schoolmaster to his king . . . the policy of the one and the history of the other are inextricably bound together. To suggest that both men reached the same conclusion independently while the one was the retainer of the other would be arbitrary and unconvincing.'[259] The evidence for this view lies partly in the remarks of Pausanias on Hieronymus' bias, partly in the belief that Hieronymus' entire literary effort belongs to the end of his life—a questionable assumption.[260] A realistic estimate of Hieronymus' political views must depend on close examination of manner and diction in Diodorus.

A series of passages in Diodorus xviii analyse the political aspirations and the intentions of the Diadochi, and these are unlikely to be the work of Diodorus himself: he rarely speculates on motivation in other books, and where he does offer an extended estimate of an individual—Themistocles—it can be shown that he was copying his source, Ephorus, almost word for word.[261] Hence there is a

[259] Jacoby, *RE* 'Hieronymos', cols. 1545–6; T. S. Brown, *Am. Hist. Rev.* 1947, pp. 694–5.
[260] See App. I, pp. 246 ff. on Pausanias' evidence; below, pp. 173 f. for the date of composition.   [261] Cf. ch. 2, pp. 28 f., App. II, p. 278.

prima facie case for regarding these passages as the literary device of Hieronymus.

Perdiccas is introduced at the moment when he had completed his wars in Cappadocia and Pisidia and began to plan for the future. He had at first intended to co-operate with Antipater, but when his position was secure (i.e. as a consequence of his military successes), and he had control of the kings and the regency, he changed his plans: ὀρεγόμενος γὰρ βασιλείας ἔσπευδε τὴν Κλεοπάτραν γῆμαι, νομίζων διὰ ταύτης προτρέψεσθαι τοὺς Μακεδόνας συγκατασκευάζειν αὐτῷ τὴν τῶν ὅλων ἐξουσίαν. For the present, however, he concealed his real intention by marrying Nicaea.[262]

Antigonus' case, in the period after Triparadeisos, is parallel. Having secured his position by his victory over Eumenes, μειζόνων πραγμάτων ὠρέγετο. For the present he pretended to be well disposed to Antipater, but he had determined eventually to take orders from no one (xviii.41.4–5). Then, when the death of Antipater became known, there was a general stirring of personal aspirations: τῶν ἐν ἐξουσίαις ὄντων ἰδιοπραγεῖν ἐπιβαλομένων. Among these, the foremost was Antigonus, whose power had so increased that he inspired to ἡ τῶν ὅλων ἡγεμονία (xviii.50.1–2).

This parallels the Perdiccas passage in both form and language. The grounds for the dynast's hopes are his recent military successes; he desires supreme power (the expressions ὀρέγεσθαι and τὰ ὅλα are used); he plans to abandon his alliance with Antipater, but for a while conceals his true intention; the death of a unifying figure releases high ambitions (compare Diod. xviii.2.1, on the death of Alexander, ἀναρχία καὶ πολλὴ στάσις ἐγένετο περὶ τῆς ἡγεμονίας, and xviii.50.1, on the death of Antipater, ἀρχὴ πραγμάτων καινῶν ἐγίνετο καὶ κίνησις).

---

[262] Diod. xviii.23.2–3. Bosworth's interpretation of this controversial passage (*CQ* n.s. xxi (1971), p. 135, with references to earlier discussion), in terms of a conspiracy against Alexander by his generals, must remain highly uncertain. On the face of it, Diodorus refers to the period *after* Alexander's death (for παρέλαβε τὰς . . . δυνάμεις κ.τ.λ., compare xviii.3.1, παραλαβὼν τὴν τῶν ὅλων ἡγεμονίαν κ.τ.λ.) and the improvement in his position at this moment is the result of his successful Pisidian campaign (N.B. xviii.22.8, the wealth of the booty taken at Isauria). Cf. Briant, *REA* lxxiv (1972), p. 47. For Perdiccas' earlier difficulties with his army cf. Briant, *Antigone le Borgne*, pp. 147–9, 160: hence Diodorus' μήπω . . . βεβαίως ἐστερεωμένων. The similar account of Antigonus (xviii.41.4–6), whom Bosworth does not involve in the alleged plot against Alexander, weakens his argument. The same passage calls in question also De Sanctis's thesis ('Perdicca', in *Problemi di storia antica*, pp. 137 ff.) that Perdiccas, actually an innocent victim of the jealousy of the other generals, was maligned by Hieronymus to exculpate his later master, Antigonus Monophthalmus: on the contrary, he saw Antigonus as a second Perdiccas. The murder of Cynane doubtless seemed to substantiate Antigonus' accusation: Arr. *Succ.* F9.22–4, cf. Errington, *JHS* xc (1970), pp. 49 ff.

To these ambitions the attitude of Ptolemy forms a direct contrast. The death of Perdiccas in Egypt offered Ptolemy the chance to step into his shoes and assume the supreme command. Coming before the assembled Macedonians he spoke 'in defence of his own attitude' (περὶ . . .τῶν καθ' αὐτὸν ἀπελογήσατο), and gained great applause; but though he was in a position to take over the regency, τούτου μὲν οὐκ ὠρέχθη, τῷ δὲ Πίθωνι καὶ ᾿Αρριδαίῳ χαρίτας ὀφείλων συγκατεσκεύασε τὴν τῶν ὅλων ἡγεμονίαν. He shrewdly passed the fatal gift to others. Here Ptolemy's situation parallels that of Perdiccas or Antigonus. The death of the chief man in the empire creates a vacuum; recent military success leads to power and popularity with the army; the question of supreme power arises, and Diodorus again uses the expressions ὀρέγεσθαι, and ἡ τῶν ὅλων ἡγεμονία.

The linguistic features here singled out are not unique to Diodorus' history of the Successors. The phrase τὰ ὅλα or ἡ τῶν ὅλων ἡγεμονία is used frequently both in Diodorus and Polybius with the vague connotation, 'supreme power', referring, for example, to the competence of generals or the hegemony of Greece.[263] In Diodorus xviii–xx, however, it occurs with unusual frequency–sixteen times in three books, as against nineteen times in all the preceding books of the *Bibliotheke*. Naturally this has something to do with the subject-matter. Hieronymus was surely aware of the totality of the struggle, and this Diodorus reflects. Hieronymus' way of expressing it is harder to identify; but there are some indications that he may have used the phrase τὰ ὅλα, 'the whole', as in Diodorus, signifying the whole of Alexander's empire, sometimes in a territorial sense, sometimes as a political concept, i.e. power over the whole. The speech of the Argyraspid at Gabiene uses this phrase: ''Επὶ τοὺς πατέρας ἁμαρτάνετε, ὦ κακαὶ κεφαλαί, τοὺς μετὰ Φιλίππου καὶ ᾿Αλεξάνδρου τὰ ὅλα κατειργασμένους.' The speech may well be authentic, and must at any rate derive from Diodorus' source, since it is also recorded by Plutarch (though Plutarch reproduces only the first part of it).[264] In this example, τὰ ὅλα apparently denotes the conquests of Philip and Alexander as a geographical entity. Elsewhere in xviii–xx the phrase appears repeatedly in connection with the ambitions of the Diadochi: in addition to the instances already cited, it is used of Perdiccas

---

[263] Diod. i.17.3, ii.32.2; iii.61.4; xiii.49.3; xiv.27.1; xv.8.2; xvi.59.4; xviii.23.6, etc. P. S. Derow, *JRS* lxix (1979), gives specific meaning to τὰ ὅλα in Polybius: 'On the one side there are orders and on the other obedience. Rome's possession of ἡ τῶν ὅλων ἀρχὴ καὶ δυναστεία means that everyone must in practice obey Roman orders, and ἡ τῶν ὅλων ἐπιβολή accordingly refers to Rome's intention to bring this state of affairs about' (pp. 4 f., cf. p. 6).

[264] Diod. xix.41.1; Plut. *Eum.* xvi.4.

(xviii.3.1), Cassander (xviii.49.2), Antigonus (xviii.54.4, xix.93.5), Cassander (xviii.49.2), Antigonus (xviii.54.4, xix.93.5), Ptolemy and Demetrius (xx.51.1 at Salamis), Cassander and Demetrius (xx.110.5, before Ipsus); and at xx.37.4 Diodorus says that each of the Successors wanted a connection with the royal house through Cleopatra, ὡς τὴν τῶν ὅλων ἀρχὴν περιστήσων εἰς ἑαυτόν.[265]

As early as 311 τὰ ὅλα appears in Chancery language: Monophthalmus himself used it twice in his letter to the Scepsians.[266] Arrian in the fifth book of the τὰ μετὰ Ἀλέξανδρον is quoted for the sentence 'σε δὲ εἶναι τὸν βουλεύοντά τε ὑπὲρ τῶν ὅλων τὰ ξυμφορώτατα καὶ ἐπαγγέλλοντα πᾶν ὅ τι περ ἂν ξυλλογισμῶι τύχηι ξυμβουλευθέν' (context uncertain).[267] It is perhaps significant, too, that Polybius uses the phrase in a context which alludes to the ancestors of Philip V: Philip's house, he says, had always coveted universal dominion—ἡ μάλιστά πως ἀεὶ τῆς τῶν ὅλων ἐλπίδος ἐφίεται—and this has to be taken as a reference to Antigonus Monophthalmus and Demetrius, since the later Antigonids had less obviously entertained grandiose hopes of overseas empire.[268] Finally, Nepos has possibly translated τὰ ὅλα from a Greek source in his *Life of Eumenes* with the phrase *summae res* or *summa rerum*. The strongest expression used by Latin authors to denote possession of total power is *rerum potiri*: thus Augustus in the *Res Gestae* (34.1), 'per consensum universorum [potitus reru]m om[n]ium' (=[κ]ατὰ τὰς εὐχὰς τῶν ἐ/μῶν πολε[ι]τῶν ἐγκρατὴς γενόμενος πάντων τῶν πραγμάτων).[269] Nepos, while he once writes *summi imperii potiretur* (Eum. vii.1), regularly, however, chooses the phrase *summa rerum* (*Eum.* v.1, cf. ii.1), or *summae res* (*Eum.* vii.2, x.3) to convey the sense 'supreme power.' At *Eum.* ii.1 the sentence 'Alexandro Babylone mortuo, cum . . . summa tradita esset tuenda Perdiccae', seems to correspond to Diod. xviii.3.1, οὗτος δὲ (sc. Περδίκκας) παραλαβὼν τὴν τῶν ὅλων ἡγεμονίαν; and at *Eum.*v.1, 'Perdiccas apud Nilum flumen interficitur . . . rerumque summa ad Antipatrum defertur', compares with Diodorus xviii.36.6. Possibly, then Nepos preserves this phrase in a Latin translation.

It can be said, with a slightly greater degree of certainty, that the words ἰδιοπραγία and ἰδιοπραγέω may originate with Hieronymus.

---

[265] Cf. also Diod. xxxi.19.4.
[266] Welles, *RC*, no. 1, lines 15–16, 23.
[267] Arrian, *Succ.* F8.
[268] Polyb. v.102.1. Cf. Walbank, *Philip V*, p. 260 (though see below, n. 278); Edson, art. cit., p. 222 n. 1.
[269] Cf. Lucretius ii.13; Cic. *ad fam.* viii.14.2; and Syme, *Tacitus*, p. 412: 'To denominate the regiment of the Caesars he (sc. Tacitus) singles out a term than which the Latin language knows none stronger: *rerum potiri*.'

These terms occur eight times in Diodorus xviii (including xviii.50.1:
see above), and nowhere else in the *Bibliotheke*.[270] In general, *idiopragia* characterizes the behaviour of those ambitious diadochs who tried
to make themselves independent of the central power: thus Pithon,
xviii.7.4; Antigonus, xviii.39.7, 50.1, 52.7 (cf. 58.4, Ἀντιγόνῳ . . .
ἐξιδιαζομένῳ τὴν βασιλείαν); and Eumenes, the loyal servant of the
Argeads, is contrasted explicitly with οἱ ἰδιοπραγοῦντες (xviii.42.2,
62.7). The verb ἰδιοπραγέω usually has the non-moral sense, 'acting
by oneself', 'acting independently', or even 'minding ones own business' (i.e. like ἰδιοπραγμονεύω, ἰδιοπράγμων, as opposed to
πολυπράγμων).[271] *Idiopragia* is a much rarer word. Plato coupled it
with *pleonexia*, claiming that, ἐπὶ πλεονεξίαν καὶ ἰδιοπραγίαν ἡ
θνητὴ φύσις αὐτὸν ὡρμήσει ἀεί;[272] so that, on the face of it, this is a
term embodying a moral or political judgement, and this is how
Diodorus has taken it. *Idiopragia* has the antonym *koinopragia*, a term
not unique to Diodorus xviii–xx (and it is used *passim* by Polybius), but
one especially frequent here, because it was demanded by the historical matter.[273] *Koinopragiai* were the private agreements made between the diadochs for common action in the period before they
became kings: *symmachiai*, international agreements, were concluded
at a time when they had become completely independent and negotiated as between one state and another.[274] *Idiopragia* and *koinopragia*
therefore do not have the same extension, though in the context of this
narrative they are connected: more than once a group of the generals
makes a 'compact for common action' against 'one acting on his own'.

It is thus arguable that certain key words have survived from
Hieronymus in Diodorus: τὰ ὅλα, denoting the aim and at the same
time the scope of the struggle among the diadochs; ἰδιοπραγία, and
perhaps κοινοπραγία, describing the way the generals ganged up
successively on the one strongest among them; ὀρέγεσθαι, suggesting
the grasping of the most powerful after the supreme prize. These are
the terms which define a central idea in the narrative before Ipsus; but
they do not, in themselves, imply a committed view on the part of the
historian to the dissolution of the empire. A desire for simplification
among the secondary authors must be reckoned with: hence they tend

---

[270] Diod. xviii.7.4, 9.2, 39.7, 42.2, 52.7, 62.7, 64.6. This is the only example of a word
which is unique to one section of Diodorus: cf. Palm, *Über Sprache und Stil*, p. 109.
[271] Cf. Polyb. viii.26.9; Strabo xii.3.28; Hesychius, s.v. ἰδιοπραγεῖ.
[272] Plato, *Legg.* 9, p. 875B.
[273] Diod. xvi.37.2, 50.6; xvii.3.2, 5.1; xviii.9.5, 14.2, 23.2, 25.4, 29.4, 41.6, 49.2, 53.5,
53.7, 57.3; xix.17.2, 58.5; xx.27.3, 28.3, 106.2, 107.4.
[274] Cf. Rosen, 'Die Bündnisformen der Diadochen und der Zerfall des Alexanderreiches', *AC* xi (1968), pp. 182–210.

to retroject Antigonus' great plans to an early stage in his career, although he could hardly have entertained hopes of empire until at least the death of Antipater;[275] and the evidence suggests he was slow to take the final step of proclaiming himself *basileus*.[276] Exaggerated judgements of Monophthalmus might, too, be encouraged by the encomiastic treatment of Eumenes. Again, the praise of the 'separatist' Ptolemy, cannot be disentangled from Diodorus' universally favourable picture of this dynast, and is not necessarily to be explained as a comment on the policy of Antigonus Gonatas. Condemnation of those who aspired to 'the whole' is not, therefore, to be inferred. We should rather suppose that τὰ ὅλα was an obsessive concept for Hieronymus, as the idea of ἀρχή was for Thucydides. He admired a man like Monophthalmus for the grandeur of his vision, as Thucydides admired the greatness of the Athenian empire, without concealing the brutality of the methods by which power was achieved and maintained; but he condemned the folly of a perpetual grasping after more: ὀρέγεσθαι was the word Thucydides used to describe the greed of the Athenians for further and further conquests.[277] The estimate of Antigonus at Plutarch, *Demetrius* xxviii, probably derives in substance from Hieronymus, and here the point is that his *philarchia* was *excessive*, hence he threw away a great empire. There is no suggestion that Hieronymus condemned in principle the rule of Alexander's empire by a single man; and to suppose that he would not have wished to see Gonatas master of Antigoneia is surely to misconceive the matter. We now know from the Labraunda documents that the Antigonids in the dark period before Philip V had tried to maintain a sphere of influence in Asia Minor;[278] even in the time of Cassander—to all appearances a

[275] Cf. Plut. *Eum.* iii.3; Briant, *Antigone le Borgne*, pp. 150, 229–34, etc. Similarly, Plutarch has probably exaggerated the *pleonexia* motif in his *Pyrrhus*: cf. above, p. 139 n. 141.

[276] For the stages of Antigonus' career and the development of his intentions see O. Müller, *Antigonos Monophthalmos*, pp. 45 ff. and 78 ff. But the evidence cited by Müller for an increasing inclination in the period 316–306 to the *title* to Alexander's empire is not compelling: Diod. xix.48.1 and 55.2 (Antigonus treated as a king by the peoples of Asia and by Seleucus at Babylon) suggest only the natural desire of the locals to ingratiate themselves with the conqueror of Eumenes (similarly *OGIS* 6, honours voted to Antigonus by the Scepsians); Diod. xix.97.3, the greeting of the Nabataean, 'Βασιλεῦ Δημήτριε', is surely a matter of politeness, and the speech is in any case hardly verbatim; Diod. xix.93.4, Antigonus recognized that Demetrius was βασιλείας ἄξιος, (cf. xix.81.4), i.e. saw Demetrius as *like a king*: it may be supposed that Antigonus came to desire the royal title because he thought he had in Demetrius a son able to retain it.

[277] Thuc. iv.21.2, vi.10.5, ii.65.10, iv.17.4, iv.83.1. For ὀρέγεσθαι in other books of Diodorus, cf. xvi.8.4; xvii.30.4; xvii.54.6.

[278] Trogus, *Prol.* 28, 'Cariam subiecit' (between the death of Demetrius II and Doson's capture of Sparta); cf. Polyb. xx.5.7–11, Doson sailed from Boeotia εἰς τὴν Ἀσίαν. The evidence for the Macedonian occupation of Caria c.227 is now supported

true exponent of the 'Macedon for the Macedonians' policy—there is a hint of the longing for overseas domains in Diodorus' account of the expedition to Caria in 314 (Diod. xix.68, cf. 69.1, *'Αντίγονος δ'ὁρῶν τὸν Κάσανδρον ἀντεχόμενον τῆς 'Ασίας*). Hieronymus censured in Monophthalmus not his objectives but his methods.[279]

Hieronymus' attitude to the Greeks is altogether a different problem. By Gonatas' time, the idea of a united Macedonian empire was hypothetical: territorial boundaries in and around the Aegean might shift their position, but no one after the death of Demetrius seriously thought he might reconstitute Alexander's kingdom. Relations between the Macedonian suzerains and their subjects, on the other hand, were an immediate and continuing issue. On this topic, it may be supposed, the historian was not altogether free from constraint, and in his treatment of the Lamian War and the settlements of Antipater and Cassander, he did adopt the official Macedonian line. In 322 Antipater deported 12,000 Athenian citizens to Thrace, abolished the Athenian democracy, restricted the franchise to a body of 9,000 wealthy citizens, and installed a garrison under the phrourarch Menyllus (Diod. xviii.18.4–6). Only a historian with pronounced Macedonian sympathies could say that Antipater had acted *φιλανθρώπως* and *ἐπιεικῶς* (xviii.18.4,8). The settlement of 317 was not less oppressive: the garrison remained in Munychia, the franchise was limited to possessors of at least ten minae, Demetrius of Phaleron was set up as *epimeletes* of Athens. Yet Diodorus' account of Cassander's dealings with Athens concludes: *τῆς πόλεως ἦρχεν* (sc. *ὁ Φαληρεύς*) *εἰρηνικῶς καὶ πρὸς τοὺς πολίτας φιλανθρώπως*. This may have been no more than the truth: the prosperity of Athens under Demetrius was admitted even by his most bitter enemies;[280] and Cassander himself perhaps

---

by the implication in the Labraunda documents 5–7 (mentioning correspondence between Olympichus and Antigonus Doson) that Philip V was already suzerain of Caria when he inherited the throne in 221. (J. Crampa, *Labraunda: Swedish Excavations and Researches*, iii, 1, *Period of Olympichus*, nos. 5–7, pp. 22 f.) Tarn's analysis of the 'sphere' of Antigonus Gonatas, and his conclusion that Gonatas meant to be 'a Macedonian king of Macedonians and nothing more' (*Antigonos Gonatas*, pp. 202–6) becomes less certain in the light of this new evidence for overseas interests in the following period.

[279] Rosen, 'Politische Ziele in der frühen hellenistichen Geschichtsschreibung', *Hermes* cvii (1979), pp. 460 ff., rightly sees Antigonus Gonatas as no mere practitioner of retrenchment and Stoic restraint, but an exponent of 'pleonexia' policies against the Ptolemies in the Aegean and Greece; while the peace of 278 with Antiochus, though a deal which lasted fifty years, was actually due to fear of involvement on a second front.

[280] Diod. xviii.74.3; cf. 75.2, Cassander is praised for *epieikeia*, Polyperchon is treated with contempt (cf. ch. 5, pp. 224 f.). For Athens' prosperity under Demetrius of Phaleron see Demochares *ap.* Polyb. xii.13.9 ff. = *F. Gr. Hist.* 75 F2; Duris *ap.* Athen. xii.542C = *F. Gr. Hist.* 76 F10, and Diog. Laert. v.75. Cf. W. S. Ferguson, *Hellenistic Athens*, pp. 58 f. and 59 n. 1.

deserved some credit for the ten years of good government (cf. Strabo ix.398). Nevertheless, this can hardly be viewed as an isolated concession to a peaceful regime by a liberty-loving Hieronymus:[281] φιλανθρωπία and ἐπιείκεια were words denoting the condescension of a master to his inferiors.

If Hieronymus were still revising his work in the 260s, the current situation demanded a careful handling of the great revolt of 323 to 322; no contemporary could have ignored the parallel between the Lamian and the Chremonidean War, or between the measures taken by Cassander and by Gonatas to pacify the Greek states.[282] Not only the position of Athens was still a living issue. The case of the lesser cities, Megalopolis, for example, offered a point of comparison. Aristodemus of Megalopolis, established in power at least soon after the battle of Corinth in 264, was one of the most important and most capable of the tyrants patronized by Gonatas. He was known as 'the good'—ὁ χρηστός;[283] and possibly his victory over Acrotatus of Sparta argues an established popularity and influence among the citizens of Megalopolis: it must at least have had this result, for Aristodemus celebrated his triumph by adorning the city with temples and building a pillared hall in the *agora* of Megalopolis.[284] Hieronymus' account of Damis of Megalopolis was perhaps written with Aristodemus in mind.[285] Until 323 Damis' career had followed the pattern of other Greeks who, in some cases originally enfeoffed and naturalized by Philip, and becoming (like Nearchus) friends of Alexander as prince, had later joined the Asian expedition. It is likely he had accompanied Alexander as far as India, since he had experience of elephants (Diod. xviii.71.2); and he is probably to be identified with 'Damyllus' the Megalopolitan, mentioned by Curtius as one of the envoys who negotiated between Perdiccas and the mutineers at Babylon in 323.[286] By 318 he had returned to Megalopolis: possibly he had been a follower of Perdiccas and was among the fifty who were exiled along with Eumenes and Alcetas (Diod. xviii.37.2); if so, events proved that

---

[281] So S. Mazzarino, *Il Pensiero Storico*, ii, p. 336.

[282] The theme of Diod. xviii.10.3—the Athenian ambassadors are to whip up Hellenic feeling by reminding the Greek cities of the Persian wars—is a topos reappearing in the preamble to Chremonides' decree (*Syll.*³ 434–5). Cf. W. E. Fellmann, *Antigonos Gonatas, König der Makedonen, und die griechischen Staaten*, Würzburg, 1930, p. 8.

[283] Paus. viii.27.11.

[284] Paus. viii.30–5. See generally Tarn, *Antigonos Gonatas*, pp. 277 ff. on Gonatas' tyrants, and pp. 302 ff. on Aristodemus' career. Cf. Berve, *Die Tyrannis bei der Griechen*, Munich, 1967, ii, p. 713.

[285] Cf. Diod. xviii.71, *passim*; xix.64.1.

[286] Curtius x.8.15; cf. Berve, ii, no. 240, and J. Kirchner, *RE* iv s.v. 'Damis', no. 1 (neither makes the connection between Damis and Damyllus).

he had made a shrewd choice. In his own city he was a great man and the hero of the hour: turning his military expertise to good account, he led the defence of Megalopolis against the besieging forces of Polyperchon, routed Polyperchon's elephants, and saved the city. In 315 Cassander made Damis his governor in Megalopolis, and he thus became an Arcadian counterpart to Demetrius of Phaleron. Diodorus' account of the siege of 318 is written from the point of view of the defenders, and pays tribute to the *empeiria* and *epinoia* of Damis, just as it castigates Polyperchon for his incompetence. Hieronymus perhaps knew Damis as an old campaigning acquaintance from the days of Alexander; but the connection with Cassander argues a political as well as a personal motive. Antigonid Macedon was not a police state, in which the distinguished friend of Antigonus' house might expect his work to be censored.[287] Gonatas, none the less, was hardly less autocratic than other Hellenistic rulers. Tarn's portrait of the philosophically minded philhellene is only one side of the picture: cultural philhellenism was never the same as political philhellenism, and the means through which Gonatas governed his domains were tyrants, oligarchies, *strategoi*, and *epistatai*, the latter found even in Macedon itself.[288] Athens in the 260s was held in a grip of iron; and it is hardly possible that a *philos* of the king could have suggested openly that it should be otherwise.

The treatment of Greek affairs between 323 and 317, in the earliest part of Hieronymus' work, is the only argument—*a priori* considerations apart—for the date of its final completion or revision, since Hieronymus had no cause to applaud the policies of Antipater and Cassander at the time he was serving Monophthalmus and Demetrius,

---

[287] It is sometimes suggested in connection with the debate on Phylarchus' origins that he could not have written his criticisms of Ptolemy while living at Naucratis (cf. Kroymann, *RE* Suppl. viii, cols. 471–2); but this is to misunderstand the relation between intellectuals and the state, a relation which the Ptolemies had to some extent tried to institutionalize through the Museum, but which was hardly oppressive in the sense implied. One had to go as far as Sotades for serious consequences to follow: Athen. 621A (eventually Patrocles sank him at sea in a leaden chest); cf. Fraser, *Ptol. Alex.* i, pp. 117 f.

[288] Tarn, *Antigonos Gonatas*, pp. 194 ff., 217 ff. on Gonatas' methods of government; but IG XII.4.373 and 374, unknown to Tarn at the time of *Antigonos Gonatas*, show what it meant to cities in the heart of Macedonia to have a Macedonian king. The recent discussion by Errington of royal titles in Hellenistic Macedon shows (against Aymard) that we cannot regard the rare style Βασιλεὺς Μακεδόνων as a regular title implying national kingship: *JHS* xciv (1974), pp. 20 ff. with references to Aymard. Cf. Hammond and Griffith, *Macedonia*, ii, pp. 387 ff. (Griffith's views: but cf. also Hammond, *CQ* xxx (1980), pp. 461 ff.). See also J. Briscoe, *The Antigonids and the Greek States*, on the inevitably restrictive character of Gonatas' policy towards Greece. For the two senses of philhellenism see Badian, *Titus Quinctius Flamininus, Philhellenism and 'Realpolitik'*, Semple Lecture, 1970, esp. pp. 53 ff.

both exponents of *eleutheria* policies and hostile to the house of Antipater. The argument is not conclusive, of course. At the time of the Lamian War matters were really very complicated. Not all the Greeks were moved by the same purposes, and hostilities like those between the Boeotians and Athenians (Diod. xviii.11.3) made some cities pro-Macedonian in their own interests; Sparta had led resistance to Macedon under King Agis, but held aloof in the Lamian War because of her reluctance to assist Athens to regain Samos.[289] If one assumes Hieronymus' narrative to have been much more detailed than Diodorus, more of the cross-currents could have been brought out in quite an objective way, and the 'clemency' of the Macedonians made less of a dominant motif (arguably Antipater's treatment of Athens was 'humane' compared with Alexander's of Thebes, and with what the Athenians might have expected). Indeed, no certain evidence on the date of writing can be adduced, unless one accepts the ancient testimony for a 'History of the Diadochi' (written after Ipsus) and a separate 'History of the Epigoni' (written at the end of the historian's life), which is not in itself compelling.[290] High office and a strenuous military or political life are no bar to literary output, as Caesar showed, to name but one: nothing prevented Hieronymus from writing continuously, and publishing in stages.[291] On the other hand, a historian with more leisure than Hieronymus might work quite slowly: there is no certain evidence that Polybius had progressed beyond Book xv by 146, by which time he had been an internee in Italy for more than twenty years and had probably thought of writing history even before that.[292] Naturally Hieronymus must, on any hypothesis, have kept

[289] For the role of Sparta and Samos in the Lamian War see Habicht, 'Der Beitrag Spartas zur Restitution von Samos während des Lamischen Krieges', *Chiron* v (1975), pp. 45 ff.; cf. Errington, 'Samos and the Lamian War', *Chiron* v (1975), pp. 51 ff. In contemporary inscriptions the Athenians advertised the war as a Ἑλληνικὸς πόλεμος (*IG* II² 448, 505, 506): 'Nothing shows more clearly the desire of Athens to include Sparta in the alliance' (Habicht, art. cit., p. 50 n. 30). Cf. Plut. *Phoc.* xxvi. Similarly, Grenfell and Hunt, *Hibeh Papyri*, vol. i, London, 1906, p. 55, no. 15, a rhetorical composition of the 3rd century BC (probably not later than the reign of Philadelphus), apparently a speech of Leosthenes, addressing an Athenian audience: it has the *eleutheria* motif (lines 122 and 138) and treats the war as 'Hellenic', like Diodorus and the inscriptions (contrast Dexippus, *F. Gr. Hist.* 100 F33, who regards it as a μισθοφορικὸς πόλεμος); cf. Lepore, 'Leostene e le origini della guerra lamiaca', *Parola del Passato* x (1955), pp. 161 ff. Conflict within cities, also, must have been not uncommon: thus at Sicyon the anti-Macedonian democrats, led by Euphron, expelled Antipater's garrison and presumably those partisans of his who controlled the government, and joined the Athenian alliance: *IG* II² 448 = *Syll.*³ 310, 317, cf. Diod. xviii.11.2.

[290] So O. Müller, *Antigonos Monophthalmos*, pp. 1–12.

[291] Cf. the situation of Ptolemy: Badian, *CW* Oct. 1971, pp. 39 ff., and A. B. Bosworth, *A Historical Commentary on Arrian's History of Alexander*, vol. i, Oxford, 1980, p. 23.

[292] Walbank, *Polybius*, pp. 16 ff.: the last reference to Carthage as still in existence is at xv.30.10.

detailed notes from an early stage in his career under the successors; and on the hypothesis here proposed, an attempt was made soon after 317 to write a historical encomium of Eumenes. It does not follow that he need have worked up all his notes or released a final version till a much later stage: Aristobulus, after all, is said to have claimed that he began to write at the age of eighty-four.[293] As Paul Valéry commented, 'A work of art is never completed, it is merely abandoned.' A theory of ceaseless revision, as Thucydides probably practised, is the most credible in Hieronymus' case, especially considering the frequency with which he changed masters; and the view is here taken that not only the last episodes on Pyrrhus, but also a final rewriting of earlier years, was undertaken as late as the 260s, when Athens, at peace, but politically emasculated, lay under the watchful eye of Heracleitus and Gonatas' *strategoi*.[294]

Hieronymus' personal sympathy with the Greek policy of Gonatas is not necessarily to be inferred from this account. Perhaps the demise of Athens as a political state seemed inevitable; perhaps, as a Greek from Cardia, with its traditional hatred of Athens and inclination to Macedon, he did not have a deep understanding of the aspirations of the Greek *poleis*: he had himself acted as Demetrius' governor in Thebes. Yet he seems to have been not without some feeling for the Greek 'hope of freedom' (Diod. xix.61.4), and he surely recognized in any case the material and psychological value of the Greek cities in the wars of the Diadochi.[295] Here Monophthalmus had shown himself a diplomat of genius: not merely the proclamation at Tyre, but the fact that, on the whole, he had put it into practice, gave him perhaps his greatest single advantage in the war after 315. Diodorus comments cynically on the insincerity of Ptolemy's rival professions (xix.62.1–2), and claims that Antigonus had decided to liberate the Greeks 'in very

[293] Aristobulus, *F. Gr. Hist.* 139 T3. (Brunt, *CQ* n.s. xxiv (1974), p. 65, doubts the truth of this figure: textual error is possible).

[294] For Heracleitus see *Syll.*³ 401, 454 (= F. Maier, *Gr. Mauerbauinschriften*, i, Heidelberg, 1959, pp. 112–14, no. 24): he had been a member of the pro-Macedonian party in Athens in the 270s, and under Macedonian patronage after the Chremonidean War become the leading figure in Athens, with military and civil authority like Demetrius of Phaleron under Cassander. For *strategoi* and garrisons maintained in Athens and Attica after the Chremonidean War, cf. *SEG* III.122 = Moretti, ii, no. 22 (lines 5–6, Apollodorus is appointed *strategos* 'by King Antigonus and by the people'; line 12, *isoteleia* is granted according to the *proairesis* of the king). The garrisons were kept down to the end of the reign of Demetrius II: Moretti ii, no. 25 (236–235 BC); *Syll.*³ 485; cf. *Syll.*³ 497 and Plut. *Arat.* xxxiv.

[295] J. Keil, *JOAI* xvi (1913), pp. 231–48 (inscriptions from Ephesus illustrating the part played by the Greek cities of Asia in the wars between 323 and 321); *OGIS* 4 = IG XII.2.45, 9–16, Antipater levies a contribution from the Greek cities in autumn 321; cf. Arr. *Succ.* F10.8 Cf. Briant, *REA* lxxiv (1972), p. 38 n. 5.

truth' (xix.78.2, γένεσθαι φανερὸν ὡς πρὸς ἀλήθειαν 'Αντίγονος ἐλευθεροῦν προῄρηται τοὺς "Ελληνας); this was shown in 313 when Ptolemaeus captured Chalcis, but left it without a garrison; and the epigraphic evidence confirms that 'liberation' was indeed central to Antigonus' policy.[296] Demetrius is said to have pursued the cause with zeal (Diod. xx.45.1, and an exaggerated version at Plut. *Demetr.* viii.2, where Athens is described as σκοπὴ τῆς οἰκουμένης); though one should note that what he restores to the Athenians in 307 is their *patrios politeia*, that much abused term, which could have been applied equally to the Solonian constitution set up by Antipater. It was a charge in Chremonides' decree that Gonatas had subverted ancestral constitutions; but Mazzarino's gloss on the phrase as used by Diodorus, 'la quale dunque era, per Ieronimo, la democrazia', is not the necessary interpretation.[297] It was no doubt by the use of such diplomatic phraseology that Hieronymus solved the problem presented by his allegiance at different times to Demetrius and to Gonatas.

There is ambiguity, again, in the account of the Lamian War. In his narrative of the actual events, as opposed to his account of the settlement, Hieronymus was able to judge the revolt as a military, not a political enterprise. The argument of οἱ συνέσει διαφέροντες was an argument about τὸ συμφέρον: the Athenians had revolted *too soon* (προεξανίστασθαι τῶν καιρῶν), before their preparations were complete; no one argues against the actual idea of rebellion.[298] Again, the failure of the uprising is treated as a military failure, caused by the disunity of the allied forces: at the time of Crannon the Greeks found their numbers depleted, πολλοὶ γὰρ αὐτῶν . . . εἰς τὰς πατρίδας ἦσαν ἀπεληλυθότες πρὸς τὴν τῶν ἰδίων ἐπίσκεψιν (xviii.17.1); the Aetolians had gone off during the siege of Lamia, διά τινας ἐθνικὰς χρείας (xviii.13.4); after Crannon Antipater began to take the Thessalian cities piecemeal, and each negotiated with him κατ' ἰδίαν.[299] It was the same story in 321 when the Aetolians had agreed to invade Thessaly at

296 For Antigonus' Greek policy see A. Heuss, 'Antigonos Monophthalmos und die griechische Städte', *Hermes* lxxiii (1938), pp. 133 ff.; Simpson, *Historia* viii (1959), pp. 385 ff. Cf. n. 34 above.
297 *Syll.*³ 434–5, lines 14–15; Mazzarino, op. cit., p. 337. Cf. M. I. Finley, 'The Ancestral Constitution', Inaug. Lecture, rep. in *The Use and Abuse of History*, Cambridge, 1975, pp. 34 ff.
298 Diod. xviii.10.4. Cf. Hibeh Papyrus I, no. 15 (cf. above, n. 266a): in lines 26–66 Leosthenes emphasizes the need for haste, while a chance is given. Compare Diod. xviii.8.7: ἐπιτηροῦντες καιρὸν εὔθετον, ὃν ἡ τύχη ταχέως αὐτοῖς παρεσκεύασε. The argument about the timing of the revolt must have been a major issue.
299 Philip after Chaeronea had used the same strategy: cf. Aelian, *VH* vi.1; C. Roebuck, *CP* xliii (1948), p. 73 n. 1.

the time of Perdiccas' attack on Aetolia: πυθόμενοι τὰς ἰδίας πατρίδας κινδυνεύειν τοὺς μὲν ἄλλους στρατιώτας ἀπέλιπον ἐν Θετταλίᾳ κ.τ.λ. Menon was defeated and killed; Polyperchon recovered Thessaly.[300] Possibly Hieronymus gained some insight into the chronic problem of Greek disunity through his own experience of the divisions in Eumenes' army.[301] We cannot in any case assume that Diodorus' sympathetic analysis of the difficulties the Greek generals experienced is evidence of a source different from his source at xviii.18.4–9. Diyllus is sometimes suggested: but Justin shows what a genuinely pro-Greek account would look like.[302] It should rather be supposed that Hieronymus was able to look at the question of Greek sentiment and the problem of pan-hellenic action with the objective eye which Herodotus, for example, brought to bear in describing the failure of the Ionian revolt. On this occasion Hecataeus had played the part of the 'men of understanding', foreseeing the certain futility of a war waged against the vast resources of Persia.[303]

Hieronymus' own standpoint on the question of *eleutheria*, whether sentimental or pragmatic, might find a certain oblique expression in his account of actual events. But as a burning issue of both past and present it demanded also a general statement from the historian; and this was presented by the freedom-loving Nabataeans. The speech of the Nabataean elder (Diod. xix.97.3–5) articulates a dominant theme of the history; the conflict between the *philarchia* of the conqueror and the tenacious independence of his subjects. The whole history of Monophthalmus was a lesson in the disastrous consequences of authoritarianism. His understanding of Greek reactions had not been matched in his approach to the communities of Asia: the treatment of the Cossaei, the Nabataeans, the Babylonians (testified independently by the Babylonian Chronicle on the Diadochi), meant in the end the loss of that local support which might have given him a swift victory

---

[300] Diod. xviii.38.4–6.
[301] See esp. Diod. xix.17.5–6, 21.1–2, 31.3, 43.9.
[302] Justin xiii.5.17 ('hoste pulso'); cf. Hypereides, *Epitaphios* 18 etc. (Leosthenes and his soldiers were like warriors of the Persian wars); *Syll.*³ 317 (Euphron of Sicyon died for freedom and δημοκρατία). Cf. ch. 2, p. 37. The discrepancy between Diyllus, *F. Gr. Hist.* 71 F1 and Diod. xix.49 ff., argues against a general use of Diyllus by Diodorus in his history of the Diadochi (cf. Fontana, *Le lotte*, pp. 152 ff.); and the absence of marked Athenian bias in his account of the Lamian War makes it unlikely that Diyllus was used at any point: cf. Reuss, *Hieronymos*, p. 116. At xxi.5 Diodorus mentions the end point of Diyllus' work in a notice taken from the chronograph, but naturally this implies nothing about his use of Diyllus as a source. For earlier discussion see G. F. Unger, *S. B. Münch. Akad.* 1878, i, pp. 268 ff., refuted by W. Nietzold, *Die Überlieferung*, pp. 142 ff.; E. Rhode, *De Diyllo Atheniensi Diodori auctore*, Iena, 1909; W. Schwahn, 'Diyllos', *Philologus* lxxxvi (1931), pp. 145 ff.
[303] Hdt. v.36, cf. 125–6.

over Seleucus.[304] By contrast, Ptolemy, Peucestas, above all Seleucus, knew how to value the goodwill of the native populations they aspired to rule.[305] The *logos* on the Nabataeans, with its resonance of Herodotus and its idealized setting, was a safe vehicle in which to convey a serious message to a despot;[306] 'for what friends do not dare to say to kings they write in books'—so Demetrius of Phaleron told Philadelphus.[307] Whether or not one endorsed the general policy of Gonatas to the Greek cities, it was possible to think that in the measures taken after the Battle of Corinth he had gone too far. Couched in the language of utopian theory and dressed in the exotic colours of the barbarian East, Hieronymus therefore gave his warning.

The issue was the degree of freedom, not a questioning of monarchy as such. Hieronymus wrote when the fact of kingship in the Greek world was established beyond any thought of turning back, and one only asked if it were good or bad kingship; hence discussion of the best form of constitution practically vanished, essays περὶ βασιλείας proliferated. Demosthenes was dead, and with him, liberty and oratory. It was no accident that philosophy flowered in Hellenistic Athens, and that 'the Muse who found the best entertainment in Macedonia was Klio.'[308] To understand the position of Hieronymus in Antigonid Macedon, we must look not back to the world of city-states from which he came, but forward to a parallel period of history, the Roman principate, and to the greatest historian of that period. Tacitus lived at a time when again the struggles were over and the form of government no longer in question; emperors were good or bad—Nerva could even be said to have blended the principate with liberty;[309] and the historian could record the events of the recent past without passion or bias. This

---

[304] Cf. ch. 5, pp. 217 ff. The case of the Cossaei especially illustrates the point: badly treated by Antigonus, and befriended by Seleucus, they allied themselves with the latter in his war against Antigonus after 311.

[305] Diod. xviii.14.1 (Ptolemy): xix.14.4–5 (Peucestas: cf. Arr. *Anab.* vi.30.3-2; but Diodorus was not here following an Alexander historian, since Peucestas' orientalism is not mentioned in Book xvii); xix.91.1–2 (Seleucus: for the evidence of the Babylonian Chronicle, see above, pp. 111 ff.). Bizière, *Diodore*, xix, p. xvii n. 1 notes that in Diodorus' history of the Diadochi, in contrast to his practice in Books xi, xv, and xvii, the terms οἱ ἐγχώριοι, οἱ βάρβαροι, are reserved solely for unconquered tribes like the Cossaei and the Nabataeans; the settled communities of Asia are called by their proper names—indicating greater knowledge and perhaps greater respect.

[306] On the Greek practice of idealizing peoples on the edge of the world, see Schwartz, *Fünf Vorträge über den griechischen Roman*, Berlin, 1896, p. 89; E. Rohde, *Die griechische Roman und seine Vorläufer*, Leipzig, 1914, p. 203; T. W. Africa, *Phylarchus*, p. 13; T. S. Brown, *Onesicritus*, pp. 54 ff.

[307] Demetrius Phal. *ap.* Stob. iv.7.27 (Wachsmuth-Hense, p. 225) = Plut. *Reg. et Imp. Apophth.* 189D = F. Gr. Hist. 228 T6b.

[308] Tarn, *Antigonos Gonatas*, p. 241.

[309] Tacitus, *Agricola* i.3.

is, perhaps, the true perspective in which we should see Hieronymus and his work. 'Ne Macedonum quidem ac Persarum aut ullius gentis quae certo imperio contenta fuerit eloquentiam novimus':[310] we have gained peace, but lost liberty, and great oratory cannot flourish in the conditions of our times; we must write history now.

[310] Tacitus, *Dialogus* xl.3; cf. Aelius Aristides, *In defence of oratory*, 1020 (311–313); Syme, *Tacitus*, i, pp. 109 f.

Chapter 5

Hieronymus and His Masters

GREEK HISTORIOGRAPHY AND THE INDIVIDUAL

For Hieronymus, as for the historians of Philip and Alexander, the period he treated was dominated by the individual. His history focused on the figures of the Successors—as perhaps its title reflected—and followed as its central thread the fortunes of Eumenes and the Anti-gonids.[1] This was not only a matter of the *res gestae* of individuals: Hieronymus claimed to know the thoughts and intentions of the generals whom he served, and the narrative abounds in words such as $νομίζω$ and $συλλογίζομαι$, referring to their plans and motives. Thus he regarded the dynasts as initiators of action. Divine powers had no part to play in the making of history, except in so far as a nervous man might credit an oracle or a shrewd one exploit it, and even Tyche, omnipresent in Hellenistic historiography, here had a circumscribed role. This was essentially a secular history.

Hieronymus' predecessors Theopompus and Anaximenes probably influenced the organization of his work, by showing how an individual might be kept at the centre of a general political history. However, his own perception and experience were no doubt paramount in deter-mining his approach. In the armies of the Successors all action was initiated by and final responsibility lay with a single autocratic commander;[2] and the historian who had followed in their entourage naturally saw the controlling forces of the times embodied in these powerful *hegemones*.

The general climate of individualist opinion needs little comment. Hieronymus wrote in a period which it has become customary to characterize by its emphasis on the individual, and histories which are centred on the personalities of the Macedonian dynasts can be seen as

---

[1] For Hieronymus' title see above, ch. 3, pp. 76 ff.

[2] Cf. Polyb. iv.24: the king's council makes deliberations, but it is to the king that historians must attribute the final responsibility for decisions. Cf. K. Dover, *JHS* lxxx (1960), p. 72, suggesting that Diodorus invented the idea of a system of rotating command at the time of Marathon because it was inconceivable by his own day that decisions should ever have been taken collectively rather than individually. It seemed natural to him that Miltiades should have been directly responsible for the Greek victory, and the 'rotation' idea was an attempt to reconcile this feeling with evidence that the decision actually lay with the board of generals.

one expression of Hellenistic individualism. Biography and portraiture were flourishing; the new philosophies put individual man at the centre of their doctrines; and in popular thought his path through life was made rough or smooth by the blind power of Tyche; character types evolved in New Comedy, and were given definition in the satirical sketches of Theophrastus; art showed a new realism in depicting both the beautiful and the grotesque. The phenomenon is well known;[3] though whether it has a single general origin is perhaps doubtful. It is usual to look for an explanation in the political decline of the city-state and the sudden expansion of the geographical world after Alexander, causing a reassessment of man's place in his environment. Probably Hellenistic philosophy had its genesis in such conditions; but this account does not seem to cover every manifestation, and in some cases it may rather be the logical culmination of processes which had been going on over many decades or centuries. It is the visual arts which tend to give the strongest impression of a period; but in commenting on the 'individualism' of Hellenistic coin portraits, for example, or portrait sculpture, one should not overlook the probability that techniques for expressing individuality were not fully developed in some areas before the end of the classical period.[4] Developments in literature were not necessarily parallel to artistic ones: in this field technique was not a problem of a kind to obscure interest in the individual even at the earliest stages, as can be seen from Homer's depiction of his heroes and heroines. Greek historiography, in one sense the successor of epic, but always linked to contemporary political institutions, is a different case again.

'Die naïve Geschichtsbetrachtung sieht nur die Helden; die Massen, die unter ihnen stehen, kümmern sie nicht': thus Beloch introduced his *Griechische Geschichte*. This was true of Homer and of Herodotus. Thucydides, on the other hand, made a deliberate attempt to find more profound explanations for events, and reflected the actual conditions of contemporary Athens, where power was vested in collective bodies, the *boule* and the *demos*. The early part of his history shows Thucydides fascinated by the polarization of Athens and Sparta as states with contrasting national characteristics and which are themselves the principal 'characters';[5] and while he seems to have

---

[3] See, for example, Toynbee, *Hellenism*, pp. 127 ff., for a general survey.

[4] See Pearson, *Journal of the History of Ideas* xv (1954), pp. 130 ff.

[5] Cf. Momigliano, *The Development of Greek Biography*, pp. 88 ff.: the collective approach appears also in the 5th-century view that a close connection existed between climates, constitutions, and the behaviour of individuals; the link between history and geography emphasized a concern with the community rather than the individual.

considered Pericles personally responsible for Athenian strategy at the beginning of the Peloponnesian War, and Pericles' successors responsible for later deviations from that strategy, this too was a reflection of reality, in so far as the office of *strategos* was the one office which the Athenians filled by direct election and not by the lot. But through Thucydides' work as a whole it is possible to trace an increasing awareness of the role of individual leaders, which can be connected with the decline of democracy in the last decade of the fifth century, and with the appearance of a personality like Alcibiades, the significance of which could not be overlooked:[6] the estimate of Themistocles in Book i was perhaps part of a revision made in the consciousness which came to Thucydides in the later stages of the conflict, that a single man with military and political capacity sometimes had power to determine the destiny of the state.

Alcibiades, the 'lion's whelp', whom Aristotle took as a paradigm of an individual in history, was a forerunner of the outstanding personalities of the fourth century who exploited Greek disunity and the feeling of disillusionment with democracy. Contemporaries feared that Alcibiades himself aspired to tyranny, and indeed democratic Athens suffered from a chronic fear of tyrants, which encouraged her to reject some of her most brilliant leaders. The numbers of those who were exiled or ostracized included the most distinguished of Athenian historians. 'Thucydides is linked to that older Hellas of the aristocratic tyrants and the dynastic families, to the men who were too big for the *polis* of citizens because of their power, their resources, and their fame outside their own cities. The men, it might happen, who are suitable candidates for being thrown out by ostracism.'[7] A final consequence of such suspicions was the defeat of 404. Sparta reacted in the same way to Cleomenes, Brasidas, and to the energetic Lysander, who wanted, so it was said, to reform the antiquated Spartan military system; and Sparta, too, suffered military catastrophe at Leuctra. The Greek states, it seemed, had got rid of their best men. Isocrates, like Xenophon, for a while held a misplaced hope in Agesilaus of Sparta, but his search for a pan-hellenic leader finally took him to the half-barbarian potentates on the edges of the Greek world, and Philip responded and gave the Greeks the 'tyranny' they had tried to avoid. These fourth-century kings and tyrants, forerunners of the Hellenistic kings, evoked an immediate response from Greek writers, on the one hand idealistic (Plato's *Republic* and Xenophon's *Cyropaedia* are obvious examples), in part consisting of historical encomium and histor-

[6] This is the conclusion of Westlake, *Individuals in Thucydides*, 1968.
[7] Syme, *Proc. Brit. Acad.* 1962, p. 40.

iography proper.[8] Whatever one thought of Philip, 'he clearly represented a more interesting subject than the continued bickerings of the Greek states.'[9] Isocrates' pupil Theopompus laid down his *Hellenica* to record the rise of Philip; at the same time in Sicily, where there was a development towards monarchy parallel to that in Macedon, the career of Dionysius inspired Philistus to write history centred on the individual; and a similar response to the emergence of potentates in the East during the declining years of the Achaemenid empire is shown in Isocrates' encomium of Evagoras, Callisthenes' encomium of Hermias of Atarneus, and the *epitaphios* written by Theopompus for the wealthy Carian dynast Maussollus.[10]

Accounts of Alexander and the Diadochi show the individual finally supreme in history: Alexander, as Hegel said of Napoleon, had heard the pounding of the hooves of history, and caught at the coat-tails of the rider as he passed. Probably none of the histories of Alexander was a general history, rather than a memoir of his life or campaigns; hence it is Theopompus who is the really seminal figure, and who counted in antiquity as a great historian in a way that none of the historians of Alexander did, except perhaps Callisthenes. Nevertheless, Alexander's spectacular achievements surely gave a powerful stimulus to histories of the Hellenistic period, all of which centre on the character and careers of great men, sometimes encroaching on the sphere of biography or historical encomium. The distinction between history and encomium was a matter which Polybius felt he should clarify, and Cato reacted strongly to what he saw as the cult of the individual in the writing of history.[11] True successors to Theopompus among the Hellenistic historians seem, however, to have been few, in so far as monarchs themselves were no longer the main inspiration of Greek historiography. Almost nothing survives of the histories of kings from this period. Pausanias, in the second century AD, remarked: 'The era of Attalus and of Ptolemy is so far off that the tradition which concerns

---

[8] Cf. W. Judeich, *Kleinasiatische Studien*, 1892, p. 14, describing Evagoras as the first 'Hellenistic' king.

[9] Grayson, in *The Ancient Historian and his Materials*, p. 39. On the personal character of Theopompus' *Philippica* see W. R. Connor, *Theopompus and Fifth Century Athens*, pp. 13 f.

[10] Callisthenes, *F. Gr. Hist.* 124 F2, 3; Theopompus, *F. Gr. Hist.* 115 T6, F48, cf. F297. Cf. G. Ryle, *Plato's Progress*, Cambridge, 1966, pp. 41 f. and 58 f., discussing the festivals organized by the 4th-century tyrants: the most brilliant orators and philosophers of the day were attracted by their patronage. Xenophon's *Hieron*, composed in c. 383, and referring to the tyrant Dionysius the Elder, also seems to have been inspired by interest in contemporary monarchy.

[11] Polyb. vii.8.5–9, cf. x.21.6–8. Cf. Momigliano, op. cit., pp. 77 ff., 82 f. Nepos, *Cato iii*: 'bellorum duces non nominavit, sed sine nominibus res notavit': cf. F. Leo, *gr.-röm. Biog.*, p. 234.

them is lost and the writings of the historians whom the kings had engaged to recount their exploits have fallen into oblivion even earlier.' (i.6.1). The fact, moreover, that Plutarch wrote no lives of the Ptolemies or Seleucids suggests that the historiography of these dynasties had already disappeared by his time. A few names have come down to us, and the existence of a considerable body of court historiography has to be inferred from the work of Polybius and Appian.[12] That so little survives, however, even in digest, is surely to be explained, as Jacoby believed, by the eulogistic and, no doubt, parochial

---

[12] Almost no histories of the Ptolemies remain. P. Gurob (*F. Gr. Hist.* 160) is an official account of the operations of the 3rd Syrian War; Pap. Graec. Haun. 6 (= Pack² 2210) possibly comes from a series of biographies of the Ptolemies in the framework of a genealogical tree (cf. Segre, *Rend. d. Pont. Accad. Rom. di Arch.* xix (1942–3), pp. 269–80). More is learned on Ptolemy IV from Polybius, using especially Ptolemy of Megalopolis (*F. Gr. Hist.* 161), and from Maccabees iii, and possibly the volume of Ptolemaic historiography increased towards the end of the 3rd century (cf. Jacoby, *F. Gr. Hist.* Comm. IIB, pp. 588–9). In the early Hellenistic period one should not, however, overlook the work of Cleitarchus, which flattered Ptolemy Soter at least in some episodes; nor the adulatory account of the first Ptolemy in Diod. xviii, which derives from Cleitarchus or another of his period writing for court consumption (see above, ch. 3, pp. 92 f.). Most surviving literature concerning Ptolemaic rulers is not properly historical, e.g. the panegyrics of Callimachus i.84–5, iv. 162 ff., and Theocritus, *Idyll* xvii, the *Letter of Aristeas to Philocrates* on the translation of the Bible, or the description of the Ptolemaic *pompe* by Callixeinus of Rhodes (Athenaeus 196A–203B).

On Seleucid historiography see Jacoby, *F. Gr. Hist.*, nos. 162–6. Demetrius of Byzantium wrote on Antiochus Soter and Ptolemy Philadelphus, but from the point of view of his native city: *F. Gr. Hist.* 162, and Jacoby, comm. ad loc. Simonides of Magnesia recorded the deeds of Antiochus the Great in epic verse (*F. Gr. Hist.* 163), and Mnesiptolemus of Cyme wrote probably a court history centred on Antiochus (*F. Gr. Hist.* 164). Timochares wrote on either Antiochus Epiphanes or Sidetes (*F. Gr. Hist.* 165), and Athenaeus of Naucratis a work 'On those who ruled in Syria' (*F. Gr. Hist.* 166). The existence of native historiography is shown by the 'Babylonian Chronicle', apparently an official history of the operations of Antigonus and Seleucus I in Mesopotamia (see above, ch. 4, pp. 111 ff.). In this meagre catalogue the absence of any serious history of Antiochus III is especially striking. Our knowledge is supplemented by the numerous passages in Polybius, by Books i and ii of Maccabees, used by Josephus, and by Appian's *Syriaca*, though individual sources are difficult to recover.

For the kings of Pergamum and of Macedon (after the period of Alexander and the Diadochi) Polybius, with Livy, is again our chief source, though the historiography of these dynasties was from the first probably richer. Suidas records that Phylarchus included in his work the history of Antiochus and of Eumenes of Pergamum. Of the work of Neanthes of Cyzicus (*F. Gr. Hist.* 171) on Attalus I we know only a trivial detail; Lysimachus' account of the *paideia* of Attalus (*F. Gr. Hist.* 170) was famous for its flattery; the epic poet Leschides seems to have recorded the deeds of Eumenes II. Among the kings of Macedon both Antigonus Doson and Philip V might be expected to have attracted the interest of Greek historians; yet the Macedonian history by Heracleitus of Lesbos which referred to the year 215 BC, an account of the deeds of Philip and Perseus by Straton, and Poseidonius' biography of Perseus, are all that survive, and these hardly in more than name (*F. Gr. Hist.* 167, 168, 169). The great historian of Philip V was Polybius.

For a recent survey of this literature see Préaux, *Le Monde hellénistique*, pp. 83 ff. and 215 ff. (to which add Proxenus, the historian of Pyrrhus, *F. Gr. Hist.* 703).

character of such works: the special histories of royal houses must have been lacking not only in conviction, but also in interest to the Greek world as a whole, except, perhaps, where the authorship of the king himself gave the work a curiosity value, or suggested a guarantee of veracity.[13] Kings surely hoped for worthy historians; but in so far as objectivity was indispensable to good historical writing, there must always have been a contradiction in the demands they made. How far a writer could go in his criticisms evidently depended on the circumstances and on the monarch: Cleitarchus felt free to differ from Ptolemy in his Alexander history; Sotades' obscene gibe was punishable. Antigonus Gonatas, the monarch who loved Klio, put to death the atthidographer Philochorus for his opposition to the Macedonian regime (though, admittedly, we cannot be certain that his resistance was expressed in his writings). Many may have felt it more prudent to say nothing, unless, like Simonides of Magnesia or Leschides, they retreated to epic poetry, where the genre admitted hyperbole without compromising integrity.

It is nevertheless astonishing that a ruler of vitality, whose career had important effects beyond the confines of his own kingdom, (one thinks, especially, of Antiochus the Great or Philip V), should not have inspired another Theopompus. To a remarkable degree the main stream of Greek historiography ignored the kings, and Greek historians continued to write local histories and *Hellenica* as they had always done, devoting their attention rather to national leaders like Cleomenes or Philopoemen. Agathocles of Sicily, too, though he himself hoped to be regarded as equal to the kings of the Hellenistic East, was actually a figure belonging to a traditional pattern of Western Greek history. The phenomenon becomes more intelligible once we liberate ourselves from the conventional doctrine that the Greek *poleis* suffered a marked decline after Alexander. There is abundant evidence, as Professor L. Robert has repeatedly asserted, that the Greek cities of the Hellenistic period, so far from dwindling into wretched obscurity and impotence under the shadow of the monarchies, flourished in a new-found prosperity. Released from the demands of liturgies and incessant inter-state warfare, funds, often provided (and this is the essential difference brought by the Hellenistic period) by individual *euergetai*, could be used for the development of trade, buildings, amenities of all kinds, religious festivals: civic life

[13] Ptolemy Soter wrote a memoir of Alexander's expedition, famous through Arrian's use of it. Pyrrhus of Epirus wrote an autobiographical work; likewise perhaps Ptolemy Euergetes II (cf. Jacoby Comm. IIB, pp. 589–90). On Hieronymus' use of royal sources, see above, ch. 4, p. 128 f.

boomed, and so did civic pride.[14] No doubt some historians, heads in the sand, were compensating for loss of political freedom by a display of haughty indifference to the activities of the monarchs; but in other cases there was surely a genuine conviction of the primacy of Greek and civic affairs.

In the universal history of Polybius the rulers of the non-Roman world necessarily receive clear definition: a Hannibal or a Philip V mattered historically in a way that no individual Roman did. But it was precisely the universal character of Polybius' history that endowed these figures with real historical significance, by showing the inter-action between states and personalities which formed the history of Rome's rise to power. Hieronymus' history of the Successors belongs to the same classification. As a general history of Greek and Macedo-nian affairs, anchored to the particular fortunes of those potent indi-viduals, the Antigonids, it belonged to the fourth-century tradition of Theopompus and Anaximenes, and anticipated the yet broader canvas and the striking psychological analyses of Polybius.[15] Diodorus, with his preference for 'universal' history, chose Hieronymus and Polybius as sources for the greater part of the Hellenistic period, thereby indicating the superiority of each to local and particular histories of the same period. Other interpretations of Hieronymus' period would, indeed, have been possible, and it is a possible criticism of Hieronymus that he ignored the growth of the Greek federal movement, which was, as it were, the other side of the coin that bore the face of Alexander.[16] Nevertheless, he had unquestionably a truer view of his times than the writers of patriotic *Hellenica*, since world history, for much of the period he covered, was practically synonymous with Macedonian his-tory, and the actions of the Diadochi affected all the communities of Greece and Asia.

There was, of course, a subjective element. The special relationship of the faithful servant to his masters gave his work both its weaknesses and its strengths: on the one hand, the temptation to eulogy and

---

[14] L. Robert, *CRAI* 1969, p. 42; cf. P. Veyne, *Le Pain et le Cirque, sociologie historique d'un pluralisme politique*, Paris, 1976, p. 109 and n. 130; C. B. Welles, *Studi in honore di Calderini e Paribeni*, vol. i, Milan, 1956, pp. 81 ff., 'The Greek City'; Préaux, op. cit., p. 401.

[15] The continuing popularity of Theopompus is indicated by a 3rd century BC anonymous *Philippica*, possibly an epitome of Theopompus' work (Pack[2] 2192). In the 1st century BC, Trogus called his universal history *Philippica*: if Timagenes' work *On Kings* was one of his principal sources, it may have influenced his decision to adopt the title of Theopompus, the first Greek historian of an individual monarch. Timagenes claimed to be the recreator of Greek historiography (Quint. *Inst. Or.* x.1.75), but it is not clear what this claim involved: cf. Fraser, *Ptol. Alex.* ii, p. 749 n. 215.

[16] Cf. T. S. Brown, *Am. Hist. Rev.* 1947, p. 695.

apologia, but on the other, the unique opportunity for first-hand observation and understanding of great men. In the convulsions following Alexander's death, individuals won or lost everything—the repeated phrase τὰ ὅλα seems to express Hieronymus' awareness of the totality of the struggle—and the reasons for success or failure were reasons of personality and the capacity to lead an army. In the last resort, the events Hieronymus described were to be explained in terms of the charisma of the generals and their relations with their followers—men like Hieronymus himself, who looked in vain among the so-called Diadóchi for a true successor to Alexander the Great. The subject here at issue is, therefore, Hieronymus' ideal of leadership.

THE MILITARY MILIEU

Hieronymus' military narrative was singular not only for its accuracy but also for its understanding.[17] His account of the first Successors had something of the military flavour and the spirit of adventure which characterize Xenophon's writings, and this part of the history is notable not only for comprehension of matters of strategy, tactics, and organization, but also for its depiction of the ethos of the Macedonian army. This was perhaps the most remarkable feature of Hieronymus' work. The historians of Philip were still working within the framework of the Greek city-state, most of the *personae* in their accounts were Greeks, and the values of the *polis* prevailed. Alexander and his generals left this world behind them, and with the military histories of Ptolemy and Hieronymus we are in an entirely different milieu. The scale of ambition has expanded. *Philotimia*, the rivalry between politicians in a democracy which Theopompus stressed in his account of the Athenian demagogues, gives place to the headier notions *philarchia* and *pleonexia*, denoting that lust for conquest which characterized Antigonus Monophthalmus and Pyrrhus, *par excellence*.[18] In Hieronymus' geographical introduction 'the cities of the Greeks' figured only marginally in a description of ὅλη 'Ασία, and in his history of the years between the death of Alexander and the death of Antigonus the institution which takes the place of the city is the army itself, composed increasingly of mercenaries without strong attachments to a home country, who carried all their domestic ménage and wordly

[17] See ch. 2, pp. 37 ff.
[18] *Philotimia* in Theopompus: *F. Gr. Hist.* 115 F89, 114, 66, 323. Cf. Connor, *Theopompus and Fifth Century Athens*, pp. 32 f. On *philotimia* and *philodoxia* see Welles, *RC* no.52.21 = letter of Eumenes II to the Ionian League, accepting the honours voted to him in 167–166 BC, διὰ τῶν ἔργων τὴν ἐμήν τε φιλοδοξίαν; and ibid., p. 373 on Polyb. iii.103–5. *Philarchia*: Plut. *Demetr.* xxviii.2. *Pleonexia*: Diod. xix.105.1; xx.106.4. For *pleonexia* in Plutarch's *Pyrrhus* see above, ch. 4, p. 139 with n. 141.

possessions in the *aposkeue*, the baggage train which accompanied the fighting force. The importance of the *aposkeue* is shown unmistakably on the notorious occasion in winter 317, when Eumenes' soldiers traded their general for their captured families and goods, and even in the settled conditions of Ptolemaic Egypt the families of men on garrison duty were still described as οἱ ἐν τῆι ἀποσκευῆι ὄντες—a reminiscence of earlier itinerant days.[19] While Alexander's army could be described as the Macedonian people in arms, towards the end of Alexander's reign can be seen a desire to end this situation;[20] and the return of the kings in 321 seemed to mark the division between homeland and camp. In the absence of a *patris* the armies of the Successors, now more mercenary than national, organized themselves into societies not unlike great cities on the move. Composed of many nationalities, which served alongside the kernel of Macedonian troops, they were accompanied by thousands of civilians—women, children, slaves, and traders.[21] Diodorus uses the image οἷον δημοκρατουμένη πόλις of Eumenes' army, and suggests a contrast between the 'democratic' leadership of the royalist forces and the 'tyranny' exercised by Antigonus, whose command was undisputed.[22] The idea is developed by Plutarch in his *Eumenes*—confirmation that it had its origin in Hieronymus, though Plutarch is certainly exaggerating for effect the corrupting influence of the 'demagogic' satraps on Eumenes' soldiers.[23] The idea of the camp as a 'city' goes back at least to Thucydides—ἄνδρες γὰρ πόλις. It was elaborated by Xenophon, who had personal experience of the way a wandering army creates its own institutions: he makes Cyrus in the *Cyropaedia* organize his camp in this way, and in turn, his ideal civic community is consciously modelled on the camp. The tradition continues with Polybius' account of the Roman army, and in Vegetius.[24]

[19] Holleaux, *Études*, iii, pp. 15 ff., 'Ceux qui sont dans le bagage'. In Hellenistic Egypt the word ἀποσκευή continued in use to denote the household and possessions of soldiers, whether in garrisons or settled in one of the villages of the χώρα as cleruchs. Document no. IV of Pap. Haliensis I makes legal provision for a whole class of persons, described as οἱ ἐν τῆι ἀποσκευῆι ὄντες, who are resident in Alexandria itself. For the importance of ἀποσκευή in battles of the Diadochi see also the Arrian fragment *PSI* xii.1284, with Bosworth, *GRBS* xix (1978), p. 235.

[20] Note esp. Justin xiv.4.3: 'in hoc castrensi exilio'.

[21] Rostovtzeff, *SEHHW* i, pp. 145–7; iii, pp. 134 f. (nn. 17–20); cf. Briant, *REA* lxxv (1973), pp. 66 ff. Goukowsky, *Rev. de Phil.* xliv (1975), 2, pp. 267 ff., stresses the very small number of Macedonians left in the royal army by the time of Alexander's death.

[22] Diod. xix.15.4. (At Diod. xvii.87.5 the comparison is only τὴν πρόσοψιν.)

[23] Plut. *Eum.* xiii.5: δημαγωγούμενον ἐπὶ αἱρέσει στρατηγῶν ὄχλον, ὥσπερ ἐν ταῖς δημοκρατίαις; cf. xv.3: αὖθις ἐδημαγωγοῦντο. Cf. Polyaenus iv.8.3.

[24] Xen. *Cyrop.* viii.5.2–16; cf. viii.1.13–15. Cf. N. Wood, *Class. et Med.* 1964. See also Thuc. vii.75.5, 77.4, 77.7.

The military values which pervade Hieronymus' narrative have their genesis in this military society. Qualities such as justice, wisdom, eloquence, are qualities which belong to a civic milieu: Aristeides 'the Just' and Phocion 'the Good' are figures of the *polis*. In the Macedonian armies on the other hand, the qualities prized by the society in its members are skill, strength, bravery, and experience—εὐχειρία, ῥώμη, ἀνδραγαθία, ἐμπειρία—the virtues of the professional soldier; and though it is often and rightly said that most ancient historians wrote from the point of view of the man in supreme command (Cleitarchus might be an exception, giving a 'soldier's-eye' view), the conditions of contemporary warfare obliged a writer like Hieronymus to take account of the needs and moods of the new professional armies, as well as the great autocrats who directed them.[25] The colourful figures of the Diadochi are set, as it were, in relief, against a background of the corporate and anonymous.

Identifying Hieronymus' own manner of expression is immediately a problem, since Diodorus' rhetorical training gave him the habit of making all soldiers outstanding in strength and courage.[26] Nevertheless, it is sometimes clear from the context that his comments on the prowess of a group of soldiers must be taken from his source. Repeatedly, he stresses the importance of *empeiria*, meaning, specifically, experience gained in Alexander's campaigns. The rebel Greeks of Bactria 'had been tried many times in the contests of war and were distinguished for their courage': πάντες δε τῶν κατὰ τὸν πόλεμον ἀγώνων πολλάκις πεῖραν εἰληφότας καὶ διαφόρους ταῖς ἀνδραγαθίαις. Of the mercenaries gathered at Taenarum, Diodorus says: ἐστρατευμένοι . . . κατὰ τὴν Ἀσίαν πολὺν χρόνον καὶ μεγάλων ἀγώνων μετεσχηκότες ἀθληταὶ τῶν κατὰ πόλεμον ἔργων ἐγεγένηντο. And of Attalus and his companions in their last stand: διαφέροντες . . . ταῖς τόλμαις καὶ ταῖς εὐχειρίαις διὰ τὴν μετ' Ἀλεξάνδρου στρατίαν, . . . πολὺ λειπόμενοι τοῖς πλήθεσι, διὰ τὰς ἀρετὰς ἀντείχοντο κ.τ.λ. The mercenary captain Mnasicles is said to possesss ἐμπειρίαν . . . τῶν πολεμικῶν πράξεων, and this he too must have gained on Alexander's expedition, like his rival Thibron, who had been one of the *philoi* of Harpalus.[27] Diodorus also seems to follow his source

[25] Cf. E. Rawson, *PBSR* n.s. xxvi (1971), p. 14. The line dividing commander from ranks was, of course, much sharper in the hierarchy of a Macedonian army: contrast the account of the new recruits at Xen. *Cyrop.* ii.2.6 ff., reflecting the easy-going relations between ranks in a Greek citizen army (cf. J. K. Anderson, *Military Theory and Practice in the Age of Xenophon*, Berkeley 1970, pp. 98 f.). [26] Cf. App. II, p. 277.
[27] Diod. xviii.7.2, 9.3; xix.16.1; xviii.20.1. Mnasicles had possibly been in the army of Harpalus which Thibron took over: so Berve, ii, no. 533. Compare the character of Bolis the Cretan, the double agent who betrayed Achaeus: Polyb. vii.17.1.

when he marks out the excellence of a particular corps. Thus Menon and the Thessalians are consistently depicted as the heroes of the Lamian War.[28] Again in the Asian campaigns the Macedonian troops, which seem to have retained a distinct identity for some time after Alexander's death, are regularly distinguished from mercenaries and native contingents. In 320 Antigonus had 10,000 infantry, ὧν ἦσαν οἱ ἡμίσεις Μακεδόνες, θαυμαστοὶ κατὰ τὰς ἀνδραγαθίας. At the battle of the Dardanelles Craterus had 20,000 foot, ὧν ἦσαν οἱ πλείους Μακεδόνες διαβεβοημένοι ταῖς ἀνδραγαθίαις, ἐν οἷς εἶχε μάλιστα τὰς ἐλπίδας τῆς νίκης.[29]

The most striking example of a corps praised for its military virtue is the body of 3,000 hypaspists known as the Silver Shields, the crack troops of Eumenes' army, who had formed themselves into an élite and semi-independent group with their own traditions perhaps by the time of Alexander's death. The hypaspist corps had probably been instituted by Philip, and had consisted originally of hand-picked infantrymen from the same social class as the *pezetairoi*, i.e. the Macedonian peasantry. They were organized into a single unit irrespective of local origins, with its loyalty focused on the person of the king, and the numbers were rapidly increased to 3,000.[30] The hypaspist corps, which is mentioned twenty-eight times in Arrian's *Anabasis*, acquired great prestige and was apparently used by Alexander for especially difficult tasks. After Alexander, our sources speak of both 3,000 hypaspists and of 3,000 *argyraspides*. Tarn wished to identify the two, and believed that *argyaspides* was Hieronymus' own name for the corps, which is first given this style in 321 after Perdiccas' defeat in Egypt, when Antipater made Antigenes its commander.[31] However, the two sets (3,000 hypaspists and 3,000 argyraspids) are clearly distinguished in the dispositions given by Diodorus for the battles of Paraetacene and Gabiene: in neither case does there seem any possibility of a 'doublet'.[32] Hence the hypaspists who were twice defeated under Perdiccas in 321 must, likewise, have been a body distinct from the argyraspids (who gloried in the description ἀνίκητοι), and in the reorganization after Perdiccas' death Antigenes must have been given command of both sets. It has been plausibly suggested that the hypaspists from the period of the Successors were in fact the descendants of Philip's and Alexander's original corps (the great age of the veteran

---

[28] Diod. xviii.17.4; cf. 15.2.4.
[29] Diod. xviii.40.7; 30.4.
[30] See R. D. Milns, *Historia* xx (1971), pp. 186 ff. on the origins and organization of the hypaspists.
[31] Tarn, *Alex. Gt.*, ii, pp. 148 ff., esp. pp. 151 ff.; cf. pp. 116 ff. So also now E. M. Anson, *Historia* xxx (1981), pp. 117 ff.   [32] Diod. xix.28.1; xix.40.3.

argyraspids is repeatedly stressed by Diódorus and Plutarch), which was renamed 'Silver Shields' probably by Alexander himself.[33]

Hieronymus certainly used the term *argyraspides* regularly, just as he used other technical or unusual military terms, but it is not likely that the name was his own invention, since both Arrian and Diodorus were aware of it in Alexander's lifetime.[34] In the list of Persian formations which Alexander began to draw up at Opis there was, according to Arrian, alongside the Persian *pezetairoi*, Persian Companion Cavalry, and Persian Royal Agema, also an ἀργυρασπίδων τάξις Περσική; and it seems likely that we should see an allusion to the projected formation of a Persian argyraspid corps in one of the Boscoreale wall-paintings. According to the most plausible interpretation, this painting depicts a personification of Macedonia and Persia, with a shield, obviously of Macedonian type, resting between the two figures. The shield appears to be pale and silvery in colour, decorated with the 'sunburst' motif now familiar from the royal tombs of Vergina, and is surely a picture of one of the famous Silver Shields. On this theory, the group of paintings to which this belongs depicts the marriages at Susa between the Macedonian and Persian nobility, and the theme of *homonoia*: a philosopher, perhaps Zeno, looks on at the side, representing the philosophical expression of the idea that mankind is one.[35]

The Boscoreale painting makes it plain that the hypaspist shield was a beautiful and highly conspicuous piece of armour. Doubtless the silver came out of all the Persian booty.[36] It was the distinctive visible

[33] Hammond, *CQ* n.s. xxviii (1978), 'A cavalry unit in the army of Antigonus Monophthalmus: *Asthippoi*', p. 135 ('Note on Argyraspides').

[34] Diod. xvii.57.2; Arrian, *Anab.* vii.11.3. Cf. Curtius viii.5.4: silver and gold trappings were introduced in 327 BC.

[35] M. Robertson, *JRS* xlv (1955), pp. 58 ff. This interpretation remains convincing and coherent, although the paintings continue to be the subject of controversy. E. Simon, *Die Fürstenbilder von Boscoreale*, Baden-Baden, 1958, makes the figures on the Naples wall Menedemus, and Antigonus Gonatas visiting his mother Phila in Hades, and the couple on the other wall Demetrius and Phila at their wedding. G. Kleiner, in *Studies in Classical Art and Archaeology: a Tribute to P. H. von Blanckenhagen*, ed. Kopcke and Moore, 1979, pp. 135 f., describes the Naples wall as Zeno, and Antigonus with Phila. P. von Blanckenhagen and B. Green in *Mitteilungen des archaeologischen Instituts, römische Abteilung* lxxxii (1975), pp. 83 ff. try to show that the wedding is that of Demetrius Poliorcetes and Phila. The only new evidence that bears on the problem is the recent discovery of painted tombs in Macedonia, which greatly strengthens the idea that the Boscoreale paintings are true copies of early Hellenistic wall-paintings: cf. M. Robertson, *History of Greek Art*, Cambridge, 1975, pp. 571–4 (I am grateful to Professor Robertson for his valuable help with this subject).

[36] This is one obvious difference between the armour of hypaspists and that of phalangites in Alexander's army: for this debate, see Tarn, locc. citt.; Hamilton, *CQ* n.s. v (1955), p. 218; Griffith, *PCPS* n.s. iv (1956–7), pp. 3–10; J. R. Ellis, *Historia* xxiv (1975), pp. 617 ff.

badge of an élite and independent-minded corps, whose social origins and method of recruitment conspired to set it apart from the other sectors of the royal army, and gave it from the first something of the character of a private mercenary bodyguard. The value of the Argyraspids as a veteran fighting force in the period after 323 is attested by the fact that they were persistently courted by rival generals: Seleucus is mentioned more than once as the originator of propaganda directed at the Silver Shields when they were serving Eumenes, and this is readily understandable in view of the fact that he had been 'archihypaspist' in Alexander's time.[37] Why the regiment failed to respond to its old commander we do not know. As for many of the satraps and the allied forces in Eumenes' army, the choice of allegiance was probably a difficult one at a time when there was no clear superiority on either side; though possibly the Argyraspids felt some residual loyalty to the royal house whom Eumenes represented, if it is true that many of them were old campaigners who had served under Philip.[38] The loss of the *aposkeue* at Gabiene of course decided the issue.

Hieronymus' moral indignation at the Argyraspids' betrayal of Eumenes can still be discerned in Diodorus and Plutarch; nevertheless, we find repeated tributes to their professional skill. At Paraetacene they are described as ἀνίκητοι . . . καὶ διὰ τὰς ἀρετὰς πολὺν φόβον παρεχόμενοι τοῖς πολεμίοις. In the battle at Gabiene Diodorus says that the Argyraspids could not be checked in their charge, and took on the entire opposing phalanx: τοσοῦτον ταῖς εὐχειρίαις καὶ ῥώμαις ὑπερεῖχον ὥσθ' ἑαυτῶν μὲν ἀποβαλεῖν μηθένα, τῶν δ'ἐναντίων ἀνελεῖν μὲν ὑπὲρ τοὺς πεντακισχιλίους, τρέψασθαι δὲ τοὺς πέζους πάντας.[39] The *arete* of the Argyraspids is the consequence of *empeiria*: their commander, Antigenes, claimed that the right to choose the commander-in-chief of the royalist forces should be theirs, because they were veterans of Alexander's army: τοῖς μετ' αὐτοῦ Μακεδόσιν, συγκαταπεπολεμηκόσιν Ἀλεξάνδρῳ τὴν Ἀσίαν καὶ γεγονόσι διὰ τὰς ἀρετὰς ἀνικήτοις. Eumenes' phalanx was said to have been victorious at Paraetacene διὰ τὰς τῶν Ἀργυρασπίδων Μακεδόνων ἀρετάς· οὗτοι γὰρ μὲν ἡλικίας ἤδη προεβεβήκεισαν, διὰ δὲ τὸ πλῆθος τῶν κινδύνων διέφερον ταῖς τόλμαις καὶ ταῖς εὐχειρίαις. And again at Gabiene Diodorus comments on the advanced age of the Argyraspids and says that they were πάντες . . . ταῖς ἐμπειρίαις καὶ ταῖς ῥώμαις ἀνυπόστατοι· τοσαύτη περὶ αὐτοὺς

---

[37] Diod. xix.12.2; 13.1.
[38] Cf. Diod. xix.41.1–2; Plut. *Eum.* xvi.4. See ch. 2, p. 113 for the suggestion that Eumenes' possession of the citadel of Babylon secured the loyalty of his troops at this time.
[39] Diod. xix.28.1; 43.1.

ἦν εὐχειρία καὶ τόλμα διὰ τὴν συνέχειαν τῶν κινδύνων.⁴⁰ It is certain
that Diodorus reflects the substance of Hieronymus in these passages,
because in the same context, before Gabiene, Plutarch speaks of the
Argyraspids in similar terms: καὶ γὰρ ἦσαν οἱ πρεσβύτατοι τῶν περὶ
Φίλιππον καὶ 'Αλέξανδρον, ὥσπερ ἀθληταὶ πολέμων ἀήττητοι καὶ
ἀπτῶτες εἰς ἐκεῖνο χρόνου, πολλοὶ μὲν ἑβδομήκοντα ἔτη γεγονότες,
νεώτερος δὲ οὐδεὶς ἑξηκονταετοῦς.⁴¹ (The truth of this extraordinary
statement on their age is another matter. There are similar absurdities
in Arrian, from Ptolemy, on, for example, the fight with Porus, and
one must suppose that Argyraspids, like elephants, were a kind of
military *thaumasion* which attracted hyperbole.)

The word ἀθληταί is used also by Diodorus in Book xviii: the
mercenaries whom Leosthenes hired at Taenarum were ἀθληταὶ τῶν
κατὰ πόλεμον ἔργων, an expression which effectively sums up the
contemporary military ethos. Both Diodorus and Plutarch use the
word elsewhere, and Plato has the phrase ἀθληταὶ πολέμου, 'masters
of warfare'. In particular it must have been familiar to Diodorus from
Polybius.⁴² Hence this is not definitely a Hieronyman expression. It
may be significant, however, that the narrative of Eumenes' campaigns inspired later authors on more than one occasion to use military
metaphors. Diodorus says of the Argyraspids at Paraetacene, διὸ καὶ
τότε τρισχίλιοι μὲν ὄντες οἱονεὶ στόμωμα καθειστήκεισαν πάσης τῆς
δυνάμεως: they were the 'spearhead' of the army.⁴³ The visual effect of
the army in action is stressed also in Diodorus' account of the battle
between Eumenes and Neoptolemus. When the cavalry became aware
of Neoptolemus' death, ἄπαντες πρὸς φυγὴν ὥρμησαν καὶ καθάπερ
πρὸς τεῖχος ὀχυρὸν πρὸς τὴν τῶν πεζῶν φάλαγγα κατέφυγον.⁴⁴ The

---

⁴⁰ Diod. xix.15.2; 30.5–6; 41.2.   ⁴¹ Plut. *Eum.* xvi.4.

⁴² Diod. xviii.9.3; Plato, *Rep.* 543B; cf. Laches 182A; Arist. *Pol.* vi.7.3, 1321a 26. Cf.
Diod. i.53; xii.75; xiii.82; xvii.9.3; Plut. *Fabius* xxiii.2; ibid., v.3; *De Fort. Rom.* 322A,
ibid., 326C. See also Plut. *Demetr.* v.2, of Ptolemy. Polyb. i.6.6 calls the Romans
ἀθληταὶ ἀληθινοὶ τῶν κατὰ τὸν πόλεμον, and at xv.9.4 he describes the soldiers on both
sides at Zama as ἀθληταὶ γεγονότες τῶν κατὰ πόλεμον ἔργων. Xenophon, *Lak. Pol.*
xii.5, calls the Spartans τεχνῖται τῶν πολεμικῶν.

⁴³ Diod. xix.30.6. The word στόμωμα = the more common στόμα, which is used by
the tactical writer Asclepiodotus in exactly this way: the strongest and the most skilful
ought to be file leaders, τοῦτο γὰρ τὸ ζυγὸν συνέχει τὴν φάλαγγα καὶ οἷον τῆς μαχαίρας
ἐστὶ στόμα (*Ars Tactica* iii.5, cf. ii.5). Cf. Xen. *Hell.* iv.3.4, *Anab.* iii.4.43; Polyb. x.12.7.
Xenophon in the *Hipparchikos* uses a similar figure: the formation should be arranged so
that the best men are at the front of each file, and an equal number of the oldest and the
most steady form the rear: εἰ γὰρ δεῖ καὶ ἀπεικάσαι, οὕτω καὶ σίδηρος μάλιστα
διατέμνει σίδηρον, ὅταν τό τε ἡγούμενον τοῦ τομέως ἐρρωμένον ᾖ καὶ τὸ
ἐπελαυνόμενον ἱκανόν (ii.3).

⁴⁴ Diod. xviii.32.1. Cf. Xen. *Cyrop.* v.4.6: Gadatas' advance party have been
ambushed by the Assyrians, but suddenly see Cyrus approaching with the main army:
δοκεῖν δὲ χρὴ ἀσμένους καὶ ὥσπερ εἰς λιμένα ἐκ χειμῶνος προσφέρεσθαι αὐτούς.

ὀχυϱὸν τεῖχος is common enough in a literal sense in Diodorus, and it can be found in a simile in Book xvi.[45] Therefore this is not necessarily a specimen of Hieronymus' language; but it should be noted that this battle encouraged not only Diodorus but also Plutarch to use a rhetorical figure. In a monstrous simile he compares the clash of the combatant's horses to the collision of triremes: τῶν δ' ἵππων ἐξ ἐναντίας βίᾳ συμπεσόντων ὥσπεϱ τϱιήϱων.[46] Arrian, too, as we know from Photius and from the new papyrus fragment, treated this episode in detail. Its veracity need not be doubted—single combats are conceivable in cavalry encounters, which at this period could be decisive—but the treatment is special. Evidently this was something of a set piece in Hieronymus, which attracted the attention of epitomators and inspired a certain amount of fine writing, intended to reflect the spirit of the original.

The account of this battle shows two sides to Hieronymus' military writing. On the one hand are the ranks of the phalanx massed solidly 'like a strong wall'; on the other, the figures of the two generals, Eumenes and Neoptolemus, are locked in single combat. Eumenes' *monomachia* is the only example in the narrative from Hieronymus of a heroic style of warfare. Possibly it was this episode that Beloch had in mind when he called Hieronymus' battle descriptions rhetorical, for in general they are rightly described as 'klare and verständlich';[47] and it is perhaps no accident that 'rhetoric' is to be found principally in the Eumenes narrative, where Hieronymus' own emotions were most closely engaged. Hieronymus elsewhere (in Diodorus) emphasizes the corporate spirit of the perfectly disciplined professional army, acting as a fighting machine, and the strategic skill of the general who directs it, rather than the prowess of individuals. The technological developments of the Hellenistic age, especially the use of long-range artillery, reduced the opportunities for hand-to-hand fighting and tended to obscure the individual in warfare; and the battles of the Diadochi were normally decided by weight of numbers and the expertise of the general, not by the archaic method of personal duelling. However, the system did offer a temptation to ostentatious posturing on the part of the general, as the only man in the army who did not have to keep formation. Xenophon had compared the well-disciplined army to a chorus; and sometimes, it seems, the general regarded himself as not

[45] Diod. xvi.76.2: ταῖς αἰεὶ κατωτάταις οἰκίαις ὥσπεϱ ὀχυϱοῖς τισι τείχεσιν ἐχϱῶντο (at the siege of Perinthus). Cf. xi.8.2; xix.94.6.

[46] Plut. *Eum.* vii.5. Compare, however, Xen. *Hell.* vii.5.23 for a naval metaphor at the battle of Mantineia: ὁ δὲ (sc. Ἐπαμεινώνδας) τὸ στϱάτευμα ἀντίπϱωϱον ὥσπεϱ τϱιήϱη πϱοσῆγεν. Sophocles *Elec.* 730 speaks of ναυαγίαι ἱππικαί.

[47] Jacoby, *RE* 'Hieronymos', col. 1557.

only the director but the star of the performance.[48] Demetrius' love of show and affectation of a heroic manner are well attested;[49] and there is evidence that Pyrrhus was personally convinced of his own descent from Achilles and consciously emulated a heroic life style. Plutarch speaks of special armour (Pyrrhus could always be recognized by his helmet with its goats' horns), of duelling, invective, and chivalry, all of which are characteristic of epic warfare; and even when allowance is made for the flattery and exaggerations of Pyrrhus' court historian, Proxenus, there seems no reason to doubt that Pyrrhus did habitually indulge himself in this way.[50] Real heroic fighting, as a means of deciding a battle or a war, was of course utterly impractical in the Hellenistic age, and the sophisticated Greeks of the third century were horrified when they encountered the genuinely ancient customs of the Celts in war, with their strange formal challenges and barbaric single combat. The behaviour of Pyrrhus and Demetrius, both of them in the personal tradition of Alexander, was largely a self-indulgence, both on occasion suffering enormous losses; and it is probably no coincidence that a frivolous attitude towards war is found mainly among the Epigoni, since nostalgia for an ethic based on prowess and personal glory would tend to increase as memories of the really epic deeds of Alexander faded. Hieronymus' attitude to this kind of generalship can be inferred from the last chapters of Plutarch's *Life of Pyrrhus*, in which Pyrrhus challenges Antigonus to stop skulking in the hills like a robber and come down and fight. The cool reply of Antigonus—'There are many roads to death for those that are tired of life'—is intended to show his contempt for Pyrrhus and his methods.[51]

[48] Xen. *Cyrop.* iii.3.70; cf. Onasander, *Strategikos* x.3. It was even a charge against Alexander: cf. Aymard, *Études*, pp. 51 ff.

[49] Plut. *Demetr.* xxi.3, Demetrius' special breastplate; ibid., xli.4–5, Diod. xx.93.4, his luxurious clothes. Plut. *Demetr.*xv.2, exchange of 'heroic' invective between Ptolemy and Demetrius at Salamis. Plut. *Demetr.* v.3, vi.2–3, xxxviii.1, xxxix.2, xl.3, xv.1, Diod. xx.102.1, Demetrius' chivalry and his crusading spirit.

[50] Plut. *Pyrrh.* xi.5, cf. xvi.7, Pyrrhus' horned helmet. Lindian Chronicle, *F. Gr. Hist.* 532 C40: Pyrrhus dedicated at Lindos the arms which he himself had used in action. Personal armour is also important in the cult of the heroized dead: cf. Lanckoronski-Petersen, *Städte Pamphyliens und Pisidiens*, ii, 64 ff., for Alcetas' arms in the tomb at Termessos; and Petersen, *Der Leichenwagen Alex. d. Gr.*, p. 710 for the arms of Alexander as described in Diodorus' account of his funeral carriage. Duels and personal prowess are recorded at Plut. *Pyrrh.* vii.4 ff. (Pyrrhus and Pantauchus); xvi.8–10 (Pyrrhus and Oplax); xxiv.1–3 (Pyrrhus and the Mamertine giant); xxx.5–6 (Pyrrhus and Evalcus the Spartan). For invective see Plut. *Pyrrh.* xxxi.1–2, Pyrrhus' challenge to Gonatas: cf. J. J. Glück, 'Reviling and Monomachy as Battle Preludes in Ancient Warfare', *AC* vii (1964), pp. 25–31. On Pyrrhus' heroic ancestry see Lévêque, *Pyrrhos*, pp. 251 f.

[51] Cf. Tarn, *Antigonos Gonatas*, p. 250. The display of heroic valour by a king could, of course, inspire his troops with enthusiasm which might decide the battle: see Préaux, *Monde Hell.* i, p. 197.

Special motives, therefore, must explain the highly coloured style in which Hieronymus wrote up the duel between Eumenes and Neoptolemus. This account has many of the features of heroic combat: the antagonists recognize each other by their horses and insignia; they are inspired by 'ancient hatred', the classic motive for a duel; the wounds they inflict on one another are described in detail; Eumenes reviles his fallen enemy.[52] The passage shows affinities to Pyrrhus' duel with Pantauchus or with Oplax as described by Plutarch (probably based on Proxenus), or to Diodorus' description of Ptolemy's prowess at the Fort of Camels, based on an Alexandrian historian, and seems remote from the straightforward military writing of Diodorus xviii–xx generally. Hieronymus was apparently here carried away by enthusiasm for Eumenes, and could not resist the opportunity, afforded by the fact that Eumenes had really killed Neoptolemus by his own hand, to bring his hero into the limelight. In this battle Eumenes was commanding Macedonians against the Macedonian army of Craterus: there was an especial need to distinguish himself before his troops and secure their loyalty. Moreover, writers like Duris had perhaps insisted on referring to Eumenes as Alexander's *grammateus*, ignoring or sneering at his military career;[53] and it was part of Hieronymus' defence of his fellow-countryman to demonstrate Eumenes' personal bravery in the first of the great battles which the Diadochi fought among themselves. This was the introduction to Hieronymus' ideal general—ἀληθινὸς στρατηγός, as Plutarch calls him—the charming condottiere Eumenes.

EUMENES OF CARDIA

The personal style of Hieronymus' account of his friend made this for ancient biographers and epitomizers, and still makes it, the most appealing part of his history. Many pictures of life in Eumenes' army are clearly Hieronymus' own reminiscenes: the setting up of the Alexander tent, the colourful description of Peucestas' feast, the privations at Nora, and Eumenes' invention of the horses' gymnasium, or the vivid scene in which Eumenes tries to keep up morale in face of Antigonus' propaganda by telling his troops the Aesop fable of the lion and the maiden, with the soldiers standing round shouting 'Right!' ("Ὀρθῶς')—a perfect vignette of camp life. Hieronymus' character-

---

[52] Diod. xviii.31, *passim*; Plut. *Eum.* vii.3–8; Arrian, *Succ.* F9.27, cf. *PSI* xii. 2, 1284, and above, ch. 2, n. 43.

[53] Cf. Arrian, *Succ.* F9.27: καὶ πίπτει μὲν Νεοπτόλεμος τῆι αὐτοῦ Εὐμενοῦς τοῦ γραμματέως δεξιᾶι, ἀνὴρ στρατιωτικὸς καὶ πολέμοις ἠριστευκώς. Engel, *Mus. Helv.* xxviii (1971), p. 230, on the treatment of the Battle of Orkynia in Plutarch and Diodorus, concludes that a bias in Eumenes' favour seems to show Hieronymus' authorship.

ization of his friend was a personal commemoration of a man who had not left his mark on the world like the other diadochs, and though as an apologia it is transparent, it has a peculiar interest as embodying Hieronymus' own ideal of military leadership.

It begins from the idea that Eumenes was a man faced by unusual difficulties. The enemy from without was Antigonus, a ruthless and bellicose opponent trained in Philip's school. Within his own army, Eumenes is said to have been hampered by the quarrels of the allied satraps, who envied his position as supreme commander, and by the resistance of the Macedonian troops, who supposedly resented being subordinated to a Greek. Finally, there was the incalculable and frustrating power of Tyche, which raised up kings and cast them down again without meaning or purpose. The cardinal elements in Eumenes' character are those which enable him to face these obstacles: *synesis* or *epinoia*—native wit; and *pistis*—good faith.

Eumenes' cleverness, attested by all our sources, takes various forms, ranging from plain deceit to strategical brilliance: forged letters, exploitation of superstitious belief, the alteration of the terms of an oath, all come within his repertory, and our accounts go out of their way to draw attention to these examples of δόλος. It was not, of course, something reprehensible: wiliness and deception were a hallmark of the Greek folk-hero Odysseus and of the historical Themistocles, and 'resourcefulness' in the Spartan system of education was understood to include theft. Xenophon had explicitly prescribed in the *Hipparchikos* (v.11, cf. 14) that one should overcome the enemy σὺν ἀπάτῃ; and in the *Cyropaedia* (i.6.27) Cyrus is told by his father that the good general must be ἐπίβουλον . . . καὶ κρυψίνουν καὶ δολερὸν καὶ ἀπατεῶνα καὶ κλέπτην καὶ ἅρπαγα καὶ ἐν παντὶ πλεονέκτην— attributes which perfectly describe Eumenes; and in Eumenes' stratagems we see Xenophon's precepts put into practice.

Plutarch and Diodorus refer in a general way to Eumenes' qualities as a leader: Alcetas and Neoptolemus are ordered to obey Eumenes in all things διὰ . . . τὴν στρατηγίαν αὐτοῦ; he is ἱκανώτατος of all the generals fighting Antigonus in Asia.[54] Plutarch describes the way he trained a corps of 6,000 native Cappadocian cavalry in record time, and dwells on their success in the battle with Neoptolemus, which proved Eumenes' *pronoia* and *paraskeue*.[55] Stratagems, however, are peculiarly Eumenes' province—Polyaenus here found a valuable

---

[54] Diod. xviii.29.2; xix.24.5.
[55] Plut. *Eum*. v.3. Cf. Hauben, *Ancient Society*, viii (1977), pp. 116 f., arguing against Briant's view that the Cappadocian cavalry had gone over to Antipater and Craterus when they crossed the Hellespont (*Antigone le Borgne*, pp. 223 f.).

quarry—especially those manœuvres of 317 by which Eumenes and
Antigonus tried to outwit each other. Diodorus records these campaigns at xix.26 ff.: Eumenes sent false deserters to Antigonus' camp
to spread the rumour that he would imminently attack; Antigonus
was forced to halt and prepare his defence while Eumenes stole a
march; realizing that he had been out-generalled (γνοὺς αὑτὸν
καταστρατηγημένον) Antigonus pursued Eumenes with only his
cavalry, and overtaking his rearguard at daybreak he took position on
the ridges where he was visible to the enemy; Eumenes supposed the
whole army to be behind the cavalry and halted to defend himself,
giving Antigonus time to bring up the rest of his troops and force
Eumenes to join battle.

Both the stratagems leading up to Paraetacene are types recommended by Xenophon in the *Hipparchikos*: sham deserters
(ψευδαυτόμολοι) are said to be useful on occasions; and the art of
making small numbers look large and vice versa is discussed at
length.[56] In either case distance, of course, increases the illusion: to
make cavalry seem more numerous, they should be crowded together,
since horses can easily be counted when scattered; and if need be, the
grooms can be armed with lances or imitation lances and stationed in
between the cavalrymen. Another trick is suggested in Xenophon's
proposals for a cavalry exhibition: every man should point his lance
between his horse's ears, for not only will this prevent the lances from
crossing, but the weapons will look fearsome, and at the same time will
convey the impression of numbers—πολλὰ φανεῖσθαι.[57] Perhaps this
is how Antigonus' cavalry should be imagined as it appeared over the
hills.

The game of cat-and-mouse continued after Paraetacene.[58]
Antigonus detained the heralds sent by Eumenes about recovery
of the bodies until he himself was ready to move, then stole a
march into Media. During the same winter, he decided to make
a surprise attack on Eumenes in winter quarters, and, spreading a
false report that he was moving into Armenia, suddenly set out across
the desert. But the army was detected, because some of the soldiers
lighted fires at night. Eumenes was able to check Antigonus'
advance by a counter-stratagem: stationing a few men on high ground

---

[56] Xen. *Hipp.* iv.7; v.1–11.

[57] Ibid., iii.3. Cf. Polyaen. iv.4.3 (from Hieronymus?): Antipater uses a similar stratagem during the Lamian War, placing mules among the cavalry. Ibid., iv.19, during his
war against Perdiccas, Ptolemy is said to have used a flock of sheep to stir up the dust and
give the appearance of a great army.

[58] Diod. xix.32, 37 ff.

overlooking the desert, he ordered them to burn fires at night in such a way as to simulate a camp, and Antigonus, believing that Eumenes' army was assembled and ready for him, led his men elsewhere.

The two generals outwitted each other, says Diodorus, as if taking part in a preliminary contest of skill—ὥσπερ προαγωνιζόμενος περὶ συνέσεως (xix.26.9), and in making their battle dispositions they vied with each other in tactical skill: διηλλαγμέναις δ'ἐχρήσαντο ταῖς τάξεσιν οἱ στρατηγοί, διαμιλλώμενοι καὶ περὶ τῆς ἐν τούτοις ἐμπειρίας πρὸς ἀλλήλους (xix.27.1). The soldiers were infected with the same spirit of rivalry, for their leaders had made them συναγωνισταί in the contest (cf. xix.24.3): and at Paraetacene both sides prepared to renew battle even when it was dark, 'such zeal for victory filled not only the generals but also the mass of the contestants' (xix.31.1). The long duel between Antigonus and Eumenes is represented as a game of skill played out between masters of the art of war. The rules of this game might be outlined by military theorists, but the successful player was the one with the greatest flexibility, who could take advantage of individual situations as they arose. This was the idea behind the collections of *strategemata* made by Polyaenus and Frontinus: no one can prescribe for every situation in war, and the best method of instruction is the example of generals in history. The theoretical treatise on generalship by Onasander, on the other hand, can have been of little practical use, since it gives no historical examples. Xenophon points out the standard tricks of strategy, but is always insistent that the good hipparch is the one who can adapt to the needs of the moment: 'It is always necessary for the commander to hit on the right thing at the right time, to think of the present situation and to carry out what is expedient in view of it. To write out all he ought to do is not more possible than to know everything that is going to happen.' The hipparch must be μηχανητικός.[59] Again, there are many ways of taking advantage of the enemy, when they are eating or sleeping, when they are over-confident, when they have been lured on to unfavourable ground by a sham retreat; but one should not only utilize what can be learned from others, but oneself be an inventor of stratagems—αὐτὸν ποιητὴν εἶναι τῶν πρὸς τοὺς πολεμίους μηχανημάτων—just as musicians render not only those compositions which they have learned, but try to compose others that are new. 'Now, if in music that which is fresh and new wins applause, new stratagems in warfare also win far greater applause, for such can

[59] Xen. *Hipp*. ix.1–2, v.1; cf. v.9–10.

deceive the enemy even more successfully.'[60] The idea of war as a creative art, which Xenophon was the first to express, pervades our accounts of Eumenes' generalship. Plutarch also sees Eumenes as a ποιητὴς μηχανημάτων at the battle of the Dardanelles. Craterus, he says, thought he would be able to fall on Eumenes when his soldiers were celebrating their victory over Neoptolemus' forces: now, to have foreseen such an attack and prepared against it was the part of a good general, though not especially remarkable; 'but that he should keep his enemies from getting any knowledge that would work him harm, and, besides this, that he should hurl his soldiers upon Craterus before they knew with whom they were fighting, and conceal from them the name of the opposing general, seems to me to have been an exploit peculiar to this commander' (ἴδιον δοκεῖ τούτου τοῦ ἡγεμόνος ἔργον γένεσθαι).[61]

Eumenes' creative ingenuity is typified by the invention of a mechanical system for exercising his horses in the cramped conditions of the siege of Nora.[62] This is one of many expressions in Hieronymus' narrative of the Hellenistic admiration for feats of technology—not the normal attitude of the ancient world. Craftsmanship, as opposed to the finished work of art, was generally thought to be banausic: we do not want to *be* Pheidias, says Plutarch, even though we admire his work.[63] But interest in military technology was given a powerful impetus by Alexander's siege of Tyre (cf. Diod. xvii.41 ff.), and by the end of the fourth century mechanical invention, brought to a peak of development by Demetrius Poliorcetes, could actually be regarded as a kingly activity. Plutarch recounts that some of the earlier kings of Macedon had amused themselves by making little tables or lamps, or cultivating a herb garden (*Demetr.* xx.1–3); but these were διαγωγαὶ ἄχρηστοι—'futuile pursuits'—compared with the splendid machines of Demetrius the Besieger. Biton, also, the third-century technical writer, dedicated his treatise on the construction of siege engines to Attalus I of Pergamon, evidently thinking this a subject which ought to interest a king.[64] We have to go back to the heroic period for a parallel attitude: Odysseus had made his marriage bed with his own hands and

---

[60] Xen. *Cyrop.* i.6.27 ff. esp. 35, 38. Cf. N. Wood, art. cit., p. 49: Xenophon was the first writer to regard war as a creative and productive art, rather than a purely acquisitive one, as Plato and Aristotle did.

[61] Plut. *Eum.* vi.3–4; cf. Arrian *Succ.* F9.27, κρατήσας τοῖς τεχνάσμασι, κρατεῖ καὶ τῶι πολεμῶι. Cf. Onasander, *Strategikos* x.22.

[62] Diod. xviii.42.3–4; Plut. *Eum.* xi.7–9; Nep. *Eum.* v.4–6. Cf. Anderson, *Ancient Greek Horsemanship*, p. 94; cf. p. 125 on the dancing horses of Lampsacus (described by Charon, *ap.* Athen. xii.520D, in the 5th c.) which may have given Eumenes the idea.

[63] Plut. *Per.* ii.1–2. Lucian, Περὶ τοῦ ἐνυπνίου 9: the sculptor is βάναυσος even if he is Pheidias or Polycleitus.   [64] Marsden, *Greek and Roman Artillery* II, pp. 5–6.

himself designed and constructed the boat that took him away from Calypso's island. From the Hellenistic period come stories of fierce professional rivalry between engineers: Vitruvius records the contest between Callias and Diognetus for the post of chief engineer at Rhodes, and a state like Rhodes awarded high honours to the most successful. The Rhodian kidnap of eleven engineers *en route* to assist Demetrius again illustrates the value set on master mechanicians at that time.[65] Hellenistic descriptions of *thaumasia* dwell on features of workmanship as much as on beauty; and delight in the latest developments of technology cut across the ordinary sentiments of warfare: Lysimachus got his enemy Demetrius to put on a display of his new ships of war, the 'fifteens' and 'sixteens', and the Rhodians asked to keep Demetrius' great *helepolis* as a souvenir after the siege of Rhodes (Plut. *Demetr.* xx.4–5). Of course, the patronage exercised at the courts of the fourth-century potentates and Hellenistic kings created conditions in which expensive engineering projects could be contemplated: not since Hephaestus was commissioned to make Achilles' shield had individuals been in a position to order the production of such unique and costly objects. But the mother of invention was often sheer necessity. Our accounts of the sieges at Tyre, Rhodes, and Syracuse show what might be accomplished when pressure was extreme, and Archimedes was only the most celebrated of a line of engineers who defended Hellenistic cities under siege. One who is known to us from Hieronymus is Damis of Megalopolis, a veteran of Alexander's campaigns who successfully led his city's defence against Polyperchon in 318 by employing a system of caltrops which immobilized Polyperchon's elephants: οὗτος γὰρ τὴν ἰδίαν ἐπίνοιαν ἀντίταγμα τῇ τῶν θηρίων βίᾳ κατασκευάσας ἀχρήστους ἐποίησε τὰς τῶν σωμάτων ῥώμας.[66] Ptolemy used a similar device against the elephants of Demetrius at Gaza, 'shrewdly forseeing the issue': τῶν περὶ Πτολεμαῖον συνετῶς προεωραμένων τὸ μέλλον ἐκ τοῦ χάρακος τῆς πήξεως, ἄπρακτον ἐποίει τὴν βίαν αὐτῶν (Diod. xix.84.4).

This David and Goliath motif—σύνεσις and ἐπίνοια matched against ῥώμη and βία—which could be graphically represented in stories of anti-elephant devices, is a prevailing theme of Hellenistic warfare and seems to express a general tendency of Hellenistic thought. The widening of horizons in the period after Alexander had as its correlate, as is often observed, a new emphasis on the individual man and reliance on internal resources. This is evident in the teaching

---

[65] Vitruvius x.16.3 ff.; Diod. xx.93.5. For other καταπελταφέται see ch. 2, n. 46.
[66] Diod. xviii.71.3. Cf. Goukowsky, *BCH* xcvi (1972), 'Le roi Poros, son éléphant et quelques autres', p. 483. On Damis, see ch. 4, pp. 172 f.

of the new philosophies: ἀνδραγαθία, οὐ πατραγαθία, is supposed to
have been a maxim of Antigonus Gonatas; while the Cynic Bion of
Borysthenes enjoined him, ἐπὶ τῶν φίλων ἐξέταζε οὐ πόθεν εἰσὶν
ἀλλὰ τίνες.[67] The founders of the new schools are said to have embodied the ideal of calm, unimpassioned contemplation, free from the
world and its perturbations. *Autarkeia* in Stoic thought came to signify
the principal private virtue, self-control, which was a necessary qual-
ification of the good king.[68]

But how was *autarkeia* to be interpreted by the man of action?
Alongside the quietism of Epicurus or the unruffled integrity of the
Stoics we find an immediate and vigorous response to an insecure
world in the exercise of practical intelligence, wiliness, opportunism—
qualities of doubtful moral status which are exemplified in Eumenes,
par excellence, and which constitute one aspect of the ancient Greek
character. A recent study of *metis*—cunning and intelligence—among
the Greeks attempts to delineate an entire area of Greek thought which
is occupied by the versatile and the complex, the changeable and
the many-coloured, the flexible and the twisted, the supple and the
interwoven; it is represented in the animal kingdom by the fox and
the polypus, among the gods by Zeus (who swallowed the goddess
Metis to make sure he would never by outwitted), and by the inventive
Hermes.[69] At certain periods the attributes of high intelligence
coupled with low cunning had a special value. The context in which we
find the archetypal *homo duplex*, Odysseus himself, is an age of
widening horizons and exploration of foreign lands which was in these
respects comparable with the early Hellenistic period; and the uncertainty of life under such conditions demanded the self-reliance, resourcefulness, adaptability, and practical wisdom which are associated
particularly with Homer's wandering hero. Callicrates, the admiral of
Ptolemy I, compared himself with Odysseus for cunning;[70] and Plutarch once calls Eumenes by Odysseus' epithet, πολύτροπος: it is not
impossible that he found in Hieronymus some conscious reminiscence
of the original ἀνὴρ πολύτροπος.[71]

[67] Plut. *Mor.* 534C = 183D 4; Stob. *Flor.* 86.13.

[68] Cf. Zeller, *Phil. d. Gr.* iii⁴, I, p. 224 n. 5.

[69] M. Detienne, J.-P. Vernant, *Les Ruses de l'intélligence: la métis des Grecs*, Paris,
1974, pp. 9–10 (= *Cunning and Intelligence in Greek Culture and Society*, trans. J. Lloyd,
Harvester Press, 1978). For the fox as a symbol of cunning, see also K. Varty, *Reynard
the Fox*, Leicester, 1967.

[70] Athen. vi.59, p. 251D = Euphantos, *F. Gr. Hist.* 74 F1; cf. Jacoby, *Hermes* lxix
(1934), pp. 214–17; Hauben, *Callicrates of Samos*, 1970, p. 25. Polybius saw himself as
an Odysseus in the breadth of his travels and thought that 'the dignity of history also
demands such a man', xii.28.1; cf. Walbank, *Polybius*, pp. 51 f. Cf. Polyaenus, *Praef.*

[71] Plut. *Eum.* xvi.3.

There was a further parallel in the relations of these men with their fellow captains. In the *Iliad* Homer portrays Odysseus among the other leaders of the Trojan expedition, 'consciously controlling his unusual versatility and flexibility in an uneasy environment, moving with alert circumspection among people of a different heredity and outlook'.[72] Despite his efforts, however, to avoid an impression of artfulness or self-assurance, Odysseus is a 'Man of Odium';[73] and the other chieftains do not always conceal their deep suspicion and prejudice.[74] In the same way Eumenes among the Macedonians disclaims any intention of competing for the highest prizes, puts himself in the background until called for by popular appeal, and tries to allay suspicion and create goodwill by methods which are themselves an indication of a fertile and devious mind. They called him 'Plague from the Chersonese', anticipating the contempt the Romans were to feel for the slippery diplomats they encountered in the subjugation of Greece. *Adulatio* was an aspect of the polytropic character which tended to develop as Greeks were deprived of other means of countering Roman βία, and which clashed with traditional Roman virtues.[75] In Cicero's time the epithets associated with *Graecus* were *levis, loquax, insulsus, fallax*; according to Juvenal, it was a *gens adulandi prudentissima*.[76] Ulysses in Latin literature was generally a detestable figure, and only gained respectability through an allegorical interpretation of the *Odyssey* by Stoics, who came to admire the ideal type of the *homo viator*, acquiring *virtus* through adversity.

With Hieronymus' Eumenes we are still far from this philosophical standpoint, though there is some common ground between the historian and Stoic contemporaries in their answers to the problem of how an individual might make his way in a world apparently governed by Chance (Diodorus was able to make moral capital out of the vicissitudes of Eumenes' career in a disquisition on Tyche which contains elements of Stoic thought).[77] *Metis* is 'a kind of absolute weapon, the only one which can be relied on in all circumstances';[78] but only what is calculable can be controlled. In a chancy world, cleverness, implying the isolation of the individual, is not always enough; and in the search

[72] W. Stanford, *The Ulysses Theme*, p. 14.
[73] Soph. *frg. incert.* 880 Nauck.
[74] *Iliad* iv 339, vii 309; cf. Stanford, op. cit., p. 18.
[75] C. Schneider, *Kulturgeschichte des Hellenismus* i, München, 1967, p. 47.
[76] Evidence for attitudes of Romans to Greeks and vice versa collected and discussed by T. J. Haarhof, *The Stranger at the Gate*, pp. 209 ff. (Republican period); and A. N. Sherwin-White, *Racial Prejudice in Imperial Rome*, Cambridge, 1967, pp. 62 ff.
[77] Diod. xviii.59, *passim*; ibid., 59.6, ὁ κοινὸς βίος, compare Diod i.1.3, 2.3, etc.
[78] Detienne–Vernant, op. cit., p. 20.

for *eustatheia*, 'stability' (a word Plutarch uses in connection with Eumenes), strength is to be found in the mutual support of friends and loyalty to one's leader. Hence *pistis* (*fides* in the Latin authors, and certainly Hieronymus' own word), is the constant attribute of Eumenes, describing his relations with the Argeads; and Eumenes' good faith, or supposed good faith, in turn is underlined by a recurring theme of betrayal and broken trust on the part of his troops.[79] Eumenes' soldiers appear to have taken an oath of allegiance to him at least once a year, and in one year no less than three times. Now, a recent study of relations between Eumenes and the Macedonian army between 323 and 316, has shown that these oaths, so far from being the spontaneous affirmations of loyalty which our sources represent, are in fact an expression of deep mistrust, and that the form which they take is analogous to that in later Hellenistic treaties between a king or city and a body of mercenaries in revolt, i.e. a formal engagement by which the soldiers swear to fight till the death for their employer, and he to pay them. The basis of the contract was thus financial, not personal. Furthermore, whereas the letters of a Hellenistic king to his army or garrison speak immediately to the entire hierarchy under his authority—generals, hipparchs, hegemons of infantry, soldiers—Eumenes appears to have negotiated with the *hegemones*, not with the soldiers direct. His army was 'une mosaïque de contingents de toute provenance' in which each *tagma* exercised practical autonomy, the *stratiotai* being not institutionally subject to the diadoch, but constituting a work force under the employment of their own commanders.[80] The problems arising from such a situation are self-evident. Unsupported by the prestige and the religious function of a national Macedonian king, the power of the personally ambitious diadoch rested on his ability to secure military victory, which alone enabled him to pay his army; hence the emphasis we find in Hieronymus on the *skill* of the general. Eumenes' troubles with his army arose chiefly, not, as our sources maintain, from the fact of Eumenes' nationality or from the perfidy of the Silver Shields, but from lack of cash and the failure to win a decisive military victory against Antigonus. When Antigonus captured the *aposkeue* at Gabiene, Eumenes could be said to have 'lost' it (cf. Justin xiv.3.18); and when the Argyraspids who handed over Eumenes are treated in our sources as 'oath-breakers', this is only half the picture.

However, not all references to *pisteis* and *pistis* are satisfied by the

---

[79] Xen. *Cyrop.* i.6.27 ff.: cunning and loyalty are not incompatible: *pistis* is to be exercised towards *philoi*.
[80] Briant, *REA* lxxv (1973), pp. 53 ff.

explanation of a work contract between soldiers and employer. The treacherous massacre of the Bactrian Greeks is a breach of *pistis* (Diod. xviii.7.7); the soldiers who stay with Polyperchon when his position seems hopeless are μάλιστα πιστοί (Diod. xix.36.6); Hieronymus himself was one of the 600 trusted friends who accompanied Eumenes to Nora (Diod. xviii.41.3; cf. 42.1, 50.4), and he is said to have enjoyed the trust—*pistis*—of Antigonus when he passed into his service (Diod. xix.44.3). This is not a virtue that Diodorus stressed in other parts of his work: his main interest lay in outstanding examples of piety and impiety.[81] *Pistis* is part of a military ideal, belonging peculiarly to the unstable conditions of the period after 323. Associated notions are *euergesia, eunoia,* and *homonoia: euergesia* on the part of a superior generates *eunoia* towards himself and *homonoia* among the beneficiaries, and *pistis* is the link which binds master and servant. This is the bond between Eumenes and the Argeads, between Hieronymus and Eumenes, and between soldiers and their commander.[82]

Xenophon in the *Cyropaedia* states that *euergesia* is the function of the good general: 'Do not think that men are by nature *pistoi*; rather, a leader must make them loyal to himself: ἡ δὲ κτῆσις αὐτῶν ἔστιν οὐδαμῶς σὺν τῇ βίᾳ, ἀλλὰ μᾶλλον σὺν τῇ εὐεργεσίᾳ.'[83] The account of Eumenes at Nora shows how this might be done. Eumenes devised exercises for both men and horses which would keep them healthy by making them sweat; and he used to invite his friends to dinner with him, sharing the same rations and seasoning the sparse food with the charm of his personality. And so, says Diodorus, by his constant affability and accommodating manner he ensured *eunoia* for himself and *homonoia* among all his fellow exiles (xviii.41.3–5; cf. Plut. *Eum.* xi.3–5); and in consequence he became 'much beloved'—ἀγαπώμενος . . . διαφερόντως (xviii.53.6). Xenophon's ideal general here shows some striking similarities of detail. Working and exercising together, Xenophon says, makes men more amiable to one another; and so

[81] *Pistos* and *pistis* occur 7 times in Diod. Bks i–xvii (iv.54.7; xi.66.2, 69.1; xiv.26.4, 48.1; xvi.16.3, 47.3; compare also xvi.47.4, 50.7). In the Greek and Asian sections of Books xviii–xx there are 10 instances of the same words: *pistis,* xviii.29.2, 42.2, 62.6; xix.42.5, 44.3, 50.8; *pistos,* xviii.58.2, xix.24.3, 36.6; xx.19.2. Compare also xix.25.2. Antigonus urged the Macedonians not to obey Eumenes, ἑαυτῷ δὲ πιστεύειν (ironic!); xix.44.2, Antigonus did not trust Eumenes because of the latter's known attachment to the Argeads; xx.107.5, the loyalty of Philippos.
[82] *Eunoia* and *euergesia:* see Diod. xix.62.2; xx.37.2, 81.2 ff., 93.7; Plut. *Demetr.* ix. xxx; *Syll.*³ 330, line 8. Cf. Welles, *RC indices,* pp. 390 f.; Simpson, *Historia* viii (1959), p. 403. Rostovtzeff, *SEHHW,* pp. 1343, 1347; A. Heuss, *Klio* Beiheft xxxix, p. 250; O. Murray *J. Th. Stud.* n.s. xviii (1967), pp. 353–4.
[83] Xen. *Cyrop.* viii.7.13.

Cyrus 'would contrive such sports as would make them sweat'; and at mealtimes, he used to invite a selection of guests from all the ranks, and 'the same dishes were always set before those whom he invited to dinner as before himself.'[84]

The same techniques are used by other diadochs. Alcetas' *euergesia* to the Pisidians, which had included dinner parties, ensured him a refuge in Pisidia when his fortune turned, and those who had enjoyed his benefactions repaid them with extraordinary *eunoia*, awarding him, after his death, a tomb and heroic cult.[85] Seleucus, too, at the time of his return to Babylon, accompanied by a following of only 800 men, relies on *philanthropia* to keep up morale, and invokes the supernatural—in the form of an encouraging oracle from Branchidae—as Eumenes had exploited a feeling for τὸ δαιμόνιον when he set up the Alexander tent (another device for securing *homonoia*). Seleucus likewise puts himself on an equal footing with his men—κατεσκεύαζεν αὑτὸν ἴσον ἅπασιν—an emphasis on equality and camaraderie found in the account of Eumenes at Nora.[86]

The common feature of these situations is adversity. Unable to bestow the *beneficia* of a wealthy ruler like Ptolemy, the generals who had not yet established their power were thrown back on their own ability, first to maintain an army by their strategic skill, and second to attract a personal following of devoted *philoi*. Ultimately Eumenes had little success in uniting his army. He is depicted as the smooth diplomat who helped to create *homonoia* between the rival factions at Babylon, and later as the Themistoclean politician who gets his way within the limitations of a 'democracy', creating *homonoia* by the device of the Alexander tent; but in the end these efforts could not compare with a single decisive victory and its rewards. It was a different matter, however, with the small circle of *philoi* who were bound to their leader by a sense of personal commitment: 800 followed Seleucus; 600 came to Nora with Eumenes, among whom we can name Hieronymus, perhaps the veteran soldier Philippus, praised for his loyalty at a later time when he was serving Antigonus, also Mithridates, described at the time of Gabiene as ἀνὴρ ἀνδρείᾳ διαφέρων καὶ τεθραμμένος ἐκ παιδὸς στρατιωτικῶς (Diod. xix.40.2)—a man

---

[84] Xen. *Cyrop*. ii.1.29–30; cf. Anderson, loc. cit. Cf. *Hipparchikos* vi, *passim*, on camaraderie; *Cyrop*. i.6.13, 25; *Hieron* i.33, iii, *passim*. Compare also Philip's actions at the beginning of his reign: Diod. xvi.3.1–3, he equips and drills all his soldiers, he is friendly to his men.

[85] Diod. xviii.46 ff. Cf. ch. 4, pp. 119 f., for Alcetas' tomb at Termessos, the tangible expression of Pisidian feelings for the diadoch.

[86] Diod. xix.90.5, cf. 91.5. Cf. Tarn, *Antigonos Gonatas*, p. 257: possibly this was also a feature of Pyrrhus' generalship.

brought up in warrior virtues; and in the society from which Mithridates came, this implies an ethic of honour and loyalty. Eumenes with his little band of faithful friends at Nora, or Alcetas among his devoted Pisidians, are still remote from the powerful, beneficent kings of the Hellenistic kingdoms: they recall more the type of warrior leader who was admired at Sparta, and such as Cyrus is supposed to have been.[87] The archaic institution of the Macedonian *hetairoi* gained new vitality and meaning in such circumstances, and personal loyalty was precious. Hieronymus commented on the trust which existed between Antigonus and his son Demetrius, an example of family loyalty which Plutarch thought remarkable; also on the genuine friendship of Lysimachus and Cassander—not in other ways the most attractive personalities among the diadochs.[88] 'It is not this golden sceptre which keeps the kingdom safe; no, faithful friends are the truest and surest sceptre for a king'—so Xenophon's dying Cyrus instructs his sons;[89] and the sentiment would have been sympathetic to people who had lived through the wars of the Successors. Hieronymus' own life was a remarkable illustration of the *eustatheia* of the trusty servant in a time of change and uncertainty: 'er hat recht bezeichnend ein starkes Gefühl für ein neues Element der damaligen Zeit, für der Treue des Dieners.'[90]

The image of the ideal leader which is presented in Hieronymus' portrait of Eumenes—a master of stratagem, a model of fidelity, endurance, and solicitude for his men—is one which evolved in an age of professional soldiering. The diadochs found their direct model in Alexander; but Alexander himself represented only the apex of an evolution in generalship which had begun during the later stages of the Peloponnesian War, with the need for generals to master new methods of fighting and serve for long periods away from home. Phalinus of Zacynthus, who got a job as military advisor to Tissaphernes, and Coeratadas the Theban, who turned up while the Ten Thousand were

---

[87] Cf. Nic. Damasc. *F. Gr. Hist.* 90 F66.3.

[88] Plut. *Demetr.* iii.2 (ὡς ἰσχύν τινα πραγμάτων βασιλικῶν καὶ δυνάμεως ἐπίδειξιν οὖσαν τὴν πρὸς υἱὸν ὁμόνοιαν καὶ πίστιν); cf. Diod. xxx.3.2. Lysimachus and Cassander, Diod. xx.106.3. Cassander's unpopularity, Plut. *Demetr.* xxxvii; Paus. ix.7.2; Justin xvi.1; cf. Tarn, *Antigonos Gonatas*, p. 89. The Antigonids at all times set a high value on family loyalty: cf. Plut. *Mor.* 486A, on the good relations between Gonatas and his half-brother Craterus. The integrity of Doson in preserving the throne for his nephew Philip also aroused comment: Eusebius (*Chron.* i.238, Schoene), thought that he killed off his own children as they were born in order to ensure Philip's succession.

[89] Xen. *Cyrop.* viii.7.13. For the importance attached by Xenophon to friendship, see also *Anab.* i.9.20 ff. (Cyrus the Younger); vii.7.42; *Hell.* vii.2.2. (loyalty of the Phliasians to the Spartans); etc.

[90] Jacoby, *RE* 'Hieronymos', col. 1558. *Eustatheia*, cf. Plut. *Eum.* ix.2.

at Byzantium, 'asking if any city or tribe needed a general', were doubtless men who had gained experience in the wars of the late fifth century and were trying to turn it to good account instead of returning to civilian life.[91] They are our earliest examples of the professional generals of the fourth century, a century which is commonly characterized as the age of the professional. Aristotle and Isocrates commented on the way the functions of the traditional Athenian statesman had become diversified and specialized; Plato noted the beginnings of military specialization. In an early dialogue, the *Laches,* he discusses the topic of education in warfare; and in the *Euthydemus* (set after 404), he ridicules the teaching of the sophists Euthydemus and Dionysodorus, who have taken to including military science in their curriculum. 'If it is a good thing to carry arms in war, then one ought to have as many shields and spears as possible; but if it is a good thing to have only one of each, then even Geryon and Briareus need no more' is supposed to be a sample of their instruction.[92] This same Dionysodorus appears in Xenophon's *Memorabilia*, as an itinerant teacher who once came to Athens professing στρατηγεῖν διδάσκειν: but upon investigation, he turns out to teach nothing but tactics.[93] In the *Cyropaedia,* Cyrus' father exposes the same kind of flimsy teaching, based solely on tactical theory: and what is the good of that, says Xenophon, when you know nothing about supplies, medical preparations, strategy, or discipline?[94] Xenophon's attitude is the same in the *Peri Hippikes*, which is rightly described as not so much a technical manual on horsemanship, but rather an essay written by a cultivated amateur, hostile to specialists: Simon, author of an earlier treatise on horsemanship, is dismissed as ἱππικὸς ὤν—'horsey'.[95]

Whatever their shortcomings, these people are a good barometer of the new interest in military theory. The sophists evidently found interested pupils, and the work on poliorcetics and tactics by Aeneas of Arcadia, 'the first of the Greeks after Homer to be interested in military science', must have met a need for a comprehensive handbook on the subject.[96] Xenophon, too, did not content himself with criticizing the efforts of others, but offered his own theories of generalship in the didactic work *Hipparchikos*, 'The Cavalry Commander', and in his

[91] Phalinus: Xen. *Anab.* ii.1.7; Coeratadas: ibid., vii.1.33. Cf. Griffith, *Mercenaries of the Hellenistic World*, p. 6.
[92] Arist. *Pol.* v 1305 a 7; Isoc. *De Pace* 54–5; Plato, *Laches* 179 ff., *Euthydemus* 271d, cf. 273E, 290C.
[93] Xen. *Mem.* iii.1.1 ff.   [94] Xen. *Cyrop.* i.6.14.
[95] Xen. *Peri Hipp.* i.1. Cf. Delebecque, Xenophon, *De l'art équestre*, Paris, 1950, introd., pp. 16 ff.
[96] Cf. Aelian, *Tactica Theoria* i.2.

romantic *Cyropaedia,* 'The Education of Cyrus', an essay on generalship and statecraft which enjoyed enormous popularity throughout
antiquity.[97] Scipio, famously, had the *Cyropaedia* 'always in his
hand';[98] and the obvious analogy between the conquests of Cyrus and
those of Alexander makes it likely that it was read widely in the
Hellenistic period.[99] Alexander's personal admiration for the historical Cyrus is reliably attested; and probably Onesicritus was imitating
Xenophon's *Cyropaedia* when he wrote the work reported as Πῶς
ἤχθη 'Αλέξανδρος.[100] It was a favourite book with the Cynics, and its
influence on the Stoics is possibly to be seen in Persaeus' *Peri
Basileias.*[101]

The *Cyropaedia,* and equally Xenophon's *Anabasis,* were prece-
dents to which one might turn also when marching with a diadoch into
the heart of Asia. There is a clear similarity in spirit between the
military writing of Xenophon and that of Hieronymus, and possibly
there was a direct literary connection: the description of Eumenes'
behaviour at Nora, especially, does seem to echo the *Cyropaedia,*
though other explanations are not to be excluded. An actual imitation
by the general himself is not impossible. In the period after 323
Eumenes found himself in a unique and extraordinarily lonely position: a book like this might seem to offer some sort of guidance in
circumstances in which there were no established lines of conduct.[102]

---

[97] For Xenophon's theory of leadership, see also H. R. H. Breitenbach, *Historio-
graphische Anschauungsformen Xenophons,* Freiburg, 1950; N. Wood, art. cit., *passim*;
Westlake, *Individuals in Xenophon, Hellenica,* in *Essays on the Greek Historians and
Greek History,* 1969, pp. 203 ff.

[98] Cicero, *Ep. ad. Q.fr.* i.18.23. According to Dio Chrysostom (18.4) Xenophon,
'alone of all the ancients can satisfy all the requirements of a man in public life'. Cf.
Grayson, art. cit., pp. 40 f.

[99] See K. Münscher, 'Xen. in d.gr.-röm. Literatur', *Philologus* Suppl. xiii.2 (1920),
pp. 45 ff.

[100] Diog. Laert. vi.84. Cf. Momigliano, *Development of Greek Biography,* pp. 82 f.;
contra, Pearson, *Lost Histories,* p. 87, who thinks Diogenes had confused the *Cyropaedia* with the *Anabasis.* Alexander and Cyrus: Arr. *Anab.* vi.24. 3, vi. 29–30; Strabo
xi.5.17.

[101] Diog. Laert. vii.36; cf. Münscher, op. cit., pp. 48, 53.

[102] The *Hipparchikos* might have been useful to Eumenes during the period when he
was satrap of Cappadocia. He had particular success with cavalry: Plut. *Eum.* iv.2–3, he
trains native Cappadocian cavalry which are victorious in the battle with Neoptolemus
(ibid., v.3); ibid., viii.3 he requisitions the royal horses grazing near Mt. Ida, and
displays his cavalry forces before Cleopatra on the plain of Sardis. (There was a tradition
of horsemanship in central Asia Minor: the earliest known equestrian treatise, addressed to a cavalry commander, is recorded on a Hittite inscription from Boghaz Keui: strict
application of its precepts explains the victories of the Hittites over the other peoples of
Anatolia: cf. Delebecque, op. cit. pp. 5–6.) For Eumenes' care of his horses at Nora,
compare Xen. *Hipp.* i.16, describing a cheap and clever method of keeping horses' feet
in good condition.

Again, Xenophon's idealization of the Persian monarchy—an early expression of 'disenchantment with the failed Greek democracy'[103]— was necessarily of interest to writers of kingship theory. Hieronymus, writing in the Stoic atmosphere of Antigonid Macedon, may have felt the influence of current opinion, which had assimilated this among other monarchic utopias. Whatever the role of Xenophon in the transmission, it can reasonably be inferred from the remnants of *Peri Basileias* literature that the ideas of *homonoia* and *philanthropia* which are pronounced in Hieronymus' military ideal, were also basic to the Hellenistic picture of the good king. Chrysippus wrote two or more books on *Homonoia*, and though the connection with kingship is not explicit in the fragments of the early Stoics, it is reasonable to assume that it was made in the treatises on kingship which we know to have been written by Persaeus, Sphaerus, and Cleanthes. Later it appears in Dio, and possibly affected the tradition about Alexander's famous attempt to promote *homonoia* between Macedonians and Persians.[104] For Zeno, Eros was the god of friendship who establishes *homonoia* in the state (*SVF* 1.263): hence the speculation that Zeno is the figure in the Boscoreale painting who lends a benevolent presence to the marriages at Susa, symbolizing harmony between Macedon and Persia. *Homonoia* was a matter of ἐπιστήμη κοινῶν ἀγαθῶν (*SVF* 3.292, 625, 630); and friendship was defined as the common use, κοινωνία, of everything in life: one treats one's friends as oneself. *Philanthropia* is a recurring theme in the 'questions and answers' section of the *Letter of Aristeas*: it is the love of a king for his subjects, and the most necessary possession of a king (265). It is exhibited in *euergesia*, which ensures the loyalty of his friends and subjects (190) and their love—ἀγάπησις —for the king. The bond between them will be *eunoia*, which is the best assurance of safety (230).[105]

Some of the fundamental concepts of kingship theory were already present, then, in Hieronymus' treatment of the Successors. The influences which worked together to produce the Hellenistic conception of monarchy came from more than one quarter: the philosopher-king of Plato, the practical suggestions of Isocrates, the romanticized Cyrus of Xenophon, and after Alexander, oriental notions.[106] But there was

---

[103] E. R. Goodenough, 'The Political Philosophy of Hellenistic Kingship,' *YCS* i (1928), pp. 55 ff.

[104] See M. Fisch, 'Alexander and the Stoics', *AJP* lviii (1937), pp. 59 ff. and 129 ff. Cf. W. C. West, 'Hellenic Homonoia and the New Decree from Plataea', *GRBS* xviii (1977), pp. 307 ff. on the cult of Homonoia in the 3rd century BC.

[105] Cf. O. Murray, 'Aristeas and Ptolemaic Kingship', *J. Th. Stud.* xviii (1967), pp. 353 f.

[106] Cf. Goodenough, loc. cit.

also, necessarily, a direct channel through which the third century acquired its ideal of kingly behaviour, and this was the actual behaviour of the diadochs, who were autocrats within their own armies long before the assumption of royal titles—and the armies were in their own way great cities. Notions of concord, beneficence, and goodwill, and their opposites, sprang up naturally in a military milieu where it was absolutely necessary to the success of a general to establish a relationship with his *philoi* based on personal trust, and a relationship with his 'subjects', i.e. the soldiers, based on *euergesia* and reciprocal *eunoia*. In the settled Successor kingdoms these virtues became institutionalized, and the personal bond between one man and his companions lost its importance as military leaders and their comrades in arms gave place to autocratic monarchs surrounded by courtiers and the paraphernalia of established kingship.[107] In the same way the ideal of *homonoia*, an immediate need among dissenting troops and hegemons, is tranformed into a more general goal of the king for his kingdom and acquires wide philosophical connotations. In Hieronymus' narrative we can, however, see something of the formative stage. His characterization of Antigonus and Demetrius offers further illustrations.

Antigonus Monophthalmus

Hieronymus' history of Eumenes was probably the most colourful part of his history, but not the most objective; and it was actually the death of Eumenes which emancipated Hieronymus as a historian: with it we leave the realm of apologia and memoir writing and enter upon the struggle for 'the whole', which centred on the figure of Antigonus Monophthalmus. Antigonus is shown as successor to the high ambition of Perdiccas, and his personality is the driving force behind the history of events between Triparadeisos and Ipsus:[108] the great coalitions—*koinopragiai*—of the other diadochs formed in response to his provocation, the Greeks organized themselves on his initiative. The history of this period was essentially his history. The extraordinary energy of this aggressive and indomitable man, the largeness of his vision, and the inexorable ambition which impelled him towards it, seem to have made a deep impression on Hieronymus, even though he frequently condemned his methods. His portrait of his second master was not without bias: determined that Antigonus' downfall was caused by a defect of leadership, Hieronymus perhaps unfairly judged him

---

[107] Cf. also O. Müller, *Antigonos Monophthalmos*, pp. 108 ff.

[108] The aspirations of the dynasts are analysed in a series of digressions which punctuate the narrative of Diodorus xviii: 23.2–3, Perdiccas; 41.4–5, Antigonus; 42.1–2, Eumenes; 50.1–3, Antigonus; 53, Eumenes; cf. also 36.6, Ptolemy. Cf. ch. 4, pp. 165 f.

against a preconceived ideal which he supposed to have existed in
Eumenes. Nevertheless, in contrast to the romanticized Eumenes
narrative it was realistic, in the same sense as Thucydides' representa-
tion of the Athenian empire: this was a study in politics and power.

Huge in physique, ruthless in his dealings with men, loud-voiced and
one-eyed, to the prisoners of war after Gabiene Antigonus the elder
must have presented a terrifying spectacle. Plutarch says that he was
taller even than the heroic Demetrius, and in old age so heavy that he
had difficulty in getting about; and he was accustomed to laugh loudly
and talk in a booming voice.[109] A deliberate contrast was probably
intended with the insinuating and conciliatory Eumenes: the latter,
says Plutarch, was slight and neat-featured, not a powerful speaker,
but αἱμύλος καὶ πιθανός—traits which he could at least infer from
Hieronymus' account.[110] Direct description became increasingly popular in the fourth century and Hellenistic historians, as a natural accom-
paniment to the writing of history centred on individuals, and doubtless Hieronymus not infrequently did make his judgements explicit.[111]
How far the secondary authors took them over must remain in doubt,
but our accounts of Antigonus and Demetrius allow at least some of
the original diction to be recovered.[112]

Antigonus is introduced at the time of his flight from Perdiccas as
ἀνὴρ πρακτικώτατος τῶν ἡγεμόνων and as συνέσει καὶ τόλμῃ
διαφέρων.[113] The words are Diodorus' own. The latter phrase can be
found *passim* in the *Bibliotheke*; the adjective πρακτικώτατος is
applied to Alcibiades, and elsewhere Diodorus uses πρακτικός.[114]
Diodorus here probably reflects in substance, but not verbally,
Hieronymus' introduction of a dominant character. Antigonus' milit-

[109] Plut. *Demetr.* ii.2 (height); xix.3 (weight). His great voice: Plut. *Demetr.* iii.2,
xxviii.4; Plut. *Eum.* x.4 (βοῶν), xv.2.
[110] Plut. *Eum.* xi.2. It is improbable that this judgement of Eumenes was taken from
Hieronymus himself, since Plutarch notes, ὡς ἐκ τῶν ἐπιστολῶν συμβάλλειν ἐστίν: cf.
Kaerst, *Philologus* xci (1892), pp. 618 f. (against Reuss, *Hieronymos*, p. 131). As R.
Schubert (*Jahrb. f. Phil.* ix Suppl., p. 668) pointed out, Hieronymus did not need to use
the letters of Eumenes to reach a judgement about him for the first time; however,
Schubert's own suggestion—Agatharchides—is no more fortunate. Plutarch either had
before him an apocryphal collection of Eumenes' letters (cf. Lucian, *Pro laps. in salut.* 8,
p. 274), or, if he used Hieronymus directly, he was able to judge by the letters cited in the
history.
[111] I. Bruns, *Das lit. Porträt der Griechen im fünften u. vierten Jahrhundert v. Chr.
Geburt*, Berlin, 1896; *Die Persönlichkeit in der Geschichtsschreibung der Alten*, Berlin,
1898. Cf. F. Leo, *Die gr.-röm. Biographie nach ihrer literarischen Form*, Leipzig, 1901,
pp. 242 ff.
[112] Cf. App. ii, pp. xlviii ff. By Aelian's time, the epithets of the diadochs had become
canonical: Aelian, *V.H.* xii.16; cf. Berve, ii, p. 241 n.1, Briant, *Antigone le Borgne*, p. 92
n.1.
[113] Diod. xviii.23.2–4.   [114] Diod. xiii.68.6; xv.64.5.

ary talents, also, are described, at the time of his naval victory over Cleitus, in the language which was Diodorus' own convention.[115]

The adjectives which Diodorus chiefly associates with Antigonus are ὑπερήφανος and τραχύς, and both have special reference to his manner of speaking. On four separate occasions he gives a 'harsh' or 'arrogant' reply to the ambassadors of his enemies: xviii.52.4, Arrhidaeus listened to Antigonus' ambassadors, καὶ τὸ τῶν λόγων ὑπερήφανον καταμεμψάμενος κ.τ.λ.; xix.56.2, Seleucus denounces Antigonus before Ptolemy—ὑπεδείκνυεν ὑπερήφανον γεγενημένον καὶ ταῖς ἐλπίσι περιειληφότα πᾶσαν τὴν Μακεδόνων βασιλείαν; xix.57.2, Antigonus' reply to the envoys of Ptolemy, Lysimachus, and Cassander in 315: τοῦ δ' Ἀντιγόνου τραχύτερον ἀποκριναμένου καὶ τὰ πρὸς πόλεμον εἰπόντος παρασκευάσθαι κ.τ.λ.; xx.82.3, Antigonus' reply to the Rhodian envoys, τραχύτερον δὲ τοῦ βασιλέως ἀπαντῶντος κ.τ.λ.; xx.106.3, Antigonus replied to Cassander's envoys in 302 that he recognized only one basis for a settlement, namely, that Cassander should surrender whatever he possessed; Cassander therefore sent to Ptolemy and Seleucus, περί τε τῆς ὑπερηφανίας τῆς ἐν ταῖς ἀποκρίσεσιν ἐμφανίζοντες. The adjective ὑπερήφανος is part of Diodorus' standard vocabulary for tyrannical rulers; and he speaks of ὑπερηφανία in a philosophical digression in Book xviii which must be taken as his own: τῇ γὰρ τῶν πράξεων ἀνωμαλίᾳ καὶ μεταβολῇ διορθοῦται (sc. ἡ ἱστορία) τῶν μὲν εὐτυχούντων τὴν ὑπερηφανίαν, τῶν δ'ἀκληρούντων τὴν ἀψυχίαν.[116] This suggests that Diodorus liked to collect examples of ὑπερηφανία and consequent μεταβολή; and Antigonus, of course, was an object lesson in pride and reversal of fortune. The word may, however, have been used by Hieronymus, since it is regular throughout the Hellenistic period, and particularly in connection with theories of the good ruler: ὑπερηφανία is the opposite of ἐπιείκεια and πραότης, and the philosophers regarded it as the worst possible vice of a king. There are many references in Philodemus' Περὶ Κακιῶν; and in the *Letter of Aristeas* we are told explicitly that ὑπερηφανία is the one thing the king should at all costs avoid:[117] he should cultivate ἰσότης and remember at all times that he is a man ruling men.[118]

The word τραχύς is not used of an individual in Diodorus outside xix.56.2 and *prima facie* this was Hieronymus' word. It is not rare in other authors in this sense, but was clearly less favoured by Diodorus than, for example, βαρύς, which is frequent as a personal epithet.[119]

---

[115] Diod. xviii.72.5, 73.1. [116] Diod. xviii.59.6.
[117] *Letter of Aristeas* 269. [118] Ibid., 262.
[119] For βαρύς and βαρύτης cf. xi.44.6, 48.6, 70.3; xiv.82.2; xv.16.1, 28.2, 31.1.

Perdiccas is called τραχύς in the fragments of Arrian, and Hieronymus probably saw a parallel between his personality and that of Antigonus. Plutarch, also, calls Antigonus τραχύς in a general assessment of his shortcomings; and here, as in Diodorus, the word refers to his manner of speech. 'It would seem that if only Antigonus had made some trifling concessions and slackened his excessive passion for dominion, he might always have retained the supremacy for himself and have left it to his son: φύσει δὲ βαρὺς ὢν καὶ ὑπερόπτης, καὶ τοῖς λόγοις οὐχ ἧττον ἢ τοῖς πράγμασι τραχύς, πολλοὺς καὶ νέους καὶ δυνατοὺς ἄνδρας ἐξηγρίαινε καὶ παρώξυνε.'[120] Plutarch gives an example of the sort of remark by which Antigonus gave offence: before the battle of Ipsus he said that he would scatter his enemies with a single stone and a single shout, as if they were a flock of birds. Other arrogant or cynical sayings are attributed to him in the *Moralia*.[121] Diodorus did not have Plutarch's concern with the *dicta* of famous men, but his constant allusions to the arrogant replies of Antigonus suggest that self-confidence and astringency of manner which Plutarch remarked on.

The same impression is conveyed in the phrase πλήρης ὄγκου καὶ φρονήματος, used of Antigonus at Diod. xviii.50.4. This is a regular formula in Diodorus, but occurs with unusual frequency in Book xviii, suggesting that Hieronymus anticipated in the earlier part of his work later reversals of fortune.[122] Personal disaster is often preceded by φρόνημα: this was the case with Pithon, before the collapse of his schemes in Bactria: Nicanor, before Cassander had him murdered; Ptolemaeus, before he was murdered by Ptolemy. Applied to Antigonus at the time when he was first making great plans, it seems to look forward to his final *peripeteia*. Words associated with φρόνημα and ὄγκος in Diodorus are μετέωρος and μετεωρίζομαι, μεγαλεπίβολος, περιχαρής, ἐπαρθείς. The word μετέωρος is used of Antigonus, describing his reaction to the news of Antipater's death, and again after the battle of Salamis; and Plutarch also calls him μετέωρος at the time when he refused to help Eumenes conquer Cappadocia.[123] This word is standard in the Hellenistic period, but the fact that Justin appears to

---

[120] Plut. *Demetr.* xxviii.2.

[121] Plut. *De Fort. Alex.* 330E; *Reg. et Imp. Apophth.* 182.4, 15.

[122] Diod. xviii.7.3, 50.4, 60.1, 75.1. Cf. xix.12.8; xvii.32.1, 62.5. See also xi.70.2; xiv.64.3; xv.37.2, 50.6; xviii.60.1, where the same expression is used of cities or groups of people. In a digression on the collapse of Spartan power (xv.33.3) Diodorus makes it clear that examples of οἱ μέγα φρονοῦντες were meant to be instructive. Plut. *Eum.* iv.2 speaks of Neoptolemus as ὄγκῳ τινι καὶ φρονήματι κενῷ διεφθαρμένος: it was a common formula.

[123] Diod. xviii.47.5; xx.53.2. Plut. *Eum.* iii.3; Plutarch, however, attributes these ambitions to Antigonus prematurely: cf. Briant, *Antigone le Borgne*, pp. 150, 229–34, etc.; Wehrli, *Antigone et Démétrios*, pp. 11, 35, 72 f. etc.

translate it with *elatus* suggests that it may go back to Hieronymus.[124] The linguistic debt of later writers to Hieronymus must remain an uncertain quantity. The consistency of the portrait, on the other hand, leaves little doubt about Hieronymus' general view of Antigonus. Indirect characterization is the surest guide to Hieronymus' opinion, since it could not be obscured by superficial rewriting, and it is entirely consistent with Diodorus' direct description.

The τραχύτης of Antigonus was demonstrated by his treatment of Alcetas' corpse (Diod. xviii.47.3), an episode significantly juxtaposed to the account of *eunoia* shown to Alcetas by the *neoteroi* of Termessus; and again in the burning of Antigenes (xix.44.1–3).[125] Both were incidents which Hieronymus might have omitted without detriment to the historical narrative. There was a similar instance of brutality in the Egyptian campaign of 306: when Antigonus saw that men were trying to desert across the river in punts, he stationed bowmen, slingers, and catapults on the bank to drive them back, and when he captured some, he tortured them frightfully, 'pour encourager les autres': δεινῶς ἠκίσατο, βουλόμενος καταπλήξασθαι τοὺς τῆς ὁμοίας ὁρμῆς ἀντεχομένους.[126] Hieronymus perhaps intended to recall Perdiccas' high-handed methods which alienated his army in 321 (their unsuccessful invasions of Egypt were an obvious point of comparison between the dynasts). Of Perdiccas, Diodorus says, καὶ γὰρ φονικὸς ἦν, καὶ τῶν ἄλλων ἡγεμόνων περιαιρούμενος τὰς ἐξουσίας καὶ καθόλου πάντων βουλόμενος ἄρχειν βιαίως, ὁ δὲ Πτολεμαῖος τοὐναντίον εὐεργετικὸς καὶ ἐπιεικὴς καὶ μεταδιδοὺς . . . τῆς παρρησίας: hence Perdiccas' men began to desert him for Ptolemy.[127] The epithets φονικός and βίαιος are part of Diodorus' regular vocabulary for cruel tyrants;[128] hence this looks at first like a rhetorical comparison inspired by the pro-Ptolemaic source of xviii.34. The parallel account in Arrian, however, also speaks of attempted desertions to Ptolemy: τραχὺς πρὸς τοὺς παρὰ Πτολεμαῖον ἐθέλοντας χωρῆσαι λίαν καταστάς. There was general resentment and reluctance in the army, and Perdiccas is described as τῆι στρατιᾶι ὑπερογκότερον ἢ κατὰ στρατηγὸν προσφερόμενος—perhaps an allusion to the ban on

---

[124] Justin xv.2.10 (corresponding to Diod. xx.53.2). For other examples of μετέωρος in Diodorus, cf. ii.26.4; iii.73.4; xi.1.3, 41.2; xiii.2.2, 38.4, 46.3, 52.1, 92.2; xiv.64.3, 70.1; xv.39.1, 77.4; xvi.11.5, 18.5, xix.90.1, xx.33.2, 92.4.

[125] This is not the exaggeration of a hostile tradition: cf. Diod. xix.63.2—Cassander's general, Apollonides, burnt alive 500 of his opponents in the Argive prytaneum. Cf. also Diod. xix.48.5: Antigonus executes Thespius for his exercise of *parrhesia*.

[126] Diod. xx.75.3.

[127] Diod. xviii.33.3.

[128] Cf. Diod. xi.53.2, 67.3, 67.5; xii.55.8; xv.30.3; xvii.5.3; xix.71.2; xxxii.9a.

parrhesia in Perdiccas' camp.[129] The characterization of Perdiccas, there-fore, is taken from the common source of Diodorus and Arrian. It is also consistent with behaviour which Diodorus has mentioned before: the execution of Meleager and the thirty rebels, the crucifixion of Ariarathes, the sack of Laranda and Isauria, all might be regarded as deeds that were φονικά and τραχέα. There emerges an ironic parallel between Perdiccas, first of the dynasts to try for supreme power, and Antigonus, the man who denounced Perdiccas and then stepped into his shoes, only to be denounced in his turn by the next ruler of Asia, Seleucus, and to come to grief through defects of character recalling those of Perdiccas himself. Antigonus suffered desertions not only from the ranks but also, like Perdiccas, among his officers: his nephew Telesphorus deserted in 312 through envy of another nephew, Ptolemaeus; three years later Ptolemaeus himself deserted to Ptolemy; Docimus and Phoenix, both valuable senior commanders, decamped before Ipsus.[130] This was surely the result of that tactless-ness in his personal dealings to which Plutarch alludes in his assess-ment of Antigonus, and to the lack of *parrhesia* which is attested in some of the apophthegms and in Plutarch's statement that Antigonus never consulted anyone about his plans, but expected blind obedience: if even Demetrius was not to be told at what time the trumpet would sound, the nephews may well have felt that their chances of promotion and independence in command were curtailed.[131]

The narrative of Antigonus' campaigns shows further aspects of ὑπερηφανία and a style of leadership which was the antithesis to that of Eumenes: despite his skill as a tactician, which Diodorus praises in conventional tributes to his *strategia*, Antigonus neglected those other parts of good generalship which Xenophon had demanded: knowledge of terrain, precautions against climate and native opposition, provi-sion of supplies, consideration for the welfare of his men.[132] The first sign is the forced march across Pisidia, when, if we can believe Diodor-

[129] Arrian, *Succ.* F9.28. Cf. P. Berol. 13045 D III, 280: ὁ μὲν γὰρ Περδίκκας ἦν ὠμός.

[130] Diod. xix.87.1; xx.27.3, 107.4, 107.5. For Telesphorus' relation to Antigonus, cf. Diog. Laert. v.79: Τελεσφόρος ὁ ἀνεψιὸς τοῦ Δημητρίου. Kirchner, *Prosopographia Attica* 13551, identifies this Demetrius as the Phalerian. For Ptolemaeus, see also Diod. xix.57.4; Memnon, *F. Gr. Hist.* 434 F1 (4.6); Plut. *Eum.* x.3. Cf. Bakhuizen, *Salganeus*, pp. 105–30, esp. pp. 121 f.; Momigliano, *Riv. Fil.* x (1932), pp. 480–1. For desertions among Perdiccas' officers cf. Hauben, *ZPE* xiii (1974), p. 63: Cleitus and possibly Hagnon were originally admirals of Perdiccas and later joined his enemies. Cf. Hauben, *Ancient Society*, viii (1977), pp. 108 f.: Cleitus' defection was caused by devotion to Craterus, not by his discovery of the enemy's strength (as Briant, *Antigone le Borgne*, pp. 212 ff.).

[131] Cf. Plut. *Demetr.* xxviii.5.

[132] Xen. *Cyrop.* i.6.15, cf. 6.25.

us, Antigonus covered forty miles a day for seven days. This sounds impossible; but even if the figure is false or exaggerated, we are meant to conclude, it seems, that the men were strained intolerably.[133] Antigonus was probably imitating the lightning campaigns of Alexander, which the King undertook especially in his early career. After 323, still lacking the distinction of Alexander's other generals, Antigonus likewise needed to establish an independent reputation and prove himself equal to Alexander.

Other examples of insensitive leadership can be found in the campaigns of 317: here the subtle personality of Eumenes served as a foil to that of Antigonus, the embodiment of ῥώμη.[134] During the crossing into Media Antigonus lost men first through the summer heat of Mesopotamia (ἅτε . . . τῆς ὥρας οὔσης περὶ κυνὸς ἀνατολάς) and then in the battle of the Coprates. The Coprates, says Diodorus, was a swift river, and 'needed boats or a bridge'; but Antigonus' only provision for the crossing was to seize a few punts. Eumenes was able to fall on his army as it crossed in disorder, while Antigonus could only look on like a spectator, unable to go to the aid of his troops διὰ τὴν τῶν πλοίων σπάνιν. The crossing of rivers was an elementary point of ancient strategy to which Xenophon refers more than once in the strategy section of the *Hipparchikos*: '. . . if the order of the file is not kept there is confusion wherever the roads are narrow or rivers are being crossed.' 'Halt at rivers to let the rear guard catch up.' 'In crossing rivers, again, a man with his wits about him may dog the enemy's steps without danger and regulate according to his will the number of the enemy that he chooses to attack.'[135]

Further disasters followed in the mountain passes, where Antigonus had to pass through the territory of the wild Cossaean tribesmen; for he considered it ἀγεννές to use persuasion or gifts on the natives, thereby neglecting the advice of Pithon, the satrap of Media and an expert on local conditions: εἰς τοιαύτην δ'ἀμηχανίαν συγκλεισθεὶς Ἀντίγονος μετεμέλετο μὲν ἐπὶ τοῦ μὴ πεισθῆναι τοῖς περὶ Πίθωνα, συμβουλεύουσι χρημάτων πρίασθαι τὴν πάροδον. Xenophon's advice to the cavalry commander is again instructive: 'A cavalry commander should be at pains even in time of peace to acquaint himself with hostile and friendly country alike. In case he is without personal experience, he should at least consult the men in the force who have the best knowledge of various localities. For the leader who knows the

---

[133] Diod. xviii.44.2. Cf. Brunt, Loeb edn. of Arrian, i, App. viii, p. 488, on the rate of march possible for an ancient army: it seems unlikely that Antigonus could have covered more than half this distance in the time on rough terrain.

[134] For the following, Diod. xix.18 ff.   [135] Xen. *Hipp.* ii.9, iv.5, vii.11.

roads has a great advantage over one who does not.'[136] The Cossaei were famous fighters: they had fought on Darius' side at Arbela, and were one of the last tribes to be subdued by Alexander.[137] Seleucus won their support in his war against Antigonus after 311, showing what might be done by diplomacy.[138] According to Polybius, the Cossaei, like other tribes of the Zagrus, were held διαφέρειν πρὸς τὰς πολεμικὰς χρείας: in his struggle against Antiochus in 221 to 220 the rebel Molon made use of light-armed forces from Kurdistan; and Antiochus, in his reconquest of the East, showed the right way of dealing with opposition of this kind.[139] Antigonus' error was again, perhaps, caused by the desire to copy Alexander, who had successfully treated the Uxians in this way. Alexander himself had, indeed, nearly come to grief on many occasions, and the officers who had been with him could offer advice with hindsight. Antigonus, moreover, had stayed in Phrygia while Alexander went east, hence the especial importance of Pithon's experience and local knowledge; and it is not unlikely that Hieronymus derived his account of this disastrous journey from Pithon himself.[140] When Antigonus at last came down into Media he faced mutiny in the army, and on this occasion alone he is said to have behaved 'philanthropically': φιλανθρώπως ὁμιλήσας τοῖς στρατιώταις (Diod. xix.20.1). In the same way Perdiccas tried to correct his mistakes in Egypt when he realized the feeling of the soldiers: ὁ δ'οὖν Περδίκκας . . . πάντας δὲ φιλανθρώποις ὁμιλίαις ἐξιδιοποιησάμενος.[141]

The φωναὶ δυσχερεῖς of Antigonus' soldiers seem to express the historian's criticism. It is, perhaps, no accident that these incidents are juxtaposed to the account of Eumenes' march through Persis. Where Antigonus had overridden Pithon's advice, Eumenes deferred to the wishes of the *hegemones*; and where Antigonus had squandered his men in the sweltering plains and impassable mountains, Eumenes journeyed through a land which was μετέωρος καὶ τὸν ἀέρα παντελῶς ὑγιεινὸν ἔχουσα καὶ πλήρης τῶν ἐπετείων καρπῶν. Here the soldiers found parks and streams and fruit trees, and brave Persian bowmen instead of fungus-eating barbarians; and those who travelled with

[136] Diod. xix.19.8; Xen. *Hipp.* iv.6.
[137] Diod. xvii.59.3, 111.4 ff.
[138] Babylonian Chronicle, Reverse line 11. Cf. ch. 4, p. 114: Hieronymus' characterization of Antigonus is confirmed by the Chronicle. See Smith, *Babylonian Historical Texts*, pp. 138–40, for discussion of the tribe.
[139] Polyb. v.44. For Antiochus' campaign, M. Cary, *A History of the Greek World 323–146 B.C.*, p. 71.
[140] See ch. 4, pp. 124 f. For Pithon's earlier career, Berve, ii, p. 311, no. 621.
[141] Diod. xviii.33.5. Bizière, *Diodore XIX*, p. 34 n. 1, notes the parallel between Antigonus and Perdiccas.

Eumenes lingered with pleasure in τόποις ἡδίστοις πρὸς ἀνάπαυσιν.[142]

The surprise attack on Eumenes during winter 317 to 316 was another imitation of Alexander's campaigning techniques; and here too it is implied that Antigonus made unreasonable demands on his soldiers' endurance: the cold of midwinter compelled them to light fires in the desert, and the secrecy of the expedition was spoiled.[143] Antigonus tried another winter march at the end of the year 314: he 'first tried to cross the Taurus range, where he encountered deep snow and lost large numbers of his men. Turning back, therefore, into Cilicia and seizing another opportunity, he crossed the same range in greater safety and on reaching Celaenae in Phrygia divided his army for wintering.'[144] Diodorus' account is very abbreviated at this point, but a characteristic procedure is still recognizable: Antigonus underestimates the weather conditions, takes a short cut, loses numbers of men, and finally has to go by the longer route after all.

The Arabian expedition follows the same pattern, for Antigonus underestimated the resistance of the Nabataeans as he had that of the Cossaei.[145] The Nabataeans were *phileleutheroi*, and the speech of the barbarian chieftain to Demetrius is a reply to the *phronema* of the autocrat: his words articulate the theme of skill against strength which pervades much of the narrative of Diodorus/Hieronymus. The Nabataeans, with their cunningly contrived water tanks and their ability to melt into the trackless desert, like Herodotus' Scythians retreating endlessly into the northern wastes, are the paradigm of independence and self-reliance, running circles round their cumbersome opponent: the philosophy of *autarkeia* seemed to be lived out by certain communities of noble barbarians. Three expeditions failed against the Arabs, the third led by Hieronymus himself. Here, perhaps, there was personal animus in his account. No military forces are mentioned in the instructions which Antigonus gave to Hieronymus, and such military escort as was sent with them can hardly have been larger than the forces of 4,000 under Athenaeus and Demetrius. Hieronymus' party must, then, have been inadequately protected against the 6,000 Arabs who attacked them and 'killed almost everyone'.[146]

Personal feelings may, too, have influenced Hieronymus in recounting the invasion of Egypt. By the year 306 Antigonus was very old and very obstinate, and obstinacy, as Onasander remarked, is a great defect in a general.[147] When his naval officers warned him of autumn gales,

---

[142] Diod. xix.21–2.
[144] Diod. xix.69.2.
[146] Diod. xix.100.2.

[143] Diod. xix.37: N.B. 37.5, ἐπιπόνως.
[145] Diod. xix.94 ff.
[147] Onasander, *Strategikos* iii.2–3.

Antigonus accused them of cowardice—an instance of τραχεῖς λόγοι—and in his eagerness to forestall Ptolemy, he advanced at once through the desert with the land army, μετὰ κακοπαθείας.[148] Demetrius and the fleet sailed along the coast, and after a few days were overtaken by wind and storm, as the experts had predicted: many ships were lost and others found it impossible to land on the harbourless shore around the Nile delta; and at last Antigonus was forced to agree that he should return another time, 'better prepared', when the Nile was at its lowest. Nothing had been learned, it seems, from the experience of the Achaemenid kings in their efforts to recapture Egypt. Diodorus' account of the invasions of 351 and 350 is of particular interest in this connection: in 351 Artaxerxes had called on the expert knowledge of Tennes of Sidon, because Tennes 'was acquainted with the topography of Egypt and knew accurately the landing places along the Nile';[149] the following year, having executed the useful Tennes, the king experienced grave difficulties approaching Egypt by the way of the swamps of Barathra and lost part of his army διὰ τὴν ἀπειρίαν τῶν τόπων.[150] Hieronymus probably sailed with Demetrius: doubtless, then, he blamed Antigonus' arrogance for the needless sufferings of the fleet.

It is arguable that a prejudice against Antigonus' methods affected Hieronymus' judgement of his strategy. The conclusion of Seibert's detailed study of this campaign is one to which Hieronymus would have subscribed: Antigonus' failure lay 'in der fehlerhaften Strategie und Gesamtplanung des Feldzuges'. Seibert supposes that Antigonus' plan was to make the difficult crossing of the Nile delta towards Alexandria, actively supported by the fleet on the coast, and accepts the criticism of this strategy which is implicit in Diodorus' account.[151] But on another view, Antigonus' original intention was to travel inland to Memphis, accompanied by those ships, probably about half the fleet, whose draught was shallow enough to navigate the Pelusiac branch of the Nile.[152] This imaginative plan would have had far more to recommend it strategically, and might explain why Antigonus did not hesitate to invade when the river was running high. The matter remains uncertain, since we have only the summaries of Plutarch and Pausanias to compare with Diodorus' account.[153] Diodorus makes it

[148] Diod. xx.73.3.
[149] Diod. xvi.43.2: ἔμπειρον ὄντα τῶν κατὰ τὴν Αἴγυπτον τόπων καὶ τὰς κατὰ τὸν Νεῖλον ἀποβάσεις ἀκριβῶς εἰδότα.
[150] Diod. xvi.46.4–5.
[151] Seibert, *Untersuchungen zur Geschichte Ptolemaios I*, p. 222.
[152] H. Hauben, *Orientalis Lovaniensia Periodica*, 1975–6, *Misc. in hon. Jos. Vergote*, pp. 267 ff.   [153] Plut. *Demetr.* xix.1–2; Paus. i.6.6.

clear that Ptolemy was in any case prepared against all eventualities: he had garrisoned all the strong points of the country in advance, and had already blocked off the Pelusiac mouth and mobilized a number of small, manœuvrable river boats which effectively repelled Demetrius' force and rendered it ἄχρηστος. With hindsight, or influenced by a concept of the natural *autarkeia* of Egypt such as Hecataeus expressed, Hieronymus may have felt that this country was really impregnable when held by a strong and intelligent ruler. What we miss, here, as in the account of the Arabian campaign, the purpose of which is never made explicit, is an explanation of Antigonus' point of view. Diodorus does not say, what was clearly the case, that Antigonus was in a hurry to exploit the victory at Salamis and finish Ptolemy off before he had time to build up his strength again; hence he took a gamble on the weather and Ptolemy's state of preparation. It was, perhaps, a failing of Hieronymus as a military historian that he was too ready to adopt the standpoint of subordinate officers like the κυβερνῆται in Demetrius' fleet.[154] However, if it is true, as Plutarch claimed, that Antigonus never let anyone in on his plans, the general had only himself to blame if in the end his strategy was not understood.

Diodorus may have obscured nuances in Hieronymus' portrayal of Antigonus in order to highlight his central characteristics. However, Plutarch's account substantially agrees; and the consistency of the portrait throughout Diodorus xviii, xix, and xx is one argument for a single source in these books. Even in the winter of 302, when Antigonus' end was already near, he draws a sad picture of the grim old general still battling through ὄμβροι μεγάλοι and χώρα πηλώδης hoping to catch Lysimachus (Diod. xx.109.3). Hieronymus invited his readers to see Antigonus as a man who was ruined, not, like Eumenes, by force of circumstance, but through a fault of character which expressed itself in the attempt to bully men and nature, and which vitiated his leadership. Arrogance, according to the *Letter of Aristeas*, is the worst fault of a king: he should not forget that he is a man among men, and should not be carried away by the desire for conquest;[155] his military commanders should be men of justice who think it more important to save men's lives than to gain victory by rashness. In these respects, then, Antigonus was the antithesis of the good ruler of Hellenistic theory. As a psychological observation, Hieronymus' analysis is supported at many points by a recent study in the psychology of generalship.[156] The common factor, it is argued, in the make-up of

[154] For other examples see ch. 4, pp. 129 ff. [155] *Letter of Aristeas* 222, 223.
[156] N. F. Dixon, *On the Psychology of Military Incompetence*, 1976, esp. pp. 263 ff., 318 ff.

incompetent generals who perpetrate disasters is that they are authoritarian: examples are Elphinstone of Kabul, Buller of Spion Kop, Townshend of Kut. Wrong decisions, humiliating surrenders, enormous casualties, the refusal to listen to sound advice—all these characterize the leadership of personalities who are dogmatic, inflexible, callous, conformist, and obsessive. Obviously competent generals—Montgomery and Rommel, for example—were not like this. One need not doubt Antigonus' great ability as an organizer and as a tactician; but his neglect of the humane aspects of generalship, which Xenophon had demanded, made him less than the ἀληθινὸς στρατηγός whom Hieronymus saw in Eumenes.[157] The downfall of Monophthalmus was brought about by the inflexibility of his character, and inability to adapt techniques learned from Alexander brought final military disaster, as the brilliant containing strategy of Lysimachus lured him to his doom.[158]

Modern analysis no doubt would connect Antigonus' *philarchia* with the sense that he had occupied an inferior position under Alexander. In 323 he was some twenty years older than most of the Companions, and without equal distinction. After the death of Antipater he must have felt the urgent need to make up for lost time. From the ancient evidence we know of only two weak spots in this formidable man: his misplaced faith in his impetuous son Demetrius, and his sensitivity about his single eye. An impressive array of one-eyed generals can be assembled from the pages of history: Hannibal and Nelson are only the most celebrated in a series which goes back to the half-legendary Lycurgus of Sparta and to Horatius Cocles.[159] There was even a one-eyed queen, Candace of Meroe in Upper Egypt, who was said in the records of her people to have achieved military success against the Roman armies of Cornelius Gallus and Petronius.[160] One might add, from fiction, the unforgettable Brigadier Ritchie-Hook ('I want to hear less about "denying" things to the enemy and more about *biffing* him'), whose 'single, terrible eye' marks him as heir to one of the most respectable traditions of generalship. Sallust said that Sertorius regarded his one eye as a badge of honour.[161] Antigonus, however,

---

[157] Plut. *Eum.* xiv.1.

[158] On Lysimachus' strategy see Cary, op. cit., p. 40. Possibly Antigonus followed Alexander too closely, since the latter's success had often been achieved more by luck than judgement: in general, up to 326 his iron resolution paid off, but the Gedrosian march, above all, was a military catastrophe.

[159] T. W. Africa, 'The One-Eyed Man against Rome', *Historia* xix (1970), pp. 528 ff.; cf. W. O. Moeller, 'Once more the One-Eyed Man against Rome', *Historia* xxiv (1975), pp. 402 ff.

[160] Rostovtzeff, *SEHRE*² pp. 303 and 679 (n. 56 to ch. 7) with references.

[161] Sallust, *Hist.* i.88 = Aul. Gell. ii.27.2.

was touchy enough to execute one of his guests at dinner for calling him Cyclops behind his back;[162] and he allowed artists to depict him only in profile so as to conceal his defect. Pliny records that Apelles painted him from the side view, and Charbonneaux argued that the gaunt and bony face of the 'old captain' on the Alexander sarcophagus, which is depicted in strict profile, and which seems to recur on a series of coins from Demetrias of the the late third century, is that of Monophthalmus.[163]

Antigonus should have taken more pride in his disfigurement, for the one-eyed general is a type, suggesting a military experience and personal bravery which have to be balanced against failures of judgement or of compassion. 'Prince Andrei glanced at Kutuzov', writes Tolstoy, 'and his eyes were involuntarily attracted by the deep scar . . . where a bullet had pierced his skull at Ismail, and the empty eye-socket, less than eighteen inches from him. "Yes, he has a right to speak so calmly of the death of so many men", thought Bolkonsky.' Some such admiration for the authority of the man he could clearly never quite bring himself to like, is expressed in Hieronymus' whole account of Antigonus' great deeds and his longing for $\mu\varepsilon i\zeta o\nu\alpha$ $\pi\rho\acute{\alpha}\gamma\mu\alpha\tau\alpha$. Plutarch's assessment, too, reveals the sort of ambivalence contained in Theopompus' estimate of Philip: this was a great man, the greatest of his time, yet he was corrupted by power. Whatever one thought about Antigonus' methods, it could not be denied that he had very nearly achieved his aim: he came to Ipsus from the building of Antigoneia. Glory was the final object of all the military and artistic and even commercial undertakings of the Hellenistic rulers, as it had been for the princes of the heroic age; even cities were founded in part to perpetuate the name of the builder; and Antigonus and Demetrius achieved this object, as Alexander had done. Antigonus was *praktikotatos* of the generals, the greatest performer of *praxeis*; his son Demetrius was *energos*. When Alexander, as the story has it, was asked how he had conquered Greece, he replied, $\mu\eta\delta\grave{\varepsilon}\nu$ $\dot{\alpha}\nu\alpha\beta\alpha\lambda\lambda\acute{o}\mu\varepsilon\nu o\varsigma$: 'By never putting anything off'.[164] Antigonus might have given a similar account of his successes: his later career exemplified the new spirit of warfare in the Hellenistic age which Tarn described as, not just a spirit of professionalism, but a spirit of 'getting things done'.[165]

---

[162] Plut. *De Puer. Educ.* xiv.

[163] Pliny, *NH* xxxv.90, cf. 96; J. Charbonneaux, *Rev. des Arts*, 1952, pp. 221 f.; cf. C. Wehrli, *Antigone et Démétrios*, p. 29. For another view on the cavalryman of the Alexander sarcophagus see V. v. Graeve, *Der Alexandersarcophag und seine Werkstatt*, Berlin, 1970, pp. 135 f.   [164] Schol. *Il.* iii.435.

[165] Tarn, *HMND*, p. 43. Onasander elevated this quality into a criterion for choosing a general: *Strategikos* i.2–3.

THE 'SECOND-CLASS' GENERALS

It might be said of Hieronymus, as of Thucydides, that 'concentrations of energy . . . were to his taste.'[166] The importance he attached to energy and achievement as aspects of generalship emerges also in his characterization of the so-called βασιλεῖς δευτερεύοντες, a title applied originally to Cassander and Lysimachus.[167] The latter figures very little in our accounts down to 302—it was, presumably, only after Ipsus that the expansion of his Thracian dominions made him a central character in histories of the period. Cassander, on the other hand, is clearly etched in Diodorus' narrative of European affairs as a dynast exhibiting ruthless *energeia*, an attribute the more pronounced because set against the apathy and vacillation of Polyperchon.

The account of Greek affairs during 318 shows Polyperchon unable to act without the advice of his *philoi* (xviii.55.1), and plagued by indecision. He publicly decrees that the Greeks shall be autonomous, but at the same time desires to occupy Piraeus; and yet, not daring to break his word to the most famous of Greek cities, he changes his mind: μετενόησε τῇ γνώμῃ (xviii.66.2). In his field operations he repeatedly divides his forces (xviii.68.3; 72.1); he undertakes the siege of Megalopolis, yet is discouraged at the first setback, and again, changes his mind: μετανοηθεὶς ἐπὶ τῇ πολιορκίᾳ . . . ἐφ'ἑτέρας ἀναγκαιοτέρας πράξεις ἐτρέπετο. Hence the Greeks despised him and turned towards Cassander, who had acted with decision by putting a garrison into Munychia: εἰς τὰς Ἑλληνίδας πόλεις ἐνέπεσέν τις ὁρμὴ τῆς Κασάνδρου συμμαχίας. ὁ μὲν γὰρ Πολυπέρχων ἀργῶς ἐδόκει καὶ ἀφρόνως προστατεῖν τῆς τε βασιλείας καὶ τῶν συμμάχων, ὁ δὲ Κάσανδρος ἐπιεικῶς προσφερόμενος πᾶσι καὶ τὰς πράξεις ἐνεργὸς ὢν πολλοὺς εἶχεν αἱρετιστὰς τῆς αὐτοῦ δυναστείας.[168]

Diodorus probably found simple character contrasts a convenient way of summarizing a section of his narrative: the contrast between Agesilaus and Agesipolis in Book xv, for example, serves this purpose.[169] The comparison of Perdiccas with Ptolemy in Book xviii, on the other hand, seems to have its origin in Diodorus' source, since there is a parallel in Arrian (see above). That the character contrast between Polyperchon and Cassander (including, perhaps, the explicit judgement at the end of Book xviii) also originates in his source

---

[166] Wade-Gery, *OCD*² s.v. 'Thucydides', p. 1069.
[167] Diod. xx.100.2.
[168] Diod. xviii.75.2. For ἐνεργεία, ἐνεργός, etc. in Diodorus, cf. xv.23.3; xvi.24.1; xvii.4.5, 7.2, 30.7; xix.79.3, 106.1; xx.19.5, 23.3, 84.4, 92.4.
[169] Diod. xv.19.4.

becomes clear from Diodorus' later account of the intrigues surrounding the boy pretender Heracles. Driven out of Macedon on the death
of Olympias, Polyperchon retired to Aetolia where he could await the
turn of events 'in the greatest safety' (xix.52.6). Later he accepted a
subordinate position as Antigonus' agent in the Peloponnese, but he
allowed eight years to elapse before taking another initiative. In 310,
still nursing his old grievance about the regency, he laid plans to
introduce the supposed son of Alexander, on whom many now pinned
their hopes; but at Cassander's offer of 'partnership' he at once abandoned his allies and murdered the unlucky prince (xx.20 ff.). Cassander knew how to manage the old captain; he rightly calculated, too,
how to lure Polyperchon's son Alexander from the service of Antigonus, by offering him command of the Peloponnese (xix.64.4). These
two were, perhaps, 'slight, unmeritable men', not fit to play a leading
part in affairs. Nevertheless, another tradition existed: Diodorus says
that Polyperchon was held in honour among the Macedonians
as the oldest of those who had served under Alexander, and after
the Lamian War he distinguished himself by pacifying Thessaly;
Pyrrhus is said to have cited him as an example of a good general.[170]
Hieronymus' unflattering sketch of Polyperchon, whom he could not
have known well, may reflect the prejudice of sources in Macedon or
Athens.

Pragmatic women were equally an object of admiration. Olympias
spoiled her chances at the siege of Pydna because she filled the city
with ladies-in-waiting instead of able-bodied men: πλῆθος μὲν πολὺ
σωμάτων, ἀχρείων δ'εἰς πόλεμον τῶν πλείστων.[171] Cratesipolis, on
the other hand, who seized power in Sicyon on her husband's death,
possessed σύνεσις πραγματικὴ καὶ τόλμα μεῖζον ἢ κατὰ γυναῖκα
(Diod. xix.67.2): this she manifested by slaughtering and crucifying
the rebel Sicyonians and dispensing well-judged *euergesia* to her
mercenaries. Hieronymus' iron lady was perhaps a reply to the frivolous story in Plutarch, which made Cratesipolis a celebrated beauty
who had an affair with Demetrius;[172] and Plutarch's source here was
probably Duris, since Duris had accepted the story of the comic poets
that Aspasia was the cause of the Peloponnesian War, and he went
back to Herodotus in declaring that all the greatest wars, starting with

---

[170] Diod. xviii.48.4, 38.6; Plut. *Pyrrh.* viii.3. Cf. also Schmitt, *Staatsverträge* III, no.
419 (treaty between Pallantion and Argos, 317/316 BC), showing that Argos remained
friendly to Polyperchon (despite Diod. xviii.75.2). Duris, *F. Gr. Hist.* 76 F12 seems to be
pure fantasy. Fontana, *Le lotte*, pp. 188–216 sees Polyperchon as a statesman of genius:
for a corrective, see P. Pédech's review, *REG* lxxv (1962), pp. 251 f.

[171] Diod. xix.35.5. Cf. Justin xiv.6.3, 'speciosus magis quam utilis grex.'

[172] Plut. *Demetr.* ix.3–4.

the Trojan, had come about through women.[173] Women in positions of political power were a novelty to the Greek world at the beginning of the Hellenistic period. Herodotus took account of great ladies like Artemisia, whom Xerxes prized above all his men; and Xenophon was intrigued by the woman 'satrap' Mania, who succeeded her husband as governor of the Aeolis region; he also mentions a certain Hellas, wife of Gongylus (possibly a daughter of Themistocles), who seems to have been acting independently.[174] From the mid-fourth century we know of Artemisia's namesake, the wife of Maussollus, and another Carian queen, Ada, acting as monarchs in their own right. There were few of them, however, and all orientals. Thucydides was able to ignore women, as historical agents, almost entirely (except for the priestess of Hera who accidentally set fire to the temple at Argos, and she, it could be said, came in handy for dating).[175] The Hellenistic historians were confronted with a dynastic system in which marriages marked political alliances, and in which individual princesses asserted their personalities in state affairs. The majestic figures of Olympias or Arsinoe could hardly be ignored. There were also women like Eurydice, who at the age of fifteen contested the regency with Antipater; Cleopatra, Alexander's sister, who flagrantly disobeyed Antipater and answered him back; and Phila, ambassadress on delicate matters of state between Demetrius and Cassander.[176] Every historian had to take account of the new phenomenon in one way or another; and Duris, Phylarchus, and Hieronymus show the widely differing reactions that were possible to the actual existence of important women—the vulgar, the sentimental, and the realistic.

PHILA AND DEMETRIUS

Among the spirited ladies who earned a place in the pages of Hieronymus, the most attractive figure was surely Phila, daughter of Antipater.[177] Diodorus digresses in his account of the war of 315 to sketch her character: σύνεσις is her principal quality, and Antipater,

---

[173] Duris, *F. Gr. Hist.* 76 F65, F2. Cf. Martial, *Ep.* ix.xx: Fulvia, wife of Antony, was held responsible for the Perusine War. The idea of women as the cause of wars gained currency once more at the time of Cleopatra: cf. Misch, *Hist. Autobiog.*, pp. 266 f.

[174] Herod. vii.99; viii.87–8. Mania: Xen. *Hell.* iii.1.10 ff. (Zenis and Mania were actually sub-satraps, because Pharnabazus was satrap of all Hellespontine Phrygia). Hellas: Xen. *Anab.* vii.8.8, cf. J. Six, *Num. Chron.* x (1890), p. 192 n. 27.

[175] R. Syme, *Proc. Brit. Acad.* 1962, p. 41.

[176] Eurydice: Diod. xviii.39.2–4, cf. Arrian, *Succ.* F9.22–4, 31–3. Cleopatra: Arrian, *Succ.* F11.40. Phila: Plut. *Demetr.* xxxii.3; cf. C. Wehrli, 'Phila, fille d'Antipatros', *Historia* xiii (1964), pp. 140 ff. See in general G. H. Macurdy, *Hellenistic Queens*, Baltimore, 1932, and Ferguson, *Hellenistic Athens*, pp. 70 ff. Cp. also Polyb.ii.8, on Teuta.

[177] Cf. Wehrli, art. cit.

wisest of the rulers of his time, is said to have consulted her on affairs of state while she was still a child; she also showed kindness and generosity in her duties in the camp.[178] Hieronymus must have known her well, and doubtless, as Tarn supposed, he saw more of the traits of Phila than those of Demetrius reappear in their son.[179] The description of Phila at the beginning of her second marriage is matched by that of the young Demetrius at Gaza, and these twin portraits, to which Schwartz drew attention in identifying Hieronymus in Diodorus, seem to be a special tribute by the historian to the parents of Antigonus Gonatas.[180] Plutarch parallels not only this description of Demetrius, but also Diodorus' later characterization of the prince in Book xx: in both cases, then, Diodorus may have drawn closely on his source, as he drew on Ephorus for his estimate of Themistocles.[181]

The attributes of the youthful Demetrius were his physical beauty, and his gentleness: πραότης τις ἦν περὶ αὐτὸν ἁρμόζουσα νέῳ βασιλεῖ.[182] These were qualities which won him sympathy and popularity in the army. The word πραότης is uncommon in Diodorus. It is used once here, and once of Gelon (xi.67.3), and Dionysius the Younger is described as πρᾷος τὸν τρόπον (xvi.5.1). Diodorus preferred generally the expression ἐπιείκεια.[183] Possibly, then, Hieronymus here influenced his diction. *Praotes* is one of the attributes of a good king. Isocrates in his *Letter to Philip* says that Philip has a right to control all Greece κατὰ τὸ τῆς ψυχῆς ἦθος καὶ τὴν φιλανθρωπίαν καὶ τὴν εὔνοιαν, ἣν εἶχεν εἰς τοὺς ῞Ελληνας, and he urges Philip ἐπὶ τὰς εὐεργεσίας τὰς τῶν ῾Ελλήνων κὰι πραότητας (114, 116). Antigonus Gonatas is called πρᾷος and ἄτυφος.[184] The sense is akin to ἐπιείκεια, 'clemency', the attitude which becomes a superior towards his inferiors and which Seneca recommended to Nero in his *De Clementia*.[185] *Praotes* is the opposite of ὑπερηφανία, χαλεπότης, and τραχύτης, those recurring motifs in the characteriza-

---

[178] Diod. xix.59.3–6.
[179] Tarn, *Antigonos Gonatas*, p. 249.
[180] Schwartz, *RE* s.v. 'Diodoros', no. 38, col. 684.
[181] Plut. *Demetr*. ii.3, v.3, xix.3 ff.
[182] Diod. xix.81.
[183] For Gelon, cf. T. J. Dunbabin, *The Western Greeks*, 1948, p. 428, contrasting the 'golden age' of Gelon, as later historians saw it, with the tyrannies of Hieron, Thrasybulus, and Dionysius.
[184] Aelian, *V.H.* ii.20.
[185] Seneca here probably reproduced many points which could be found in early Stoic treatises on Kingship: cf. M. Fisch, 'Alexander and the Stoics', *AJP* lviii (1937), p. 77. See also M. Griffin, *Seneca, a Philosopher in Politics*, p. 145 n. 3. Cf. Nic. Damasc. *F. Gr. Hist.* 90 F57 (based on Ephorus?) using πρᾷος of the Cypselids; and Suidas Δ 431: ὁ δὲ Πτολεμαῖος ἅτε διαφερόντως τρόπου τρᾳότητα καὶ φιλανθρωπίαν ἔργοις δηλώσας κ.τ.λ. Cf. Bakhuizen, *Salganeus*, pp. 125 f. n. 90.

tion of Antigonus Monophthalmus; and this portrait was surely intended to contrast the terrifying old man with his splendid son, in
whom all now placed their hopes for the future. Indeed, the remarks
about generals of long standing may allude obliquely to Antigonus:
'Because Demetrius had just been placed in command, neither soldiers nor civilians had for him any ill-will such as usually develops
against generals of long standing when at a particular time many minor
irritations are combined in a single mass grievance; for the multitude
becomes exacting when it remains under the same authority, and every
group that is not preferred welcomes change' (xix.81.3). Generaliza-
tions in Diodorus are frequently his own work: this is, however, a
military, not a moral judgement, and the sentiment is closely related to
the passage as a whole. Instances of just such a feeling were the
desertions of Telesphorus and Ptolemaeus, and the near mutinies of
317 in Media and 306 in Egypt. Those who saw the brilliant figure of
Demetrius in the assembly at Gaza or fighting on the poop of his galley
at Salamis, may well have felt that Antigonus had produced something
better than himself, a second Alexander who would be able to fulfil the
dream of world empire. Disappointment was in store.

   The second portrait is set six years later at the time of the siege of
Rhodes, and presents a more warlike figure, still of heroic beauty and
dignity, but now skilled in poliorcetics, energetic and cool-headed in
war: κατὰ τοὺς πολέμους ἐνεργὸς ἦν καὶ νήφων (xx.92.4). The word
ἐνεργός is regular in Diodorus, but in the same context Plutarch uses
ἐνεργότατος: again, therefore, perhaps Hieronymus' epithet, expressing the characteristic dynamism of Antigonus' house.[186] At the same
time Demetrius had learned the pleasures of peace, and in his capacity
to indulge himself alternately in the pursuits of war and peace, he was
compared to Dionysus. The man who shows this versatility is a type
which goes back to Alcibiades, and to Philip II, as seen by Theopompus, and which is later exemplified in Mark Antony, whom Plutarch
took as his Roman parallel to Demetrius. Less attractive traits also
now emerge: τῇ ψυχῇ μετέωρος καὶ μεγαλοπρεπὴς καὶ καταφρονῶν
οὐ τῶν πολλῶν μόνον, ἀλλὰ καὶ τῶν ἐν ταῖς δυναστείαις ὄντων. This
associates Demetrius with the typical faults of Antigonus, and suggests
a development of character. The inexperienced prince whom the army
at Gaza had loved for his 'mildness' had had his head turned by his
successes over Cillas and Ptolemy and the sycophantic reception of the
Athenians.

   From the time of Gaza Demetrius' behaviour, as characterized by

---

[186] Diod. xx.92.4; compare Plut. *Demetr.* ii.3 with xix.6. For νήφων cf. Plut. *Eum.*
xvi.5, of Antigonus: αὐτῷ . . . νήφοντι χρησάμενος παρὰ τὰ δεινά.

Diodorus and Plutarch, often recalls that of Antigonus. He showed his father's obstinacy when he refused to take the advice of his friends at Gaza and insisted on fighting against superior forces and an experienced general. Hieronymus was probably among the *philoi* whose advice was ignored; and the enumeration of the good men killed in the battle can be read as a reproach.[187] Forced marches and κακοπάθεια are also recorded of Demetrius; the lightning march to Cilicia in 313, for example, which failed to achieve its object and which lost him most of his horses: for in six days he covered twenty-four stages and not one of his sutlers and grooms could keep up the pace, διὰ τὴν ὑπερβολὴν τῆς κακοπαθείας (xix.80.1–2). Other futile expeditions were his campaign against the Nabataeans, and the dashing, ineffective, attack on Babylon in 311 (xix.97; 100.5–7). An instance of brutality was the crucifixion of Strombichus, the garrison commander of Arcadian Orchomenus, and 'at least eighty of the others who were hostile to him'; and this contrasts directly with Ptolemy's treatment of the garrison commander of Tyre, Andronicus, in similar circumstances (xix.103.5–6; cf. 86.2). Again, Plutarch's description of Demetrius at the siege of Thebes shows his disregard for the sufferings of his soldiers, and his reply to Gonatas' reproach, τί δυσχεραίνεις; ἢ διάμετρον ὀφείλεις τοῖς ἀποθνήσκουσιν; qualifies as an example of Antigonid τραχεῖς λόγοι (Plut. *Demetr.* xl.2). The use of the very rare word διάμετρον is some guarantee of the authenticity of the remark. For Demetrius' career after 302 we are dependent mainly on Plutarch, who used sources other than Hieronymus; the tradition seems to be unanimous, however, in detecting a tendency to *hauteur* and callousness in Demetrius' later years.

There are some signs, then, that Hieronymus traced an evolution in Demetrius' character—a rare thing in ancient writers. There is certainly little awareness of character development in the historiography of the fifth and fourth century. 'Cleon', as Cornford says, 'is a good instance. He is allowed no individuality, no past history, no atmosphere, no irrelevant relations. He enters the story abruptly from nowhere. A single phrase fixes his type, as though on a play-bill . . . Pericles is introduced in the same way, with a single epithet.'[188] Xenophon's portraits of the generals in the *Anabasis* are also static descriptions, and his encomium of Agesilaus, like Isocrates' encomium of Evagoras, contains only a generalized account of the subject's virtues. Theopompus, too, while recognizing the dual aspect

---

[187] Diod. xix.85.1–3. The casualties perhaps included Nearchus the Cretan, who is not heard of again. Cf. ch. 1, p. 12, ch. 4, p. 124, on Nearchus and Hieronymus.

[188] F. M. Cornford, *Thucydides Mythistoricus*, London, 1907, pp. 146 f.

of Philip's nature, does not seem to have traced any progress in his character. Even so sophisticated a writer as Tacitus did not see character as a changing thing: Tiberius 'dissimulated', and the corruption he gradually revealed was part of the nature he had always possessed.[189]

The portrait of Demetrius must have been founded on the avuncular relationship between the historian and his subject. Whereas Hieronymus met the other generals when most were already in middle age, he first knew Demetrius as a boy of eighteen, and was at his side throughout a formative period of the prince's life. It was natural that he should watch keenly for the way the boy was turning out. There was perhaps also a conscious reminiscence of Alexander. While the improvement of character, beyond the stage of youthful *paideia*, held little interest for ancient writers, in some cases there can be no doubt that they saw a *deterioration*: Alexander, Demetrius, and Philip V are three parallel cases. The Peripatetics regarded Alexander in the later part of his life as a barbarized megalomanic tyrant, corrupted by oriental decadence and violence;[190] and this view was not confined to the philosophers who had a grievance over the death of Callisthenes. The early Stoics thought that Alexander had been full of $τῦφος$;[191] and Arrian, while in general he refused to speculate on the character and thoughts of Alexander (*Anab.* vii.1.4), did hold the view, or take it from his sources, that some kind of change for the worse occurred during the last years of Alexander's life, especially after the psychological defeat at the Hyphasis and the hardships of the return from India—$\mathring{η}ν$ $γὰρ$ $δὴ$ $ὀξύτερός$ $τε$ $ἐν$ $τῷ$ $τότε$ $καὶ$ $ἀπὸ$ $τῆς$ $βαρβαρικῆς$ $θεραπείας$ $οὐκέτι$ $ὡς$ $πάλαι$ $ἐπιεικὴς$ $ἐς$ $τοὺς$ $Μακεδόνας$.[192] In tracing Demetrius' development from eager youth to harsh autocrat, Hieronymus may have had in mind the corrupting influence of power on Alexander. Demetrius bore a closer resemblance to Alexander in brilliance and energy than any other of his Successors, and was the one man who might have

[189] A. R. Hands, *CQ* n.s. xxiv (1974), pp. 312 ff. argues that Tacitus' account of the 'dissimulation' of Tiberius is partly derived from his training for the law-courts, where it was a regular argument that, if the defendant had shown uncharacteristic behaviour in committing his crime, he must nevertheless always really have been that sort of man. Cf. Syme, *Tacitus*, i, pp. 421 ff. Tac. *Hist.* i.50.4: 'et ambigua de Vespasiano fama, solusque omnium ante se principum in melius mutatus est'; with Syme, *Tacitus*, i, p. 37 and n. 2: '. . . it stood as a notable exception if an emperor improved.' Seneca could suggest that Augustus' clemency was 'exhausted cruelty'. So too in Plutarch, Pericles *discloses* his better and true nature in his later career.

[190] Agatharchides *ap.* Phot. cod. 249.17 gives a picture of Alexander destroyed by flattery: cf. Fraser, *Ptol. Alex.* ii, p. 777 n. 177. The Peripatetics were not peculiarly hostile: cf. Brunt, 'From Epictetus to Arrian', *Athenaeum* n.s. lv (1977), pp. 19 ff.

[191] J. Stroux, *Philologus* lxxxviii (1933), pp. 222–40, esp. pp. 232 f.

[192] Arrian, *Anab.* vii.8.3. The fact that there is no hint of a development in Arrian's obituary notice (vii.29) suggests that this was not his own comment.

reconstituted Alexander's empire, if he had not been distracted by showy exploits and inflated by the megalomania that resulted from divinization.[193]

Another power for evil which Hieronymus may have seen as hastening moral decline was the bad advice of counsellors and flatterers. This was the chief explanation Polybius gave for the moral deterioration of Philip V, a king who showed many resemblances to his great-grandfather, Demetrius. Philip is described at the début of his career in terms reminiscent of Demetrius in the scene at Gaza: καλὰς ἐλπίδας ὑποδεικνύων πρᾳότητος καὶ μεγαλοψυχίας βασιλικῆς (Polyb. iv.27.10): and his prestige with the Peloponnesian symmachy in 217 after the Social War earned him the title of 'beloved of the Greeks' (Polyb. vii.11.8). But only two years later he made his first attempt to garrison Ithome, and early promise and philhellenism were followed by periods in which the king was exposed to the bad influence of men like Demetrius of Pharos and Heracleides of Tarentum, and in which he experienced reversal of fortune. Increasingly autocratic and violent behaviour ensued, until by the year 200, when he drove the population of Abydos to commit suicide, 'he had apparently come to find pleasure in the mere outraging of Hellenic sentiment.'[194] Like Demetrius, he suffered final disillusionment and death in obscurity, brought to bay by a foreign power. The theme of the wicked counsellor is prominent in Polybius' analysis of Philip's μεταβολή; and it has been observed that the actual importance of counsellors at the Hellenistic courts is frequently reflected in the accounts of Hellenistic historians, who sometimes exaggerate their sinister influence.[195] Kingship writings stress the importance of listening to *philoi* or *phronimoi*.[196] The *Letter of Aristeas* advises the king to choose counsellors who are men of practical experience and absolute loyalty: they should be δίκαιοι and σώφρονες and should have παρρησία (246, cf.270).[197] Hieronymus no doubt saw himself in such a role; and the various stories of Monophthalmus and Demetrius ignoring their advisors suggest a certain pique on the part of

---

[193] Cf. Tarn, *Antigonos Gonatas*, p. 18: *CAH*, vi, p. 499. For the deification of Demetrius, K. Scott, *AJP* xlix (1928–9).

[194] Walbank, *Philip V*, p. 136.

[195] Polyb. v.50, vii.14.3, xiii.4.1–5, 6; Walbank, *Polybius*, pp. 93 f.; Pédech, *Méthode*, p. 234.

[196] Dio, *Orat.* lvi (Agamemnon in the *Iliad* is obedient to Nestor and attempts nothing without his council of elders); cf. O. Murray, *JRS* lv (1965), p. 176.

[197] Cf. O. Murray, *J. Th. Stud.* n.s. xviii (1967), p. 358. The idea became especially important for writers of the Roman period, with the Senate as a model. Momigliano, *Alien Wisdom*, pp. 31 f. draws attention to Cicero, *De Offic.* i.26.90, implying that Panaetius believed, with Scipio, that the more powerful a man is the more he needs the ⁀ounsel of his friends; this was the relation Panaetius saw between Scipio and himself.

the historian, whose own wisdom, perhaps, had too often been proffered and rejected. The good counsellors of Demetrius' early years whom we meet at Gaza may have been contrasted with the Athenian *kolakes* to whom Demetrius later did give a ready ear.

The hero of Salamis and darling of the army, the second Alexander on whom men had fastened their hopes, turned out to be an adventurer who had no time to be king, and who drank himself to death in a gilded captivity. Some explanation was necessary. The introduction of Tyche, or flatterers, or theories about the inevitably corrupting effects of power, are attempts to lighten the responsibility of the individual; for nature and circumstance interact to produce the adult character, but the choice in any particular action lies ἐφ᾽ ἡμῖν, so Aristotle had told his contemporaries. If a man with Demetrius' gifts could not claim Alexander's inheritance, who could? When the message came to Corinth, 'Regard me as dead', the last dreams of empire faded, and Demetrius' historian turned, in disillusionment or relief, to the unglamorous figure of Demetrius' heir, a man whose true virtues, put in the shade by his father's brilliance, were to become apparent with Demetrius's eclipse.

ANTIGONUS GONATAS

Gonatas' character was brilliantly reconstructed by Tarn, whose classic study builds up from the miscellaneous evidence a coherent picture of a prudent, efficient, cool-headed man, who knew his limitations and concentrated on what was possible.[198] He is called πρᾷος, μέτριος, ἄτυφος.[199] He showed kindness to Cleanthes and Bion when they were ill and impoverished;[200] he was an admirer of Zeno. It is not necessary to dwell on the contrast he formed to his father and grandfather, which was pointed out by ancient moralists, and which, it is usually assumed, was implicit in the general tenor of Hieronymus' history.[201] The few details about Gonatas which may be supposed to derive from Hieronymus are consistent with other accounts: the sober common sense implied in his answer to Pyrrhus; the humanity of his treatment of Pyrrhus' son Helenus, and in his reaction to the way Demetrius squandered lives.[202] Hieronymus' censure of Monophthalmus and Demetrius presupposes an ideal of clemency, and this he may have seen or claimed to see in Antigonus Gonatas.

[198] See esp. Tarn, *Antigonos Gonatas*, pp. 249–50; though Tarn underestimated Gonatas' long-term aspirations: see above, pp. 170 f. with nn. 278 and 279.

[199] Plut. *Mor.* 545B, Aelian, *V.H.* ii.20.

[200] Diog. Laert. vii.169; iv.23 ff.

[201] Plut. *Mor.* 562F; cf. Tarn, loc. cit.

[202] Plut. *Pyrrh.* xxxi.2; xxxiv.5; *Demetr.* xl.2.

Pausanias thought that he went further than this. Hieronymus'
history, he asserted, was hostile to all the other kings, but bestowed
undue praise on Antigonus, that is, Gonatas—not unimpeachable
testimony, though the concluding chapters of Plutarch's *Life of Pyrrhus* possibly give some substance to the remark: the characterization
of a living monarch was, perhaps, less than totally frank.[203] But how
exactly Hieronymus made the transition from *strategos* to *basileus* has
to be imagined. 'It is neither nature nor institutions which give men
royal power', reads the entry in Suidas under *Basileia* (no. 2), 'but the
ability to lead an army and the knowledge of how to conduct the affairs
of state: such was the case with Philip and the Diadochi.'[204] This
statement on the nature of authority, almost certainly from a work on
kingship, articulates a point of view implicit in Hieronymus' writing. In
the century spanned by the historian's life the national kingship of the
Macedonians had been transformed into a personal leadership founded on ability and individual magnetism, under which the king's
servant was not *philobasileus* but *philalexandros*; and this, by a natural
evolution, hardened again into institutionalized monarchy. Hieronymus had recorded the period of transition; and possibly he handled the
king returned to the *patris* with less confidence than the great marshals
of earlier days, lending a tone of artificiality to his account of Gonatas
which was interpreted as flattery. Xenophon wrote with greater conviction when describing Cyrus' conquests than when working out the
details of his civic administration. Hieronymus' ideal of leadership was
also essentially military, the models for 'the true general' being Cyrus
and Alexander, the conquerors of Asia. It remained for philosophers
in the peace of the Hellenistic cities to adapt the values of wartime and
set up a new model, appropriate to the ruler bound in noble servitude
to the state.

[203] Hier. F6, 15; cf. App. I, p. 248; ch. 2, p. 71. See above, pp. 171 ff., for the
possibility that Hieronymus had reservations about Gonatas' policy towards his Greek
subjects, which he expressed obliquely.
[204] Suidas s.v. Βασιλεία no. 2: (B 147 Adler) οὔτε φύσις οὔτε τὸ δίκαιον
ἀποδιδοῦσι τοῖς ἀνθρώποις τὰς βασιλείας, ἀλλὰ τοῖς δυναμένοις ἡγεῖσθαι
στρατοπέδου καὶ χειρίζειν πράγματα νουνεχῶς. οἷος ἦν Φίλιππος καὶ οἱ διάδοχοι
Ἀλεξάνδρου.

Conclusion

The best Greek histories were all to some extent external histories: Thucydides, Timaeus, and Polybius wrote in exile; Herodotus looked at the states of mainland Greece with an Ionian perspective; and it was perhaps his position as an outsider in Athens that enabled Theopompus to perceive the figure of Philip looming from the north. Hieronymus of Cardia holds a place among this distinguished group. Exile gave him, like Polybius, a horizon beyond the confines of the *polis*, and his history has a claim to be called universal. Much in his point of view was un-Greek: the Cardian background, his close relation to the Antigonids, on whose behalf he governed liberty-loving Thebes, and the astonishing span of his career, combined to make his experience different from that of other Greek historians. Cardian partisanship, other than his admiration for Eumenes, cannot be detected; Greek problems and Greek aspirations were not ignored, but the orientation was Macedonian.

Probably Hieronymus planned to be a historian from an early stage, his idea of *historia* maturing from the simple project of an encomium on Eumenes to the grand plan of a political history of his times. One of the influences on his final conception may have been the appearance of narrow or mistaken accounts by others. The relative dates of Hieronymus and Duris cannot be established; but Duris' *Makedonika* seems to have covered approximately the same events as Hieronymus, and it is at least likely, as Droysen and Jacoby believed, that Hieronymus was partly stimulated to write, as one with the authority of first-hand knowledge, to correct Duris' errors, as he saw them, and perhaps to improve on his historiographical method. One or other of these objects was probably incidental to the writing of many Greek histories: Ptolemy, if he wrote late rather than early, may have done so with the wish to rectify Cleitarchus' picture; criticism of their predecessors is implicit and not infrequently explicit in Herodotus and Thucydides, not to mention Polybius. Indeed, the contentious spirit of Greek historians can be considered a significant catalyst in the development of Greek historiography.

Information on other historians of Hieronymus' period is severely limited. Polybius' censure of their 'sensationalism' has received wider acceptance than, from so captious a critic, it really deserves; neverthe-less, the fragments of Duris do not encourage confidence, nor those passages of later writers which may plausibly be derived from him. Whether through patriotism or parochialism, there was a tendency, it seems, in this historian to reduce the stature of great personalities by stories of scandal and private vice (Eumenes, Demetrius, and Cratesi-polis became victims of such anecdotes), and to institutionalize the unpredictability of life under the name of the goddess Tyche.[1] These were attempts to tame and render palatable a historical evolution which Greeks either could not tolerate or could not comprehend. Resenting the domination of the monarchs, which deprived them of independent foreign policy, at the same time the Hellenistic Greeks were dependent for the continued blossoming of the city, as a form of cultural and social life, upon their distant benefactors;[2] Duris himself must have been reliant on the support of Antigonus and Demetrius, while they controlled the East Aegean, for the maintenance of his Samian tyranny. Hieronymus, placed at the eye of the storm, could not share the complicated reaction of the Greek *poleis* to its effects. Hence two incompatible but intelligible views of the world of the Successors coexisted. More remarkable, perhaps, is the difference in Ptolemy's approach. The Macedonian general, with the opportunity to write from knowledge about one of the greatest conquerors of all time, produced, so far as we can tell, nothing more than a military chronicle, in which he failed to interpret, explain, and evaluate, and in which he omitted what was unfavourable to Alexander, as well as the successes of his own later enemies. Hieronymus' far wider concept of history shows that among his Macedonian friends he still retained the ways of thought of a Greek education.

The dominant influence on his work ultimately must have been Thucydides: in his account of *aitiai* and his analysis of the struggle for total power Hieronymus shows his desire to be a political historian. No single literary influence, however, could have directed him in describ-ing a period which was itself without precedent. Theopompus was a direct predecessor, suggesting ways of embedding an individual's career within general history; Herodotus gave the paradigm for a study of an outlandish people; and Xenophon was a faithful guide through the weary campaigns across the Asian hinterland. In the last analysis,

---

[1] Cf. R. Kebric, 'In the Shadow of Macedon: Duris of Samos', *Historia Einzelschrift* xxix (1977), for an estimate of Duris as patriot and apologist.

[2] C. B. Welles, *Studi in hon. di Calderini e Paribeni*, Milan, vol. i, 1956, p. 95: 'The Hellenistic monarchy . . . was not designed to extinguish the Greek city but to preserve it.'

of course, Hieronymus was writing only a history of his life and times as he personally had perceived them; but reconstruction of his work discloses a complexity and historical insight which precludes the idea of a naïve or unselfconscious historian.

'Es gehört zu den schwersten Verlusten die die griechischen Historiographie erlitten hat, dass gerade dieses Werk zu Grunde gegangen ist': so lamented Wachsmuth.[3] Among later authors it came to be regarded as a useful book, but not a classic. Doubtless it was the model for Nymphis' work on the Diadochi; Phylarchus could have used it for events in the Peloponnese at the start of his history. It was known to the rhetorical writer Moschion at the end of the second century (Hier. F2); to Agatharchides of Cnidus, who wrote under Ptolemy Soter II (Hier. T2); and to Artemidorus (fl. *c*.100 BC), if the latter was Strabo's source for his citations of Hieronymus.[4] Polybius, however, never mentions Hieronymus—a remarkable fact considering the similarities in their historiographical approach and the relevance of third-century Macedonian history as background to Polybius' own theme. The passages at v.102.1, where he speaks of the perennial desire of the Antigonid house for dominion of empire, and at i.63.7, where he patronizes 'those who have spoken with wonder at the sea-battles of an Antigonus, a Ptolemy or a Demetrius', perhaps allude obliquely to Hieronymus; but the latter is spared, with Thucydides, Polybius' tirades on the subject of historiographical method.[5] Was Hieronymus really too unimportant to mention? Or was this the one historian with whom even Polybius could find no fault?

A century later both alike faced sentence of oblivion, or the fate of being pickled in Diodorus' *Bibliotheke*. Dionysius inveighed against the degenerate style of Hellenistic historiography (in a treatise shackled by rhetorical convention, which fails even to recognize the reasons for Herodotus' appeal), and urged historians to follow his own model in the *Antiquities*.[6] If one questioned Dionysius' judgement, the silence of Quintilian, at least, was decisive: for him, in so far as he was prepared to consider this period at all, Cleitarchus and Timagenes were the high points of Hellenistic history-writing.[7] Hieronymus found his last and most sympathetic reader in Arrian, and after this brief

---

[3] *Einleitung*, pp. 580 f.

[4] Cf. Reuss, *Hieronymus*, p. 180.

[5] Cf. v.55, on the Pontic region 'overlooked by Alexander': a reminiscence of Hieronymus? (cf. Hier. F3). Compare also v.43, on the descent of Mithridates, with Diod. xix.40.2. Gomme, *Commentary on Thucydides* vol. iii, p. 523 (and cf. p. 733) remarks on the 'silent compliment' paid to Thucydides by Polybius.

[6] Cf. S. Bonner, *The Literary Treatises of Dionysius of Halicarnassus*, Amsterdam, 1969.   [7] Quintilian, *Inst. Or.* x.1.74.

renaissance became a name noticed in late antiquity only by lexico-graphers. 'Men and dynasties pass; but style abides.'[8] Where style was lacking, and time has done its work, it is the task of later historians to try to recapture spirit and intention.

[8] Syme, *Tacitus*, p. 624.

Appendix I

Commentary on the Fragments of Hieronymus

FI = ATHEN.V.58, P. 217DE

Brückner (p. 257) and Müller (p. 452) uncertainly attributed this to Hieronymus of Cardia. Athenaeus is discussing Plato's *Symposium*: he objects that the characters who figure in it belong to different generations, because at the time when Agathon the tragic poet won his victory, Plato was only fourteen years old; and in citing other instances where Plato's chronology is at fault, he is led to speak of the reign of Perdiccas of Macedon. The allusion to Agathon suggested to the earlier commentators that Athenaeus may refer to Hieronymus of Rhodes, who wrote a treatise Περὶ Ποιητῶν and whom he frequently cites elsewhere (x.424F, xi.499F, xiii.566B, xiii.604D, xiii.602A; cf. x. 435A, xiii.557E, xiv.635F). The reference to 'Hieronymus' at v.40, p. 206DE is undoubtedly to the Cardian, however (cf. Hier. F2), whereas Hieronymus the Peripatetic was last cited at ii.48B and is not mentioned again until x.424F; and Athenaeus' other authorities on Perdiccas are all historians. Wehrli, *Die Schule des Aristoteles*, x (1959) does not include this text among the fragments of Hieronymus of Rhodes.

Jacoby, IID, p. 545, sees it as part of an introduction to Hieronymus' history in which he reviewed the history of Macedon down to 323 BC. This is possible, though other contexts can be imagined: a survey of the earlier kings of Macedon would have been appropriate in an account of the accession of Antigonus Gonatas and the celebrations at Pella in winter 276 to 275, when Antigonus married Phila, daughter of Seleucus, and perhaps instituted the games called *Basileia*: cf. A. Körte, *Rh. Mus.* iii (1897–8), pp. 174 ff. on the Βασιλεία ἐν Μακεδονίᾳ mentioned in IG II² 3779: Attalus I instituted *Basileia* at Nakrasa after his victory over the Gauls and assumption of the royal title in 241 to 240 (OGIS 268). The Macedonian *Basileia* were perhaps birthday festivals, which also marked the anniversary of the king's accession, like the Ptolemaic *Basileia*: cf. Fraser, *Ptol. Alex.* i, p. 232.

The widely differing estimates of the length of Perdiccas' rule in Macedon reflect an oddity about his reign. The king is Perdiccas, the son and successor of Alexander I, who is mentioned several times by Thucydides. He was on the throne by 432, and still alive by 414, but he died during the next two years, since his son Archelaus was king by 411 to 410 (Thuc. i.56, vii.9.1; Diod. xiii.49.1). His coins are scarce and mostly uninscribed, so that it is difficult to draw a distinct line between his coinage and that of his predecessor; but the coins of Alexander I appear to run from *c.* 500 to *c.* 450, which is consistent with the statement of the chronographers that he reigned from 498 to 454: *BMC Macedon* etc., p. xlviii; H. Gaebler, *Die Antiken Münzen Nordgriechenlands* iii.2, p. 148; Euseb. i.227, 229; Syncell. 469, 498. Cf. Geyer, *Makedonien bis zur Thronbesteigung Philipps II*, Berlin, 1930, pp. 50f.; and *RE* xix s.v. 'Perdikkas', no. 2, cols. 590ff. If Alexander's son Perdiccas succeeded in 454 and reigned until 413, he was on the throne for 41 years, which is the span given by Nicomedes of Acanthius, and Anaximenes is near enough with 40 (no doubt inclusive and exclusive reckonings respectively). Perdiccas' succession was not a straightforward matter, however, because Thucydides refers to an ἀρχή of his brother Philippus and Plato to an ἀρχή of his brother Alcetas which was taken from him by Perdiccas (Thuc. ii.100.3, cf. 95.2; Plato, *Gorgias*, p. 471 a,b; cf. Geyer, *RE*, loc. cit., col. 591). Evidently Alexander on his death divided his kingdom between his sons, of whom Perdiccas, the eldest or the strongest, gradually appropriated the whole. For the stages by which this may have happened see O. Abel, *Makedonien vor König Philipp*, Leipzig, 1847, pp. 166ff.; Momigliano, *Filippo il Macedone*, Florence, 1934, pp. 16f. The diversity of views among the six historians cited by Athenaeus (cf. also *Marmor Parium, F. Gr. Hist.* 239 A61: 41 years, as Nicomedes) shows in any case that there was an anomaly about Perdiccas' reign which made the date of his 'real' accession ambiguous. Cf. Hammond and Griffith, *Macedonia*, ii, pp. 103 f., suggesting that 40 or 41 represents the standard way of reckoning at the time of Philip II, 23 or 28 that of historians in the period of Alexander and after; Theopompus, with 35, is a 'headstrong individualist'.

F2 = ATHEN.V.40, P. 206 DE

Moschion justifies his own description of the ship built by Hieron II by citing other writers who had described *thaumasia*. This suggests that Hieronymus' description of Alexander's funeral car was an elaborate *ekphrasis* like Moschion's own, and there is a strong prima-facie case for Hieronymus as the source of Diod. xviii.26.2ff., where the funeral car is described at length: cf. ch. 2, pp. 40 ff. This is one of four coincidences between the fragments of Hieronymus and Diodorus.

The carriage took two years to build (Diod. xviii.26.1) and Hieronymus must have described it as it looked on completion when the funeral cortège set out from Babylon in 321. Hence this fragment belongs chronologically after F3, which deals with the campaign against Ariarathes in summer 322 (this is the order followed by Diodorus: cf. xviii.16.1ff.).

F3 = APPIAN MITH.VIII. F4 = PS.-LUCIAN MACROB. XIII

Compare Diod. xviii.16.1–3: an account of the war of Perdiccas and Eumenes against Ariarathes, apparently derived from Hieronymus (cf. ch. 2, pp. 46 f.). Hieronymus seems to have prefaced this narrative with a brief account of the earlier history of Cappadocia.

The text raises a problem of historicity: cf. Reuss, *Hieronymus*, p. 2. According to Appian, Hieronymus said that Alexander in his journey through Asia Minor travelled along the coast of Pamphylia and Cilicia and 'never touched the Cappadocians at all—ὅλως' (cf. Polyb. v.55, and above, p. 236 n. 6). The rival version, which Appian seems to prefer, stated that Alexander restored its ancestral constitution to Amisus on the Pontus—implying that he travelled along the northern coast—and that he exacted tribute from the rulers of Cappadocia. The account in Arrian (*Anab.* ii.4.1–2) differs from both of these. Arrian records that Alexander marched from Gordium to Ancyra, received the submission of the Paphlagonians, and continued to Cappadocia, where he became master of 'the whole of the land within the river Halys and also some of the country beyond the Halys'; then leaving Sabiktas as satrap of Cappadocia he pressed on to the Cilician Gates. Arrian and Hieronymus therefore disagree about the submission of Cappadocia, but have the same route: Alexander marched from Ancyra to the south-west corner of Cappadocia, and to reach the Cilician Gates must have dropped down into Pamphylia and along the Cilician coast, as Hieronymus said, since the mountainous country of inland Cilicia was impassable from east to west; he does not, in Arrian, travel beyond the Halys and on to the Pontic coast, and the reference in Appian to Alexander's restoration of the constitution of Amisus looks like local Amisan propaganda. Curtius knows of an Abistamenes who was left by Alexander as satrap of Cappadocia (iii.4), and says that tribute was imposed on the Paphlagonians. A distinction between north and south Cappadocia is first made explicitly by Strabo (xii.534), who says that there were two Cappadocian satrapies at the time of the Macedonian conquest, each of which later became a kingdom. We hear of Persian governors of Cappadocia going back to the time of Darius; a Persian was given Cappadocia as a δωρεά by Artaxerxes 'or some other king', as a reward for saving the king from a lion (Polyb. F54 Büttner-Wobst; cf. Walbank, *HCP* iii, p. 472); and there was still a satrap of Cappadocia in 334, Mithrobouzanes, named among the Persian nobility who died at the Granicus (Arr. *Anab.* i.16.3: ὁ τῶν Καππαδόκων ὕπαρχος. On the terminology, see Bosworth, *CQ* n.s. xxiv (1974), pp. 155 f., showing that in certain contexts in Arrian, of which this is a paradigm, ὕπαρχος means 'satrap'. Cf. L. Robert, *CRAI* 1975, p. 312 f.) At no point under Achaemenid rule is it stated that the province was subdivided, but a *de facto* division is implied by the history of Cappadocia during the thirty years before Alexander's crossing: cf. T. Reinach, *Trois Royaumes de l'Asie Mineure*, Paris, 1888, p. 9; cf. p. 57; A. Baumbach, *Kleinasien unter Alexander dem Grossen*, Diss. Iena, 1911, pp. 58 ff.

Southern Cappadocia, bordering on the Taurus, was governed during the early part of the fourth century by the half-Carian Camisares, and granted to his son Datames on Camisares' death (Nep. *Datames* i.2). During the 370s Datames seems to have extended his territory northwards (Nep. *Dat.*v.6, 'Paphlagoniam occupat'; vi.7, conquest of the Pisidians), and after joining the revolt of the western satraps in 362 he struck coins at Sinope and planned to set up a mint at Amisus: *BMC Pontus etc.*, p. 96, no. 8; Polyaen. vii.2.1; Ps.-Arist, *Oecon.* ii.24, 1350b, cf. D. Magie, *Roman Rule in Asia Minor*, Princeton, ii, 1950, n. 24, p. 1078; E. Meyer, *Geschichte des Königreichs Pontos*, Leipzig, 1879, p. 26. The little empire he had created in the north was perhaps inherited by his son. In the period after Datames' assassination the coins of Sinope, which in normal times were inscribed with the initials of the prytaneis, bear a name in Aramaic letters which was transcribed by Head as Abd—Susin, who is possibly to be identified with Sysinas, the son of Datames who betrayed his rebel father to the king: Six, *Num. Chron.* 1894, pp. 302 ff.; cf. G. Fogazza, 'Datame di Cappadocia', *Par. d. Pass.* xxvii (1972), pp. 130f. (Arr. *Anab.* i.25.3; Curtius iii.7; Berve, ii, no. 710. Cf. Arrian, *Succ.* F4).

A short tradition of hereditary satraps in Cappadocia might help to explain the origins of the genealogy of Cappadocian 'kings' at Diod. xxi.19ff. The earlier part of this king-list is chronologically impossible and was evidently invented in order to confer legitimacy and antiquity on the dynasty of the later Cappadocian monarchs. Datames, however, is a perfectly historical character; likewise Ariarathes; though the connection between them has been blurred by the interpolation of the names Ariamnes and Arimnaios, and there is no mention of Sysinas, unless a memory of him survives in the name 'Aryses' son of Holophernes. The names Ariamnes and Arimnaios are suspiciously similar. Moreover, Ariamnes or Ariaramnes is the name of the first satrap of Cappadocia known to us (Ctesias, *F. Gr. Hist.* 688 F13a, 20; cf. von Gutschmid, *Kl. Schr.* iii.510), and a common name among the later kings of Cappadocia—a name, therefore, which had the ring of authenticity. But the compiler of the list was unable to find a single event 'worthy of mention' in all the fifty years of Ariamnes' reign, and this span is, in any case, ruled out on chronological grounds, since Ariarathes has to be fitted in before 322. The compiler has tried to connect Ariarathes, the real founder of the Hellenistic dynasty of Cappadocian kings, with the famous historical character Datames, in a line of direct descent; apparently he used the name Ariamnes to gloss over a period when the affairs of Cappadocia were in confusion and Datames' line in all probability broken (Beloch, *Gr. Gesch.*, iii² 2, p. 155, thinks that Ariamnes is real). Sysinas, if he is to be identified with 'Sisines the Persian', the double agent involved in a plot against Alexander's life, who had earlier spent time in Egypt and at Philip's court, was doubtless excluded from the official king-list and replaced by the impeccable Ariamnes on account of his disreputable career (Arr. *Anab.* i.25.3; Curtius iii.7; Berve, ii, no. 710).

Ariarathes may have been a usurper (hence Sysinas sought refuge at the Macedonian court). His succession was dated by Six to the 350s on the evidence of the coins of Sinope which bear his name in Aramaic letters, and which seem from the details of their design to follow directly upon those struck by Abd-Susin (Six, *Num. Chron.*, 1885, pp. 15ff. The coins alleged by Reinach, op. cit., pp. 9f. to bear the names of a series of otherwise unknown governors of Sinope in the period after Datames, are very inferior to the usual coins of Sinope and are probably imitations: cf. Six, *Num. Chron.*, 1894, p. 303 n. 13). Six's interpretation is supported by Diodorus' king-list, according to which Ariarathes took the 'throne' in the reign of Artaxerxes Ochus, and sent his brother Holophernes to help the king in his invasion of Egypt in 343 (Diod. xxxi.19.2: the μεγάλαι τιμαί which the king bestowed on Holophernes must be the consequence of a successful campaign, i.e. that of 343, not the defeat of 351). It is also consistent with the statement of Hieronymus *ap.* Ps.-Lucian, *Macrob.* 13 (F4) that Ariarathes was 82 years old when he died in 322 BC: cf. Niese, *RE* s.v. 'Ariarathes', no. i, col. 816. Other silver coins of Ariarathes have been found from Gazioura on the Iris, depicting the seated figure of Baal of Gazioura, and again bearing Ariarathes' name in Aramaic: these seem to date from the 330s, as they imitate the later coinage of Mazaeus: E. Babelon, *Les Perses Achéménides*, Paris, 1893, pp. 57 f.; W. Wroth, *BMC Galatia* etc., pp. xxiv f.; B. V. Head, *HN²*, Oxford, 1911, pp. 749ff.; *SNG von Aulock,* Berlin, 1966, Tafel 215. These coins probably signal the extension of his power at the time of Alexander's invasion, and Gazioura was, no doubt, the centre of his domain, for Strabo (xii.3.15) says there was an ancient palace there: Meyer, op. cit., p. 28, suggested that a small independent kingdom might have existed in the valley of the upper Iris since the time of Otanes/Anaphas, which formed the kernel of the territory of Ariarathes and later of the Pontic kings.

During the 330s and 320s Ariarathes seems to have extended his power as far as Trapezus, because this was the limit of the Cappadocian satrapy assigned to Eumenes in 323: and in 322 he is described as master of great wealth and able to muster an army of 30,000 foot and 15,000 horse, composed both of native troops and mercenaries: Diod. xviii.16.1–2. His relation to the central government is unclear. Diodorus, loc. cit., describes him as 'dynast': he is 'king' only in the genealogy at xxi.19; and Reinach suggested that the rulers of Cappadocia did not take the title of king until 256. His minting of his own coins does not necessarily indicate that he was a rebel like Datames, because new satrapal coinage sometimes marked only a moment of political crisis: Pixodarus of Caria, for example, seems to have struck gold as an emergency measure on the death of Ochus in 338, and possibly

Ariarathes' decision to coin at Gazioura arose from the same situation (Pixodarus' coinage: *BMC Caria and Islands*, p. lxxxiv, pl. 28, nos. 9–12. Cf. Hamilton, *Plut. 'Alex.'*, p. 25). He is alleged to have sent help to Ochus in 343, and if we may identify him with the otherwise unknown Ἀριάκης who commanded a contingent of Cappadocians at Gaugamela, he was willing to help Darius against Alexander: Arr. *Anab*. iii.8.5; cf. Berve, ii, nos. 111, 113. (Berve's view, that 'der nach Selbständigkeit strebende Ariarathes sich kaum noch 331 zur Heeresfolge für Dareios bequemt hätte', begs the question. He is listed next to Orontes of Armenia: these semi-independent governors had little to gain from the defeat of Darius.) He was not the appointed satrap of Cappadocia, however, because Arrian is clear that until his death at the Granicus Mithrobouzanes had been hyparch of the Cappadocians. Apparently Darius claimed to rule all Cappadocia, but in practice a semi-independent kingdom had evolved on the northern coast since the time of Datames.

Arrian's account shows that it was south-west Cappadocia which submitted to Alexander: the recent death of Mithrobouzanes probably meant that there was little organized resistance. Alexander's own nominee, Sabiktas, replaced Mithrobouzanes, and no doubt Alexander claimed, like Darius, to rule all Cappadocia, because the Cappadocians, *tout court,* are listed among his subject peoples in his speech at the Hyphasis (Arr. *Anab*. v.25.4), and Diod. xviii.16.1 ff. implies that Ariarathes' defiance of Alexander was a *casus belli* in 322. Alexander's real control over the province may have been very limited, however. Curtius names 'Abistamenes' instead of Sabiktas, and Berve conjectured that this was Sabiktas' successor, dating his appointment to 331 (Berve, ii, nos. 4, 690); but the simple substitution of one name for another in Curtius is common (cf. Brunt, *CQ* n.s. xii (1962), p. 144 n. 4), and it is unlikely that the Macedonian governors of Cappadocia survived for long after Alexander's departure for the East. Ariarathes' great power in 322, and the implication in our sources that the whole of the province granted to Eumenes needed to be reconquered, suggests that Ariarathes had encroached south-west of the Halys. Hence Hieronymus' statement about the earlier state of Cappadocia (if, indeed, it did not refer merely to the northern kingdom ruled by Ariarathes) showed no more than a grasp of political realities; although doubtless he also wished to maximize the task which faced Eumenes in conquering his satrapy, in order to enhance his victory and perhaps to establish that Cappadocia was 'spear-won' by Eumenes. See now Bosworth, *Hist. Comm. Arr.*, on *Anab*. ii.4.1–2.

F3 = APPIAN MITH IX. F7 = PS.-LUCIAN, MACROB. XIII

Μιθριδάτης . . . ἀνὴρ γένους βασιλείου Περσικοῦ: Mithridates, later king of Pontus. He succeeded to the kingdom of Cius in Mysia in 302 after the death of Mithridates II of Cius, who was son of the

Ariobarzanes who died in 337: Diod. xx.3.4. The Florentine manuscript of Diodorus describes Mithridates of Cius and Mithridates the Founder as father and son (ὁ υἱὸς αὐτοῦ deleted by Fischer), but they were more probably uncle and nephew, since Plutarch calls the younger Mithridates son of Ariobarzanes: Plut. *Demetr.* iv. A Mithridates fought on Eumenes' side at the battle of Gabiene (Diod. xix.40.2), and this was probably Mithridates the younger, since Diodorus' allusion to his famous ancestry recalls that in Appian. (Cf. also Polyb. v.43, and above, p. 236 n. 6.) He must have transferred to Antigonus' camp after the defeat of Eumenes, along with Hieronymus and many others, for he appears in Antigonus' army in Syria as a friend of the prince Demetrius: Plut. *Demetr.* iv. At some time during the following period Mithridates of Cius was executed by Antigonus on suspicion of rebellion (Diod. loc. cit) and Antigonus decided to get rid of the heir as well: according to Plutarch, Demetrius warned Mithridates, who escaped to a mountain fortress in Cappadocia and survived to found the powerful kingdom of Pontus in the period after Ipsus. The relative dates of these events are not certain. Plutarch implies that Antigonus' prophetic dream and Mithridates' flight took place while Antigonus and Demetrius were still in Syria, and Appian mentions the expulsion of the former satrap of Syria, Laomedon, as though it were a recent event: this suggests the period between 315, when Antigonus took over Phoenicia, and the battle of Gaza in 312. Meyer, op. cit., p. 37, regards the flight of Mithridates and the execution of Mithridates the elder as falling in winter 302 to 301: certainly there is more point to Appian's ἐν τῇῖδε τῶν Μακεδόνων ἀσχολίαι if it refers to the marshalling of Macedonian forces before Ipsus; and it is preferable to have Mithridates shut up at Kimiata not longer than one or two years. Appian's telescoping of events prevents a definite conclusion, however.

Pseudo-Lucian's citation of Hieronymus for the age of Mithridates 'Ktistes' is muddled. Diodorus xx.3.4, in a notice probably taken from the chronograph (cf. Jacoby, *F. Gr. Hist.* IID, p. 546; *contra,* Meyer, op. cit., p. 37, who thinks it comes from Hieronymus), says that Mithridates Ktistes reigned 36 years after succeeding Mithridates the elder in 302; and if Hieronymus recorded his death, he must have been writing or revising his history after 266 BC, which is in itself by no means impossible. However, the wording of the *Macrobioi* implies that Mithridates' death followed directly upon his flight from Antigonus, and this is inappropriate to Ktistes. Meyer's view (p. 36) should be followed, that Mithridates II of Cius is unlikely at any time to have been regarded as 'Founder'; and no simple emendation of the text reconciles it with historical fact: cf. Jacoby, *RE* 'Hieronymus', col. 1543. Pseudo-Lucian or his source has confused or conflated the two men, no doubt in the attempt to reconcile Hieronymus with the ἄλλοι συγγραφεῖς. Hieronymus cannot in any case have used the title 'King of Pontus' which appears in Pseudo-Lucian: the Pontic kingdom was not called by this name until a later period, and until at least the time of Polybius was spoken of as Euxine Cappadocia, or Cappadocia and Paphlagonia (cf. Diod. xxiii.4; Polyb. v.43.1; Meyer, op. cit., p. 37; Strabo xii.1.4).

Hieronymus' interest in the house of Mithridates no doubt originated in personal acquaintance with Mithridates as a young man in Eumenes' army, (there is a special tribute to him at Diod. xix.40.2, ἀνὴρ ἀνδρείᾳ διαφέρων καὶ τεθραμμένος ἐκ παιδὸς στρατιωτικῶς: cf. ch. 5, pp. 206 f.) and in the fact that Cappadocia was Eumenes' satrapy: later his historical importance became apparent. Antigonus' dream about Mithridates which Appian and Plutarch record seems to belong to a tradition favourable to the Pontic house, which evolved after Antigonus' defeat at Ipsus. By 296 Mithridates was already so powerful that he took the title of king, and the next fifteen years, while the Macedonian dynasts were occupied in wars among themselves, saw the extension of his kingdom over most of northern Anatolia (Meyer, op. cit., p. 39): thus the witticism that Mithridates reaped the crop that Antigonus had sown was probably in circulation by the time Hieronymus wrote, and the 'dream' is embedded in the accounts of Appian and Plutarch in such a way that it may well derive from their common historical source, Hieronymus.

F5 = PARADOX. FLOR. DE AQ. MIR. 33. F6 = JOSEPH. C. APION. 1.213–14

The length and nature of Hieronymus' excursus on the Dead Sea is not specified by the paradoxographer; but at least part is preserved by Diodorus (xix.98–9, cf. T6): cf. Strabo xvi.2.45 ff. (Xenophilus, the Hellenistic author of a history of Lydia, also gave an account of the Dead Sea, but the fragment which deals with this subject is too short to allow conclusions about his source: *F. Gr. Hist.* 767; cf. Herter, *RE* s.v. 'Xenophilus', no. 7, cols. 1566–7). Hieronymus' expedition to southern Syria thus had literary results despite its failure as an expansionist venture (cf. ch. 1, pp. 12 f.) It was probably part of Hieronymus' task to prepare a written report on the Asphalt Lake for Antigonus: we may compare the account of his voyage round the Persian Gulf which Nearchus wrote for Alexander, or the account of his journey to the Caspian Sea which Patrocles wrote for Seleucus or Antiochus, and which was part of a larger work, as it also contained an account of India: *F. Gr. Hist.* 712; F. Gisinger, *RE* xviii s.v. 'Patrokles', no. 5, col. 2263. Arrian's version of Nearchus' 'Periplus' shows that such reports were not so technical in character as to make them unsuitable material for a historical work; and a tradition going back to Herodotus sanctioned the inclusion of geographical and ethnographical elements in historiography (cf. ch. 4, pp. 144 ff.).

Strabo and Dionysius show that throughout Hieronymus' work

there were descriptions of peoples and places, and Josephus' complaint that Hieronymus failed to give an account of the Jews, although he was 'governor' of Syria, (cf. ch. 1, p. 13), implies that Hieronymus had written about other nations. Josephus no doubt had in mind specifically Hieronymus' study of the Nabataean Arabs (Diod. xix. 94 ff.), to which the description of the Dead Sea was annexed.

F8 = PS.-LUCIAN, MACROB. XIII. F10 = PS.-LUCIAN, MACROB. 11

On the sources and reliability of Pseudo-Lucian's *Macrobioi* see F. Rühl, *Rh. Mus.* lxii (1897), pp. 421 ff.; cf. ch. 1, pp. 5 f. and n. 7. In the section on kings and commanders he seems to have used an already existing compilation, which was also used by Phlegon, and which took its material from historical sources (ch. 17, ἱστορήκασι). Each notice therefore has to be taken on its own merits. For the age of Ariarathes (F4) and of Mithridates (F7) we have no other evidence; but for the ages of Antigonus and Lysimachus (F8, 10) the sources disagree.

F8: App. *Syr.* 55: at Ipsus Antigonus was ὑπὲρ ὀγδοήκοντα ἔτη. Porphyrius *ap.* Euseb. i.247 (Schoene): τὰ πάντα βίωσας ἒξ καὶ ὀγδοήκοντα. Porphyrius also records the length of Antigonus' rule over Asia, and was apparently well informed about him. The corruption of ἒξ into ἓν at any point in the transmission might explain this discrepancy. On copying errors in the *Macrobioi* cf. Brunt, *CQ* n.s. xxiv (1974), p. 65.

F10: Lysimachus' age at the time of Corupedion is given as 70 by App. *Syr.* 64; as 74 by Justin xvii.1.10; and by Hieronymus *ap.* Pseudo-Lucian as 80. Beloch, *Gr. Gesch.* iv² 2, p. 129 points out that Lysimachus must have been quite young at the time of Alexander's crossing into Asia, because he achieved no position of prominence until the time of the Indian campaign; and he plausibly concludes that, of the figures given, 'die erste Zahl wird nach unten, die letzte nach oben abgerundet sein, und die Angabe des Iustin etwa das richtige geben.' Rühl, art. cit. demonstrated that where Pseudo-Lucian has made his own calculations or is confronted with two conflicting traditions he tends to compromise rather than to 'round' the figure. His source for the section where Hieronymus is cited apparently used a different method, and perhaps exaggerated Lysimachus' age in order to get him into his list of famous octogenarians. Justin may have preserved the true figure given by Hieronymus.

F9 = PAUS. I.9.7. F15 = PAUS. I.13.7

F9: Pausanias gives three reasons for disbelieving Hieronymus' story that Lysimachus despoiled the royal Epirot tombs: 1) the common descent of Pyrrhus and Alexander from the Epirot kings would have dissuaded Lysimachus from such an action; 2) the subsequent alliance between Pyrrhus and Lysimachus precludes it; 3) Lysimachus' destruction of Cardia caused Hieronymus to hate him.

1) is a trivial reason, possibly thought up by Pausanias himself.

2) The allusion to the ὕστερον . . . συμμαχία makes the whole setting unclear. The obvious time for Lysimachus' alleged attack on Epirus is the period of general hostility in spring 283, after Lysimachus' moral victory at Edessa and the expulsion of Pyrrhus from Macedon (Plut. *Pyrrh.* xii.6–7): so Tarn, *Antigonos Gonatas*, p. 120; K. Klotzsch, *Epeirotische Geschichte*, pp. 212f.; G. N. Cross, *Epirus*, p. 65; cf. Lévêque, *Pyrrhos*, p. 167. But it is Pausanias' normal practice to keep chronological order in his historical excursuses, and he definitely places the invasion of Epirus before the joint action of Pyrrhus and Lysimachus against Demetrius in 288, i.e. at the very beginning of Pyrrhus' reign; and the first part of Paus. ch. 10, following the Hieronymus citation, concerns the period of their alliance. Pausanias' review of Pyrrhus' career in ch. 11 also mentions a war against Lysimachus before the war against Demetrius, showing that Pausanias was personally convinced of this order of events and has not made a simple slip in ch. 9. The difficulty of supposing an otherwise unknown war between Pyrrhus and Lysimachus before 288 leads Lévêque, op. cit., pp. 170f., to regard the war as spurious and accept Pausanias' judgement that Hieronymus invented the whole story out of spite against Lysimachus. Jacoby, however, points out the suspicious similarity between this story and the (true) story of Pyrrhus' mercenaries plundering and despoiling the royal Macedonian tombs at Edessa during Pyrrhus' war against Antigonus Gonatas in 274–3 (*F. Gr. Hist.* IID, pp. 546–7; Plut. *Pyrrh.* xxvi.6–7); and it seems likely that the incident has been duplicated in the process of transmission and become attached to Pyrrhus' rival, Lysimachus. Significantly, Pyrrhus was in camp at Edessa in 284 to 283 when Lysimachus attacked him, and at this moment Hieronymus might have digressed on the later behaviour of Pyrrhus at Edessa: the accidental substitution of one name for another in copying the text might then lead to further changes in the interests of rationalization.

3) We may accept that Hieronymus had reasons for disliking Lysimachus: as well as eclipsing Cardia, he was the enemy of Demetrius and had attempted to have Demetrius assassinated by Seleucus (these were perhaps the ἄλλα ἐγκλήματα). That he did hate him is only a supposition, however. The words Ἱερώνυμος οὗτος ἔχει . . . καὶ ἄλλως δόξαν suggest that Pausanias knew Hieronymus only at second hand, since he normally expresses his own opinion in words such as δοκεῖ μοι, δόξῃ ἐμῇ: cf. Segre, *Historia* ii (1928), pp. 217ff. Paus. i.6.1 speaks of οἱ συγγενόμενοι τοῖς βασιλεῦσιν, but no single writer is specified by name. Pausanias' direct source on the Diadochi is unknown; but the hostile judgement on Hieronymus may derive ultimately from Hieronymus' contemporary Timaeus, who is the common source

for criticisms of Philistus, Ephorus, and Theopompus in later authors and who earned the nickname 'Epitimaeus' for his fault-finding: Segre, art. cit.

Hence the charge of bias against Lysimachus must be regarded with scepticism. References to Lysimachus in Diodorus, based on Hieronymus, are by no means unfavourable (cf. xx.106.3; xxi.12); and Diodorus records the founding of Lysimacheia at xx.29.1 without comment. For Hieronymus' treatment of the other kings, see ch. 5.

F15 διάφορα δὲ ὅμως κ.τ.λ.: The sense is ambiguous. Pausanias has given two versions of the death of Pyrrhus: 1) Pyrrhus defeated Antigonus outside the walls of Argos and pursued the fugitives inside the city, where he was killed by a tile thrown from the rooftops by a woman; 2) according to the Argives, it was not a real woman, but Demeter who killed him. (Demeter was thought to have a grievance against Pyrrhus because he had once plundered a sanctuary of Persephone: Dion. Hal. *Ant. Rom.* xx.9.1–2; cf. Frazer, *Pausanias' Description of Greece,* ii, p. 111.) Hieronymus' version apparently differed from both of these, and following Tarn's view, it is the latter which Plutarch used at *Pyrrhus* xxxiv.1–3 (Tarn, *Antigonos Gonatas,* App. VIII, pp. 447ff.). In Plutarch's account there is no mention of Gonatas' defeat in battle, and Pyrrhus is only stunned by the tile, and then decapitated by one of Gonatas' soldiers. Pausanias does not specify the form taken by Hieronymus' bias: Pyrrhus is not treated unfairly in Plutarch's account (cf. Jacoby, *F. Gr. Hist.* IID, p. 547). But if Hieronymus failed to record Pyrrhus' victory over Gonatas or in some way palliated its importance, it might reasonably be claimed that he had distorted the truth in the interests of his patron.

F13 = DION. HAL. A.R. 1.5.4.
F11 = PLUT. PYRRH. XVII.7. F12 = PLUT. PYRRH. XXI.7

It is one of Hieronymus' claims to fame that he was the first Greek to write ἀκριβὴς ἱστορία about the Romans. Dionysius' allusion to a 'treatment of the Epigoni' indicates that his 'archaeology' of Rome was a digression set in the context of Pyrrhus' war in Italy: Hieronymus needed to characterize Pyrrhus' enemies and explain why he failed to win an easy victory in Italy. It was an early reflection, therefore, of the new and detailed knowledge of Rome and the West which came to the Greeks as a result of Pyrrhus' Western expedition.

The first Greek historian to mention the Romans was Theopompus (*F. Gr. Hist.* 115 F317), and there are allusions to the foundation legends of Rome in Heracleides Ponticus (Plut. *Camill.* xxii.2), in Theophrastus' contemporary, Callias of Syracuse, and in the early third-century historian Xenagoras (*F. Gr. Hist.* 240 F29, drawing on a tradition that must go back to a period before Rome's sack of Antium in 337). Duris mentioned the battle of Sentinum (*F. Gr. Hist.* 76 F56). For Peripatetic knowledge of the West, see Fraser, *Ptol. Alex.* i, pp.

763 ff., showing that Callimachus' material for the legends of Sicily and Italy derives chiefly from fourth-century Peripatetic sources. For contacts between Rome and Greece in general before Pyrrhus, W. Hoffmann, 'Rom u.d.gr. Welt im 4 Jahrhund.', *Philol. Suppl.* xxvii (I), 1934, pp. 1 ff.; Thiel, *A History of Roman Sea Power Before the Second Punic War,* Amsterdam, 1954, rev. Forrest, *JRS* xlvi (1956), pp. 169 ff.; H. H. Schmitt, *Rom und Rhodos,* Munich, 1957, rev. Fraser, *CR* n.s. ix (1959), pp. 64 ff.; Neatby, *TAPA* lxxxi (1950), pp. 89 ff. (relations between Rome and Egypt); Fraser, *Ptol. Alex.,* loc. cit. It is now clear that Romans, or Italians who wanted to be thought of as Romans, made their appearance in the East Mediterranean from the early third century: Diehl, *Altlat. Ins.* (4), no. 183 = Degrassi, *Inscr. Lat. lib. rei pub.* i.245 (a bilingual inscription in Greek and Latin set up on Rhodes to Athena Lindia by L. Folius); A. Kondoleon, *Praktika,* 1953, 271 = *Akte des IV Epig. Kongresses,* Wien, 1964, pp. 192 ff. (an honorary decree of Chios for ? Hermokles, who had been to Rome as envoy and done something involving the Romulus and Remus legend: though L. Robert, *REG* lxxviii (1956), p. 146, maintains that it is to be dated after the peace of Apamea). Knowledge of a casual sort could have been acquired by Greeks from traders and settlers like these: cf. Fraser, *Ptol. Alex.,* loc. cit.

Knowledge of the non-Greek West remained indefinite, however, before 280, when Roman expansion in South Italy and Pyrrhus' invasion of Italy and Sicily drew attention to Rome (cf. F. Altheim, *Epochen der röm. Gesch.* ii, 1934, p. 212). The new place which Rome occupied in Greek thought by the mid-third century can be illustrated by Greek use of the word 'Roman': Diodorus xvi.82 records under the year 342 that an 'Etruscan', called by the distinctively Roman name of Postumius, was captured by Timoleon while privateering in Sicilian waters; by contrast, just before the year 263 to 262, the Aetolians gave proxeny status to someone, described as Ῥωμαῖος, with the Italian but not Roman name Volceius, showing that this was the term by now more familiar in the Greek world (IG IX²I, 17A, line 51). That Lycophron's *Alexandra* is evidence of exaggerated respect for Rome's power in the first quarter of the third century remains the subject of debate: see especially A. Momigliano, *JRS* xxxii (1942), pp. 53 ff. = *Secundo Contributo,* pp. 431 ff., for the view that the author of the *Alexandra* was the court poet of Ptolemy Philadelphus; Fraser, *Ptol. Alex.* ii, p. 1065 n. 331 for other literature. See now Fraser 'Lycophron on Cyprus', *Report of the Department of Antiquities, Cyprus,* 1979, pp. 328 ff., arguing from the Cypriote episode in the *Alexandra* that the poet drew on Eratosthenes, hence wrote in the late third or early second century, a date which would justify the famous allusions to Rome's sway over land and sea, and which demands the hypothesis of a deutero-Lycophron distinct from the Alexandrian poet of Philadelphus' reign. The place held by Rome in Greek consciousness during the first half of the third century is probably more accurately reflected by the frequent but incidental references to Rome in Timaeus' account of the history and legends of the West. This highly influential work, the first general and large-scale treatment of the subject, was used by many of the Alexandrian writers and eclipsed the brief earlier effort of Hieronymus, whose account of Rome is mentioned only by Dionysius.

The scope of Hieronymus' excursus on Rome can only be guessed. Dionysius, whose own 'Roman Archaeology' filled twenty books, could dismiss it as one of the κεφαλαιώδεις ἐπιτομαὶ πανὺ βραχεῖαι, and the word ἐπιδραμόντος implies that Hieronymus gave only an outline of Rome's early history. It was perhaps comparable to his account of early Thebes, which Diodorus partly preserves at xix.53.4 ff., and the early history of Thessaly (F17). If Hieronymus is the source for the passage at Pausanias i.ii.7 ff., where Pyrrhus reflects that he, a descendant of Achilles, will be fighting against a colony of the Trojans, it is likely that Hieronymus spoke of the Trojan origins of Rome in his 'archaeology'. Aristotle, Xenarchus, and Heracleides Ponticus had apparently regarded Rome as a Greek city, but it is not certain that a πόλις Ἑλληνὶς might not have a Trojan origin in Greek thought. The thesis of Perret, *Les origines de la légende troyenne de Rome (281–31)*, Paris, 1942, pp. 409 ff., that Pyrrhus was personally responsible for creating the legend of a Trojan foundation, was definitely refuted by the discovery of fifth-century votive statuettes from Veii, depicting the group of Anchises and Aeneas (Lévêque, *Pyrrhos,* p. 254, with references), and the literary evidence from before 281 that Rome was regarded as a Trojan foundation cannot be dismissed: cf. Momigliano, *JRS* xxxv (1945), pp. 99 ff. = *Terzo Contributo*, pp. 677 ff. Stories of Greek and Trojan origins might easily be reconciled: Pyrrhus himself believed that he was a descendant of Achilles on one side and of Priam on the other: cf. Lévêque, *Pyrrhos*, p. 255.

F14 = PLUT. PYRRH. XXVII.8

Hieronymus tends to give the more conservative of rival statistics: compare F11, 12. He may have accompanied Antigonus on the Peloponnesian campaign against Pyrrhus and seen the Spartan trench for himself (cf. Africa, *Phylarchus*, p. 47). Phylarchus possibly exaggerated its size in order to maximize the achievement of the Spartan women.

Pausanias states that Sparta was already surrounded by a ditch and palisade when Demetrius attacked the city (i.13.6 ff.); Plutarch perhaps refers to the refortification of a limited section of the circuit opposite to Pyrrhus' camp: so Tarn, *Antigonos Gonatas*, App. VIII, p. 488.

F16, 17, 18 = STRABO VIII.6.21; IX.5.22; X.4.3
Brückner, p. 259 attributed these fragments to Hieronymus of
Rhodes; followed by H. L. Jones in the Loeb edition of Strabo, vol. iv,
p. 191 n. 4, and Daebritz *RE* viii s.v. 'Hieronymos', no. 12, col. 1564.
Editors of the fragments of Hieronymus of Rhodes have not followed
this view: cf. F. Wehrli, op. cit., E. Hiller, *Satura Philologa Hermanno
Sauppio*, Berlin, 1879, pp. 85 ff. for discussion of the problems of
identification. Strabo certainly refers to the Cardian in all three cases.
The similarities between the description of the Dead Sea in Strabo
(xvi.11.45 ff.) and in Diodorus (xix.98–9) show that Strabo knew
Hieronymus' work, as do the similarities between Strabo's topography
of Corinth and Diodorus xx.103 (the capture of Corinth by Demetrius
in 303 BC: cf. Jacoby, *F. Gr. Hist.* IID, p. 547). Strabo's account of
Corinth is compiled from several authors and from his own observation, but Hieronymus' was perhaps the principal contribution since he
is named first. Whether the *topothesia* of Corinth was an independent
excursus or part of the military narrative is not clear.
    The excursus on the plain of Thessaly (F17) must have been a
self-contained section, since Strabo alludes to legends and early history which could have had no place in Hieronymus' main narrative.
For the context, cf. Jacoby, loc. cit. It is not certain where the citation
ends: the infinitives of indirect speech which follow Hieronymus' name
govern the words down to *καὶ Μαγνῆτις*; if Hieronymus is also the
source for the legends about Mopsion, son of the Argonaut Lapithos,
his treatment of Thessalian 'archaeology' must have been quite extensive. Strabo's mention of 'later writers'—later, that is, than Homer—
who wrote about the early history of the Magnetians, Crannonians,
and Aenianians, might include Hieronymus (ix.5.21 *τοὺς ὕστερον
ἀνθρώπους*, cf. 5.22 *τῶν ὕστερον ἐπὶ χρόνον συχνόν*).
    The context of F18 is unkown. Crete was a recruiting ground for
mercenaries in this period; it was mentioned, too, in connection with
the murder of Harpalus (Diod. xviii.19ff.; Arrian, *Succ.* F9.16). If the
excursus on Thessaly can be taken as a model, the measurements of
Crete would have been followed by an account of its ancient history;
but Strabo cites Staphylus and Ephorus for his early history of Crete
and does not mention Hieronymus again. (Strabo x.4.6; x.4.8 f.:
Hieronymus could be among the unnamed writers who did not accept
Andron's account of Thessalian immigrants in Crete.)

F19 = PHILODEMUS *Περὶ τῶν Στωικῶν* VI

The *Περὶ τῶν Στωικῶν* is partially preserved in two copies on papyri
from Herculaneum, one of which contains this passage (edited by W.
Crönert, 'Kolotes und Menedemus', *Studien für Palaeographie und
Papryuskunde*, Leipzig, 1906, pp. 24, n. 136, 27, 53 ff. The opening
columns of the papyrus seem to have dealt with historical and

biographical material and were evidently polemical in character: col. 2
relates something unfavourable about the Epicureans, col. 3 mentions
Antigonus Gonatas' conquest of Athens, col. 4 deals with the life and
times of Zeno. Using the second papyrus as a supplement, where it
refers to the death of Lysimachus, Crönert reconstructed the argument of the beginning of the treatise as follows: 'der dem Epikur
befreundete Lysimachos hat den Athenern nicht geschadet, wohl aber
der stoiker König Antigonos Gonatas.' (op. cit., p. 54). The beginning
of col. 6 mentions Cleanthes, though it is possible that the main subject
is still Zeno. The text becomes certain with the words ἃ γὰρ λέγομεν,
Ἱερώνυμός τε μαρτυρεῖ κ[αὶ] ὁ Χαλκιδεὺς Εὔφαντος, ἔτι δ' Ἡγήμων,
κ.τ.λ., the large number of authorities cited suggesting that the matter
was especially controversial.

Hegemon is otherwise unknown, and the ethnic following his name
is uncertain (Jacoby, Ἀθηναῖος; cf. Crönert, p. 28: Σμυρναῖος?
Μυριναῖος?). The date for this group of writers is suggested by
Euphantos 'the Chalcidian', who must be Euphantos of Olynthus,
pupil of the eristic philosopher Euboulides of Miletus. He wrote tragic
poetry and a history of his times, and was the teacher of 'Antigonus the
King', to whom he addressed a treatise Περὶ Βασιλείας; according to
Athenaeus he also wrote about Ptolemy III Euergetes: Müller, *FHG*
iii, pp. 19–20, Jacoby, *F. Gr. Hist.* 74. His dates have been disputed.
Schwartz's argument (*Hermes* xxxv (1900), p. 128, followed by Pearson, *Lost Histories*, pp. 61, 260) that Euphantos must have been born
before 348 in order to call himself an Olynthian will not do, since the
epigraphic evidence shows a number of people calling themselves
Olynthians at the end of the fourth century and later: IG II(2) 1263,
1956; other references given by P. Perdrizet, *BCH* xxi (1897), p. 118;
cf. Tarn *JHS* xxxi (1911), p. 256 n. 32 (F. Hampl, *Der König der
Makedonien*, Weida, 1934, p. 30 n. 2, cites the absence of archaeological evidence at Olynthus for the late fourth and third centuries in
support of Schwartz's view, but does not dispose of the third-century
inscriptions referring to Olynthians). Hence, despite the implication at
Diod. xix.52, that the Olynthians who survived by 316 were absorbed
in the new foundation of Cassandreia, it must be supposed that Olynthus in fact recovered a large measure of her former prosperity during
the third century. Euphantos should, nevertheless, be dated early,
because his teacher Euboulides was the personal antagonist of Aristotle (Diog. Laert. ii.109); and although he is said to have had a long
life (ibid., ii.100) it seems most unlikely that he could have been the
teacher of Antigonus Doson, born in 262, and have written about
Ptolemy Euergetes, who reigned 247 to 222 (so Müller, *FHG*, loc.
cit.). The conjecture of Mallet, *Histoire de l'école de Megare*, 1845, p.
96 (followed by Zeller, *Philos. der Griechen* ii(4), I, p. 248 n. 1,
Natorp, *RE* vi s.v. 'Euphantos', col. 1166) that for Πτολεμαίου . . .
τοῦ τρίτου at Athen. vi, p. 251D we should read Πτολεμαίου . . . τοῦ

πρῶτον, accommodates all the other evidence on Euphantos. The pupil of Euboulides could have been the teacher of Antigonus Gonatas (born *c.* 319) and it was then for Gonatas that he wrote the treatise *On Kingship*: so Jacoby, loc. cit.; cf. Tarn, *Antigonos Gonatas,* p. 25. Crönert, op. cit., p. 26 n. 142 points out that Euphantos was a fellow pupil of Alexinos (Diog. Laert. ii.109–10) who was a friend and contemporary of Menedemus of Eretria, the early friend and mentor of Gonatas. Euphantos' history of his times must have mentioned Ptolemy Soter, not Ptolemy Euergetes; and the Callicrates whom he described as a flatterer of Ptolemy (Athen. vii.318B) was not the famous admiral of Ptolemy II, who made dedications to Philadelphus and Arsinoe, but another Callicrates, possibly the admiral of Ptolemy I who was sent to Cyprus in 310: Diod. xx.21; cf. Tarn, *JHS* xxxi (1911), pp. 253–6; Hauben, *Callicrates of Samos*, Leuven, 1970, pp. 21 ff.

Euphantos was therefore an exact contemporary of Hieronymus of Cardia, and a historian of the period of the Diadochi; and it is possible that Philodemus consulted two historians of the period who had a special connection with Antigonus Gonatas, either of whom might have had occasion to mention Gonatas' philosopher friends, though perhaps not his conquest of Athens (cf. ch. 3, p. 103). It is more likely, however, that Philodemus would have drawn on the philosopher Hieronymus of Rhodes. It is certainly the Rhodian whom he cites in his work on rhetoric, where he attacks Isocrates, because Hieronymus the Peripatetic wrote a polemic against Isocrates: Philod. *Rhet.* iv, col. 16, p. 198 Sudhaus, 1.9 ff. = Wehrli, frg. 52a; Cic. *Or.* 189 = frg. 51; Dion. Hal. *De Isocrate* 13 = frg.52b. Hieronymus of Rhodes was nominally a Peripatetic, but he was at odds with Lycon, the leader of the Peripatos in the early third century (Diog. Laert. v.68; Tarn, *Antigonos Gonatas*, pp. 329 f.), and he seems in practice to have inclined to the school of Epicurus, notably in his views on the *summum bonum* (Plut. *De Stoic. Repugn.* ii, p. 1033c = frg.11; Cic. *De Fin.* v.14 = frg. 8c; etc.): this tendency in his thinking would naturally recommend him to the Epicurean Philodemus, and his writings evidently appealed to Cicero, who cited them many times, and who, though more eclectic in his philosophy than the Epicureans of Naples, was associated with Philodemus' circle (Momigliano, *Secundo Contributo*, pp. 379 ff.). The Rhodian Hieronymus lived in Athens where he celebrated annually the festival of Gonatas' son Halcyoneus with funds supplied by Gonatas (Diog. Laert. iv.41; cf. Ferguson, *Hellenistic Athens*, p. 233, Tarn, *Antigonos Gonatas,* pp. 335 f.); probably he was there at the time when Gonatas captured the city, and he must have been well informed about the philosophers who are mentioned in the fragment of Philodemus. His work *Περὶ Ποιητῶν* contained historical biographies of the Greek poets in the Peripatetic manner, and he is not infrequently cited for the lives of philosophers, also. He would, therefore, have been a useful source to Philodemus in his discussion of the early Stoics, and there is a strong case for identifying him as the Hieronymus Philodemus here cites: so Crönert, p. 28; Daebritz, *RE* viii s.v. 'Hieronymos', no. 12, col. 1563; Wehrli, frg. 47 and comm. ad loc., p. 42.

P. OXY. I XIII = PACK² 2203 = JACOBY F. GR. HIST. 153 FI

The text is part of a letter written to a king of Macedon, attacking the behaviour of the Thebans and apparently urging harsher treatment of Thebes. Grenfell and Hunt suggested Antigonus or Demetrius as the addressee, but drew no conclusions about the authorship beyond remarking that the style is thoroughly Isocratean. Rühl, *Rh. Mus.* liv (1899), pp. 152 ff. argues that it is an imaginary letter written to Alexander on the occasion of his destruction of Thebes. De Sanctis (*Riv. Fil.* ix, 1931, pp. 330 ff. = *Scritti Minori* i, Rome, 1966, pp. 345 ff.) followed by P. Treves (*Riv. Fil.* x, 1932, pp. 194 ff.) claimed that it is a fragment of a real letter written by Hieronymus of Cardia to Demetrius Poliorcetes at the time of the Theban revolts of 293 to 292, to warn him, in his capacity as governor of Thebes, of the dangers of leniency: on this view Hieronymus later included the letter in his history as he included many other documents from the Macedonian archives. Treves contrasts Demetrius' policy towards the Greek states with the traditional policy of Philip, Cassander, and Antigonus Gonatas, which was particularist and divisive: Demetrius abandoned the hated method of controlling the Greek cities through local tyrants and factions, and instead installed his own governors, seeking an over-all solution to the problem of governing the Greeks, as Alexander did. He sees Hieronymus as advocate of the traditional methods, and suggests that Thebes constituted an especial threat to Demetrius at this time, as a *point d'appui* for Pyrrhus in his hostilities against Macedon (Plut. *Pyrrh.* xxxix–xi; Pyrrhus' invasion of Thessaly seems to be linked with the Theban revolt of 291; cf. Beloch, *Gr. Gesch.* iv² 1, p. 226. Pyrrhus is not mentioned in the papyrus.)

The hypothesis that this is a true fragment of Hieronymus cannot be maintained, however. Documents of this kind are suspect *a priori* (cf. the cautious remarks of Pearson, *Historia* iii (1954–5), p. 444), and the general tone of the fragment indicates that it is a rhetorical exercise. The words εἰ καὶ τυγχάνεις εἰδώς κ.τ.λ. are only an excuse for introducing a review of Theban relations with Macedon, and the reminder that Amyntas was the father of Philip seems inappropriate in a real letter to a Macedonian king: cf. Jacoby, IID, p. 540. It is also unlikely that Hieronymus would write to Demetrius on so serious a matter διὰ βραχέων. The allusion to the alliance of Thebes with Olynthus in the time of Amyntas has more relevance to the situation of 336 than to that of the 290s, and the fact that Philip is not identified as father of Alexander perhaps suggests a date before the accession of Philip

Arrhidaeus in 323: Rühl, op. cit., pp. 153–4. The corrections in the text (Rühl, p. 152) are possibly the mark of an exercise, though the papyrus comes from the second to third century AD and may in any case be a copy of an earlier work. The phrase τὴν οἰκίαν τὴν τῶν σῶν ἑταίϱων also is so strange that it seems to indicate an incompetent author or one who did not understand the terminology of the Macedonian court and wrote only for effect. Attempts to give sense to this expression, as a compliment to the addressee (so De Sanctis, art. cit., p. 331) or by assuming that the Macedonian king was himself one of the *hetairoi* (G. S. Stagakis, *Observations on the ἕταιϱοι of Alexander the Great* in *Archaia Makedonia*, 1st Int. Symp. Thessaloniki, 1968, pp. 86 ff.) are not persuasive.

Anaximenes included in his history a version of the letter written by Philip to the Athenians (*F. Gr. Hist.* 72 Anhang. cf. IIC, p. 112), and it is certain that Hieronymus did incorporate, at least in paraphrase, many political documents in his work, but he was not a rhetorical writer who would have tried to improve on their literary quality. The official letter of the Hellenistic period was in general non-rhetorical and uninfluenced by the epistolary style of the fourth-century philosophical schools. Cf. Welles, *Royal Correspondence*, p. xlii: the Τύποι Ἐπιστολικοί of Demetrius, a Hellenistic handbook for state secretaries, says that letters may be written ὡς ἔτυχεν, i.e. no rhetorical training is required. If at one time Hieronymus had acted as *grammateus* (ch. 1, p. 10, he would have been trained by chancellery work to use a practical and straightforward style in his correspondence. The letter of this papyrus fragment certainly belongs to the genre of counterfeit letters which flourished in the Hellenistic period (see especially R. Merkelbach, *Die Quellen des gr. Alexanderromans*, München, 1954, pp. 32 ff., on the letters in the *Alexander Romance*), and should be assigned to the limbo of anonymous Alexander literature.

THE TESTIMONIA AND FRAGMENTS OF HIERONYMUS OF CARDIA
The following text is reproduced from F. Jacoby, *Die Fragmente der griechische Historiker*, IIB, no. 154, pp. 829–35, by kind permission of E. J. Brill, Leiden. For discussion of the *testimonia* see above, ch. 1.

T

1 SUID. s. Ἱερώνυμος Καρδιανός· ὃς τὰ ἐπ᾽ Ἀλεξάνδρωι πραχθέντα
5 συνέγραψε. Καρδία δὲ ὄνομα πόλεως.

2 [LUKIAN.] Macrob. 22 (= PHLEGON 257 F 37 c. II): Ἱερώνυμος
δὲ ἐν πολέμοις γενόμενος καὶ πολλοὺς καμάτους ὑπομείνας καὶ τραύματα
ἔζησεν ἔτη τέσσαρα καὶ ἑκατόν, ὡς Ἀγαθαρχίδης ἐν τῆι ἐνάτηι τῶν Περὶ
τῆς Ἀσίας ἱστοριῶν (86 F 4) λέγει· καὶ θαυμάζει γε τὸν ἄνδρα ὡς μέχρι
10 τῆς τελευταίας ἡμέρας ἄρτιον ὄντα ἐν ταῖς συνουσίαις καὶ πᾶσι τοῖς
αἰσθητηρίοις, μηδενὸς γενόμενον τῶν πρὸς ὑγίειαν ἐλλιπῆ.

3 DIOD. XVIII 42, 1: μετὰ δὲ ταῦτα ὁ Εὐμένης πρὸς τὸν Ἀντί-
πατρον πρεσβευτὰς ἀπέστειλε περὶ τῶν ὁμολογιῶν (a. 320), ὧν ἦν ἡγούμενος Ἱερώνυμος ὁ τὰς τῶν Διαδόχων Ἱστορίας γεγραφώς.

15 **4** — XVIII 50, 4 (a. 319/8): ταῦτα δὲ διανοηθεὶς (sc. ὁ Ἀντίγονος)
Ἱερώνυμον μὲν τὸν τὰς Ἱστορίας γράψαντα μετεπέμψατο, φίλον ὄντα
καὶ πολίτην Εὐμένους τοῦ Καρδιανοῦ τοῦ συμπεφευγότος εἰς τὸ χωρίον
τὸ καλούμενον Νῶρα. τοῦτον δὲ μεγάλαις δωρεαῖς προκαλεσάμενος
ἐξαπέστειλε πρεσβευτὴν πρὸς τὸν Εὐμένη .... PLUT. Eum. 12.

20 **5** — XIX 44, 3 (a. 316/5): nach der gefangennahme des
Eumenes ἀνήχθη δ᾽ ἐν τοῖς τραυματίαις αἰχμάλωτος καὶ ὁ τὰς Ἱστορίας
συνταξάμενος Ἱερώνυμος ὁ Καρδιανός, ὃς τὸν μὲν ἔμπροσθεν χρόνον
ὑπ᾽ Εὐμένους τιμώμενος διετέλεσεν, μετὰ δὲ τὸν ἐκείνου θάνατον ὑπ᾽
Ἀντιγόνου ἐτύγχανε φιλανθρωπίας καὶ πίστεως.

25 **6** — XIX 100, 1–3 (a. 312/1): ὁ δ᾽ Ἀντίγονος ἐπανελθόντος
τοῦ Δημητρίου καὶ τὰ κατὰ μέρος τῶν πεπραγμένων ἀπαγγείλαντος ἐπὶ
μὲν τῆι συνθέσει τῆι πρὸς τοὺς Ναβαταίους ἐπετίμησεν αὐτῶι .... ἐπὶ
δὲ τῶι κατασκέψασθαι τὴν λίμνην (F 5–6) καὶ δοκεῖν εὑρηκέναι τινὰ
τῆι βασιλείαι πρόσοδον ἐπαινέσας ἐπὶ μὲν ταύτης ἐπιμελητὴν ἔταξεν

---

4 ⟨ἱστορικός·⟩ ὅς? ἐπ᾽ Ἀλεξάνδρωι Leopardi (vgl. F 3 Περδίκκας δέ,
ὃς ἐπὶ Ἀλεξάνδρωι τῆς Μακεδόνων ἦρχεν) ἐπ᾽ Ἀλεξάνδρου V ἐπ᾽ Ἀλεξανδρείαι cett
18 προσκαλεσάμενος F   21 τραυματίαις: ἑαλωκόσι F   27 Ναβαταίους: νομάδας F

Ἱερώνυμον τὸν τὰς Ἱστορίας συγγράψαντα (F 6). τούτωι δὲ συνετέτακτο πλοῖα
παρασκευάσασθαι καὶ πᾶσαν τὴν ἄσφαλτον ἀναλαβόντα συνάγειν εἴς τινα
τόπον. οὐ μὴν ἀπέβη γε καὶ τὸ τέλος κατὰ τὴν ἐλπίδα τοῖς περὶ τὸν
Ἀντίγονον· οἱ γὰρ Ἄραβες συστραφέντες εἰς ἑξακισχιλίους, ἐπιπλεύσαντες
5 ἐν ταῖς δέσμαις ἐπὶ τοὺς ἐν τοῖς πλοίοις, σχεδὸν ἅπαντας κατετόξευσαν.
ἐξ οὗ δὴ συνέβη τὸν Ἀντίγονον ἀπογνῶναι τὰς προσόδους ταύτας διὰ
τὸ γεγονὸς παράπτωμα καὶ διὰ τὸ τὸν νοῦν ἔχειν πρὸς ἑτέροις μείζοσι.
　　7 [LUKIAN.] Macrob. 11 (= F 8): ὁ συστρατευόμενος αὐτῶι
(sc. Ἀντιγόνωι, bei Ipsos a. 301) Ἱερώνυμος.
10　　8 PLUT. Demetr. 39, 3—7: ὡς δὲ ταῖς Θήβαις ἐπαγαγὼν τὰς μηχανὰς
ὁ Δημήτριος (a. 293) ἐπολιόρκει καὶ φοβηθεὶς ὑπεξῆλθεν ὁ Κλεώνυμος,
καταπλαγέντες οἱ Βοιωτοὶ παρέδωκαν ἑαυτούς. ὁ δὲ ταῖς πόλεσιν
ἐμβαλὼν φρουρὰν καὶ πραξάμενος πολλὰ χρήματα καὶ καταλιπὼν αὐτοῖς
ἐπιμελητὴν καὶ ἁρμοστὴν Ἱερώνυμον τὸν ἱστορικόν, ἔδοξεν ἠπίως κεχρῆ-
15 σθαι ..... οὐ πολλῶι δὲ ὕστερον ἁλίσκεται Λυσίμαχος ὑπὸ Δρομιχαίτου,
καὶ πρὸς τοῦτο Δημητρίου κατὰ τάχος ἐξορμήσαντος ἐπὶ Θράικην ...
πάλιν ἀπέστησαν οἱ Βοιωτοὶ ... ταχέως οὖν καὶ πρὸς ὀργὴν ἀναστρέψας
ὁ Δημήτριος εὗρεν ἡττημένους ὑπὸ τοῦ παιδὸς Ἀντιγόνου μάχηι τοὺς
Βοιωτοὺς καὶ τὰς Θήβας αὖθις ἐπολιόρκει.
20　　9 THEON VIT. ARAT. p. 147, 18 M: Ἀντίγονος ὁ Γονατᾶς, παρ' ὧι διέτριβεν
αὐτὸς καὶ σὺν αὐτῶι Περσαῖος ὁ Στωικὸς καὶ Ἀνταγόρας ὁ Ῥόδιος ... καὶ Ἀλέξανδρος ὁ Αἰτωλός, ὡς αὐτός φησιν ὁ Ἀντίγονος ἐν τοῖς †περὶ Ἱερώνυμον.
　　10 DIOD. I 3, 3: τῶν δὲ τὴν ἐπιβολὴν ταύτης τῆς πραγματείας πεποιημένων
οὐδεὶς προεβίβασε τὴν ἱστορίαν κατωτέρω τῶν Μακεδονικῶν καιρῶν· οἱ μὲν γὰρ εἰς
25 τὰς Φιλίππου πράξεις, οἱ δ' εἰς τὰς Ἀλεξάνδρου, τινὲς δ' εἰς τοὺς διαδόχους ἢ
τοὺς ἐπιγόνους (F 13) κατέστρεψαν τὰς συντάξεις.
　　11 PAUS. I 9, 8: ὁ δὲ Ἱερώνυμος οὗτος ἔχει μὲν καὶ ἄλλως δόξαν
πρὸς ἀπέχθειαν γράψαι τῶν βασιλέων πλὴν Ἀντιγόνου, τούτωι δὲ οὐ
δικαίως χαρίζεσθαι. s. F 9; 15.
30　　12 DION. HAL. De comp. verb. 4, 30: τοιγάρτοι τοιαύτας συντάξεις κατέλιπον οἵας οὐδεὶς ὑπομένει μέχρι κορωνίδος διελθεῖν, Φύλαρχον
λέγω .... Ἱερώνυμόν τε .... s. 76 T 10.

F
⟨ΤΑ ΕΠΙ ΑΛΕΞΑΝΔΡΩΙ ΠΡΑΧΘΕΝΤΑ?⟩

35　　1 (II 452) ATHEN. V 58 p. 217 DE: Περδίκκας τοίνυν πρὸ Ā
Ἀρχελάου βασιλεύει, ὡς μὲν ὁ Ἀκάνθιός φησιν Νικομήδης (III), ἔτη μ̄α,

---

1 Ἱερώνυμον: Ἀντίγονον RX　　3 τέλος ⟨εἷλε⟩ Rhodomanus　　6 ταύτας
om RX　　22 περὶ: apud quem Hieronimus vers Lat πρὸς Ruhnken περὶ
Ἱερωνύμου?

Θεόπομπος (115 F 279) δὲ λε̄, Ἀναξιμένης (72 F 27) μ̄, Ἱερώνυμος κη̄,
Μαρσύας (135—136 F 15) δὲ καὶ Φιλόχορος (III) κγ̄.

2   — V 40 p. 206 DE: γράφει οὖν ὁ Μοσχίων (III) οὕτως· ᵃ· ³²⁵/¹
Διοκλείδης μὲν ὁ Ἀβδηρίτης (VI) θαυμάζεται ἐπὶ τῆι πρὸς τὴν
₅ Ῥοδίων πόλιν ὑπὸ Δημητρίου ⸱ προσαχθείσηι τοῖς τείχεσιν ἑλεπόλει,
Τίμαιος (III) δ᾽ ἐπὶ τῆι πυρᾶι τῆι κατασκευασθείσηι Διονυσίωι ....,
καὶ Ἱερώνυμος ἐπὶ τῆι κατασκευῆι τῆς ἁρμαμάξης, ἧι συνέβαινε κομι-
σθῆναι τὸ Ἀλεξάνδρου σῶμα, Πολύκλειτος (128 F 4) δὲ ....

3 (1 a)   APPIAN. Mithrid. 8: Καππαδοκίας δὲ πρὸ μὲν Μακεδόνων ᵃ· ³²²
₁₀ οἵτινες ἦρχον, οὐκ ἔχω σαφῶς εἰπεῖν εἴτε ἰδίαν ἀρχὴν εἴτε Δαρείου
κατήκουον. Ἀλέξανδρος δέ μοι δοκεῖ τοὺς ἄρχοντας τῶνδε τῶν ἐθνῶν
ἐπὶ φόρωι καταλιπεῖν, ἐπειγόμενος ἐπὶ Δαρεῖον. ..... Ἱ ε ρ ώ ν υ μ ο ς
δ ὲ ο ὐ δ᾽ ἐ π ι ψ α ῦ σ α ι τ ῶ ν ἐ θ ν ῶ ν ὅ λ ω ς , ἀ λ λ᾽ ἀ ν ὰ τ ὴ ν π α ρ ά -
λ ι ο ν τ ῆ ς Π α μ φ υ λ ί α ς κ α ὶ Κ ι λ ι κ ί α ς ἑ τ έ ρ α ν ὁ δ ὸ ν ἐ π ὶ τ ὸ ν
₁₅ Δ α ρ ε ῖ ο ν τ ρ α π έ σ θ α ι . Περδίκκας δέ, ὃς ἐπὶ Ἀλεξάνδρωι τῆς Μακεδόνων ἦρχεν, Ἀριαράθην Καππαδοκίας ἡγούμενον εἴτε ἀφιστάμενον εἴτε
τὴν ἀρχὴν αὐτοῦ περιποιούμενος Μακεδόσιν, εἷλε καὶ ἐκρέμασε (F 4)·
καὶ ἐπέστησε τοῖς ἔθνεσιν Εὐμένη τὸν Καρδιανόν. Εὐμένους δὲ ἀναι-
ρεθέντος ὅτε αὐτὸν οἱ Μακεδόνες εἵλοντο εἶναι πολέμιον, Ἀντίπατρος
₂₀ ἐπὶ τῶι Περδίκκαι τῆς ὑπὸ Ἀλεξάνδρωι γενομένης γῆς ἐπιτροπεύων,
Νικάνορα ἔπεμψε Καππαδοκῶν σατραπεύειν. (9) Μακεδόνων δὲ οὐ πολὺ
ὕστερον ἐς ἀλλήλους στασιασάντων, Ἀντίγονος μὲν ἦρχε Συρίας Λαομέδοντα
ἐκβαλών, Μιθριδάτης δ᾽ αὐτῶι συνῆν, ἀνὴρ γένους βασιλείου Περσικοῦ.
καὶ ὁ Ἀντίγονος ἐνύπνιον ἔδοξε πεδίον σπεῖραι χρυσίωι, καὶ τὸ χρυσίον
₂₅ ἐκθερίσαντα τὸν Μιθριδάτην ἐς τὸν Πόντον οἴχεσθαι. καὶ ὁ μὲν αὐτὸν
ἐπὶ τῶιδε συλλαβὼν ἐβούλετο ἀποκτεῖναι, ὁ δ᾽ ἐξέφυγε σὺν ἱππεῦσιν ἕξ,
καὶ φραξάμενός τι χωρίον τῆς Καππαδοκίας, πολλῶν οἱ προσιόντων ἐν τῆι-
δε τῆι Μακεδόνων ἀσχολίαι, Καππαδοκίας τε αὐτῆς καὶ τῶν ὁμόρων περὶ
τὸν Πόντον ἐθνῶν κατέσχεν, ἐπί τε μέγα τὴν ἀρχὴν προαγαγὼν παισὶ
₃₀ παρέδωκεν (F 7). [[οἳ δ᾽ ἦρχον ἕτερος μεθ᾽ ἕτερον ἕως ἐπὶ τὸν ἕκτον
ἀπὸ τοῦ πρώτου Μιθριδάτην, ὃς Ῥωμαίοις ἐπολέμησεν]].

4 (2)   [LUKIAN.] Macrob. 13: Ἀριαράθης δὲ ὁ Καππαδοκῶν ᵃ· ³ ₂
βασιλεὺς δύο μὲν καὶ ὀγδοήκοντα ἔζησεν ἔτη, ὡς Ἱερώνυμος ἱστορεῖ·
ἐδυνήθη δὲ ἴσως καὶ ἐπὶ πλέον διαγενέσθαι, ἀλλ᾽ ἐν τῆι πρὸς Περδίκκαν
₃₅ μάχηι ζωγρηθεὶς ἀνεσκολοπίσθη.

5 (3 a)   PARADOX. Flor. De aq. mir. 33: Ἱερώνυμος ἱστόρησεν ἐν ᵃ· ³¹⁵/¹
τῆι Ναβαταίων χώραι τῶν Ἀράβων ᾽εἶναι λίμνην πικράν, ἐν ἧι οὔτ᾽

---

13 ⟨τῶνδε⟩ τῶν Schweighaeuser *ne has quidem gentes* vers. Candidi
15—16 τῶν Μακεδόνων Reiske   26 ἐβούλετο i *conatus est* Cand ἐβούλευεν O

ἰχϑῦς οὔτε ἄλλο τι τῶν ἐνύδρων ζώιων γίνεσϑαι, ἀσφάλτου δὲ πλίνϑους
ἐξ αὐτῆς αἴρεσϑαι ὑπὸ τῶν ἐπιχωρίων.

6 (13) JOSEPH. c. Apion. I 213—214: ὅτι δὲ οὐκ ἀγνοοῦντες a. 315/2
ἔνιοι τῶν συγγραφέων τὸ ἔϑνος ἡμῶν, ἀλλ' ὑπὸ φϑόνου τινὸς ἢ δι'
5 ἄλλας αἰτίας οὐχ ὑγιεῖς τὴν μνήμην παρέλιπον, τεκμήριον οἶμαι παρέξειν·
Ἱερώνυμος γὰρ ὁ τὴν Περὶ τῶν διαδόχων ἱστορίαν συγγεγραφὼς κατὰ
τὸν αὐτὸν μὲν ἦν Ἑκαταίωι (III) χρόνον, φίλος δ' ὢν Ἀντιγόνου τοῦ
βασιλέως τὴν Συρίαν ἐπετρόπευεν (Τ 6)· ἀλλ' ὅμως Ἑκαταῖος μὲν καὶ
βιβλίον ἔγραψεν περὶ ἡμῶν, Ἱερώνυμος δ' οὐδαμοῦ κατὰ τὴν ἱστορίαν
10 ἐμνημόνευσε καίτοι σχεδὸν ἐν τοῖς τόποις διατετριφώς.

7 (3) [LUKIAN.] Macrob. 13: Μιϑριδάτης δὲ ὁ Πόντου βασιλεὺς a. 302/1
ὁ προσαγορευϑεὶς Κτίστης Ἀντίγονον τὸν μονόφϑαλμον φεύγων ἐπὶ
Πόντου ἐτελεύτησε βιώσας ἔτη τέσσαρα καὶ ὀγδοήκοντα, ὥσπερ Ἱερώνυμος
ἱστορεῖ καὶ ἄλλοι συγγραφεῖς.   s. F 3—4.

15 **8 (4)** — — 11: Ἀντίγονος δὲ ὁ Φιλίππου ὁ μονόφϑαλμος βασι- a. 301
λεύων Μακεδόνων περὶ Φρυγίαν μαχόμενος Σελεύκωι καὶ Λυσιμάχωι
τραύμασι πολλοῖς περιπεσὼν ἐτελεύτησεν ἐτῶν ἑνὸς καὶ ὀγδοήκοντα,
ὥσπερ ὁ συστρατευόμενος αὐτῶι Ἱερώνυμος ἱστορεῖ.

9 (6) PAUS. I 9, 7: Λυσίμαχος δὲ καὶ ἐς πόλεμον πρὸς Πύρρον a. 285/4
20 κατέστη τὸν Αἰακίδου· φυλάξας δὲ ἐξ Ἠπείρου ἀπιόντα, οἷα δὴ τὰ πολλὰ
ἐκεῖνος ἐπλανᾶτο, τήν τε ἄλλην ἐλεηλάτησεν Ἤπειρον καὶ ἐπὶ τὰς ϑήκας
ἦλϑε τῶν βασιλέων. (8) τὰ δὲ ἐντεῦϑεν ἐμοί ἐστιν οὐ πιστά,
Ἱερώνυμος δὲ ἔγραψε Καρδιανὸς Λυσίμαχον τὰς ϑήκας
τῶν νεκρῶν ἀνελόντα τὰ ὀστᾶ ἐκρῖψαι. ὁ δὲ Ἱερώνυμος οὗτος
25 (Τ 11) ἔχει μὲν καὶ ἄλλως δόξαν πρὸς ἀπέχϑειαν γράψαι τῶν βασιλέων πλὴν Ἀντιγόνου, τούτωι δὲ οὐ δικαίως χαρίζεσϑαι· τὰ δὲ ἐπὶ τοῖς τάφοις τῶν Ἠπειρωτῶν
παντάπασίν ἐστι φανερὸς ἐπηρείαι συνϑείς, ἄνδρα Μακεδόνα ϑήκας νεκρῶν ἀνελεῖν.
χωρὶς δὲ ἠπίστατο δή που καὶ Λυσίμαχος οὐ Πύρρου σφᾶς προγόνους μόνον ἀλλὰ
καὶ Ἀλεξάνδρου τοὺς αὐτοὺς τούτους ὄντας· καὶ γὰρ Ἀλέξανδρος Ἠπειρώτης τε ἦν
30 καὶ τῶν Αἰακιδῶν τὰ πρὸς μητρός, ἥ τε ὕστερον Πύρρου πρὸς Λυσίμαχον συμμαχία
δηλοῖ καὶ πολεμήσασιν ἀδιάλλακτόν γε οὐδὲν πρὸς ἀλλήλους γενέσϑαι σφίσι. τῶι
δὲ Ἱερωνύμωι τάχα μέν που καὶ ἄλλα ἦν ἐς Λυσίμαχον ἐγκλήματα, μέγιστον δὲ
ὅτι τὴν Καρδιανῶν πόλιν ἀνελὼν Λυσιμάχειαν ἀντ' αὐτῆς ὤικισεν ἐπὶ τῶι ἰσϑμῶι
τῆς Θραικίας χερρονήσου.

35 **10 (4)** [LUKIAN.] Macrob. 11: καὶ Λυσίμαχος δὲ Μακεδόνων a. 281
βασιλεὺς ἐν τῆι πρὸς Σέλευκον ἀπώλετο μάχηι ἔτος ὀγδοηκοστὸν τελῶν,
ὡς ὁ αὐτός φησιν Ἱερώνυμος.

11 (7) PLUT. Pyrrh. 17,7: (schlacht bei Herakleia) Διονύσιος μὲν a. 280
οὖν ὀλίγωι τῶν πεντακισχιλίων· καὶ μυρίων ἐλάσσονας πεσεῖν ἱστορεῖ
40 Ῥωμαίων, Ἱερώνυμος δὲ μόνους ἑπτακισχιλίους· τῶν δὲ περὶ Πύρρον ὁ

---

20 τὸν om L   27 ἐπηρείαι Siebelis —αν Paus   30 ἥ τε om L

μὲν Διονύσιος μυρίους καὶ τρισχιλίους, ὁ δὲ Ἱερώνυμος ἐλάττονας τῶν
τετρακισχιλίων· κράτιστοι δὲ ἦσαν οὗτοι. καὶ τῶν φίλων ὁ Πύρρος καὶ
τῶν στρατηγῶν οἷς μάλιστα χρώμενος διετέλει καὶ πιστεύων ἀπέβαλεν.

12 (8) PLUT. Pyrrh. 21, 7: ἐκ τούτου μάχης ἄλλης τῶν πραγμάτων a. 279
5 αὐτῶι δεομένων ἀναλαβὼν τὴν στρατιὰν ἐχώρει, καὶ περὶ Ἄσκλον πόλιν
τοῖς Ῥωμαίοις συνάψας καὶ βιαζόμενος πρὸς χωρία δύσιππα καὶ ποταμὸν
ὑλώδη καὶ τραχύν, ἔφοδον τῶν θηρίων οὐ λαβόντων, ὥστε προσμεῖξαι τῆι
φάλαγγι, τραυματ⟨ί⟩ων πολλῶν γενομένων καὶ νεκρῶν πεσόντων, τότε μὲν
διεκρίθη μέχρι νυκτὸς ἀγωνισάμενος. (8) τῆι δ' ὑστεραίαι στρατηγῶν δι'
10 ὁμαλοῦ τὴν μάχην θέσθαι καὶ τοὺς ἐλέφαντας ἐν τοῖς ὅπλοις γενέσθαι
τῶν πολεμίων, προέλαβε τὰς δυσχωρίας φυλακῆι, καὶ πολλὰ καταμείξας
ἀκοντίσματα καὶ τοξεύματα τοῖς θηρίοις ἐπῆγε μετὰ ῥώμης καὶ βίας
πυκνὴν καὶ συντεταγμένην τὴν δύναμιν. (9) οἱ δὲ Ῥωμαῖοι τὰς διακλίσεις
καὶ τὰς ἀντιπαραγωγὰς τὰς πρότερον οὐκ ἔχοντες ἐξ ἐπιπέδου συνεφέ-
15 ροντο κατὰ στόμα· (10) καὶ σπεύδοντες ὤσασθαι τοὺς ὁπλίτας πρὶν ἐπιβῆναι
τὰ θηρία, δεινοὺς περὶ τὰς σαρίσας τῶν ξιφῶν ἀγῶνας εἶχον, ἀφειδοῦντες
ἑαυτῶν καὶ ⟨πρὸς⟩ τὸ τρῶσαι καὶ καταβαλεῖν ὁρῶντες, τὸ δὲ παθεῖν εἰς οὐδὲν
τιθέμενοι. (11) χρόνωι δὲ πολλῶι λέγεται μὲν ἀρχὴ τροπῆς κατ' αὐτὸν γενέσθαι τὸν Πύρρον ἐπερείσαντα τοῖς ἀντιτεταγμένοις, τὸ δὲ πλεῖστον ἀλκῆι
20 καὶ βίαι τῶν ἐλεφάντων κατειργάσατο, χρήσασθαι τῆι ἀρετῆι πρὸς τὴν
μάχην τῶν Ῥωμαίων μὴ δυναμένων, ἀλλ' οἷον ἐφόδωι κύματος ἢ σεισμοῦ
κατερείποντος οἰομένων δεῖν ἐξίστασθαι μηδὲ ὑπομένειν ἀπράκτους ἀπο-
θνήσκειν, ἐν τῶι μηδὲν ὠφελεῖν πάντα πάσχοντας τὰ χαλεπώτατα. (12) τῆς
δὲ φυγῆς οὐ μακρᾶς εἰς τὸ στρατόπεδον γενομένης
25 ἑξακισχιλίους ἀποθανεῖν φησι τῶν Ῥωμαίων Ἱερώνυμος,
τῶν δὲ περὶ Πύρρον ἐν τοῖς βασιλικοῖς ὑπομνήμασιν
(229 F 2) ἀνενεχθῆναι τρισχιλίους πεντακοσίους καὶ
πέντε τεθνηκότας.

13 (8) DION. HAL. AR I 5, 4: οὐδεμία γὰρ ἀκριβὴς ἐξελήλυθε a. 280/79
30 περὶ αὐτῶν (sc. τῶν Ῥωμαίων) Ἑλληνὶς ἱστορία μέχρι τῶν καθ' ἡμᾶς
χρόνων, ὅτι μὴ κεφαλαιώδεις ἐπιτομαὶ πανὺ βραχεῖαι, (6, 1) πρῶτον μέν,
ὅσα κἀμὲ εἰδέναι, τὴν Ῥωμαϊκὴν ἀρχαιολογίαν ἐπιδραμόντος Ἱερωνύμου
τοῦ Καρδιανοῦ συγγραφέως ἐν τῆι Περὶ τῶν Ἐπιγόνων πραγματείαι·
ἔπειτα Τιμαίου (III) ......
35 **14 (9)** PLUT. Pyrrh. 27, 8: ἦν δὲ τὸ μὲν πλάτος αὐτῆς (des von a. 272
den Lakedaimoniern gegen Pyrrhos aufgeworfenen grabens) πήχεων
ἕξ, τὸ δὲ βάθος τεττάρων, τὸ δὲ μῆκος ὀκτάπλεθρον, ὡς ἱστορεῖ Φύλαρχος
(81 F 48), ὡς δ' Ἱερώνυμος, ἔλαττον.

---

8 τραυματίων Jac　　17 ⟨πρὸς⟩ Ziegler　　20 κατειργάσατο Reiske —αντο
Pl —αστο?　　24 μακρὰν Ziegler　　33 ἐπιγόνων: ἐπειγομένων B

15 (10) PAUS. I 13, 7: *ὑπὸ δε τοῦτον τὸν χρόνον καὶ τὴν τοῦ* a. 272
πολέμου τοῦ Λακωνικοῦ τριβὴν Ἀντίγονος τὰς πόλεις τῶν Μακεδόνων
ἀνασωσάμενος ἠπείγετο ἐς Πελοπόννησον οἷα ἐπιστάμενος Πύρρον, ἢν
Λακεδαίμονα καταστρέψηται καὶ Πελοποννήσου ⟨τὰ⟩ πολλά, οὐκ ἐς Ἤπει-
5 *ρον ἀλλ᾽ ἐπί τε Μακεδονίαν αὖθις καὶ τὸν ἐκεῖ πόλεμον ἥξοντα· μέλλοντος*
δὲ Ἀντιγόνου τὸν στρατὸν ἐξ Ἄργους ἐς τὴν Λακωνικὴν ἄγειν, αὐτὸς
ἐς τὸ Ἄργος ἐληλύθει Πύρρος. κρατῶν δὲ καὶ τότε συνεσπίπτει τοῖς
φεύγουσιν ἐς τὴν πόλιν καί οἱ διαλύεται κατὰ τὸ εἰκὸς ἡ τάξις. (8) *μαχο-*
μένων δὲ πρὸς ἱεροῖς ἤδη καὶ οἰκίαις καὶ κατὰ τοὺς στενωποὺς καὶ κατ᾽
10 *ἄλλο ἄλλων τῆς πόλεως, ἐνταῦθα ὁ Πύρρος ἐμονώθη καὶ τιτρώσκεται τὴν*
κεφαλήν. κεράμωι δὲ βληθέντα ὑπὸ γυναικὸς τεθνάναι φασὶ Πύρρον·
Ἀργεῖοι δὲ οὐ γυναῖκα τὴν ἀποκτείνασαν, Δήμητρα δέ φασιν εἶναι γυναικὶ
εἰκασμένην. ...... (9) .... *δ ι ά φ ο ρ α   δ ὲ   ὅ μ ω ς   ἐ σ τ ὶ   κ α ὶ   τ α ῦ τ α*
ὧ ν   Ἱ ε ρ ώ ν υ μ ο ς   ὁ   Κ α ρ δ ι α ν ὸ ς   ἔ γ ρ α ψ ε ν·   ἀνδρὶ γὰρ βασιλεῖ
15 *συνόντα ἀνάγκη πᾶσα ἐς χάριν συγγράφειν. εἰ δὲ καὶ Φίλιστος* (III)
αἰτίαν δικαίαν εἴληφεν, ἐπελπίζων τὴν ἐν Συρακούσαις κάθοδον, ἀπο-
κρύψασθαι τῶν Διονυσίου τὰ ἀνοσιώτατα, ἦ που πολλή γε Ἱερωνύμωι
συγγνώμη τὰ ἐς ἡδονὴν Ἀντιγόνου γράφειν.

16 (5) STRAB. VIII 6, 21: *τὴν δὲ τοποθεσίαν τῆς πόλεως* (sc. *Κορίν-* a. 303/2 ?
20 *θου), ἐξ ὧν Ἱερώνυμός τε εἴρηκε καὶ Εὔδοξος* (V) *καὶ ἄλλοι, καὶ αὐτοὶ δὲ*
εἴδομεν, νεωστὶ ἀναληφθείσης ὑπὸ τῶν Ῥωμαίων, τοιάνδε εἶναι συμβαίνει.
ὄρος ὑψηλὸν ὅσον τριῶν ἥμισυ σταδίων ἔχον τὴν κάθετον, τὴν δ᾽ ἀνάβασιν καὶ
τριάκοντα σταδίων, εἰς ὀξεῖαν τελευτᾶι κορυφήν· καλεῖται δὲ Ἀκροκόρινθος, οὗ τὸ
μὲν πρὸς ἄρκτον μέρος ἐστὶ τὸ μάλιστα ὀρθίον, ὑφ᾽ ὧι κεῖται ἡ πόλις ἐπὶ τραπε-
25 *ζώδους ἐπιπέδου χωρίου πρὸς αὐτῆι τῆι ῥίζηι τοῦ Ἀκροκορίνθου. αὐτῆς μὲν οὖν*
τῆς πόλεως ὁ κύκλος καὶ τεσσαράκοντα σταδίων ὑπῆρχεν, ἐτετείχιστο δ᾽ ὅσον τῆς
πόλεως γυμνὸν ἦν τοῦ ὄρους· συμπεριείληπτο δὲ τῶι περιβόλωι τούτωι καὶ τὸ ὄρος
αὐτὸ ὁ Ἀκροκόρινθος, ἧι δυνατὸν ἦν τειχισμὸν δέξασθαι ... ὥσθ᾽ ἡ πᾶσα περίμετρος
ἐγίνετο περὶ πέντε καὶ ὀγδοήκοντα σταδίων. ἀπὸ δὲ τῶν ἄλλων μερῶν ἧττον ὀρθιόν
30 *ἐστι τὸ ὄρος, ἀνατέταται μέντοι ἐνθένδε ἱκανῶς καὶ περίοπτόν ἐστιν. ἡ μὲν οὖν*
κορυφή ναίδιον ἔχει Ἀφροδίτης, ὑπὸ δὲ τῆι κορυφῆι τήν τε Πειρήνην εἶναι συμβαίνει
κρήνην, ἔκρυσιν μὲν οὐκ ἔχουσαν, μεστὴν δ᾽ ἀεὶ διαυγοῦς καὶ ποτίμου ὕδατος.
φασὶ δὲ καὶ ἐνθένδε καὶ ἐξ ἄλλων ὑπονόμων τινῶν φλεβίων συνθλίβεσθαι τὴν πρὸς
τῆι ῥίζηι τοῦ ὄρους κρήνην, ἐκρέουσαν εἰς τὴν πόλιν, ὥσθ᾽ ἱκανῶς ἀπ᾽ αὐτῆς
35 *ὑδρεύεσθαι. ἔστι δὲ καὶ φρεάτων εὐπορία κατὰ τὴν πόλιν, λέγουσι δὲ καὶ κατὰ*
τὸν Ἀκροκόρινθον ..... τοῦ δ᾽ οὖν Εὐριπίδου (F 1084) *φήσαντος οὕτως· 'ἥκω περι-*
κλυστον προλιποῦσ᾽ Ἀκροκόρινθον ἱερὸν ὄχθον πόλιν Ἀφροδίτας,' τὸ περίκλυστον
ἤτοι κατὰ βάθους δεκτέον, ἐπεὶ καὶ φρέατα καὶ ὑπόνομοι λιβάδες διήκουσι δι᾽
αὐτοῦ, ἢ τὸ παλαιὸν ὑποληπτέον τὴν Πειρήνην ἐπιπολάζειν καὶ κατάρρυτον ποιεῖν τὸ
ὄρος. ἐνταῦθα δέ φασι πίνοντα τὸν Πήγασον ἁλῶναι ὑπὸ Βελλεροφόντου, πτηνὸν

4 *τὰ* add V   14 *ὧν* Clavier *ὡς* Paus   *ἄνδρα* Facius   16 *εἰς* Συρα-
κούσας Hitzig   17 *τῶν* ς *τὴν* cett   30 *μέντοι* ⟨καὶ⟩ Corais *μὲν τὸ* Str   31 *τε*
om E   37 [*πόλιν*] Valckenaer   38 *δεκτέον* Casaubonus *λεκτέον* Str

ἵππον ἐκ τοῦ τραχήλου τοῦ Μεδούσης ἀναπαλέντα κατὰ τὴν Γοργοτομίαν· τὸν δ᾽
αὐτόν φασι καὶ τὴν Ἵππου κρήνην ἀναβαλεῖν ἐν τῶι Ἑλικῶνι, πλήξαντα τῶι ὄνυχι
τὴν ὑποπεσοῦσαν πέτραν. ὑπὸ δὲ τῆι Πειρήνηι τὸ Σισύφειόν ἐστιν, ἱεροῦ τινὸς ἢ
βασιλείου λευκῶι λίθωι πεποιημένου διασῶζον ἐρείπια οὐκ ὀλίγα. ἀπὸ δὲ τῆς
5 κορυφῆς πρὸς ἄρκτον μὲν ἀφορᾶται ὅ τε Παρνασσὸς καὶ ὁ Ἑλικών, ὄρη ὑψηλὰ καὶ
νιφόβολα, καὶ ὁ Κρισσαῖος κόλπος ὑποπεπτωκὼς ἀμφοτέροις, περιεχόμενος ὑπὸ
τῆς Φωκίδος καὶ τῆς Βοιωτίδος καὶ τῆς Μεγαρίδος καὶ τῆς ἀντιπόρθμου τῆι Φωκίδι
Κορινθίας καὶ Σικυωνίας· πρὸς ἑσπέραν δὲ * * ὑπέρκειται δὲ τούτων ἁπάντων τὰ
καλούμενα Ὄνεια ὄρη, διατείνοντα μέχρι Βοιωτίας καὶ Κιθαιρῶνος ἀπὸ τῶν
10 Σκειρωνίδων πετρῶν, ἀπὸ τῆς παρὰ ταύτας ὁδοῦ πρὸς τὴν Ἀττικήν.

17 (11) STRAB. IX 5, 22: Ἱερώνυμος δὲ τῆς πεδιάδος Θετταλίας a. 303/2
καὶ Μαγνήτιδος τὸν κύκλον τρισχιλίων ἀποφαίνεται σταδίων· ὠικῆσθαι
δ᾽ ὑπὸ Πελασγῶν, ἐξελαθῆναι δὲ τούτους εἰς τὴν Ἰταλίαν ὑπὸ Λαπιθῶν.
εἶναι δὲ τὸ νῦν καλούμενον Πελασγικὸν πεδίον, ἐν ⟨ὧι⟩ Λάρισα καὶ Γυρ-
15 τώνη καὶ Φεραὶ καὶ Μόψιον καὶ Βοιβηὶς καὶ Ὄσσα καὶ Ὁμόλη καὶ Πήλιον
καὶ Μαγνῆτις. Μόψιον δ᾽ ὠνόμασται οὐκ ἀπὸ Μόψου τοῦ Μαντοῦς τῆς
Τειρεσίου, ἀλλ᾽ ἀπὸ τοῦ Λαπίθου τοῦ συμπλεύσαντος τοῖς Ἀργοναύταις·
ἄλλος δ᾽ ἐστὶ Μόψος, ἀφ᾽ οὗ ἡ Ἀττικὴ Μοψοπία.

18 (12) — X 4, 3: Ἱερώνυμος δέ, μῆκος (sc. τῆς Κρήτης) δισχιλίων
20 φήσας, τὸ δὲ πλάτος ἀνώμαλον, πλειόνων ἂν εἴη λέγων τὸν κύκλον ἢ
ὅσων Ἀρτεμίδωρος (V).   s. 244 F 206.

Zweifelhaftes.

19 (—) PHILODEM. Περὶ τῶν Στωικ. VI: ... a .. πολλάκις ἐξ [.... Κλεάν]θην.
ἃ γὰρ λέγομεν, Ἱερώνυμός τε μαρτυρεῖ κ[αὶ] ὁ Χαλκιδεὺς Εὔφαντος (74 F 3), ἔτι δ᾽
25 Ἡγήμων ὁ Ἀθηναῖος (?) ....

---

1 τῆς Μεδούσης B   8 πρὸς ἑσπέραν δὲ om E * * Kramer   10 καὶ
τῆς Pleth   13 τῶν Πελασγῶν B   τὴν om BE   ἰταλίαν A¹ αἰτωλίαν A²BE
14 ⟨ὧι⟩ Politus   15 φεραῖς A (comp) BE   16 ὠνομάσθαι Groskurd   τοῦ
Μάντους τῆς Kuhn τοῦ μάντεως τοῦ Str   18 Μόψος Str E Steph Byz s. Μόψιον
Μόψοπος Casaubonus   21 ὅσων Corais ὅσον Str

Appendix II

Diodorus and Hieronymus: The Problem of Language

Strictly speaking, we do not possess a word of Hieronymus. None of the fragments is a direct quotation, and allusions to items in his history are generally not even paraphrases. Means of discerning his diction are, nevertheless, available. A detailed comparison of the surviving narratives of the Diadochi, as made by Kallenberg or Nietzold, shows that in certain passages the authors must be very close to their common source.[1] Verbal resemblances rarely extend for more than the occasional phrase or sentence, but some of the dominant themes of Hieronymus' history can be inferred on the basis of such parallels, for example, the *pistis* of Eumenes, translated by Nepos as *fides*; likewise description of the dynasts sometimes appears to derive from Hieronymus (cf. ch. 5). Again, the repeated use of a word in Diodorus xviii–xx, when it seldom occurs elsewhere in the *Bibliotheke*, suggests that it was Hieronymus' word. A notable example is *idiopragia*. Technical terms, too, were sometimes taken over: Diodorus' use of *asthippoi*, *katapeltaphetai*, also of *hetairoi, somatophylakes*, and *synedrion* in xviii–xx but not in xvii, indicates the influence of his source.[2] Diodorus did not 'write out' his sources: where comparison can be made (cf. ch. 2) it shows him rendering the original in his own words; and the regularity of his language throughout the *Bibliotheke* was demonstrated by J. Palm in his study of Diodorus' language and style.[3] The sort of process by which he must have converted Hieronymus may, however, be suggested by a survey of Diodorus' style and comparison with parallel texts.

THE HAUPTPROEM

His proem to Book I, where it is certain that he is speaking in his own person, can be taken as a paradigm of Diodorus' language.[4] His style here is that of a typical late Hellenistic writer. He uses the Hellenistic

---

[1] H. Kallenberg, *Philologus* xxxvi and xxxvii; W. Nietzold, *Die Uberlieferung der Diadochengeschichte*, Würzburg, 1905.

[2] Cf. ch. 4, pp. 168 ff. (ἰδιοπραγία); ch. 2, pp. 34 f. and n. 53.

[3] Palm, *Uber Sprache und Stil Diodoros von Sizilien*, Lund, 1955.

[4] The use of the first person does not always indicate that Diodorus is speaking in his own person: at iii.41, 38, iv.20.2–3, v.35 he has reproduced the personal comments of his sources (cf. ch. 2, p. 29). The word ἡμεῖς naturally refers to Diodorus himself where he announces the plan of a new book or a change of subject. There is a genuine autobiographical allusion at xvii.52.4–5, where Diodorus describes Alexandria as he had seen it.

διό καί or διόπερ four times in five chapters: 1.4, 3.1, 3.4, 4.1.
Relative clauses are favoured: 1.4, ἧς τοσοῦτον ὑπερέχειν, 4.2, δι᾽ ἣν
πᾶσιν ἀνθρώποις κ.τ.λ., 4.7, καθ᾽ ὃν ἡγούμενος κ.τ.λ., 5.1, ἣν
τελευτὴν πεποιήμεθα κ.τ.λ. Likewise impersonal and periphrastic
expressions: 2.1, ἀποδοτέον, 2.2, ὑποληπτέον, ἡγητέον, 3.8,
ἡγητέον; 4.2, ἀφορμῇ . . . ἐχρησάμεθα . . . τῇ . . . ἐπιθυμίᾳ, 1.4,
συμβέβηκε, 2.7, συμβαίνει, 4.2, τυγχάνει 4.6, τυγχάνουσιν. The
words ἴδιος and οἰκεῖος are regularly substituted for the possessive
pronoun: 1.1, τοῖς ἰδίοις πόνοις, 3.2, τοὺς οἰκείους χρόνους, 3.7,
πρὸς τὴν ἰδίαν ὑπόστασιν. The pronouns αὐτός and οὗτος are used
extensively: 1.1, διὰ τῆς πραγματείας ταύτης, 1.4, τὴν ταύτης
ἀνάληψιν, 2.2, εἶναι ταύτην φύλακα κ.τ.λ., 2.6, διὰ μόνου τούτου,
etc.; compare also the formulae πρὸς δὲ τούτοις (2.6, 3.8), and χωρὶς
δὲ τούτων (1.5). We find a rich use of the prepositions κατά and δία:
1.4, κατὰ τὸν βίον, 2.3, τὰ κατὰ τὸν βίον, 2.4, κατ᾽ ἀνθρώπους, 3.2,
διὰ τὴν δυσχέρειαν, 3.3, διὰ τὸ μέγεθος τῆς ὑποθέσεως, 3.8, διὰ τὴν
ἀνωμαλίαν, etc. The preposition πρός frequently accompanies a verb
or participle: 1.4, πρὸς διόρθωσιν χρῆσθαι, 1.5, στρατιώτας . . .
ἑτοιμοτέρους κατεσκεύαζει πρὸς τοὺς . . . κινδύνους, etc. The
general tendency to strengthen plain cases and verbs with prepositions
is apparent again in the extensive use of verbs compounded with
prepositions: 1.1, ἀπονέμειν, 1.3, ἀπέδειξαν, 1.4, ἐπεγνώκαμεν 2.1,
ἐξευρεῖν, συμπληρουμένης, 2.3, συναποθνήσκει, 2.4,
ἀπαθανατιζούσης, 2.8, προτρεπομένην ἐπί, 4.6, προδιορίσαι περί,
etc. Diodorus also uses compound adjectives of a type which in classical Greek occur only in poetry: 3.4, δυσπερίληπτος, δυσμνημόνευτος,
3.8, δυσκατάληπτος, δυσέφικτος.[5] Again the object is to make the
sense crystal clear. Diodorus shows the same desire for clarity and
emphasis in his use of the expressions καθόλου (2.1, 2.6, 3.8)
παντελῶς (3.8), τὸ σύνολον (2.8), ὅλος (2.2, 4.6, 5.1, 5.2), and πᾶς or
ἅπας (1.3, 1.4, 2.3, 2.4, 2.5, 2.6, 2.7, 3.6, 4.2, 4.4, 4.7); these add little
to the sense, and are merely an attempt to give added weight to his
words. The word κοινός, though it was relevant to the theme of the
proem, also tends to be used pleonastically: 1.1, κοινὰς ἱστορίας, 1.3,
κοινὴν ἀναλογίαν, κοινὰς πράξεις, κοινὸν χρησματιστήριον, 2.1, τῷ
κοινῷ βίῳ 2.2, τοῦ κοινοῦ γένους, 3.2, κοινὰς πράξεις.

The characteristics noted here are typical of late Hellenistic Greek:
Diodorus excels in the excessive use of prepositions and prefixes, of
the demonstrative pronoun, of the emphatic ἴδιος, κοινός, καθόλου,
ὅλος, and ἅπας, all of which represent the general striving of Hellenistic prose after clarity of expression.[6] An extension of this tendency is
the actual repetition of words or phrases, an irritating and distinctive

---

[5] Palm, op. cit., p. 193 gives a list of such adjectives from all books of the *Bibliotheke*.
[6] Hellenistic papyri show that ἴδιος was commonly used as a possessive reflexive
pronoun in official documents where clarity was of the first importance: cf. Palm, op.
cit., p. 80.

feature of Diodorus' prose. The following examples are again taken from the proem to Book One.

πραγματεία: 1.1, 1.3, 3.1, 3.2, 3.3, 3.4, 3.6, 3.8, 4.2, 4.6, 5.1, 5.2.
πραγματεύω: 1.1, 3.1, 3.3, 3.5, 4.1.
ἐμπειρία: 1.1, 1.4, 1.5, 2.8, 4.4, cf. 1.2, τῆς πείρας, πολυπειρότατος, ἀπείρατον.
ἀνάληψις: 1.4, 3.4, 3.8.
ἐπιβολή: 3.2, 3.3, 3.3, ἐπεβάλετο, 3.8, τοῖς . . . ἐπιβαλλομένοις, 4.2.
ὑπόθεσις: 2.2, 3.1, 3.3, 3.5, 4.1, 4.2, 4.6.
περίστασις: 1.4, 2.5, 3.2.
περιποιοῦμαι: 1.1, 1.5, 2.3, 2.6, 2.8, 4.4.
προδιορίσαι: 4.6, 5.2, cf. 5.1, διοριζόμεθα.
τὸ συμφέρον: 1.1, 2.7, 3.1.
χρήσιμος: 1.2, τῶν χρησίμων, 1.4, χρησιμωτάτην, 2.7, χρήσιμα, 3.6, εὐχρηστοτάτην, 3.7, τὸ χρήσιμον, 4.1, χρησιμωτάτην.
ἀξιόλογος: 2.2, 2.3, 2.6.
συμβάλλομαι: 2.2, 2.5, 2.7.
προτρέπομαι: 1.5, 2.8.
περιγίγνομαι (= acquire): 1.2, 1.4.
περιέχομαι: 2.1, 4.6, 5.1.
περιλαμβάνομαι: 2.7, 5.1.
σύνεσις: 1.2, 1.5.
ἱστορία: 1.1, 1.2, 2.1, 2.2, 2.3, 2.5, 2.7, 3.8, 5.2.
πάντες ἄνθρωποι: 1.1, 1.3, 2.3, 4.2.
κοινὸς βίος: 1.1, 1.2, 2.1.
κοιναὶ πράξεις: 1.3, 3.2, 4.6.
ἅπαντα τὸν αἰῶνα: 1.3, 2.3, cf. 1.5, ταῖς αἰωνίοις βλασφημίαις, 2.3, τοῦ πάντος αἰῶνος, 2.5, τῆς αἰωνίου παραδόσεως.
πάντα χρόνον: 2.3, πάντα τὸν ὕστερον χρόνον, 2.4, πάντα τὸν γενόμενον αὐτῷ . . . χρόνον.
τὸ γένος τῶν ἀνθρώπων: 2.1, 2.2, 2.4.
μία πόλις: 1.3, 3.2, 3.6.
πόνοι καὶ κίνδυνοι: 1.2, μετὰ πολλῶν πόνων καὶ κινδύνων, 2.4, μεγάλους καὶ συνεχεῖς πόνους καὶ κινδύνους, 3.6, πόνον . . . πολὺν ὑπομεῖναι, 4.1, πολλοῦ . . . πόνου καὶ χρόνου προσδεομένην, 4.1, μετά . . . πολλῆς κακοπαθείας καὶ κινδύνων.

Compare also the following:

1.1, ἀκίνδυνον . . . διδασκαλίαν, 1.2, ἀπείρατον κακῶν . . . διδασκαλίαν.

2.1, πρὸς εὐεργεσίαν τοῦ γένους τῶν ἀνθρώπων, 2.4, τὸ γένος τῶν ἀνθρώπων εὐεργετήσας.

3.2, τῶν καθ' αὐτοὺς καιρῶν, 3.3, τοῦ καθ' ἡμᾶς βίου, 3.6, τῶν καθ' αὐτὸν καιρῶν.

3.2, ἀπὸ τῶν ἀρχαίων χρόνων ἀρξάμενοι, 3.6, ἀρξάμενος ἀπὸ τῶν ἀρχαιοτάτων χρόνων.

3.3, μιᾶς συντάξεως περιγραφῇ, 3.8, μιᾶς συντάξεως περιγραφῇ.

4.6, περὶ ὅλης τῆς πραγματείας, 5.1, τὴν ὅλην πραγματείαν, 5.2, τῆς ὅλης προθέσεως, 5.2, παρ᾽ ὅλην τὴν ἱστορίαν.
1.4, τὰ . . . κατὰ τὸν βίον, 2.3, τὰ κατὰ τὸν βίον.
2.2, φύλακα . . . τῆς . . . ἀρετῆς, 2.5, φύλακα τῆς αἰωνίου παραδόσεως κ.τ.λ.
5.1, δυσὶ λείποντα τῶν τριακοσίων; ἔτη δυσὶ λείποντα τῶν χιλίων.
2.5, ἡ δὲ τῆς ἱστορίας δύναμις ἐπὶ πᾶσαν τὴν οἰκουμένην διήκουσα, 4.3, ἡ γὰρ ταύτης τῆς πόλεως ὑπεροχή, διατείνουσα τῇ δυνάμει κ.τ.λ.

Sometimes Diodorus merely repeats vocabulary: for example he seems obsessed with the word πραγματεία, and hardly less with ἐμπειρία, ὑπόθεσις, χρήσιμος, περιποιοῦμαι, and ἅπας. Sometimes a noun and adjective become linked together in a cliché, like ὁ κοινὸς βίος, ἡ ὅλη πραγματεία. Again, the repetition may be regular throughout several chapters, as in the case of πραγματεία, or there may be a short 'run': ἐπιβολή occurs twice in twelve words at 3.2 and 3.3; and in 5.1 and 5.2 we find successively τὴν ὅλην πραγματείαν, τῆς ὅλης προθέσεως, παρ᾽ ὅλην τὴν ἱστορίαν. Even more striking is the repetition of longer phrases like μετὰ πολλῶν πόνων καὶ κινδύνων, or τὸ γένος τῶν ἀνθρώπων, in the space of five chapters. The nature of his theme in the opening proem made it inevitable that there should be a high incidence of words like ἱστορία, συγγραφεύς, κοινός; but most of the repetitions suggest only someone at a loss for a synonym or a different thing to say: they do not have a rhetorical function like the repetitions in Plato or Demosthenes.[7]

The same tendency to overemphasize leads to a frequent use of pairs of words: 1.2, πόνων καὶ κινδύνων; 1.3, τόποις καὶ χρόνοις; 3.2, πλείστας καὶ ποικιλωτάτας; 3.3, πολλῶν καὶ μεγάλων; 3.4, πλείοσι πραγματείαις καὶ διαφόροις συγγραφεῦσιν; 4.1, πόνου καὶ χρόνου; 4.1 κακοπαθείας καὶ κινδύνων; 4.3, ἑτοιμοτάτας καὶ πλείστας; 4.7, πλεῖστα καὶ μαχιμώτατα.[8]

STYLISTIC FEATURES OF BOOKS XVIII–XX

The same stylistic features can be observed throughout the *Bibliotheke*. This can be demonstrated in a sample section from Book xviii and Book xix, of the same length as the main proem (five chapters). The sections xviii.65–9 and xix.20–4 manifest again the excessive use of prepositions, the unnecessary use of πᾶς and of demonstrative pronouns, a marked preference for periphrasis, especially with the verb ποιεῖσθαι, instead of a simple verb. In the narrative sections, also, Diodorus achieves a peculiarly monochrome style by an excessive use of participles leading up to the main verb: e.g. xviii.65.2, οἱ δὲ Ἀθηναῖοι πεπολυωρηκότες . . . καὶ νομίσαντες . . . ἐλπίζοντες . . . περιχαρεῖς ἦσαν; xviii.66.2, αἰσχυνόμενος . . . νομίζων . . .

[7] See J. D. Denniston, *Greek Prose Style*, Oxford, 1952, pp. 78 ff.
[8] Cf. Palm, op. cit., pp. 143 f.

μετενόησε τῇ γνώμῃ; xviii.68.3, σπανίζων . . . ὑπολαμβάνων . . . ἠναγκάσθη.

We find also in these chapters the stylistic trait, amounting almost to an eccentricity, which characterizes the main proem and which seems to be peculiarly Diodoran, namely, the use of repeated words and phrases.

xviii.65–9

65.3, αὐτὸς ἰδίᾳ, 65.4, αὐτὸν ἰδίᾳ, 65.5, ἰδίᾳ δέ.

65.3, τὰς . . . ἐν τῷ πολέμῳ χρείας, 66.2, τὰς ἐν τοῖς πολέμοις χρείας.

66.5, τοῖς θορύβοις, 66.6, τοῦ θορύβου, 67.1, τῶν θορυβούντων, 67.2, τοῖς θορύβοις.

66.6, πικρῶς διέκειτο, 67.5, πικρῶς διεκειμένων, 67.5, πικρῶς ὠνείδιζον.

67.1, διὰ τὸ μέγεθος τῆς κραυγῆς, ibid. διὰ τὸ μέγεθος τοῦ κινδύνου.

68.2, Πολυπέρχων . . . διατρίβων περὶ τὴν Φωκίδα, 69.1, τοῦ δὲ Πολυπέρχοντος περὶ ταῦτα διατρίβοντος.

69.1–2, εἰς τοὺς ἐσχάτους κινδύνους ἤγαγε τοὺς Σαλαμινίους· κινδυνευούσης δὲ τῆς πόλεως κ.τ.λ.

xix.20–4

20.1, κατασκευασάμενος δαψιλῆ χορηγίαν, 21.3, διεδίδου δαψιλῆ, 22.3, χορηγούσης τῆς Περσίδος δαψιλῆ.

20.2, ὑποζυγίων πλῆθος, 20.4, πλῆθος τῶν ὑποζυγίων.

21.2, εἰς Περσέπολιν τὸ βασίλειον, 22.1, εἰς Περσέπολιν τὸ βασίλειον.

20.4, ἀνεκτήσατο τὴν παρὰ τῶν στρατιωτῶν εὔνοιαν, 21.3, ἐκκαλούμενος αὐτῶν τὴν εὔνοιαν, 24.5, τὰ μὲν πλήθη πρὸς εὔνοιαν προεκαλέσατο.

22.2, ἐπλήρωσε . . .ἣν ἀνεπλήρουν . . . ἀναπληροῦσθαι.

22.1, τῶν . . .χρησίμων πλῆθος, 23.1, τὸ πλῆθος, ibid. πρὸς τὸ πλῆθος, ibid. παρὰ τοῖς πλήθεσι, 23.4, ὑπὸ τοῦ πλήθους, 24.5, τὰ μὲν πλήθη.

23.1, στρατηγίας ὀρεγόμενον, 23.4, στρατηγίας ὀρεγομένους.

23.1, ὄγκον καὶ τὸ πρόσχημα, 24.1, ὄγκον καὶ πρόσχημα.

23.4, ἔλαθε . . .λαθών.

24.5, καταβαρούμενος ὑπὸ τοῦ πάθους, ibid. ὑπὸ τῆς νόσου πιεζουμένου.

24.1, ἑαυτῷ . . . ἑαυτῷ, 24.4, αὐτοῦ . . . αὐτός, 24.5, αὐτός, 24.6, αὖτον . . . αὐτός.

Some further examples from Books xviii–xx illustrate the tendency to pointless repetition.

Book xviii

5.2, προσηγορίας, 5.5, τὰς προσηγορίας, 6.2, τὴν προσηγορίαν, 6.3, τῆς προσηγορίας.

8.1, χάριν, 8.5, χάριν, χαρὰν.

24.2, ἀνωχύρους . . . ὀχυρότητι, 25.1, τόπους ὀχυροὺς . . . τὴν ἐν τοῖς τόποις ὀχυρότητα.

44.2, τὴν παρουσίαν . . . 44.3, τὴν παρουσίαν.

46.5, δι' ἀκροβολισμῶν, 46.6, διὰ τῶν ἀκροβολισμῶν.

47.3, ὁ δ' Ἀντίγονος . . . ἀνέζευξεν ἐκ τῆς Πισιδικῆς, 47.4, ὁ δ' οὖν Ἀντίγονος ἀναζεύξας ἐκ τῆς Πισιδικῆς.

49.4, παραλαβὼν τὴν . . . ἐπιμέλειαν . . . τὴν ἐπιμέλειαν παραλαβεῖν.

50.4, τῆς ὅλης ἐπιβολῆς, 50.5, τῆς τῶν ὅλων ἐπιβολῆς . . . τὰς ἰδίας ἐπιβολάς, 51.1, αὐτοῦ τὴν ἐπιβολήν, 52.1, τὰς μελλούσας ἐπιβολάς, 52.2, τῆς δὲ ὅλης ἐπιβολῆς.

51.5, ὁ δὲ Ἀρριδαῖος καταστρατηγηθείς, 51.7, Ἀρριδαῖος μὲν οὖν καταστρατηγηθείς.

57.3, τῶν βασιλέων . . . τοὺς βασιλεῖς . . . τῶν βασιλέων . . . τῶν βασιλέων . . . τοὺς βασιλεῖς, 57.4, τῶν βασιλέων.

59.5, τῆς κατὰ τὸν ἀνθρώπινον βίον ἀνωμαλίας, 59.6, τῇ γὰρ τῶν πράξεων ἀνωμαλίᾳ.

70.6, διὰ τοῦ πτώματος, 70.7, διὰ τοῦ πτώματος.

71.2, τὸν τοῦ πτώματος τόπον, 71.4, τὸν τόπον τοῦ πτώματος.

72.2, μετὰ τοῦ στόλου πάντος, 72.3, μετὰ πάντος τοῦ στόλου.

72.8, αὐτάνδρων . . . αὐτάνδρων.

74.3, καταστῆσαι δ' ἐπιμελητὴν τῆς πόλεως . . . παραλαβὼν τὴν ἐπιμέλειαν τῆς πόλεως.

Book xix

11.5, παρανομήσασα, 11.6, παρανομουμένης, 11.9, παρανομήμασι.

17.7, τὸ δοθὲν παραδοθῇ.

21.2, εἰς Περσέπολιν τὸ βασίλειον, 22.1, εἰς Περσέπολιν τὸ βασίλειον, cf. 46.6, εἰς τὸ βασίλειον, ὃ καλεῖται Περσέπολις.

31.3, ἀναμφισβήτητον, 31.4, ἀμφισβητούντων . . . ἠμφισβήτει.

39.2, τοὺς δ' ἐλέφαντας . . . μεμονωμένους, 39.3, μεμονωμένοις τοῖς θηρίοις.

56.4, ἀρχὴ διαφορᾶς ἐφύετο καὶ μεγάλων πολέμων, 57.3, τὸ μέγεθος τοῦ φυομένου πολέμου.

56.4, Ἀντίγονος . . . συλλογισάμενος, 57.3, Ἀντίγονος . . . συλλογιζόμενος.

58.5, κοινοπραγοῦντες, 58.6, κοινοπραγοῦντες.

79.1, ἐνεργέστερον, 79.3, ἐνεργῶς.

83.3, παραγγείλαντες τοῖς τε ἀκοντισταῖς καὶ τοξόταις συνεχῶς κατατιτρώσκειν τὰ θηρία καὶ τοὺς ἐπ' αὐτοῖς ἀναβεβηκότας, 84.1, τὸ μὲν πλῆθος τῶν ἀκοντιστῶν καὶ τοξοτῶν συνεχῶς βαλλόντων κατετίτρωσκε τὰ σώματα τῶν ἐλεφάντων κ.τ.λ.

84.3, ἄπρακτον ἔχει τὴν ἀλκήν, 84.4, ἄπρακτον ἐποίει τὴν βίαν.

Book xx

20.2, κατάγειν τὸ μειράκιον ἐπὶ τὴν πατρῷαν βασιλείαν, 20.3,
   συγκατάγωσι τὸ μειράκιον ἐπὶ τὴν πατρῷαν βασιλείαν.
82.4, βραχὺ λειπόμενοι, 82.5, βραχὺ λειπόμενοι.
98.7, τῆς ἰδίας τάξεως, 98.9, τῆς ἰδίας τάξεως.
Diodorus seems to have had little feeling for the sound of his prose.
At xx.106.4 he writes πλεονάκις . . . πλεονέκτης (hardly a deliberate
play on words), and at xviii.36.2 the talk of θηρία (crocodiles) inspires
ἀποθηριοῦσθαι metaphorically of Perdiccas' soldiers; their comrades
are θηριόβρωτοι. Diodorus shows some fondness for the cognate
accusative, e.g. xix.17.7, τὸ δοθὲν παραδοθῇ, and the frequent
δωρεὰς ἔδωκεν, but it is unclear whether he liked the similarity in
sound or just wanted to amplify the sense.

PHRASEOLOGY IN BOOKS XVIII–XX

Diodorus' consistency of vocabulary and construction extends also to
phraseology; and here again the repetitive, formulaic character of his
language is striking. Palm took a sample of the first twenty chapters of
Book xi and showed that 64 phrases from these chapters can be
paralleled in other books. In the following section phrases from
Books xviii, xix, and xx are compared with the phraseology of other
books.

Book xviii

2.3, τοὐναντίον δέ: 33.3, 65.3; xvi.58.5, 91.3, xviii.10.6, 12.2.
2.4, εὐθὺ δέ, beginning a sentence: 10.2, 25.5, 55.4, 70.1, 50.5, 59.1,
   61.1, 61.4, xix.42.4, xx.83.3, xvi.4.3, 30.3, 31.1, 49.8, 52.3, 91.4,
   xviii.29.3, 31.1, 40.5, xi.12.2, 17.2, 47.1, 71.3, 71.6.
4.1, τῶν ἐπιφανεστάτων ἀνδρῶν: 37.2, xix.85.3, xvii.77.4, 89.1,
   107.6.
4.4, μνήμης ἄξια: 22.4, xvi.31.7, 40.2, xvii.5.6, 38.4, 99.1, 100.1,
   xi.88.4.
5.1, οὕτως γὰρ μάλιστα εὐπαρακολούθητος . . . ἡ διήγησις ἔσται: cf.
   i.3.8, τὴν δ᾽ ἀνάληψιν ἔχει παντελῶς εὐπαρακολούθητον.
7.7, κελεύων τὰ μὲν ὅπλα καταθέσθαι, αὐτοὺς δὲ τὰ πιστὰ λαβόντας
   ἐπὶ τὰς ἰδίας κατοικίας ἀναχωρῆσαι: cf. xi.5.4, κελεύει τὰ μὲν
   ὅπλα πάντες ἀποθέσθαι, αὐτοὺς δὲ ἀκινδύνους εἰς τὰς πατρίδας
   ἀπιέναι.
8.2, ἰδίους ταῖς εὐνοίαις: 40.4, 46.2; xix.11.1, cf. 46.1: xvi.69.8, 89.2;
   xvii.24.2.
9.5, τῆς αὐτονομίας ἀντέχεσθαι: 51.3; xix.20.2, 66.4, 73.1; xvi.41.3;
   xvii.3.2, 62.1, 74.1; xi.71.3.
9.5, διαπρεσβευόμενος κοινοπραγίαν συνέθετο: 14.2, 25.4,
   πρεσβεύειν . . . περὶ κοινοπραγίας, 29.4, διεπρεσβεύσατο . . . καὶ
   συνθέμενος κοινοπραγίαν; xvii.3.2, διαπρεσβευσάμενοι . . .
   συνέθεντο κοινοπραγίαν, 5.1, συνετίθετο κοινοπραγίαν.

15.3, *πολλοῖς τραύμασι περιπεσών*: xi.7.3, *πυκνοῖς τραύμασι περιέπιπτον*; xix.4.6; xx.12.3, 98.9.

15.7, *ἐπιφανεῖ μάχῃ νικήσας*: 32.4; xvi.38.1, *νικήσας . . . ἐπιφανεῖ παρατάξει*; xvii.89.1; xi.82.4.

17.1, *πολὺ τοῖς πλήθεσι λειπόμενοι*: 44.5, *πολὺ τοῖς . . . πλήθεσιν ὑπερέχοντες*, cf. 45.1: xix.13.3, 16.5, 88.4, 89.2; xvi.47.5; cf. xvii.75.7, 87.2, 95.4; xi.4.7, 5.2.

18.1, *ἐν ἀπορίᾳ πολλῇ καθειστήκει*: cf. 35.5; xvi.3.1, *ἐν ἀπορίᾳ τῇ μεγίστῃ καθειστήκεισαν.*

19.5, *ἐκκαλούμενος αὐτῶν τὰς προθυμίας εἰς τὸν πόλεμον*: xix.21.3, *ἐκκαλούμενος αὐτῶν τὴν εὔνοιαν*, 24.4, *πρὸς εὔνοιαν προσεκαλέσατο*, cf. 91.2, 79.7; xx.84.4, cf. 94.5; xvi.37.4, *ὁ γὰρ χρυσὸς τὰς πλεονεξίας τῶν ἀνθρώπων ἐκκαλούμενος*; 1.72,2, *ἀνακαλούμενοι τὴν ἀρετήν*, 64.9, *ἐκκαλεῖσθαι τὴν τοῦ πλήθους πρὸς αὐτὸν εὔνοιαν*; xiv.42.1, *τὴν γὰρ προθυμίαν τό τε μέγεθος τῶν μισθῶν ἐξεκαλεῖτο*, cf. 18.6, 43.3.

22.3, *τῶν πρὸς πολιορκίαν ἀνηκόντων*: 51.1, 51.6; xx.45.1; xvi.48.7, 92.3, *τῶν ἀνηκόντων πρὸς τὴν . . . στρατείαν*; xvii.16.4, *τὰ πρὸς τὴν εὐωχίαν ἀνήκοντα*; cf. i.36.10, *τῶν πρὸς ἡδονὴν ἀνηκόντων*.

23.4, *φανερὸς ἦν ἀναιρήσων αὐτόν*: 65.6, 67.2, 52.3, 55.2; xix.23.1; xx.28.3; xvi.28.2, 54.1; xvii.5.4, 15.3, 28.2, 43.2.

25.1, *εἰς ἐσχάτους . . . κινδύνους*: 41.3, 69.1; xvi.35.2; xvii.55.4, 81.1, 97.2, 103.3.

32.1, *πολὺν ἐποιοῦντο φόνον*: 17.4, 30.6; xi.10.2, 31.1, 80.5; xvi.35.5; xvii.12.5, 19.6, 25.2, 84.2, 88.4.

32.1, *τὸ μὲν πρῶτον ἰσόρροπος ἦν ὁ κίνδυνος*: xi.7.2; xvi.4.6, 12.3; xvii.11.5, 88.2; xix.104.2; cf. xi.19.2, 36.4.

33.5, *τοὺς ἐπιφερομένους κινδύνους*: xi.9.1; xvi.3.1, 3.3; xvii.56.4; xix.79.7; xx.108.4.

34.5, *διημερευσάντων <ἐν> τοῖς κινδύνοις*: xi.8.3, 83.1; xvii.70.4.

34.5, *διὰ τὴν ὑπερβολὴν τῆς . . . φιλοτιμίας*; cf. 42.2, 45.5, 47.1; xix.18.2, 20.1; xi.11.6, 47.2; xvi.4.6; xvii.11.5, 20.5, 26.5, 42.4, 85.1, 101.1; etc.

35.2, *ἴδιον δέ τι καὶ παράδοξον συνέβη γενέσθαι*: xix.32.2; xvi.66.3, 88.3; xvii.5.6, 7.5, 63.4, 66.3, 90.1, 100.1, 103.7.

40.6, *εὐθέτοις πεδίοις πρὸς ἱππομαχίαν*: i.18.5, 87.4; ii.57.3, iii.10.1, 31.1, 49.5; v.37.3; xi.4.1; xvi.47.6; xx.4.8.

40.8, *μετὰ πάσης τῆς δυνάμεως*: 44.1, 46.3, 52.1, 57.4, 63.2, 70.4, 72.2, 73.1; xix.32.2, 93.3; xx.100.5, 103.1; xvi.48.7; xvii.8.3, 9.1, 24.1, 30.1, 49.1, 63.1, 64.3, 95.3; xi.5.1.

41.4, *διαγωνίσασθαι περὶ τῶν πρωτείων*: xi.9.1, *ὑπὲρ τῶν πρωτείων ἀγωνιζόμενος*; xvii.6.3, *ἀγῶνας . . . περὶ τοῦ πρωτείου*; xx.31.3, *ἀμφισβητεῖν τῶν πρωτείων.*

42.1, *πολλαῖς καὶ ποικίλαις . . . τοῦ βίου μεταβολαῖς*: xvi.85.6, *πολλὰς . . . καὶ ποικίλας παρατάξεις*; xvii.13.1, *πολλαὶ καὶ ποικίλαι περιστάσεις*; xi.80.4, *πολλοὺς καὶ ποικίλους ἀγῶνας.*

46.2, τιμῶν δωρεαῖς ἀξιολόγοις: xi.8.1, δωρεὰς ἀξιολόγους δώσει; xx.34.1, δωρεὰς ἀξιολόγους δώσειν; xix.64.8, δωρεαῖς μεγάλαις ἐτίμησε; xvi.51.3, cf. 53.3; xvii.68.6, 74.4.

46.5, περὶ τὴν μάχην ἐκτὸς τῆς πόλεως ἀσχολουμένων: 64.4; xix.2.9, 68.5; xi.1.5; ii.40.4; iv.25.3; xvi.20.4, 27.2.

47.5, μετέωρος ἦν ταῖς ἐλπίσιν: xix.90.1, μεμετεωρισμένος ταῖς ἐλπίσιν:; xx.8.5, 33.2; xvii.29.3, μετέωροι ταῖς ἐλπίσιν.

59.6, ὁ κοινὸς βίος: i.1.1, 2.1, 8.8, 9.2.

59.6, πάντα τὸν αἰῶνα: i.1.3, 2.3, 2.3.

70.7, ταχὺ τῶν ἔργων συντελουμένων διὰ . . . τὴν πολυχειρίαν: xi.2.4, ταχέως ἤνυον διὰ τὴν πολυχειρίαν τῶν ἐργαζομένων; xvii.40.5, ταχὺ διὰ τῆς πολυχειρίας ἠνύετο τὰ τῶν ἔργων, 89.6; xx.92.1.

71.1, τῆς νυκτὸς περικαταλαβούσης: xi.7.4; xvii.27.4, 35.1, 43.5, 50.5, cf. 13.6; xx.75.4, 5.4, 26.3, 69.1.

75.1, κεκοσμημένῳ τῷ στόλῳ τοῖς ἀπὸ τῆς νίκης ἀκροστολίοις: xx.52.4, τὰς ἰδίας ναῦς κοσμήσας τοῖς ἀκροστολίοις, cf. 87.4.

Book xix

14.3, κοινωνεῖν τῶν αὐτῶν ἐλπίδων: xvii.29.4, κοινωνεῖν τῶν Περσικῶν ἐλπίδων.

15.5, τῷ μὲν λόγῳ . . . τῷ δ᾽ ἔργῳ: 48.3; xi.4.4; cf. ii.24.7, τῷ μὲν λόγῳ . . . τῇ δ᾽ἀληθείᾳ.

19.1, τὸ στρατόπεδον εἰς ἀθυμίαν ἐνέπεσεν: cf. 24.5; xvi.76.4; xvii.49.4.

26.6, σύντονον τὴν πορείαν ποιούμενος: xviii.44.2; xix.32.2, 93.2; xx.108.2; xvii.19.1, 32.3.

48.2, κατ᾽ ἀνδρείαν καὶ σύνεσιν θαυμαζόμενον: ii.22.5, 33.1; xvi.18.1.

52.6, καραδοκήσειν . . . τὰς τῶν πραγμάτων μεταβολάς: xi.3.4, καραδοκοῦντες τὸ τοῦ πολέμου τέλος; xvii.8.6, καραδοκοῦντες τὴν ῥοπὴν τοῦ πολέμου; xx.39.2, 55.3, 60.2, 110.5.

57.3, συλλογιζόμενος τὸ μέγεθος τοῦ φυομένου πολέμου: xviii.55.1, Πολυπέρχων . . . προεώρα μὲν τὸ μέγεθος τοῦ . . . ἐσομένου πολέμου, 21.4, θεωροῦντες τὸν πόλεμον αὐξόμενον; xvi.28.1, προορώμενος τὸ μέγεθος τοῦ πολέμου.

74.4, πολλοὺς μὲν ἀνεῖλεν, οὐκ ὀλίγους δ᾽ἐζώγρησεν: xvi.28.3; xvii.68.7.

81.2, μίᾳ φωνῇ: xi.9.3, 92.4; xvi.79.3; xvii.33.4.

81.6, παρακαλέσας . . . τοῖς οἰκείοις λόγοις; xvi.4.3; xvii.2.2, 33.1, 56.4.

90.5, πάντα γίνεται τὰ καλὰ καὶ παρ᾽ ἀνθρώποις θαυμαζόμενα διὰ πόνων καὶ κινδύνων :i.1.2, 2.4, 4.1; xvi.76.3, 40.4; xvii.56.4, 94.1.

94.3, θάνατον . . . πρόστιμον εἶναι: xx.58.5, θάνατος ὥριστο πρόστιμον; i.77.2, θάνατος . . . ἦν τὸ πρόστιμον; v.34.3, θάνατον τὸ πρόστιμον τεθείκασι; xi.8.1, θάνατος ἔσται τὸ πρόστιμον.

Book xx

48.5, ἀμφίδοξος ἦν ὁ κίνδυνος: xvi.39.5, τῆς νίκης ἀμφιδόξου γενομένης, 86.2, ἀμφιδοξουμένας τὰς ἐλπίδας τῆς νίκης; cf. xvii.33.6.

51.3, πρύμναν ἀνεκρούοντο πρὸς ἄλλην ἐμβολήν: cf. xi.18, xii.78.

52.1, τοῖς σκεπαστηρίοις ὅπλοις: i.24.3; v.18.3; xi.7.3.

73.2, παραδοὺς τὸν στόλον συνέταξε συμπαραπλεῖν ἅμα πορευομένῃ τῇ δυνάμει: xi.51; iv.18.2.

81.1, διὰ τοιαύτας τινας αἰτίας: xvi.2.1, 23.1, 29.2, 39.1, 41.1.

81.3, ἐπὶ τοσοῦτον γὰρ προεληλύθει δυνάμεως: xi.8.2, ἐπὶ τοσοῦτο δὲ προέβησαν ταῖς προθυμίαις; xvii.12.2, ἐπὶ τοσοῦτο δὲ ταῖς ἀνδραγαθίαις προέβησαν; iv.54.7, ἐπὶ τοσοῦτο προελθεῖν ὀργῆς; cf. xii.50.1; xiv.46.4; xix.1.7, 49.2.

88.8, γενομένης . . . μάχης . . . ἰσχυρᾶς: xi.7.1, 12.6, 13.2, 19.2, 32.2, 78.1, 79.3, 79.4; xvi.16.1, 31.3, 35.5, 86.2; xviii.40.8, 44.4, 15.3; xx.22.5.

Diodorus made up his own clichés and applied them everywhere mechanically, even when they were actually inappropriate to the context: for instance, the common formula μετὰ πάσης τῆς δυνάμεως, as used at xviii.70.4 is not merely empty but untrue, for it was said at xviii.68.3 that Polyperchon had divided his force.[9] Formulaic language was more suited to epic than to history; and in his efforts to silhouette the general moral truth behind a historical situation, Diodorus took much of the colour out of the narrative he drew upon. His main purpose being instructive, it did not matter if battles were standardized or individuals stereotyped: rather, this method facilitated his didactic aims. He has a style of his own, but it is a style characterized by monotony and repetition, the colourless style of bureaucratic prose. As Palm concluded: 'wir haben nicht ein Kunstwerk vor uns, wohl aber ein bequemes und vielseitig verwendbarer Werkzeug für praktische Zwecke, nicht unähnlich der modernen Verwaltungsprose mit ihren vielen praktischen Vorteilen und ästhetischen Schrecklichkeiten.'[10]

---

[9] The formula ἐκ διαδοχῆς—'in relays'—as at xviii.34.4 and frequently in earlier books, seemed to Diodorus an appropriate description for siege warfare; but in fact relays were not exploited to the full until the end of the fifth century, and the terminology is anachronistic for the battles at Thermopylae and Pylos (xi.7.2, 8.2–3; xii.61.3): Thucydides and Herodotus did not mention relays in their accounts, though their language may have suggested the idea to Diodorus. Cf. R. K. Sinclair, *CQ* n.s. xvi (1966), pp. 249–55, rightly viewing phrases with διαδοχή as Diodorus' own cliché; cf. Y. Garlan, *Recherches de poliorcétique grecque*, Paris, 1974, pp. 158 ff.

[10] Palm, op. cit., pp. 207 f. Cf. the summary of Diodorus' style by A. M. Croiset, *Histoire de littérature grecque*, v, 1900, p. 349: 'Comme écrivain, son principal mérite est d'être clair. Il écrit avec une facilité banale, dans une langue sans couleur. Sans cesse, il se sert des mots abstraits et vagues qui remplacaient alors dans l'usage les manières de dire précises et vivantes d'autrefois.' Diodorus' language in fact bears much resemblance to that of Hellenistic bureaucratic prose (Cf. Robert, *REG* lxxi (1958), no. 130, censuring Palm for his failure to consider this aspect of the subject), as does that of Polybius (cf. E. Norden, *Die Antike Kunstprosa*, Leipzig, 1898, pp. 152 f.).

Occasionally a grammatical or syntactical usage is not found uniformly throughout the work, but it is impossible to relate this to changes of source. Palm gives the following statistics for the relative occurrence of the optative:

i   ii iii iv v xi xii xiii xiv xv xvi xvii xviii xix xx
45 18 13 20 11 11 11 28 20 10 7   5   5   12 37

The optative was used more widely in classical than in Hellenistic Greek, but the unevenness which these figures show does not correspond to any division of sources ever proposed. Furthermore, there are considerable differences within particular books: in Book xx, 24 out of 37 instances belong to the history of Agathocles, which occupies 53 out of 113 chapters; 5 belong to the proem, 1 to Roman history, and 7 to the narrative of the Diadochi. The proportions seem to be connected with the subject matter, for the history of Agathocles is full of reflections and philosophical comment, in contrast to the straightforward political and military narrative of the Diadochi. In Book xix, only one of the twelve optatives occurs in the history of Agathocles, which here occupies 20 out of 110 chapters; so that if we are to assume one source for the Agathocles section, the optatives cannot be connected with this source. The large number in the first book is perhaps to be explained by Diodorus' desire to make a stylish beginning to his work.

Relative clauses are a similar case. Palm counts the following:

xi xii xiii xv xvi xviii xix xx
12 10 53   4 12   10   53 33

Here again the variation in numbers can hardly be connected with the use of different sources, and considerable irregularities can be found within individual books: xix has 3 instances in chapter 2, 2 in chapter 3, 3 in chapter 36, 3 in chapter 73, etc.; xx has two instances in chapter 24.1, 2 in chapter 97 etc.[11] In his use of constructions as in his use of vocabulary and phrases it seems that Diodorus has a tendency to concentrate many instances within a short space of the text.

THE ADAPTATION OF SOURCES

It remains to be considered how Diodorus transformed his sources so as to produce this bland effect. Palm's analysis of Diodorus Book iii and Photius' epitome of Agatharchides shows the general tendency of Diodorus to clarify and expand the language of the original. His use of conjunctions and particles, especially μέν, δέ, γάρ, and οὖν is richer than that of Agatharchides. He favours participles (about 890 participial constructions, to Agatharchides' 560), and sometimes changes a finite verb to a participle, e.g. οὓς καλοῦσι Σίμους—οἱ προσαγορευόμενοι Σιμοί. He favours the accusative at the expense of the genitive: e.g. νυκτὸς μὲν, ἡμέρας δέ—τὰς μὲν νύκτας, τὰς δ' ἡμέρας; and uses the prepositions κατά and περί more frequently than

[11] Palm, op. cit., pp. 68–9.

Agatharchides. Prepositions are often added to verbs, as in tragedy, for greater clarity of meaning, and Diodorus tends to substitute complex for simple verbs, e.g. περιγίγνεται for νικᾷ. He prefers the more modern Hellenistic usage, e.g. ἀμφοτέρων rather than ἀμφοῖν, and in general replaces unusual with usual words.[12] A simple verb in Agatharchides is sometimes turned into a lengthy periphrasis: Agatharchides' ὑπνοῦσιν becomes ποιεῖται τὴν διὰ τῶν ὕπνων ἀνάπαυσιν; and he doubles the number of expressions with παράδοξος, θαυμαστός, καθ'ὑπερβολήν (about 40 in Diodorus to 20 in Agatharchides). 'Padding' of this kind makes Diodorus' account rather longer than the original, and very much weaker in impact. Although Diodorus and Agatharchides are both Hellenistic historians writing within a century of one another and using almost identical vocabulary and syntax, Diodorus' dilution of the language of Agatharchides has quite altered the original lively style.

A similar process seems to have taken place in Book xx, where for two chapters we can compare the text of the second-century papyrus which epitomizes a Hellenistic historian's account of the siege of Rhodes.[13] As always, Diodorus makes use of many compound verbs: 93.2, ἐξέπεμψαν, διακελευσάμενοι, ἀφηγουμένους, ἐκπλευσάντων; 93.3, ἀφηγούμενος, ἐπιφαινομένους, 93.5, περιτυχών, 94.3, ἐξαπεσταλμένος. The author of the papyrus (P) does not use compounds unnecessarily (though at line 19 he has διορύξαντες, and at lines 30–1 παρεσάξειν), and more than once uses a plain verb, e.g. line 6, στελλομένους, line 32, δοὺς καὶ λαβών; at line 27 he has ἀποσταλείς for Diodorus' ἐξαπεσταλμένος. There is little difference in the number of participles used: 35 in Diodorus to 32 in P; and of these Diodorus has 15 in the nominative, P has 12; Diodorus has 7 genitive absolutes, P has 6; but Diodorus has a greater number of participles in an attributive position—4 compared to 1 in P. Diodorus also has a richer use of conjunctions and particles: 23 to P's 14, excluding καί and τε. Diodorus' relation to P is thus comparable wih his relation to Agatharchides, in so far as it can be measured in statistical terms. A line-by-line comparison of the texts suggests that Diodorus also amplified the language of his source by the use of the same linguistic devices by which he amplified the language of Agatharchides.

Diodorus xx.93.5: τῶν δ' ὑπολοίπων νεῶν τριῶν Ἀμύντας ἡγούμενος ἔπλευσεν ἐπὶ νήσων. P has only Ἀμύντας δὲ πλέων ἐπὶ νήσων. Ibid: καὶ πολλοῖς πλοίοις περιτυχών . . . εἰς τὴν πόλιν. Omitted by P, who goes directly from πλέων ἐπὶ νήσων to καταπελταφέτας . . . αἴρεε. Diodorus expands the sentence by using the compound verb

[12] Ibid., pp. 48 f. for a comparative list of vocabulary in Diodorus and Agatharchides.

[13] Cf. ch.2, pp. 42 ff. In the following discussion references are to the parallel texts as set out in Hiller von Gaertringen's edition, *SB d. preuss. Akad.*, 1918, pp. 752 ff. (see below).

περιτυγχάνω and the relative clause ἐν οἷς κ.τ.λ. The clauses ἃ μὲν αὐτῶν κατέδυσεν, ἃ δὲ κατήγαγεν εἰς τὴν πόλιν, are an imitation of 93.2, ἃ μὲν βυθίζειν τῶν ἁλισκομένων πλοίων, ἃ δὲ κατάγειν εἰς τὴν πόλιν. Diodorus sometimes repeats himself by expressing an order and its fulfilment in the same words (compare for example xix.83.3 and 84.1). 93.5: τεχνῖται τῶν ἀξιολόγων πρὸς βέλη. Contrast P's πολλούς τε βελέων δημιοργούς. Diodorus characteristically enhances the merits of the engineers: ἀξιόλογος is found *passim* in the *Bibliotheke*. For the construction, cf. xx.92.3, τοὺς ἀφικνουμένους τῶν ξένων. The καταπελταφέται are also made more interesting by the addition τῶν ἐμπειρίᾳ διαφερόντων: for this formula cf. xviii.10.4, συνέσει διαφέροντες, xix.40.2, ἀνδρείᾳ διαφέρων, xviii.13.6. συνέσει στρατηγικῇ καὶ ἀνδρείᾳ διαφέρων, etc.

xx.94.1: Δημητρίου δὲ διὰ τῶν μεταλλέων ὑπορύξαντος τὸ τεῖχος. P has only Δημητρίου τὰ Ῥοδίων τείχεα ὑπορύσσοντος. Diodorus may have added the prepositional phrase: cf. xviii.8.5, διὰ τὴν χαρὰν ἠμείβοντο τὴν εὐεργεσίαν, xix.93.2, διὰ τῶν σκόπων ἀκούσας, etc.

ibid.: τῶν αὐτομόλων τις ἐμήνυσε τοῖς πολιορκουμένοις ὡς οἱ ταῖς ὑπονομαῖς χρώμενοι σχεδὸν ἐντός εἰσι τοῦ τείχους. Compare P lines 16–18, μηνυσάντων αὐτομόλων τὸ γεινόμενον τόν τε χῶρον τὸν ὑπορυσσόμενον ὑποδεξάντων. Diodorus has a more personal form of expression with τις and οἵ for his main subjects; he also uses a characteristic periphrasis with χρῆσθαι: cf. i.1.4, 4.2.

xx.94.2: Diodorus clarifies the sense with διόπερ; P's sentence is unbroken. οἱ Ῥόδιοι τάφρον ὀρύξαντες βαθεῖαν: cf. P. line 19 (Ῥόδιοί τε) διορύξαντες ἐς τὠυτόν. The clauses παράλληλον . . . τείχει and διεκώλυσαν . . . πορείας also amplify the sense of P, and in each clause Diodorus adds an attributive phrase: τῷ δοκοῦντι πεσεῖσθαι (sc.τείχει), and εἰς τοὔμπροσθεν. The emphatic use of αὐτός (καὶ αὐτοί) is not in P.

Ibid.: ταῖς μεταλλείαις χρώμενοι. The periphrastic construction with χρῆσθαι is repeated from 94.1—ταῖς ὑπονομαῖς χρώμενοι. The sense is repeated from 94.1—διὰ τῶν μεταλλέων. Diodorus uses μεταλλεία (as at 94.1, μεταλλεύς) instead of the unusual word μεταλλωρύχος in P (the latter a *hapax legomenon*).

xx.94.3: . . . Ἀθηναγόραν. οὗτος δ'ἦν Μιλήσιος μὲν τὸ γένος. Cf. P. lines 26–7, Ἀθηναγόρης γάρ τις Μιλήσιος. Diodorus' new sentence, opening with the demonstrative and a finite verb, is more emphatic. The accusative of respect using γένος, φύσις, etc. is common throughout Diodorus: cf. xi.8.5, 50.6, 69.1, 78.5, 86.4; xvii.67.4, 68.5, 20.2, 69.3, 72.2, 74.5, 77.1, 79.1, 95.1, 100.2; xviii.20.1, 67.4. For P's ἀποσταλείς he has ἐξαπεσταλμένος.

xx.94.4: τινα ἀξιολόγων ἡγεμόνων. P line 31, στρατὸν ἀντίπαλον. Cf. e.g. Diod. xviii.40.2, τινος τῶν ἐπιφανῶν ἡγεμόνων; and for ἀξιόλογος cf. 93.5 and note.

Ibid.: διὰ τοῦ ὀρύγματος εἰς τὴν πόλιν. Contrast P line 31, ἐς τὸ ἄστυ.

For Diodorus' addition διὰ τοῦ ὀρύγματος cf. 94.5, διὰ τῆς διώρυχος. P's ἄστυ is certainly correct as against Diodorus' πόλιν: Demetrius would not have opened his attack by land with an assault on the acropolis itself. Diodorus has used πόλις under the influence of εἰς τὴν πόλιν at 93.2 and 93.5.

xx.94.5: εἰς ἐλπίδας δὲ μεγάλας ἀγαγών. An allusion to the oath-giving which is described in P but omitted altogether from Diodorus' account. For the phrase, cf. xix.46.3, μεγάλας ὑπογραφόντων ἐλπίδας.

Ibid.: τοῦτον μὲν ἀναβάντα διὰ τῆς διώρυχος. Diodorus adds the demonstrative τοῦτον, and the prepositional phrase: the latter recalls διὰ τοῦ ὀρύγματος at 94.4. The verb συνέλαβον is weaker that P's ἐνεχείρισεν.

Ibid.: ἐστεφάνωσαν χρυσῷ στεφάνῳ καὶ δωρεὰν ἔδωκαν ἀργυρίου τάγαντα πέντε. δίδωμι with the cognate accusative is regular in Diodorus: cf. xi.8.1, δωρεὰς ἀξιολόγους δώσει; xx.34.1, δωρεὰς ἀξιολόγους δώσειν. The formula here supplements P's ἐστεφάνωσαν . . . ἀργυρίου ταλάντοισι πέντε. But comparison with the formulae of other Rhodian documents shows that P's source and P have transcribed the decree correctly: Diodorus has made an unnecessary 'improvement': cf. Larfeld, *Gr. Epig*, p. 382, para. 228.

Ibid.: σπεύδοντες καὶ τῶν ἄλλων μισθοφόρων καὶ ξένων ἐκκαλεῖσθαι τὴν πρὸς τὸν δῆμον εὔνοιαν. Larfeld, *Gr. Epig.*, pp. 380 f. gives many examples of the 'Zweckformel' following directly upon the account of the honours in honorary decrees; but all his examples begin with ἵνα or ὅπως, leading to a subjunctive verb; so that both Diodorus' σπεύδοντες and P's ἅμα, if this word is correctly restored, appear to deviate from the normal formula. Hiller von Gaertringen suggested that the word ἐκκαλεῖσθαι in Diodorus and P, introducing the formula of exhortation, might be 'ein Charakteristikum der rhodischen Volkesbeschlüsse'.[14] He compared the similar expressions at Diod. xx.84.4 and Polybius xvi.9.5 in the context of Rhodian public decrees. However, the formula is also characteristic of Diodorus himself: cf. xiv.42.1, 44.3; xvi.37.4; xviii.19.5; xix.21.3, 24.4, 79.7, 91.2; and above p. 270. The fact that it occurs not only outside Book xx, but also outside xviii and xix, shows that this is not a phrase Diodorus has picked up from his source and used over a limited section only. If Hiller's guess is right, this is a coincidence between a Diodoran cliché and a Rhodian documentary formula; but it has not yet appeared on a Rhodian inscription.

Direct comparison between Diodorus and his main source for xviii–xx as yet eludes us, for the common source of Diodorus and P was almost certainly not Hieronymus but a working over of Hieronymus by a (second-century?) Rhodian historian: hence comparison between

---

[14] Hiller von Gaertringen, op. cit., p. 759.

the language of Diodorus and that of P is still at more than one remove from the original. Indeed, in some places it is evident that it is not Diodorus who has added material, but P who has omitted it: for example, Diod. xx.93.5, τὰ πρὸς μηχανὰς ἁρμόζοντα, can be explained by the first draft of P, ὄργανα πρὸς τὴν πολιορκίην τὴν τῶν πολίων φερόμενα, which he later erased. Sometimes Diodorus has kept an unusual word or phrase: 93.5, ἐπὶ νήσων, as at P, lines 3–4, without the definite article; and ibid., the technical word καταπελταφέται. Both are very Rhodian expressions, and suggestive of a Rhodian source.[15] However, the general technique of substituting the more for the less common expression, and of diluting language by means of prepositions, demonstratives, and all sorts of periphrasis, is apparent here as it is in Book iii where Photius/Agatharchides is the control. Diodorus shows the tendency to repeat himself, observed in the *Hauptproem* and elsewhere in xviii–xx; and almost every clause in these two chapters can be paralleled in other parts of the *Bibliotheke*.

DIODORUS' LANGUAGE OF PERSONAL DESCRIPTION

This aspect of Diodorus' style illustrates a further problem in isolating the language of his source, for his descriptions of historical figures are the product of the rhetorical school, and with few exceptions are highly conventionalized.

The finite verb and complement is not uncommon: e.g. xi.67.4, ἦν γὰρ καὶ φιλάργυρος καὶ βίαιος (Hieron); xiii.66.6, ἦν γὰρ ὁ Κλέαρχος χαλεπός; xv.19.4, ὁ δ᾽ Ἀγησίλαος . . . φιλοπόλεμος ἦν; xviii.33.3, καὶ γὰρ φονικὸς ἦν (Perdiccas); xx.92.4, ἐνεργὸς ἦν καὶ νήφων (Demetrius).

More often he uses some periphrasis with a stock noun or adjective. The use of φύσει, or τὴν φύσιν, with a participal from εἰμί (e.g. ii.7.2, Ἡ δὲ Σεμίραμις, οὖσα φύσει μεγαλεπίβολος), or of hyperbolic phrases like διὰ τὴν ἰδίαν ἀνδρείαν, διὰ τήν ὑπερβολὴν τῆς εὐσεβείας (cf. xii.50.1; v.7.7, etc.), or of διαφέρω with the dative, or θαυμαζόμενος, διαβεβοημένος with ἐπί, κατά, or the dative (e.g. i.94.3, Σάσυχιν, ἄνδρα συνέσει διαφέροντα; ii.33.1, Παρσώνδην τὴν Πέρσην, θαυμαζόμενον ἐπὶ ἀνδρείᾳ καὶ συνέσει καὶ ταῖς ἄλλαις ἀρεταῖς), provided Diodorus with formulae which are endlessly repeated throughout his work. The legendary founders of the Egyptian and Assyrian kingdoms, gods and demigods, women, and the historical characters of Greece and Persia, are all characterized by the same stock epithets. Strong men excel in σώματος ῥώμη, good men are outstanding in φιλανθρωπία and ἐπιείκεια, generals in στρατηγικὴ σύνεσις, soldiers in εὐχειρία and ἀνδραγαθία; tyrants are βίαιοι and ὑπερήφανοι, the reckless and ambitious are φρονήματος πληρεῖς or μεγαλεπίβολοι. These stereotyped heroes and villains were required

---

[15] See ch. 2, p. 57. Cf. Diod. xx.93.2: ναῦς τὰς καλουμένας παρὰ Ῥοδίοις φυλακίδας.

by Diodorus' didactic purpose. 'Throughout our entire history,' he says, 'we have made it our practice in the case of good men to enhance their glory by means of the words of praise we pronounce over them, and in the case of bad men, when they die, to utter the appropriate obloquies.' (xi.46.1: the statement is prompted by the κακία and προδοσία of Pausanias). The figures of myth and legend in the early books are necessarily conventional, being artificially constructed; but Diodorus makes no serious attempt of his own at the characterization even of historical figures. This was the consequence partly of his desire to be instructive, and partly of a rhetorical training. In some cases the tradition on an individual may have been inadequate;[16] but it cannot be supposed that all his sources were deficient in this respect.

The process by which he transformed the language of his source can occasionally be detected. Agatharchides, otherwise our most important control source, is not illuminating here, because his subject-matter is purely ethnographic; the papyrus fragment of Ephorus, however, suggests the sort of technique which Diodorus used.[17] In lines 27-31, Ephorus' σο[φωτάτην καὶ δικαι]οτά[την . . .]τα[τ]η[ν] κ[αὶ/χαλεπ]ώτατ/ην, [γενομένη]ν πρὸς/ἐκε[ῖνον], (discussing Athens' treatment of Themistocles), becomes in Diodorus (xi.59.3), σοφωτάτην καὶ ἐπιεικεστάτην χαλεπωτάτην πρὸς ἐκεῖνον εὑρίσκομεν γεγενημένην. Ephorus had balanced two contrasting pairs of adjectives; Diodorus has destroyed the balance by omitting one of the second pair, and has substituted ἐπιεικεστάτη for Ephorus' δικαιοτάτη: ἐπιεικής was one of his favourite words.[18] The method of abbreviation suggests that Diodorus had evolved a 'code' of description. There is no fundamental difference between the diction of Diodorus and that of his Hellenistic sources, except that Diodorus confines himself to a limited and monotonous selection. Hence the language of his sources is translated into set formulae of his own; and while these formulae represent something said in the same sense by his source, they inevitably weaken the force of the original.

A one to one relation between a 'code' word in Diodorus and a word in his source cannot, of course, be assumed. Diodorus may anticipate, repeat, or make explicit a characteristic deducible from the narrative. For example, he anticipates his estimate of Epaminondas (xv.88) before describing the rise of Thebes (xv.39.3), concluding with a remark in the first person which suggests independence of his source.

---

[16] Cf. L. Pearson, *Journ. Hist. Ideas*, xv, no. 1 (1954), pp. 136 ff. suggesting that lack of information about individuals, rather than lack of interest in them, was a major reason for the poor characterization of many historical personalities by ancient historians. Hence they were often treated in the same way as mythological characters, sometimes, like Solon, becoming the symbol of a particular ideal.

[17] Cf. ch. 2, pp. 28 f.

[18] Diodorus' fondness for the word ἐπιεικής is unusual: it occurs only seven times in Polybius, and only three times of a person in a moral sense. Cf. A. Mauersberger, *Polybios-Lexicon*, s.v. ἐπιεικής.

Similarly in Book xix he gives a brief sketch of Phila, while looking forward to a later point in his narrative where her character will be more fully revealed.[19] Cases where Diodorus singles out a minor character are perhaps to be explained in the same way. At xix.48.2, the previously unknown Evagoras is singled out from Antigonus' satraps as ἄνδρα . . . κατ᾽ ἀνδρείαν καὶ σύνεσιν θαυμαζόμενον—a regular formula in the Diodoran code. Such formulae were not distributed at random, however. At xix.92.4 Evager (*sic*), evidently the same man, appears as commander of the Persian contingent which resisted Seleucus on his return to Babylon.[20] Evidently Diodorus knew when he first mentioned Evagoras that this satrap was to play a more important role later in his history. Conversely, there are cases of repetition, where Diodorus became obsessed with a certain epithet: Agesilaus is described as δραστικός three times within fourteen chapters;[21] Gelon is always ἐπιεικής, even in allusions to him after his death. The dominant qualities of these men, which Diodorus was so eager to underline, may have been mentioned only once or twice by his source.

These limitations in his manner of expression have to be taken into account in considering Diodorus' descriptions of the Diadochi. Even the best epitomizer finds it difficult to remove all traces of a historical portrait which is implicit in the narrative of a man's actions and the general slant of the history, and Diodorus could not help preserving indirect characterization, embedded in Hieronymus' account of the Successors.[22] Direct description, on the other hand, has to be treated with reservation. In many cases, while doubtless it reflects the substance of Hieronymus' words, it may have been transformed into the terms of Diodorus' own 'code'. We can only feel confident that a word was used by Hieronymus if it appears in exactly the same context in another author, or if it is used consistently by all authors as the epithet of one man. However, the fact that Diodorus copied Ephorus' assessment of Themistocles must influence our view of those extended passages in Books xviii, xix, and xx where individuals are characterized directly, and the motives of action analysed: in these passages it is possible that Diodorus was reproducing his source with few alterations.

[19] Diod. xix.59.6.
[20] In 316 Antigonus made Evagoras satrap of Aria, and Asclepiodotus satrap of Persis; but Asclepiodotus is not heard of again, and may have died or been removed. The temporary re-allocation of a province to a neighbouring satrap under such circumstances was not uncommon: cf. Tarn, *Alex. Gt.* ii, App. 7, pp. 310 ff.
[21] Diodorus' use of the word δραστικός is peculiar. It is not found in Polybius. Usually it refers to the active or efficient element of something, and as a medical term means 'drastic'. Cf. Plut. *Coriol.* xxi. 2, though there too the word is virtually technical.
[22] Cf. ch. 5, p. 215.

P. Berl. 11632 and Diodorus xx.93–4

The following text is reproduced from Hiller von Gaertringen, 'Aus der Belagerung von Rhodos 304 v. Chr.', *Sitzungs Berichte der Preussischen Akademie* xxxvi (1918), pp. 755 f., by kind permission of the Akademie der Wissenschaften der D.D.R.

- - ‖[1] [. . . . β]ΑϹΙΛΙΚΟΙ̑ϹΙ ΓᾺΡ

ἐΟΎϹΙ ΧΡΈ[2][ΕϹΘΑΙ ΟΥ̑] ϹΦΙϹΙΝ

Η̑Ν. Κ[Α]ὶ ΤᾺ ΜὲΝ ΟΥ̑[3][ΤΩϹ Ἐ-

ΠΡΗΞΑ]Ν. Ἀμύντηϲ Δὲ ΠΛΈΩΝ

ἐπὶ [4][ΝΗϹΩ]Ν ΚΑΤΑΠΕΛΤΑΦΈΤΑϹ

ἔΝΔΕΚΑ ΠΡὸϹ ΤῊΝ ΠΟΛΙΟΡΚΙ-

[5][ΗΝ ΤῊΝ ΤΩ̑Ν] ΠΟΛΊΩΝ Δ ΗΜΗ-

ΤΡΊΩΙ [6][ϹΤΕΛΛΟΜΈΝΟ]ΥϹ ΑΙ̑ΡΕΕ

ΠΟΛΛΟΎϹ ΤΕ ΒΕΛΈΩΝ ΔΗ[7][ΜΙ-

ΟΡΓΟΎ]Ϲ. ΟΥ̑ϹΠΕΡ Δ ΗΜΗΤΡΊΩΙ

ΛΥΟΜΈ[8][ΝΩΙ ΛΎΤ]ΡΩΝ ΤΩ̑Ν ΤΕ-

ΤΑΓΜΈΝΩΝ Ῥ[9][Ό]ΔΙΟΙ ΟΥ̓Κ Ἀ̓-

ΠΕΔΊΔΟϹΑΝ, ΧΡΕΊΖΕΙΝ ΑΥ̓ΤΩ̑Ν

[10][ΦΆϹΚΟΝΤΕϹ]· ὁ Δὲ ΤΩ̑ΝΔΕ

ἈΠΑΜΑΡΤ[Ὼ]Ν [11][ΟΥ̓Δ᾽ ΑΥ̓ΤΌϹ]

ϹΦΙϹΙΝ ἜΦΗ ΛΎϹΕΙΝ ἜΤΙ, Η̑Ν

[12][ἜΛΗΙ. ΜΕΤᾺ] Δὲ ΤΑΥ̑ΤΑ Δ Η-

ΜΗΤΡΊΟΥ ΤᾺ Ῥο[13][Δίων Τ]ΕΊΧΕΑ

ὙΠΟΡΎϹϹΟΝΤΟϹ ἐΝ [14][ΤΌϹ ΤΕ

Τ]Ω̑Ν ΤΕΙΧΈΩΝ ᾔΔΗ ἐΌΝΤΩΝ

[15][ΤΩ̑Ν ΚΑΤ]ὰ Γῆϲ ἜΡΓ[ΑΖ]Ο-

ΜΈΝΩΝ, ῬόΔΙ[16][Οί ΤΕ, ΜΗΝΥ-

Ϲ]ΆΝΤΩΝ ΑΥ̓ΤΟΜΌΛΩΝ Τὸ [17][ΓΕΙ-

ΝΌΜ]ΕΝΟΝ ΤΌΝ ΤΕ ΧΩ̑ΡΟΝ

ΤὸΝ [18][Ὺ̓ΠΟΡΥ]ϹϹΌΜΕΝΟΝ Ὺ̓ΠΟ-

ΔΕΞΆΝΤΩ(Ν), [19][ΔΙΟΡΎΞΑ]ΝΤΕϹ

ἐϲ ΤΩΥΤὸΝ ΤΟΙ̑[20][ϹΙ ΜΑΚΕ-

Δ]ΌΝΩΝ ΜΕΤΑΛΛΩΡΎΧΟΙϹΙ(Ν)

[21][Ὺ̓ΠΗΝΤΊ]ΑϹΑΝ ΟἸ̑ ΤΕ Ὺ̓ΠΌΝΟ-

ΜΟΙ ΠΑ[22][Ρὰ ΜΙΚΡὸ]Ν ἐϲ ΤΩΥ-

ΤὸΝ ϹΥΝΕΜΙΞΑΝ ἈΛΛΉΛΟΙϹΙ(Ν).

[23][ἜΡΓΟΥ Δ᾽ ἐ]ΚΑΤΈΡΩΝ ΤΟΥ̓

ϹΦΕΤΈΡΟΥ ΦΎΛΑ[24][ΚΑϹ ἐΠΙϹΤΗ-

Ϲά]ΝΤΩΝ, ἈΛΛΉΛΟΙϹΊ .ΤΕ ΤΩ̑Ν

Diodor XX 93, 2. ἐξέπεμψαν δὲ καὶ τῶν νεῶν ἐννέα (Ῥόδιοι), διακελευσάμενοι τοὺς ἀφηγουμένους πανταχῇ πλεῖν καὶ παραδόξως ἐπιφαινομένους ἃ μὲν βυθίζειν τῶν ἁλισκομένων πλοίων, ἃ δὲ κατάγειν εἰς τὴν πόλιν. ἐκπλευσάντων δὲ τούτων καὶ τριχῇ διαιρεθέντων Δαμόφιλος μὲν ἔχων ναῦς τὰς καλουμένας παρὰ Ῥοδίοις φυλακίδας ἔπλευσεν εἰς Κάρπαθον - - (3) Μενέδημος δὲ τριῶν ἀφηγούμενος τριημιολιῶν πλεύσας τῆς Λυκίας ἐπὶ τὰ Πάταρα - - (4) εἷλε δὲ καὶ τετρήρη πλέουσαν μὲν ἐκ Κιλικίας ἔχουσαν δ᾽ ἐσθῆτα βασιλικὴν καὶ τὴν ἄλλην ἀποσκευήν, ἣν ἡ γυνὴ Δημητρίου Φίλα παρασκευασαμένη φιλοτιμότερον ἀπέσταλκει τἀνδρί. τὸν μὲν οὖν ἱματισμὸν ἀπέστειλεν εἰς Αἴγυπτον, οὐσῶν τῶν στολῶν ἀλουργῶν καὶ βασιλεῖ φορεῖν πρεπουσῶν - - (5) τῶν δ᾽ ὑπολοίπων νεῶν τριῶν Ἀμύντας ἡγούμενος ἔπλευσεν ἐπὶ νήσων καὶ πολλοῖς πλοίοις περιτυχὼν κομίζουσι τὰ πρὸς τὰς μηχανὰς ἁρμόζοντα τοῖς πολεμίοις ἃ μὲν αὐτῶν ἱμῆν κατέδυσεν, ἃ δὲ κατήγαγεν εἰς τὴν πόλιν, ἐν οἷς ἑάλωσαν καὶ τεχνῖται τῶν ἀξιολόγων καὶ πρὸς βέλη καὶ καταπέλτας ἐμπειρίᾳ διαφέροντες ἔνδεκα (τῶν ἀξιολόγων πρὸς βέλη καὶ καταπελταφέτας [corr. 2.m] τῶν ἐμπειρίᾳ διαφερόντων ἔνδεκα F).

(6. 7 Protokoll einer rhodischen Volksversammlung; nicht im Papyrus berücksichtigt.)

Diodor XX 84. 6 συνέθεντο γὰρ οἱ Ῥόδιοι πρὸς τὸν Δημήτριον ὥστε ἀλλήλοις διδόναι λύτρον ἐλευθέρου μὲν χιλίας δραχμάς, δούλου δὲ πεντακοσίας.

Diodor XX 94. 1. Δημητρίου δὲ διὰ τῶν μεταλλέων ὑπορύξαντος τὸ τεῖχος τῶν αὐτομόλων τις ἐμήνυσε τοῖς πολιορκουμένοις ὡς οἱ ταῖς ὑπονομαῖς χρώμενοι σχεδὸν ἐντός εἰσι τοῦ τείχους.

(2) διόπερ οἱ Ῥόδιοι τάφρον ὀρύξαντες βαθεῖαν, παράλληλον τῷ δοκοῦντι πεσεῖσθαι τείχει, ταχὺ καὶ αὐτοὶ ταῖς μεταλλείαις χρώμενοι συνῆψαν ὑπὸ γῆν τοῖς ἐναντίοις καὶ διεκώλυσαν τὰς εἰς τοὔμπροσθεν πορείας. (3) τῶν δὲ διορυγμάτων παρ᾽ ἀμφοτέροις τηρουμένων ἐπεχείρησάν τινες τῶν παρὰ τοῦ Δημητρίου διαφθείρειν χρήμασι τὸν τεταγμένον ἐπὶ τῆς

ΦΥΛΆΚΩΝ ἐϹ ΛΌΓΟΥϹ ἈΠῸ ΤῶΝ
ΠΡΟΤΕΙΧΙϹΜΆΤ(ΩΝ) ἈΠΙΚΝΕΟ-
Μ(ΈΝ)ΩΝ, ΠΡΟΔΟϹΊΗ ‖ ²⁵ΤΙϹ   **II**
ΔΗΜΗΤΡΊΩΙ ΔΌΞΑϹΑ [ἈϹΦΑΛῊϹ
ΚΆΡΤΑ] ²⁶ΜΙΝ ἨΠΆΤΗϹΕΝ. ἈθΗ-
ΝΑΓΌΡΗ[Ϲ] Γ[ἀΡ] ²⁷ΤΙϹ ΜΙΛΉ-
ϹΙΟϹ [ἈΠΟϹΤΑΛΕῚϹ ἐΞ ΑἸΓΎ]-
²⁸ΠΤΟΥ ῾ΡΟ[ΔΊΟΙϹΙ, ΤῊΝ ΤΟῦ
ΤΕΊΧΕΟϹ ΦΥ]²⁹ΛΑΚῊΝ ἔΧῼ[Ν,
ΔΗΜΗΤΡΊΩΙ ἐΠῚ] ³⁰ΧΡΉΜΑϹΙΝ
ὠΜ[Ο]ΛΌΓΗϹΕΝ [ΠΑΡΕϹ]³¹ΆΞΕΙΝ
ϹΤΡΑΤῸΝ ἈΝΤΊΠΑΛΟΝ ἐϹ ΤῸ
ἌϹΤΥ· ὍΡΚΙΑ ΔῈ ἐ³²ΠῚ ΤΟῖϹΙΔΕ
ΔΟΎϹ ΤΕ ΚΑῚ ΛΑ[ΒῺΝ, ΕὐθῈϹ]
³³ΔῈ ϹΗΜΉΝΑϹ ΤΟῖϹΙ ῾ΡΟ[ΔΊΩΝ
ἌΡΧΟΥ]³⁴ϹΙ, ΝΥΚΤῸϹ ΤῆϹ ἐΠΙ-
ΓΕΙΝΟ[ΜΈΝΗϹ] ΠΑΛΙΜΠΡΟΔΟϹΊΗΝ
ἐΡΓΆ[ΖΕΤΑΙ·] ³⁵ἐϹΑΓΑΓῺΝ ΓΑΡ
(Rasur) [ἈΛΈΞΑΝ]³⁶ΔΡΟΝ ἌΝ-
ΔΡΑ ΜΑΚΕΔΌΝΑ [ΤῶΝ ἈΜ]³⁷ΦῚ
ΔΗΜΉΤΡΙΟΝ ἐΌΝΤΩΝ [ΤᾺ ἔΝ]-
³⁸ΔΟΝ ΠΡῸ ΤΟῦ ΠΕΜΦθῆΝΑΙ[ἰ
ΜΕΤᾺ] ³⁹ϹΤΡΑΤΟῦ ΚΑΤΟΥΌΜΕ-
ΝΟΝ ῾ΡΟ[ΔΊΟΙϹΊ] ⁴⁰ΜΙΝ ἐΝΕΧΕΊ-
ΡΙϹΕΝ. ῾ΡΌΔΙΟ[Ι ΔῈ ΤῸΝ ⁴¹ΜῈΝ
ἈθΗΝΑΓΌΡΗΝ [ἐϹΤΕΦΆΝΩϹΑΝ]
⁴²Χ[ΡΥϹ]ΈῼΙ ΤΕ ϹΤΕΦ[ΆΝΩΙ ΚΑῚ
ἈΡΓΥ]⁴³ΡΊΟΥ ΤΑΛΆΝΤΟΙϹΙ ΠΈΝ-
Τ[Ε, ἅΜΑ ΤΟῖϹΊ]⁴⁴ΔΕ ΤΟῪϹ ἌΛ-
ΛΟΥϹ ΞΈ[ΝΟΥϹ ΠΡῸϹ] ⁴⁵ΤᾺ ὅ-
ΜΟΙΑ ἐΚΚΑΛΕΌΜΕ[ΝΟΙ· ΤῸΝ ΔῈ]
⁴⁶ἈΛΈΞΑΝΔΡΟΝ ΚΤΕΊΝΕΙΝ Μ[ΈΛ-
ΛΟΝΤΕϹ Ἀ]⁴⁷ΠΕΤΡΆΠΟΝΤΟ ΚΉ-
ΡΥΚΟϹ [ΠΑΡᾺ ΔΗΜΗ]⁴⁸ΤΡΊΟΥ
ΕἼϹΩ ΚΑΤᾺ ΛΎΤΡΩ[ϹΙΝ] ἈΠΙΚΟ-
ΜΈΝ[ΟΥ - - - -] ‖ - -

ΦΥΛΑΚῆϹ ὙΠῸ ΤῶΝ ῾ΡΟΔΊΩΝ Ἀθ ΗΝΑΓΌΡΑΝ· ΟὖΤΟϹ Δ᾽ ἦΝ
ΜΙΛΉϹΙΟϹ ΜῈΝ ΤῸ ΓΈΝΟϹ, ὙΠῸ ΠΤΟΛΕΜΑΊΟΥ Δ᾽ ἐΞΑ-
ΠΕϹΤΑΛΜΈΝΟϹ ἩΓΕΜῺΝ ΤῶΝ ΜΙϹθΟΦΌΡΩΝ. (4) ἐΠΑΓΓΕΙ-
ΛΆΜΕΝΟϹ ΔῈ ΠΡΟΔΏϹΕΙΝ ϹΥΝΕΤΆΞΑθ᾽ ἩΜΈΡΑΝ ΚΑθ᾽ ἣΝ
ἔΔΕΙ ΠΑΡᾺ ΔΗΜΗΤΡΊΟΥ ΠΕΜΦθῆΝΑΊ ΤΙΝΑ ΤῶΝ ἈΞΙΟ-
ΛΌΓΩΝ ἩΓΕΜΌΝΩΝ ΤῸΝ ΝΥΚΤῸϹ ἈΝΑΒΗϹΌΜΕΝΟΝ ΔΙᾺ ΤΟῦ
ὈΡΎΓΜΑΤΟϹ ΕἰϹ ΤῊΝ ΠΌΛΙΝ, ὅΠΩϹ ΚΑΤΑϹΚΈΥΗΤΑΙ ΤῸΝ
ΤΌΠΟΝ ΤῸΝ ΜΈΛΛΟΝΤΑ ΔΈΞΑϹθΑΙ ΤΟῪϹ ϹΤΡΑΤΙΏΤΑϹ.

(5) ΕἰϹ ἐΛΠΊΔΑϹ ΔῈ ΜΕΓΆΛΑϹ ἈΓΑΓῺΝ ΤΟῪϹ ΠΕΡῚ
ΔΗΜΉΤΡΙΟΝ ἐΜΉΝΥϹΕ Τῇ ΒΟΥΛῇ· ΚΑῚ ΠΈΜΨΑΝΤΟϹ ΤΟῦ
ΒΑϹΙΛΈΩϹ ΤῶΝ ΠΕΡῚ ΑὐΤῸΝ ΦΊΛΩΝ ἈΛΈΞΑΝΔΡΟΝ ΤῸΝ
ΜΑΚΕΔΌΝΑ ΤΟῦΤΟΝ ΜῈΝ ἈΝΑΒΆΝΤΑ ΔΙᾺ Τῆ Ϲ ΔΙΏΡΥΧΟϹ
ϹΥΝΈΛΑΒΟΝ Οἱ ῾ΡΌΔΙΟΙ, ΤῸΝ Δ᾽ Ἀθ ΗΝΑΓΌΡΑΝ ἐϹΤΕΦΆ-
ΝΩϹΑΝ ΧΡΥϹῷ ϹΤΕΦΆΝῼ ΚΑῚ ΔΩΡΕᾺΝ ἔΔΩΚΑΝ ἈΡΓΥΡΊΟΥ
ΤΆΛΑΝΤΑ ΠΈΝΤΕ, ϹΠΕΎΔΟΝΤΕϹ ΚΑῚ ΤῶΝ ἌΛΛΩΝ ΜΙϹθΟ-
ΦΌΡΩΝ ΚΑῚ ΞΈΝΩΝ ἐΚΚΑΛΕῖϹθΑΙ ΤῊΝ ΠΡῸϹ ΤῸΝ ΔῆΜΟΝ
ΕὔΝΟΙΑΝ.

Select Bibliography

AFRICA, T. W., *Phylarchus and the Spartan Revolution*, Berkeley, 1961.

ANDERSON, J. K., *Military Theory and Practice in the Age of Xenophon*, Berkeley, 1970.

BABELON, E., *Les Perses Achéménides*, Paris, 1893.

BAKHUIZEN, S. C., *Salganeus and the Fortifications on its Mountains, Chalcidian Studies*, ii, Groningen, 1970.

BARBER, G. L., *The Historian Ephorus*, Cambridge, 1935.

BARTOLETTI, V., 'Framento di Storia dei Diadochi (Arriano?); *Papiri della Societa Italiana*, xii.2 (1951), no. 1284, pp. 158 ff.

BAUMBACH, A., *Kleinasien unter Alexander dem Grossen*, Iena, 1911.

BELOCH, K. J., *Griechische Geschichte²*, vols. i–iv, Berlin–Leipzig, 1914–27.

BENGTSON, H., *Die Strategie in der hellenistischen Zeit*, vols. i–ii, München, 1964.

BERVE, H., *Das Alexanderreich auf prosopographischer Grundlage*, vols. i–ii, München, 1926.

——, *Die Tyrannis bei der Griechen*, vols. i–ii, München, 1967.

BEVAN, E. R., *The House of Seleucus*, vols. i–ii, London, 1902.

BILABEL, F., 'Die kleineren Historikerfragmente auf Papyrus', no. 8, p. 20, in *Kleine Texte für Vorlesungen und Übungen*, ed. Lietzmann, 149, Bonn, 1922.

BIZIÈRE. F., *Diodore de Sicile, Bibliothèque Historique, Livre XIX*, edition and French translation (Budé), Paris, 1975.

BOARDMAN, J.: see Kurtz and Boardman.

BOTTIN, C., 'Les sources de Diodore de Sicile pour l'histoire de Pyrrhus, des successeurs d'Alexandre le Grand et d'Agathocle', *Revue Belge de philologie*, vii (1928), pp. 1307 ff.

BOUCHÉ-LECLERQ, A., *Histoire des Lagides*, vols. i–iv, Paris, 1903–7.

BREITENBACH, H. R. H., *Historiographische Anschauungsformen Xenophons*, Freiburg, 1950.

BRIANT, P., 'D'Alexandre le Grand aux Diadoques: le cas d'Eumène de Cardia', *Revue des études anciennes*, lxxiv (1972), pp. 32 ff. and lxxv (1973), pp. 43 ff.

——, *Antigone le Borgne*, Paris, 1973.

BRISCOE, J., *The Antigonids and the Greek States,* in *Imperialism in the Ancient World*, ed. Garnsey and Whittaker, Cambridge, 1978.

BROWN, T. S., *Onesicritus, A Study in Hellenistic Historiography*, Berkeley, 1949.

——, 'Hieronymus of Cardia', *American Historical Review*, liii (1947), pp. 684 ff.

BRÜCKNER, C. A. F., 'De Vita et Scriptis Hieronymi Cardiani', *Zeitschrift für die Alterthumswissenschaft*, 1842, pp. 252 ff.

BRUNT, P. A., *Arrian, 'Anabasis Alexandri'*, Books i–iv, Loeb edition, vol. i, Harvard, 1976.

BURTON, A., *Diodorus Siculus; Book I: a commentary*, Leiden, 1972.

CONNOR, W. R., *Theopompus and Fifth Century Athens*, Harvard, 1968.

CRÖNERT, W., 'Kolotes und Menedemus', *Studien für Palaeographie und Papyruskunde*, Leipzig, 1906.

DE SANCTIS, G., 'Una lettera a Demetrio Poliorcete', *Rivista di Filologia* xi (1931), pp. 330 ff. = *Scritti Minori* i, Rome, 1966, pp. 345 ff.

——, 'Perdicca,' in *Problemi di Storia Antica*, Bari, 1932, pp. 137 ff.

DELEBECQUE, E., *Xenophon, de l'art équestre*, text, translation, and notes, Paris, 1950.

DETIENNE, M., and VERNANT, J. P., *Les Ruses de l'intelligence: la Métis des Grecs*, Paris, 1974, = *Cunning and Intelligence in Greek Culture and Society*, translated J. Lloyd, Harvester Press, 1978.

DIXON, N. F., *On the Psychology of Military Incompetence*, London, 1976.

DREWS, R., 'Diodorus and his Sources', *American Journal of Philology*, lxxxiii (1962), pp. 383 ff.

DROYSEN, J. G., *Geschichte des Hellenismus*[2], vols. i–iii, Gotha, 1877.

ERRINGTON, R. M., 'From Babylon to Triparadeisos, 323–320 B.C.', *Journal of Hellenic Studies* xc (1970), pp. 49 ff.

FELLMAN, W. E., *Antigonos Gonatas, König der Makedonen, und die griechischen Staaten*, Wurzburg, 1930.

FERGUSON, W. S., *Hellenistic Athens*, London, 1911.

FISCHER, C. T., *Diodorus Siculus*, Teubner edition, Stuttgart, 1964, vols. iv–v.

FONTANA, M. J., *Le lotte per la successione di Alessandro Magno*, Palermo, 1960.

FORBES, R. J., *Bitumen and Petroleum in Antiquity*, Leiden, 1936.

FRASER, P. M., *Ptolemaic Alexandria*, vols. i–ii, Oxford, 1972.

FRAZER, J. G., *Pausanias' Description of Greece*, vols. i–ii, London, 1898.

FURLANI, G., and MOMIGLIANO, A., 'La Cronaca Babilonese sui Diadochi', *Rivista di Filologia*, x (1932), pp. 462 ff.

GARLAN, Y., *Recherches de poliorcétique grecque*, Paris, 1974.

GEER, R., Diodorus Siculus, Loeb edition, vols. ix–xx, Harvard, 1962–9.

GLUECK, N., *Rivers of the Desert*, New York, 1959.

GOODENOUGH, E. R., 'The Political Philosophy of Hellenistic Kingship', *Yale Classical Studies* i (1928), pp. 55 ff.

GOUKOWSKY, P., *Diodore de Sicile, Bibliothèque Historique, Livre XVIII*, edition and French translation (Budé), Paris, 1979.

GRAMMAN, C., *Quaestiones Diodoreae*, Göttingen, 1907.

GRAYSON, C., 'Did Xenophon Intend to Write History?', in *The Ancient Historian and his Materials, Essays in Honour of C. E. Stevens*, ed. B. Levick, 1975, pp. 31 ff.

GRIFFITH, G. T., *Mercenaries of the Hellenistic World*, Cambridge, 1933.

—— (ed.), *Alexander the Great: The Main Problems*, Cambridge, 1966.

——: see Hammond and Griffith.

HAMILTON, J. R., *Plutarch, 'Alexander': a commentary*, Oxford, 1969.

HAMMOND N. G. L., 'The Sources of Diodorus Siculus xvi', *Classical Quarterly* xxxi (1937), pp. 79 ff., and xxxii (1938), pp. 137 ff.

—— and GRIFFITH, G. T., *A History of Macedonia*, vols. i–ii, Oxford, 1972 and 1979.

HAMMOND, P. C., *The Nabataeans*, Göteborg, 1973.

HAUBEN, H., *Callicrates of Samos*, Leuven, 1970.

HELLY, B., *Gonnoi*, vols. i–ii, Amsterdam, 1973.

HEUSS, A., 'Antigonos Monophthalmos und die griechische Städte', *Hermes* lxxiii (1938), pp. 133 ff.

HILLER, E., 'Hieronymi Rhodii Peripatetici Fragmenta', in *Satura Philologa Hermanno Sauppio*, Berlin, 1879, pp. 85 ff.

HILLER VON GAERTRINGEN, 'Aus der Belagerung von Rhodos 304 v. Chr.', *Sitzungsberichte der preussischen Akademie*, xxxvi (1918), pp. 752 ff.

HOFFMAN, W., 'Rom und die griechische Welt im 4 Jahrhundert', *Philologus*, Suppl. xxvii.1, (1934), pp. 1–144.

JACOBY, F., *Atthis, the Local Chronicles of Ancient Athens*, Oxford, 1949.

——, 'Die Beisetzungen Alexanders des Grossen', *Rheinisches Museum*, lviii (1903), pp. 461 f.

KAERST, J., 'Untersuchungen über Timagenes von Alexandria', *Philologus* lvi (1897), pp. 621 ff.

——, *Geschichte des hellenistischen Zeitalters*[2], vols. i–ii, Leipzig, 1926–7.

KALINKA, E., *Tituli Asiae Minoris*, Vindobonae, 1920–44.

KALLENBERG, H., 'Die Quellen für die Nachrichten der alten Historiker über die Diadochenkämpfe bis zum Tode des Eumenes und Olympias', *Philologus* xxxvi (1877), pp. 305 ff., 488 ff., 637 ff., and *Philologus* xxvii (1878), pp. 193 ff.

KLEINER, G., 'Diadochengräber', *Sitz. Wiss. Gesell. Johann Goethe*, i, Frankfurt-Main, 1963, pp. 71 ff.

KÖHLER, U., 'Über die Diadochengeschichte Arrians', *Sitzungsberichte der Berlin Akademie*, 1890, pp. 557 ff.

KRUMBHOLZ, P., 'Wiederholungen bei Diodor', *Rheinisches Museum*, xliv (1889), pp. 286 f.

KUNZ, M., *Zur Beurteilung der Prooemien in Diodors Bibliothek*, Zurich, 1935.

KURTZ, D., and BOARDMAN, J., *Greek Burial Customs*, London, 1971.

LANCKORONSKI, K., and PETERSEN, E., *Städte Pamphyliens und Pisidiens*, vols. i–ii, Wien, 1892.

LAUNEY, M., *Recherches sur les armées hellénistiques*, vols. i–ii, Paris, 1949–50.

LEO, F., *Die griechische-römische Biographie nach ihrer literarischen Form*, Leipzig, 1901.

LÉVÊQUE, P., *Pyrrhos*, Paris, 1957.

LUCAS, A., *Ancient Egyptian Materials and Industries*[4] (ed. Harris), London, 1962.

MACURDY, G. H., *Hellenistic Queens*, Baltimore, 1932.

MARSDEN, E., *Greek and Roman Artillery*, vols. i–ii, Oxford, 1969–71.

MAUERSBERGER, A., *Polybios-Lexicon*, Bd. I, Lieferung 1–4, Berlin, 1956–75.

MAZZARINO, S., *Il Pensiero Storico*, vols. i–ii, Bari, 1966.

MERKELBACH, R., *Die Quellen des griechischen Alexanderromans*, München, 1954.

MEYER, E., *Geschichte des Königsreichs Pontos*, Leipzig, 1879.

MISCH, G., *A History of Autobiography in Antiquity*, vol. i, translated Dickes, London, 1950.

MOMIGLIANO, A.: see Furlani and Momigliano.

MOMIGLIANO, A., *The Development of Greek Biography*, Harvard, 1971.

——, *Alien Wisdom*, Cambridge, 1976.

MORETTI, L., *Iscrizione storiche ellenistiche*, vol. ii, Florence, 1975.

MÜLLER, O., *Antigonos Monophthalmos und 'das Jahr der Könige'*, Bonn, 1973.

MÜNSCHER, K., 'Xenophon in den griechisch-römisch Literatur', *Philologus*, Suppl. xiii.2 (1920), pp. 45 ff.

MURRAY, O., 'Herodotus and Hellenistic Culture', *Classical Quarterly* n.s. xxii (1972), pp. 207 ff.

NIESE, B., *Geschichte der griechischen und makedonischen Staaten seit der Schlacht bei Chäronea*, vols. i–ii, Gotha, 1893–1903.

NIETZOLD, W., *Die Überlieferung der Diadochengeschichte bis zur Schlacht bei Ipsus*, Würzburg, 1905.

PALM. J., *Über Sprache und Stil Diodors von Sizilien*, Lund, 1955.

PEARSON, L., *The Lost Histories of Alexander the Great*, American Philological Association Monograph, New York, 1960.

PÉDECH, P., *La Méthode historique de Polybe*, Paris, 1964.

PERRET, J., *Les Origines de la légende troyenne de Rome*, *(281–231)* Paris, 1942.

PETERSEN, E.: See Lanckoronski and Petersen.

PICARD, CH., 'Le trône vide d'Alexandre dans la cérémonie de Cyinda et le culte du trône vide à travers le monde gréco-romain', *Cahiers Archéologiques* vii (1964), pp. 1 ff.

——, 'Sépultures des compagnons de guerre ou successeurs macédoniens d'Alexandre', *Journal des Savants*, 1964, pp. 208 ff.

POWELL, J. U. and BARBER, E. A., *New Chapters in Greek Literature*, vol. ii, Oxford, 1929.

PRÉAUX, C., *L'économie royale des Lagides*, Brussels, 1939.

——, *Le monde hellénistique*, vols. i–ii, Paris, 1979.

RAWSON, E., 'The Literary Sources for the Pre-Marian Army', *Papers of the British School at Rome*, n.s. xxvi (1971), pp. 13 ff.

REINACH, T., *Trois royaumes de l'Asie Mineure*, Paris, 1888.

REUSS, F., *Hieronymos von Kardia*, Berlin, 1876.

ROBERTSON, M., 'The Boscoreale Figure-Paintings', *Journal of Roman Studies* xlv ((1955), pp. 58 ff.

ROSEN, K., 'Political Documents in Hieronymus of Cardia', *Acta Classica* x (1967), pp. 41 ff.

ROSTOVTZEFF, M., *Caravan Cities*, Oxford, 1932.

SCHACHERMEYR, F., *Alexander in Babylon und die Reichsordnung nach seiner Tod*, Wien, 1970.

SCHMITT, H. H., *Die Staatsverträge des Altertums*, iii, München, 1969.

SCHMITTHENNER, W., 'Über eine Formveränderung der Monarchie seit Alexander d. Gr.', *Saeculum* xix (1968), pp. 31 ff.

SCHNEIDER, C., *Kulturgeschichte des Hellenismus*, vols. i–ii, München, 1967.

SCHUBERT, R., *Die Quellen zur Geschichte der Diadochenzeit*, Leipzig, 1914.

SEIBERT, J., *Untersuchungen zur Geschichte Ptolemaios I*, München, 1969.

SIMPSON, R. H., 'A Possible Case of Misrepresentation in Hieronymus of Cardia', *Historia* vi (1957), pp. 504 ff.

——, 'Antigonus the One-Eyed and the Greeks', *Historia* viii (1959), pp. 385 ff.

——, 'Abbreviation of Hieronymus in Diodorus', *American Journal of Philology* lxxx (1959), pp. 370 ff.

SMITH, L. C., 'The Chronology of Books xviii–xx of Diodorus Siculus', *American Journal of Philology* lxxxii (1961), pp. 283 ff.

SMITH, S., *Babylonian Historical Texts Relating to the Capture and Downfall of Babylon*, London, 1924.

SPOERRI, W., *Späthellenistische Berichte über Welt, Kultur and Götter*, Basel, 1959.

SYME, R., *Tacitus*, vols. i–ii, Oxford, 1958.

TARN, W. W., *Antigonos Gonatas*, Oxford, 1913.

——, *Hellenistic Military and Naval Developments*, Cambridge, 1930.

——, *Alexander the Great*, vols. i–ii, Cambridge, 1948, reprinted 1979.

THONKE, E., *Die Weltkarte des Eratosthenes und die Feldzüge Alexanders*, Strasburg, 1914.

TOYNBEE, A. J., *Hellenism*, London, 1959.

TREVES, P., 'Jeronimo di Cardia e la politica di Demetrio Poliorcete', *Rivista di Filologia* x (1932), pp. 194 ff.

VERNANT, J. P.: see Detienne and Vernant.

VEZIN, A., *Eumenes von Kardia,* Münster, 1907.

VITALE, G., 'Testi recentemente pubblicati: papiri letterari, 170,' *Aegyptus* ii (1921), pp. 207 ff.

VOSS, G. J., *De Historicis Graecis,* ed. Westermann, Leipzig, 1838.

WACHSMUTH, C., *Über das Geschichtswerk des Sikelioten Diodors,* Leipzig, 1892.

——, *Einleitung in das Studium des alten Geschichte,* Leipzig, 1895.

WALBANK, F. W., *Philip V of Macedon,* Cambridge, 1940.

——, *Polybius,* Sather Classical Lectures, xiii, Berkeley, 1972.

WEHRLI, C., *Antigone et Démétrios,* Geneva, 1968.

WEHRLI, F., *Die Schule des Aristoteles: Texte und Kommentar, X, Hieronymos von Rhodos, Kritolaus und seine Schüler,* Basel, 1959.

WESSELING, P., Diodorus Siculus, edition, vols. i–ii, Amsterdam, 1746.

WESTLAKE, H. D., 'Eumenes of Cardia', in *Essays on the Greek Historians and Greek History,* New York, 1969, pp. 313 ff.

WILL, E., *Histoire politique du monde hellénistique,* vols. i–ii, Nancy, 1966–7.

ZELLER, E., *Philosophie der Griechen in ihrer geschichtlichen Entwicklung,*[4] vols. i–vi, Hildesheim, 1963.

Index of Greek Terms

General Index